NEWNES'
PICTORIAL KNOWLEDGE

VOLUME FOUR

NEWNES'
PICTORIAL KNOWLEDGE

General Editors
R. H. POOLE
PETER FINCH, M.A.
WALTER SHEPHERD

Art Editor
A. H. J. HUMPHREYS

VOLUME 4

GEORGE NEWNES LIMITED
CARLTON HOUSE, GREAT QUEEN STREET,
LONDON, W.C.2

PRINTED IN GREAT BRITAIN
BY THE WHITEFRIARS PRESS LTD., LONDON AND TONBRIDGE, AND
BOUND BY HAZELL, WATSON & VINEY LTD., AYLESBURY AND LONDON
N.P.K. 7055.   W.P. 5316

CONTENTS OF VOLUME FOUR

Colour Plates

Photo=tone Supplements

The Story
of the
World and
its Peoples

Our Neighbours
and Friends
Across
the Channel

E.N.A.

Our islands are part of the continent of Europe. France is our nearest neighbour and a stretch of her northern coast—so very like our own south coast—is seen in this picture. The town is actually Fécamp in Normandy.

THE CONTINENT OF EUROPE

MODERN INVENTION has made the World seem a much smaller place to the people who live in it. Not so many years ago, before the coming of the Air Age, and before the invention of wireless and the telephone, east and west and north and south were distant and remote from one another. To travel abroad, to see foreign lands and peoples, was a long and arduous business of days and weeks by sea and land. But to-day, when planes span continents within the space of hours and high-speed communication systems can flash a message round the World in a fraction of time, the peoples of the World have become much more closely knit and much more aware of one another.

To-day we can be transported from the Old World of Europe to the New World of the Americas within twenty-four hours or can talk to the people of the Americas even though they are thousands of miles away. The World has suddenly become small because our thoughts and our bodies can travel across its vast distances at much greater speeds. Yesterday, we of these British Isles were citizens of Britain who, had we wished, could have turned our backs upon the other nations of the World. To-day, we are as much citizens of Europe and of the World, whose daily life, hopes and fears are intimately bound up with the lives, hopes and fears of our neighbours.

In particular, we look to the Continent of Europe of which we are part, for it is here that we find our nearest friends and our nearest foes. Europe is to Britain what the houses in our street are to the home in which we live.

Its Mountains, Valleys and Forests

Europe is a continent which stretches from the rugged Caucasus in the east to the Atlantic shore in the west, from the Mediterranean in the south to Lapland and Iceland in the North.

Europe presents many contrasts—regions that are mountainous and cold, plains that are blanketed in winter snow, plains that are parched under a merciless sun, sheltered valleys and shorelands that are the gardens of the continent where grow the good fruits of the earth that feed us, vast forests where men's axes strike sharply against the sturdy trees, seas and lakes where the keen bows of fishing craft and merchantmen cleave the water. In all these different regions we shall see how man's life is ruled by the type of climate and the kind of country in which he lives, for everywhere throughout the World the story of man is the story of how he has adapted himself to the conditions imposed upon him by nature.

In western Europe—our own country, much of France, Belgium and Holland, and the coastal lands of the North Sea—man lives in a region of temperate climate. Here he can work in the open the year round, and even in winter can travel upon unfrozen seas. His lands are forest and meadow, farmlands and dairylands. To the north-east are the Baltic Lands where life is more difficult because the climate is less kind and the land more inhospitable. Here dwell the hardy Scandinavians, the west Russians, the peoples of the eastern Baltic shore and of the North German Plain.

E.N.A.

THE BELGIAN COUNTRYSIDE

These farmlands of northern Belgium are typical of western Europe where the climate is temperate and man can work in the open all the year round. In the Baltic Lands to the north-east life is more difficult because the climate is harsher.

PLAIN, FOREST, AND MOUNTAIN

Here we are on one of the great steppes of Europe, the Hortobagy Plain in Hungary where *csikos* (Hungarian cowboys) tend their herds. In this photograph we see one of them with his *komondor* or sheep dog. Behind the cart (left) is a typical well.

Photos : E.N.A.

Forest and mountain typify the region of Central Europe where snow-capped peaks are joined to fertile valleys by forest carpets of dark green spread across the mountain slopes. Here is a scene in the Austrian Tyrol; notice the peasant costume of the farmer.

I—2

Central Europe is a region of forest and of mountain where mighty peaks capped perpetually by snow rear into the thin air and where dark green carpets of trees are spread across the mountain slopes to link them to fertile valleys. Coniferous forestland is typical of north-eastern Europe where Russia dominates. Southwards are the Steppes, wide grasslands where Cossacks and Hungarian *csikos* tend their herds.

Round the northern and eastern shores of the Caspian Sea are barren tracts of salt desert where few people can live and they but poorly. But the greatest contrast of all is between the pleasant sun-kissed Mediterranean lands, where winters are mild and summers warm, and the cold desolate Arctic lands of Europe that geographers call the Tundra.

All these different regions containing many different peoples go to make the Continent of Europe. Separated from one another by differences in language and outlook : by political divisions which have come about as much by war as by any other means, they are yet one. They are the Europeans, whose story is told in the following pages.

Europe's Part

What an immensely important part these Europeans have played in the history and progress of the world! At one time Asiatic peoples led the world in culture and in human knowledge, but afterwards it was Europe's task to point the way forward. From the glorious times of Ancient Greece and Imperial Rome to the days when Europeans first crossed the vast Atlantic in their wooden ships : from the times when little bands of adventurers first carved out the colonies and empires until the present day, Europe has been the source and fountainhead of human progress, the mother of new nations which have taken over and developed her high ideals of civilisation.

E.N.A.

IN EUROPE'S ARCTIC LANDS

The greatest contrast in European climate and scenery is between the Mediterranean lands and those of the cold, desolate Arctic. This picture shows something of the ice and snow of northern Europe where dwell such people as the Lapps with their reindeer.

FRANCE

THE PLACE DE L'OPÉRA, PARIS

E.N.A.

Paris is the heart, as well as the capital of France, and this picture shows us one of the most famous squares in the French capital. Facing us is the magnificent Opera House which looks out on busy thoroughfares where the traffic is controlled, not only by lights, but by a small army of gendarmes equipped with white batons and shrilly-sounding whistles.

LA BELLE FRANCE—Beautiful France! Throughout the civilised world France is spoken of with affection, not merely because of the beauties of her land, but because she has made immeasurably generous contributions to the knowledge and culture of mankind. French artistic and cultural standards have spread across the world enriching humanity and adding lustre to the name of France. The unique spirit of France, the atmosphere that is found only in France herself, draw visitors to her land as much as do the villages, cities, buildings, monuments and showplaces that are so significant in the story of the French people and the world. France is not only a land of romance and scenic beauty — France is a country of enlightenment whose thinkers and artists have sped the course of intellectual progress.

France first enters history as Gaul, a land peopled by warlike tribes who had migrated westwards from the Danube. The Gaulish domains of these migrants gradually crumbled, the pieces being swallowed up in the expanding Roman Empire. After Julius Caesar's triumph over the Gaulish chieftain Vercingetorix, Gaul was for five centuries one of the principal centres of Roman civilisation, and despite the changes which later ages brought, the influence of Rome upon French religion, law, language and customs remains to-day.

When Paris Began

With the collapse of the Roman Empire, Gaul suffered new invasions. Fierce tribes from the east mastered her countryside, the Visigoths in Aquitaine, the Burgundians in Rhenish Gaul and west of the Jura mountains,

5

and the Franks in the north-east. The Franks, or Free Men, were the strongest. Led by a chieftain called Clovis, they conquered territory as far south as the Loire. From the Franks came the modern name *France*, and from a tribe of the Gauls called Parisii, the present capital, Paris. For Clovis made the Ile de la Cité—the islet on the River Seine which is now the very heart of the great French capital—his seat of government.

There were other great Frankish leaders—Charles Martel (Charles the Hammer), whose defeat of the Arabs at Tours in 732 confined Muslim conquest to Spain and preserved France for Christendom, and Charlemagne (Charles the Great) who ruled not only over France, but over most of what we now call Germany, and over parts of Spain and Italy. Charlemagne was more than a conqueror, for he tried to unite his dominions in peace by spreading learning and religion and by developing trade. But when he died, there was none strong enough or wise enough to carry on his rule and his empire fell apart.

The Franks, themselves once raiders, were attacked in the north by the Normans, the " Northmen." These sea-rovers were eventually allowed to settle near the mouth of the Seine where their leader, Rollo, became the first Duke of Normandy, founding a ducal dynasty that was to produce a future king of England, William the Conqueror. By the time William had conquered England, France had come to accept the house of Capet as her ruling family. Hugh, the first Capet king (987–996) had been born in France and spoke French ; the line he founded was to give France her kings for eight hundred years.

E.N.A.

THE HEART OF PARIS

This fine aerial picture shows (foreground) the Ile de la Cité where, many centuries ago, Clovis built his capital. Notre Dame's noble entrance faces on to the Place du Parvis Notre Dame which was the scene of bitter fighting between the Germans and the French Resistance in the Second World War when the French capital was liberated by its own citizens.

As a result of the Norman Conquest, kings of England ruled in parts of France, and for four hundred years they tried to keep and extend their hold upon France, actually claiming the French throne itself and styling themselves Kings of France. Fortunes in the long struggle swayed from one side to the other. We all remember the great English victories at Creçy, Poictiers, and Agincourt, and the new faith which Joan of Arc inspired in her countrymen and her tragic end in the market-place of Rouen; then the final victory of French armies which placed securely on the French throne a king of their own race.

When Tyrants Ruled

The seeds of future events lie in the distant past. King Francis the First (1515–1547) not only revived religious persecution which ultimately led to the terrible massacre of Saint Bartholomew's Day, when Protestants were murdered in French streets and homes: he began the policy of royal extravagance which, just over two hundred years later, was to be one of the prime causes of the French Revolution that brought Capet rule to its end.

The French people lived under a feudal system long after that system had begun to decay in other countries. What rights and liberties they had were denied peaceful growth by the stern rule of the French kings and their ministers. The despotic Cardinal Richelieu, first minister to King Louis

NOTRE DAME DE PARIS

Notre Dame, the beautiful Cathedral of Paris, stands on the eastern end of the Ile de la Cité, not far from the Pont de l'Archevêché (The Archbishop's Bridge). There has been a cathedral church on this site since A.D. 365, but Notre Dame itself was not begun until 1163 and not completed until 1235, and since then has been extensively altered through the centuries.

the Thirteenth (1610–1643), made France poor by the savage taxes which he imposed, and ruled the country like a police state. Louis' successor was guided along the same fatal path by Cardinal Mazarin, so that when the Cardinal died in 1661 and Louis the Fourteenth (1643–1715) took full control, he ruled as rigidly, and as extravagantly, as any dictator of modern times. *"L'État c'est moi!"* exclaimed Louis. *"The State? I am the State!"*

His power over the lives of his subjects was absolute and he thought only in terms of his own glory. His armies, led by many famous generals, marched and fought to make his kingdom greater, draining the royal treasury which had to be replenished by cruel taxes on the French people. War was not their only burden; they had to pay to satisfy the royal taste for luxury. Louis, the *Grand Monarque* as he was called, stressed his own greatness by making his Court renowned for its wealth and splendour.

To glorify himself he built the sumptuous Palace of Versailles where the highest nobles of France, even royal princes, served as members of his household and where he lived a life of wasteful magnificence, squandering vast sums of money through his extravagant tastes and love of show. Ten thousand soldiers, four thousand servants, and five thousand horses served him at Versailles whose pomp and ceremony was the visible expression of his greatness and of the supremacy of France over all European countries. The redeeming feature of this period was France's true greatness in art and literature. The *Louis Quatorze* period, which is named from the *Grand Monarque*, was the age of great French dramatists—Corneille, Racine, and Molière—the portrait painter Mignard, and the architect and sculptor Charles le Brun.

Free Men in Chains

With the accession of Louis the Fifteenth, France moved swiftly towards a crisis. Wars stripped her of her colonies, while at home the plight of the ordinary people became piteous. The country was ripening for revolution and the way to rebellion was shown by the great writers of this Age of Enlightenment—Montesquieu, Voltaire, and Rousseau—whose work condemned the corrupt and poverty-stricken state of the country and proclaimed the true freedom of mankind—a revolutionary creed that also characterised the work of Diderot and the Encyclopædists. "Man is born free, and

Donald McLeish.

A MASSIVE "ARCH OF TRIUMPH"

The Arc de Triomphe, Paris, is upwards of 160 feet in height, 147 feet in width and 72 feet in depth. It is the largest arch of its kind in existence, and was built to commemorate the military triumphs of Napoleon. Beneath the great central archway is the Tomb of the Unknown Soldier of France, corresponding to the British Unknown Warrior's grave in Westminster Abbey.

WHERE HISTORY HAS BEEN WRITTEN

One of the most interesting buildings in Europe, if not in the world, the Palace of Versailles was built by Louis XIV in 1661–1683. Here in 1871 was signed the Peace Treaty at the conclusion of the Franco-Prussian War; and, in 1919, the Peace Treaty after the War of 1914–18.

Photos: Will F. Taylor.

The Palace of Fontainebleau, which stands some thirty-seven miles S.E. of Paris, was the favourite residence of Napoleon I. There has been a palace on this site since the tenth century.

everywhere he is in chains." With such words did Rousseau begin his *Social Contract* which has been called " the Bible of the Revolution."

On one side was the wasteful luxury and frivolity of the royal Court, on the other the wretched misery of countless thousands in town and countryside. Louis the Sixteenth was too weak a monarch to heed the warnings; when at length he tried to act, the people were beyond his control and there came about the French Revolution which overthrew by violence everything which was seen by the unhappy French to have caused their poverty and oppression. The feelings of the people were expressed in the *Marseillaise*, an inspiring revolutionary song that afterwards became the national hymn of France. The Bastille, fortress-prison of Paris and symbol of royal tyranny, and the Palace of the Tuileries were stormed by the mob, and the king and his family were cast into prison and later executed with many of their nobles during the Reign of Terror.

Napoleon Bonaparte

Meanwhile other nations had taken up arms against the Revolution. France was attacked and from the fires of revolt produced a new leader, Napoleon Bonaparte, who would not only hurl back her assailants but would lead French armies to military glory the length and breadth of Europe. Napoleon nearly mastered the whole Continent. One nation alone never yielded to his armies and that nation was Britain. At times, she stood singly against him, and it was her faith and endurance that eventually led to Napoleon's defeat at the battle of Waterloo.

French leadership of Europe was soon challenged by young and thrustful Prussia. By 1870 Prussia, guided by the crafty Bismarck, was virtual master of Germany; only the possibility of French opposition prevented Bismarck from completing his great plan. In the war that came about, France was defeated utterly. Her province of Alsace was taken from her and she suffered the humiliation of seeing the first German Emperor, Kaiser Wilhelm I, proclaimed in the magnificent Hall of Mirrors at the Palace of Versailles.

But Germany was not content. She wished to become the greatest Power in Europe. War came again in 1914 and for four terrible years the lifeblood of the nations was poured out on the fields of Flanders. With the defeat of Germany in 1918 peace came, and the world thankfully turned its thoughts from battle and destruction. But in Germany it was not long before a new and completely ruthless leader came to power. He was Adolf Hitler, whose Nazi Party took control of the country and in 1939 again brought war to Europe.

In this, the Second World War, France was overrun and occupied. Not until 1944 did the Allied armies, aided by the gallant French Resistance Movement, drive out the invaders. Shortly after, all Europe was freed and France, like many of her neighbours, was faced with making good her losses and repairing the destruction of the war. She was more fortunate than many; only in the north were her towns and villages laid in ruins. The rest of the country, including Paris, suffered little.

The City of Light

What the brain is to the body, Paris is to France. For many foreigners, Paris is a city which gathers together in one place all the charms and qualities that are peculiarly French.

Paris is a centre of European culture, a city where her greatest artists and writers have lived and worked; Paris is a gay city, a city of light and of fashion; Paris gives us a wonderful first sight of France and her people.

To explore Paris thoroughly would take a long time, for she has always new things to tell and old secrets to reveal. We notice from the very first how different the streets are from ours—the

A UNITED NATIONS MEETING-PLACE

The imposing Palais de Chaillot is the scene of UNO Assembly meetings when these are held in Paris. Elaborate fountains lie between the Palace and the Pont de Jena which leads across the Seine to the Eiffel Tower, from the first floor of which this picture was taken.

tree-lined boulevards, the busy cafés, where all Paris seems to meet in the evening, the tall houses in which most people live in flats or apartments rather than in little houses in the suburbs like the Londoners, and the hurrying traffic which bothers us a bit when we cross the road, because it keeps to the right and not to the left as in England.

How Paris Grew

The oldest part of Paris—" the City "—is on an island in the Seine, which is bordered by clean stone quays and embankments and crossed by many beautiful bridges. On this island stand the great cathedral of Notre Dame and the Palace of Justice, which once upon a time was the palace of the kings of France.

From this island, Old Paris spread to the banks, and you can trace the growth of the city through the ages by the successive " rings " of boulevards made along the lines of the old forti-fications. On the right bank is the busiest part of the city, where we can see the Palace of the Louvre, which to-day is the " National Gallery " of France ; the site of the old palace of the Tuileries, burned in 1871, in its lovely gardens ; the Elysée, where the President lives, and the theatres and great *magasins* or shops. Paris has no great parks within its boundaries as London has, but its fine squares are among the best in Europe. From the Place de la Concorde, one of these squares, the splendid avenue of the Champs Elysées leads up to the Arc de Triomphe—a great triumphal arch which was set up to commemorate Napoleon's victories, and which to-day shelters beneath its mighty arch the tomb of France's Unknown Soldier. Napoleon himself, and Foch, the great general of France in the war of 1914–18, sleep beneath the golden dome of the Invalides.

The park of Paris is the Bois de Boulogne, outside her western borders.

Not far from the city is the great Palace of Versailles, and away to the south-west the forest of Fontainebleau with its royal palaces built by the monarchs of France from Francis the First to Napoleon.

The Real France

What is this country of France whose busy heart is Paris, where all roads and railways converge, and where life is so very different from that of London? We shall be wrong if we think of France only as a place for tourists and holiday makers, although she has more perhaps to give them than any other country in Europe—beautiful scenery, wonderful old towns, priceless art treasures, and endless gaiety.

First of all France is the home of over 42 millions of people, many of whom are farmers, for France is one of the leading farming countries of Europe. To-day about forty in every hundred Frenchmen are farmers. Their farms are mostly small and have not nearly so much farm machinery as, for example, the farms of Britain. Although much is being done to provide tractors and implements, most French farmers are still peasant farmers using the ways of old in working their land and raising their crops.

France is farther south than Britain, and on the whole is much warmer, especially on her sheltered Mediterranean shores, where mild winters bring crowds of visitors to the French Riviera, to Cannes, Nice, Mentone and others of its brilliant string of seaside resorts. But in north-eastern France winters are more severe than ours, although summers are hotter.

The pastures of Normandy and Brittany are the homes of fruit-growers and dairy farmers. Flax and sugar-beet are grown in the cooler northern and eastern plains.

E.N.A.

A PARISIAN CAFÉ

Every French town has its cafés where you can sit at your table in the street and watch the world go by, and Paris especially is famous for its boulevard cafés. From about mid-morning onwards trade will be brisk until the evening when every table will be taken and the conversation of the customers will join with the music of the orchestra inside the café and the noise of the traffic and passers-by.

The Breton and Norman farmers also keep many pigs and breed horses. If you travelled from Cornwall, in south-western England, to Brittany, you would notice at once that the Cornish and Breton countrysides are alike in many ways. You would learn, too, that the old Cornish tongue was very like that used in Brittany; both were Celtic in origin.

Wheat, " the bread crop," is the most important crop in France. It flourishes on the rich plains of the north, and in Aquitaine, in the warmer south, where maize is another important crop.

" The Garden of France "

The most important farming region in France is the basin of the River Loire, which is often called " The Garden of France." The Loire is the longest river in France.

French Government Tourist Office.

MAKING CAMEMBERT CHEESE

Since it was first made in the district of Camembert, near Vimoutiers, in Normandy, Camembert has become one of the most famous French cheeses. It is a soft cheese ripened by mould. Its manufacture is a skilled art. The freshly-made cheeses in this picture are standing upon mat-covered, sloping draining tables. When they are firm enough to be handled, the cheeses are salted by a dusting process.

It rises high up in the Gerbier de Jonc (Ardèche) and flows north, and then west to the Atlantic. On its estuary stand Nantes and the port of St. Nazaire.

The Loire basin is another important wheat-growing region. Cattle are raised along the lower reaches of the river. But it is not the fertile land that brings visitors to this part of France. They come to see the beautiful old castles for which the Loire is famous. And what a number there are! Some, like Langeais (which is said to be the oldest in France), are fortified castles ; others, like Azay-le-Rideau, are more like mansions or palaces. One of the most amazing of the Loire castles is Chambord, which stands on the banks of the Cosson, a tributary of

the Loire. Nearly two thousand men laboured for fifteen years to complete this great château. Among its features is a strange " double staircase," by which two people can ascend or descend without seeing one another.

France is famous for its vineyards. Vines flourish in most parts of the country, except the north. The best-known vineyards are those in the warm lands of the Garonne basin around the busy port of Bordeaux, in Burgundy and in Champagne. These give their names to the wines that they produce.

The Mediterranean lands of south-eastern France, with which we must include the French island of Corsica, are different from the rest of the country. Here, the winters are less severe and the

St. MICHEL d'AIGUILLE

In the town of Le Puy, in France, stands the remarkable church of St. Michel d'Aiguille, built on a high needle-like rock.

mulberry and olive can thrive. In the very south, along the Riviera, the farmers have terraced the hillsides and grow flowers and vegetables, as well as olives and vines. In northern France we saw oaks, chestnuts and similar trees ; along the Riviera we find palms and oranges, beautiful flowering creepers and other trees and plants that need the sunshine.

Have you ever seen shepherds walking about on stilts? If not, you should travel to the *Landes*, a coastal region of sand dunes and marshes lying south of Bordeaux. The shepherds of the *Landes* use stilts because the ground is so wet. Besides flocks of sheep, their countryside supports herds of cattle. There are also large pine forests, which were planted to prevent the sand dunes spreading inland and which yield valuable timber.

The Core of France

The core of France is the old block of the Auvergne Plateau, on whose top are the broken-down cones of prehistoric volcanoes, known locally as " puys." From this central core the great tributaries of the Loire and the Garonne come down. The eastern edge of this plateau is called the Cevennes, from the top of which you can look eastward across the Rhône valley to the snowy peaks of the Alps. The Mont Cenis Tunnel bores through these Alps to provide a way from France into Italy.

Between this central core, which the French call the *Massif Central*, and the Alps is the deep valley of the rivers Saône and Rhône. This valley runs south to open out into the French Mediterranean lands and carries road and railway south to the important manufacturing centre of *Lyons*, the great port of *Marseilles* and the Mediterranean coast.

Lyons, the third largest city in France, is the chief silk centre. It has other industries, too, including engineering, and can power its works and factories with coal from the St. Etienne field and with cheap hydro-electric power from the Alps.

Photos: Will F. Taylor.

St. MALO

Quaint old St. Malo is a seaport of Normandy. The town itself is particularly picturesque, with an ancient cathedral.

E.N.A

THE CHÂTEAU OF LANGEAIS

France has many fine old castles and many of the most famous lie along the banks of the River Loire. Here we see the château of Langeais, built during the second half of the fifteenth century by Jean Bourée, minister of Louis XI. Near the château are the ruins of an older fortress, built by Fulk the Black, Count of Anjou, in the tenth century.

Hydro-electric power is of rapidly growing importance in this part of France, for the Rhône itself, which is probably the most turbulent and swift-moving river in France, is being harnessed.

From the snow-capped Alpine peaks along her frontiers with Italy and Switzerland to her sun-kissed Mediterranean coast, France is working to complete a great system of dams and turbines that will produce vast supplies of electricity and control the waters of this great river. These dams and power stations that are being built at eighteen points along the course of the Rhône from the Lake of Geneva to the Mediterranean will also help the irrigation of the lower Rhône valley and so increase farm production there. A system of locks and canals is also being built which will make the Rhône navigable for 354 miles of its course.

Typical of the work being done are the great dam at Génissiat, in the upper Rhône valley, which was completed in 1948, and the huge power station at Donzère-Mondragon, on the lower Rhône. It has been said that the Génissiat dam is the largest completed work of its kind in western Europe.

A Village Submerged

Among the tributary rivers being harnessed is the Isère, on whose upper reaches stands the new dam of Tignes, inaugurated by the French President in July, 1953. This dam is the highest in Europe. It is 600 feet high, contains 850,000 cubic yards of concrete and took six years to build. The building of the dam meant submerging the old village of Tignes. The new village which is now being built will not only rehouse the inhabitants of the old, but will be developed as a winter sports resort.

It will be many years before this

great scheme is complete. But when it is finished France will have not only bountiful electric power, but a navigable river Rhône linked *via* the Aar and Lausanne with the Rhine.

Although France is a leading farming country, she has many manufactures and important industries, especially on the northern coal-field, where such centres as Lille, Roubaix, Tourcoing and Cambrai make linens, woollens and cottons as well as goods of iron and steel. This northern coal-field produces more than 60 per cent. of all French coal. Dunkirk is its port, and its manufacturing centres are linked by a network of canals. But France cannot produce all the coal she needs, and this is why she has to import coal and why she is developing her reserves of water power in the French Alps and the Pyrenees.

France produces plenty of iron ore from her mines in Lorraine (Longwy, Briey, Nancy and Luneville), in Normandy (Caen) and elsewhere. Coal and iron are at hand to serve her iron and steel works at Le Creuzot and Alais, which are also important centres for glass manufacture. Interesting local industries are found at Besançon (watch-making), Grenoble (glove-making), Nîmes (shawls) and Montpellier (blankets). Everyone who knows anything about fine china and porcelain has heard of Sèvres and Limoges.

Great French Ports

With a population of over 600,000, *Marseilles* is second in size only to Paris (population over 2,725,000) and a centre of trade with the overseas territories of the French Union. To Marseilles comes such produce as tobacco, sugar, hides and skins, vegetable oils and cacao. As a result important local industries have been developed, including cigarette making, sugar refining, tanning, oil refining, and the manufacture of cocoa and chocolate.

Bordeaux does great business with the Latin republics of South America, as well as with Northern Africa and Western Europe to whose ports she sends her clarets and brandies.

Brest, which figures in the stories of both the World Wars, is too far

E.N.A.

WASHING DAY AT ANNECY

These French housewives use the waters of the Thioux canal when washing day comes. Annecy is the chief town of the department of Haute Savoie. It stands at the northern end of the lake of Annecy which is linked by the Thioux canal to the Fier, a tributary of the Rhône.

W. Suschitzky.

CHENONCEAUX, ONE OF THE LOVELIEST CHÂTEAUX IN THE LOIRE VALLEY

Like some fairy-tale castle set against the green of field and forest, Chenonceaux stands proudly on the banks of the Cher, which is a tributary of the river Loire. The Loire is the longest river in France and is known throughout the world for the many wonderful castles to be found along its course. The main part of the castle was built during the period 1515–24 by Thomas Bohier, financial minister in Normandy. Later, the castle was taken over by the French kings. Catherine of Medici, Mary Queen of Scots, Rousseau and Voltaire are some of the famous names to be found in its history.

MONT SAINT MICHEL, FRANCE

Like the castle from some fairy story, the Benedictine fortress-abbey of Mont St. Michel rises as if from
the sea-bed itself. It is built upon a granite mass, 165 feet high, which stands off the coast of the French
department of the Manche, and is linked with the mainland only by a narrow causeway. Mont St. Michel
has been sacred from early times, for it was here, in the eighth century, that St. Michael appeared to
St. Aubert of Avranches and commanded him to build an oratory. The oldest part of the present
buildings, however, dates from the thirteenth century.

VINEYARDS OF FRANCE

The making of wine is an important industry in France, where vineyards may be seen in many parts of the country. The vines in this picture grow near Epernay, and are of the " black pinot " stock whose greenish-white juice is used in this district for the manufacture of Champagne.

Photos: Planet News.

In this picture of a Calvet farm near Bordeaux, we see grapes being pressed, the skins and stems being extracted by this operation. Bordeaux and Burgundy are regions providing the most famous of French wines. In Bordeaux alone there are over 300,000 acres of vineyards.

from Paris and too much out of the way at the end of the peninsula of Brittany to become a really important commercial centre. Cherbourg is better off and nearer Paris; it is a regular port of call for many Atlantic liners.

France has much to offer those who love beautiful things, and all who are interested in her past history. Brittany and Normandy are not only pleasant in their little villages, their pastures and orchards and flowers, and their delightful seaside places, but in their towns are fine old castles and churches, and old houses and streets that recall the days of Norman William and of the Plantagenet kings who had dominions there in the Middle Ages.

Roman France

Southern France has wonderful old buildings that remind us of the times when Imperial Rome was mistress of Gaul—the magnificent Roman arena at Arles, the great Roman aqueduct at Pont du Gard, the Temple of Diana and the arena at Nîmes, are well-known examples. There are, too, many ancient buildings that give us far-off glimpses of the France of the Middle Ages— Avignon, where the Popes had their palace in the third quarter of the fourteenth century; Tarascon and the Château of King Réné, and Boulbon with its stronghold of Raymond, Count of Toulouse.

On the western side of the Auvergne, too, are more old cities, and other fine old castles and churches, some perched dizzily on the very pinnacles of volcanic stumps, like the church of St. Michel d'Aiguille in Le Puy of the Haute Loire. But perhaps the most marvellous sight in all France to the student of history is the old city of Carcassonne—a complete fortified city of the Middle Ages existing in almost perfect condition at the present day. The old defences are mainly those of the sixth, twelfth and thirteenth centuries. The place was a stronghold in the days of Roman Gaul.

Such is France: a land of beauty, of romance, of history, of culture. From the towns and villages that we have seen—above all, from the great cultural centre of Paris—came men and women whose contributions to enlightenment have won them international fame. Matthew Arnold once wrote " France is versed in all the arts, in none supreme," and while it is true that she has produced no one of the stature of Shakespeare or Dante, her men and women of the arts have influenced the minds of Europe and the world.

From Rabelais and Calvin in the sixteenth century to the Romantic nineteenth century, France has produced writers whose thought and power has resounded through Europe: Montaigne, the philosopher, the playwrights of the *Louis Quatorze* age, the Revolutionary writers and philosophers whose creed of freedom blazed across the oppressed peoples of the Continent, the literary giants of the nineteenth century—Victor Hugo, Mérimée, Dumas, de Maupassant, Flaubert, Daudet, and Zola. Other fields of art are peopled by Frenchmen of genius—painters like Watteau, Fragonard, Greuze, Delacroix, Manet, and Degas: sculptors like Rodin: musicians like Berlioz, Debussy, and Ravel. For the living greatness of France springs from the natural genius of her men of culture.

The French Union

Before passing from France to other European countries, let us look briefly at France overseas, at territories ruled by her and states associated with her in what is now known as the *Union Française*, or French Union. It is this new grouping which embraces the former French colonial empire and which, in very general terms of course, may be likened to a French equivalent of the British Commonwealth of Nations. It includes, besides France herself, five groups of overseas territories and departments. These are: Algeria and the Southern Territories; Martinique, Guadeloupe, Réunion, and French

TOWERS AND BATTLEMENTS

Dorien Leigh.

Romans, Visigoths, Saracens, Franks, and Feudal Counts played their part in the history of Carcassonne, the fortified town which by its very completeness stands to-day as one of the finest examples of medieval military architecture. Strong defences guard the gates of the town which has within its walls a baronial castle and a wonderful church, the Basilica of Saint-Nazaire.

E.N.A.

Everyone who has read Dumas' " Count of Monte Cristo," knows the Château D'If as the island fortress off Marseilles where Edmond Dantes was imprisoned. Built in 1529 by order of Francis I, the castle has had many distinguished prisoners, including The Man in the Iron Mask, Mirabeau, and Philippe Egalité. The rocky island on which it stands cannot be reached in stormy weather.

2–2

Guiana; French West and Equatorial Africa, Madagascar and its dependencies; Togoland and the Cameroons, which are held under trusteeship; and the New Hebrides which France administers jointly with us. In addition, there are French associated states within the French Union; under this heading come the French protectorates of Morocco and Tunisia, and the Federation of Indo-China (including the Republic of Viet-Nam). France also retains a foothold in India, her chief settlement there being Pondicherry, and in the Americas, where she has the islands of St. Pierre and Miquelon, near the south coast of Newfoundland. In addition she rules certain Pacific islands, including Tahiti.

Best-known to us of these lands are those in North Africa (Algeria, Morocco, and Tunisia) which have been painted colourfully in stories of the famous French Foreign Legion; and French Guiana, on the north-east coast of South America, whose port of Cayenne was once a notorious penal settlement but is no longer used for this purpose. Of the remainder, Martinique is a West Indian island producing sugar and rum; Guadeloupe, too, is in the West Indies; and the island of Réunion lies in the Indian Ocean some four hundred and twenty miles east of Madagascar. Madagascar, which has been a French possession since 1885, owes its modern name to a spelling mistake made by Marco Polo many centuries ago.

This is what happened. Madagascar was discovered by the Portuguese in 1500. The King of Portugal, hearing of the discovery, concluded that the island must be the " Madagascar," mentioned by Marco Polo. But Marco Polo had never been there. Believing information given him by Arabs, he assumed the island of which they spoke to be the kingdom of Mogadisho, on the east coast of Africa. His way of spelling the name was " Madagascar."

Tananarive is the capital and chief town of Madagascar. Most of the inhabitants of the island belong to tribes of the Malagasy races.

E.N.A.

A FAMOUS PLACE OF PILGRIMAGE

Ever since 1858 when a peasant girl, Bernadette Soubirous, announced that the Blessed Virgin Mary had repeatedly revealed herself to her in a grotto near the town, Lourdes has been a place of pilgrimage. This picture shows the Church of the Rosary and the Grotto, built above the grotto and its spring of healing water, which was consecrated in 1876.

THE LOW COUNTRIES

WINDMILLS DRAIN THE RICH FARMLAND

Taken in southern Holland, this picture shows windmills used to draw off water from a *polder* lying eight to twelve feet below the sea-level. A single mill could raise the water only a few feet, and several mills are required here to make an ascending "water stairway." A *polder* is land reclaimed from the sea. Electric pumps are now more commonly used for draining than windmills.

THE life and story of the Low Countries are intimately connected with those of France, for the Low Countries have been a partial buffer between France and her traditional foes, a questionable privilege for which they have had to pay a heavy price. Time and again through centuries of history, nations have fought for possession of the Low Countries or come to grips across them.

The "Cockpit of Europe"

Their people have themselves had to fight desperately and repeatedly for their liberty, not only against foreign aggressors but against that mighty force of nature, the sea. For Holland and, to some extent, Belgium are lands preserved in defiance of the ocean deeps by the patient skill and abiding labour of their people who themselves have gained in wisdom and determination from the endless work of draining and dyking to keep back the menacing waters. Thus the Low Countries, the "Cockpit of Europe" as history has called them, are lands born of struggle.

Once part of Charlemagne's great empire, the Low Countries later became a number of small and independent feudal states and cities which rose to high prosperity on a tide of industry and commerce. The chartered towns, cities given charters by their local lord or prince, were more or less independent and, by the thirteenth century, had made the Low Countries the marketplace of the Western World. Bruges was a central exchange for world trade and shared this leading position with Ghent and Ypres.

These were the most renowned of the Netherlands trading cities, but there were many others which were no less prosperous—Antwerp, Louvain, Brussels, Malines, Delft, Haarlem, Rotterdam and Amsterdam. At such places craftsmen and merchants gathered, making money from many trades and industries, but above all from wool shipped from England which Flemish weavers made into fine cloth. To-day, these ancient centres still contain the stately town halls, lofty belfries and graceful churches which were built at the peak of their prosperity, and while some have lost the life and bustle of their golden age, others, like Antwerp, Brussels, Rotterdam, and Amsterdam, have gained even greater importance.

It was as well that the people of the Low Countries had large reserves of stubborn courage, for in the fifteenth and sixteenth centuries they suffered under the tyrannical rule of Charles the Fifth and his successors. Charles' wide empire embraced Austria and Spain, and the sturdy independence of the Netherlands craftsmen and merchants seemed an affront to his royal prestige. He did his utmost to rob them of their liberties and made repeated demands upon their rich cities for money for his treasury. Those towns which opposed him were robbed of their charters and witnessed the execution of their leading citizens.

What was even worse was the religious persecution of the Low Countries. Their people were Protestants and suffered terrible cruelties at the hands of the Inquisition which Charles set up in their midst. Driven to desperation, they planned revolt when it was seen that Charles' heir, his son, Philip the Second, intended to continue this cruel policy. A famous Spanish soldier, the Duke of Alva, was therefore sent to the Low Countries with orders to stamp out the rebellious spirit of the people. He was a man without pity and without the smallest shred of human kindness, whose brutalities made the Netherlanders even more firm in their opposition. Luckily they had a leader, William the Silent, Prince of Orange, who bravely guided them through the years of the War of Independence and became head of the Dutch Republic that was declared in 1581. Three years later he was murdered by a hired Spanish assassin.

Meanwhile war with Spain continued and the southern Low Countries were savagely brought to subjection. North and South now went separate ways. The North became the United Provinces; the South—the Belgic provinces

Donald McLeish.

THE BELFRY OF BRUGES

In the Grand Place of Bruges stands the famous Belfry, here seen from the calm waters of one of the many canals which intersect the city. The Belfry rises to a height of 352 feet and was commenced in the year 1282, being completed two centuries afterwards. Bruges is the chief town of West Flanders.

BRUSSELS' PALACE OF JUSTICE

Donald McLeish.

One of the largest buildings in Europe, the Palais de Justice at Brussels has an area actually exceeding that of the famous St. Peter's at Rome and is so vast that it makes one think of the mighty structures of Ancient Greece. The building was completed in 1883 and towers to a height of 400 feet—as great as that of the spire of Salisbury Cathedral. The figures at the corners beneath the dome represent respectively Justice, Clemency, Strength and Law.

—reverted to Spain and became the Spanish Netherlands. Hostile to Spain, the United Provinces naturally cast their lot in with the French, and this, with wider considerations of European politics, made the southern Netherlands a battleground for many years.

How Belgium Became a Kingdom

The sweeping changes in political geography made by Napoleon were a major problem for the Congress of Vienna which assembled to remake the map of Europe. The Low Countries were once more united under the Prince of Orange as the Kingdom of the Netherlands. But north and south had been apart for a hundred and thirty years and had become radically different in ideas, outlook, and religion. These differences, and the resentment of the Belgians at what seemed nothing more than Dutch domination, led them to demand a separate government and full rights and liberties. Nothing came of this, and in 1830 the Belgians revolted. Belgium was declared independent and a national congress was called to draw up a constitution. From these events emerged the Kingdom of Belgium.

But the Low Countries were "the Cockpit of Europe," and when the mighty clash of arms came in 1914, Belgium was a victim of German aggression. Holland escaped and preserved her neutrality, but Belgium became the battlefield of nations. Countless thousands of our soldiers fell "in Flanders fields" where to-day memorials and war cemeteries remind us of the frightful toll in human life that our first victory against Germany cost us.

That victory gave us no more than an armistice, as we now know. In 1939, war again came to the Low Countries, and this time both Holland and Belgium were occupied by Nazi Germany. Both fought back through their Resistance Movements and through

Donald McLeish.

HELD AGAINST NAPOLEON

In the Battle of Waterloo (June 18th, 1815), fought at the village of that name near Brussels, two farms played an important part. They were called Hougoumont and La Haye Sainte. Above is seen the gateway of Hougoumont, which was repeatedly attacked by Napoleon's troops during the battle. It was, however, held by Coldstream Guards and some Belgian troops, and defied the French.

Donald McLeish.

THE LION OF WATERLOO

That brilliant commander, the Duke of Wellington, had at the Battle of Waterloo (1815) a large force of Belgians among the Allied troops with which he opposed Napoleon. The campaign took place on Belgian territory, and the site of the battlefield is marked to-day by this huge mound of earth which rises to a height of 200 feet near the farm of La Haye Sainte. The mound commemorates the part played by Belgians in the conflict, and is surmounted by their national Lion.

their troops serving with the Allies, and at length regained their freedom.

The Fields of Belgium

At first sight, Belgium seems a land of many villages with fine old towns here and there at nodal points gathering up the trade of the surrounding country-side in their ancient market places. Belgium is a busy land cultivated like a garden, for about three-quarters of her area is rich farmland lying between the sandy coastal strip and the old crust-block of the wooded Ardennes. First and foremost, the Belgians are farmers; women and children toil in the fields and gardens as they never toil in Britain; even the dogs are pressed into service as beasts of burden.

The fields of Belgium, with their crops of wheat and rye, sugar-beet and tobacco, roots and vegetables, hops and flax, are, like the Dutch fields, drained by canals and fortified against the in-rush of the sea by dykes, especially in the west. Roads and canals are verged with trees, which are also planted as wind-breaks to protect the young crops. Here the farmers, many of them living cheaply and poorly in humble dwellings, produce the fruit and vegetables for the town markets and for export to Britain, and the seeds and young plants which are an equally important export. Their ploughs, carts, and farming machinery are drawn by the sturdy, noble horses of Brabant which are world famous.

The people of Belgium have two national tongues, French and Flemish. French is the language of the Belgian Walloons living mostly in the south-west. Flemish is more the language of the north and of the countryside. In some villages along the German border, a dialect of German is spoken. Like Holland, Belgium is one of the most thickly-populated countries of Europe.

Almost without exception, Belgian towns are rich in history, and new and old stand side by side to join past with present. *Ghent*, with its grim island castle of the Counts of Flanders, its famous old Cloth Hall, once the centre of the wool-trade, and its ruined Abbey of St. Bavon, where John of Gaunt was born in 1340, is the very heart of the Belgian cotton industry. *Malines*, one of the famous old charter towns, is still renowned for its lace.

Textiles and Heavy Industry

The woollen industry which made Flanders famous is now centred at Verviers. Linen is manufactured at Tournai and Oudenarde, and at Courtrai where the river Lys was once blocked by rafts of retting linen; nowadays, retting—the cleansing of the linen fibres—is done in tanks of heated water.

The heavy industry lies on or near the Belgian coalfield in the valleys of the Sambre and the Meuse along the northern edge of the Ardennes. Here are *Namur* and *Liège* with their iron and steel works: *Mons* with its coalpits and iron foundries: and *Charleroi* with its great plate-glass factories.

Brussels, the Belgian capital, is sometimes called " Little Paris," because it is the centre of Belgian fashion and culture and because, perhaps, it has the same friendly cosmopolitan welcome for its visitors. But Brussels has charms which Paris lacks. Nowhere in the French capital is there the equal of Brussels' Grand Place, a square bordered by fine old buildings. Nor has Paris so imposing an edifice as Brussels' Palais de Justice rising above the city on its terraced hill as if gods and not men had placed it there.

Brussels is a central point. Roads, railways, canals and rivers converge upon it on the Belgian plain. It has its own link with the sea in the Willebroek Ship Canal along which travel towering sea-going barges of a kind never seen in our country. Forty minutes away, by electric train, is Belgium's great port of Antwerp, on the river Scheldt, whose Cathedral tower is a landmark to vessels bound for her great docks. Also within easy reach of Brussels are the seaside resorts of Ostend, Blankenberghe, Zeebrügge and Knocke-Zoute, which have long been favourite holiday places for British tourists.

Like Holland, Belgium is a land of bells. Many a town or city takes great pride in its carillon, or peal of bells, and many employ *carillonneurs* (bell-masters) to give regular recitals. For carillons are not rung as church bells are in England. They are operated by a mechanically worked cylinder, which causes them to play certain tunes; or they are played by the bell-master, who sits at his keyboard and pedals high up in the belfry. Malines, Bruges, Ghent and Antwerp have particularly fine carillons; the carillon at Ghent comprises more than fifty bells.

Belgium is fortunate in having a very rich colony in Africa—the Belgian Congo, which is the home of 70,000 Europeans and 11 million native peoples (mostly Bantu). The prosperity of the colony comes largely from its mineral wealth, much of which lies in the Katanga Province, where the Union Minière du Haut Katanga produces about 170,000 tons of copper every year. Large quantities of cobalt, industrial diamonds, tin and palm oil also are produced. The entire uranium output is bought by the United States and represents more than half the quantity used annually by the U.S.A.

Léopoldville, the capital, stands on the river Congo opposite Brazzaville (French Equatorial Africa). It has fine modern buildings and a spacious roadway, the Boulevard Albert I. The chief town of the Katanga mining region is *Elisabethville*, which stands on the main railway from Cape Town.

Holland, Land of Dykes

The most amazing feature of Holland

IN HOLLAND AND BELGIUM

Associated Press.

A large part of Holland is less than a hundred feet above sea level and canals for drainage and transport are a feature of the country. Here is a scene when the cold weather had frozen the canals and so provided ice skating for the inhabitants. This picture shows Dutch skaters enjoying their sport against a typical landscape with its familiar windmill.

Reece Winstone.

Beyond the old buildings forming the heart of Brussels are many fine blocks of offices, shops and flats in the modern style. Here are the Radio Staff Centre and (right) Broadcasting House, in the southern suburb of Ixelles on the banks of the Etangs d'Ixelles. *Etang* means " pond."

is the intricate system of dykes and canals by which the Dutch have protected their low-lying country and have actually added to it. Indeed, there is a saying that " God made the earth, except Holland, which the Dutchmen made for themselves." At times in their history, though, the Dutch have used the sea as a weapon against their enemies, breaking the dykes they had laboriously built and flooding the countryside to check the advance of some aggressor. Leyden was so defended against the Spaniards in 1574, and in quite recent times the dykes were cut and parts of Holland flooded to stem the German onslaught.

But for the most part the sea has been the enemy of Holland, taxing the skill of her engineers who are working to-day on reclamation schemes and the construction of new *polders* (areas of reclaimed land). Most impressive of these has been in the Zuider Zee, now known as Ijsel Lake, since at last it has been completely enclosed and considerably reduced in area.

Two large areas, the Wieringermeer Polder and the Noordoost Polder, have already been won from the sea. Further areas are to follow, bringing the total of reclaimed land to more than half a million acres. Imagine living on an island, then finding that your island home has become part of the mainland! That is what happened to the fishermen of Urk, an island which is now incorporated in the Noordoost Polder. In time the picturesque island of Marken also will be absorbed and quaint fishing villages like Volendam and Monnikendam will no longer look out over a vast stretch of water, but face new-won farmland.

Reece Winstone.

FINE OLD GUILD HOUSES IN BRUSSELS' GRAND PLACE

Few cities have a medieval square to equal the Grand Place at Brussels. Rebuilt after the bombardment of 1695, these richly-decorated buildings were the headquarters of trade and craft organisations. Notice (left) the House of the Shippers' Guild whose gable represents the stern of an old-time sailing ship

E N.A.

IN THE BELGIAN ARDENNES

In the wooded valley of the Lesse, not far from where it joins the Meuse, the walls and pinnacles of the castle of Walzin rise from a precipitous rock. The thirteenth-century castle was destroyed by Henry II in 1554, but was rebuilt in its present form in 1581.

But the sea fights back. The great floods of February, 1953, caused enormous destruction and much suffering in Holland, and vast areas of the country again went under water. So terrible was the damage that the work of reclaiming the Zuider Zee had to be stopped and cranes, dredgers and other equipment rushed to the coast elsewhere to make good the yawning gaps in the dykes.

A typical example of what happened is found on the island of Schouwen, where, at Schelphoek, the sea tore a gap a quarter of a mile wide. Four months after the floods sea water was still flowing through this gap, through a channel a hundred feet deep. It was said that 120 million tons of sea water came in with every tide. The gap could not be sealed where it was made; instead the defenders had to work on a new sea wall farther " inland," sinking willow mats and caissons as a foundation for this work.

How Land is Reclaimed

Willow mats play an important part in winning land from the sea and in repairing the dykes that protect land already recovered. They are quite large and are made of willow faggots fastened together. The mats are then filled with sand and clay, loaded with stone and sunk to prevent the sea from scouring the gap that is to be closed. Upon such foundations will the sea wall be built. Stakes and sandbags are used to protect the dyke, which is also reinforced by sand, pumped with water through large pipes. When the sea has thus been held back successfully, water can be pumped out from within the dyke, which will be protected further by the grasses planted upon it. These grasses are tough and specially chosen for their ability to grow quickly and so bind together the soil of the dyke.

Land reclaimed in this way is supervised by a government department called the Waterstaat, whose scientists study the soil and advise on how it can best be made fertile, as well as helping with the actual work of reclamation.

We may expect to see further changes in the map of Holland as more land is wrested from the sea. One project that is now being studied by Dutch engineers is the " Three Islands Plan," which would join the islands of North and South Beveland and Walcheren together.

Perhaps you know the famous story of the little Dutch boy who saved the dyke by stopping a small hole with his finger to prevent the water trickling through and causing a break in the sea defences. The story tells us that he kept back the water all through the night, only leaving his post when help came in the morning. The little Dutch boy never actually existed, but his story so typifies the struggle of the Dutch against the sea that a statue now commemorates the young hero of fiction. It was unveiled in 1950 at Spaarndam, near Haarlem, " to honour the boy who symbolises the perpetual struggle of the Netherlands against the water."

Fighting the sea is costly. Repairs to the dykes of Schouwen-Duiveland after the floods of 1953 were not nearing completion until March, 1954. The work required over 600,000 tons of stone, more than 3 million sandbags and 5 million osier bundles. More than 400 small caissons and five large caissons, and huge quantities of sand and clay were also used.

A large part of Holland is less than a hundred feet above sea level; much of the west is many feet below it; the eastern areas are higher, rising at one point to 1,000 feet above sea level. Like Belgium, western Holland is protected in many places by sand dunes on which marram and other hardy grasses have been planted; these form as much a bulwark against the sea as do the imposing man-made dykes found elsewhere.

The work of dykes and dunes is completed by the canals which are both highways and drainage channels. They carve the countryside into a thousand patterns, drawing the water off the rich farmland and linking towns and villages in a transport

Reece Winstone.

AN OLD LADY FROM S'HERTOGENBOSCH

But for her modern glasses, this dignified old lady might be a figure from one of the masterpieces of some Flemish painter such as Rembrandt. National costume and the kindly lines of her worn face suggest the quiet of those older times rather than the bustle and hurry of the modern world.

AN OLD DUTCH TOYSELLER

Reece Winstone.

This genial old fellow with a handsome handlebar moustache sells toy windmills in the square outside the Royal Palace at Amsterdam. Amsterdam is officially the capital of Holland and is one of her great seaports. It is linked to the North Sea by a ship canal, which begins with the great sea locks at Ymuiden. It is also an important manufacturing town and is a famous centre for diamond cutting and polishing.

system that is uniquely Dutch. With sentinel-like windmills upon their high banks, the canals in summer are alive with *schuyts*, *boiers*, and the *marktschepen* (market boats) in which the farmers take their produce to market. In winter they are glassy roads over which sledges glide and skaters skim like swallows.

Holland is a neat, trim country with all the small freshness of some gaily painted toyland. The woodwork on the houses is painted with bright colours that would seem out of place in staid Britain; bright shutters flank the windows; and everywhere there is cleanliness. Even the pavements, roads, and *rijwielenpads* (special bicycle roads) are spotlessly clean, and it is nothing to see a Dutch villager and his family cleaning down the front of their house in the early hours of the morning. As in Belgium, many of the towns cluster round high belfries which past generations of Dutch have reared as if to defy the flatness of their lush meadows. Some towns are built round networks of canals so that there are as many, if not more, waterways than streets.

Holland is a country of bulb gardens and dairy farms where land, as soon as it is reclaimed from the sea and fit for use, is turned to agriculture. Looking at the famous *polder* near Haarlem with its rich, multi-coloured carpet of flowers it is hard to realise that this fertile stretch was once the sea bed. To-day, this Haarlem *polder* is a flourishing bulb centre whence bulbs are sent to all parts of

Donald McLeish.

HERE FORTY-TWO BELLS RING OUT

The city of Utrecht, in Holland, is partly divided by the Oude Canal, affording one many glimpses of placid waters, quaint bridges and ancient houses. On the right is seen the tower of Utrecht Cathedral, carried to a height of 338 feet and containing no fewer than forty-two bells. Bells assembled in such numbers are known as a " carillon."

A Shell Photograph.

IN THE HARBOUR OF MARKEN ISLAND, HOLLAND

An island of fishing hamlets off the north of Holland, Marken stands in the Ijsel Lake, formerly known as the Zuider Zee before the great enclosing dam was completed in recent years. The sailors in the picture are wearing the traditional blue waist-length shirts which cover the warm red woollen vests. Baggy knee breeches, usually black, navy blue stockings and "klompen" (clogs) are as characteristic of these fishing villages as the wooden houses seen in the background.

A. F. Kersting.

IN NORWAY'S "HOME OF THE GIANTS"

If you travel from Fortun, at the head of the Sogne Fiord, to Grotli you may use this winding road through the foothills of the Jotunheim country of southern Norway. This mountainous region has an area of about nine hundred and fifty square miles and contains Galdhöpiggen, Glittertind and other great peaks, which make this part of Norway a favourite playground for climbers. The name Jotunheim means "Giants' Home" and makes us think of Thor and the other mountain-dwelling giants of Norse legend. Notice the typical scenery—small pastures, conifer trees and barren peaks.

FISHERFOLK OF THE NETHERLANDS

Little change has taken place in the costumes of the villagers and fisherfolk of the Netherlands, but there have been changes in other ways. This scene was taken by the side of the Ijsel Lake, formerly part of the Zuider Zee. Gradually the reclamation of this area from the sea is being accomplished and Ijsel Lake has become fresh water. The great enclosing dam or dyke will bring over half-a-million fertile acres of farmland into existence.

the world where there are gardens and where the climate will permit tulips and hyacinths to grow.

Over a third of Holland is grassland and dairy-farming is the country's most important business, particularly in the Friesland provinces around Utrecht, and in North Holland. Dutch cheese is famous, and the two best-known cheese centres are Edam and Alkmaar.

There is cultivation, of course, as well as dairy-farming, and the chief crops are rye and oats, sugar-beet and potatoes. The Dutch farmlands are gay, for the people still wear their traditional costumes which add brightness and colour to the landscape.

Dutch Industries

Though Holland has little coal (only in Dutch Limburg and the Kempenland on the Belgian border), and few raw materials, she maintains her factories with supplies brought from abroad. Coal from Britain and elsewhere makes steam power for her factories and electrical plants. Her timber comes from the Baltic, her cotton from the United States, her wool from the Argentine; and to these are added the raw materials from her own dominions overseas, from the East Indies and from Dutch Guiana (Surinam). Thus she feeds her cotton and linen industry at Almelo, her woollen and artificial silk factories at Utrecht, her linen mills at Tilburg and Haarlem, and her imposing electric light bulb and radio factories at Eindhoven and Venlo.

Since the war, Holland has developed her own oilfields. She produces, in the Schoonebeek region of the province of Drenthe, about a quarter of the oil that she needs. The chief refinery for handling this " black gold " is at Pernis. Since 1952 she has been tapping her natural gas; by the end of 1953 some 300 miles of pipeline had been laid to carry the supply.

Her overseas trade, on which these industries depend, comes to two great ports, Rotterdam and Amsterdam. Of these, the greater is Rotterdam which is itself a manufacturing city for margarine, soap, cocoa and chocolate, tobacco and cigars, and rubber manufactures. Rotterdam, standing on the " new waterway " some few miles from its outport of the Hook of Holland, was mercilessly attacked by German aircraft early in the Second World War and a great area of the city was completely destroyed. The Germans, too, did their utmost to destroy the docks in 1944, before they were driven from Rotterdam, but all their efforts could not prevent the quick revival of the city as a leading European port. In 1953, 16,000 ships entered Rotterdam. This was a record number for the port.

Amsterdam is the official capital of Holland, although The Hague is the seat of government (and so the political capital). Like many Dutch cities, it lies below sea level and its larger buildings rest on huge piles. The Royal Palace, for example, has almost 14,000 piles as its foundation.

Amsterdam has its outlet to the sea in its North Sea Ship Canal which begins with the great sea-locks at Ymuiden. It has manufactures similar to those of Rotterdam and is world-famous as a centre for diamond-cutting and polishing. Because of its canals, Amsterdam is sometimes called " The Venice of the North."

The airport for Amsterdam is Schiphol, which is a European crossroads of the air used by the airlines of many continental countries.

The correct name of The Hague is 's Gravenhage, which means " the Count's Hedge." It is said that the city owes its name and beginnings to the hunting lodge of Count William, which stood there in the thirteenth century and which became the residence of the counts of Holland. Not far from The Hague is the seaside holiday town of Scheveningen. Between The Hague and Amsterdam, especially in the district north of the historic university city of Leiden, are the fields of bulbs and other flowers.

SANTA CLAUS ON HORSEBACK

Sport and General.

St. Nicholas is called Santa Claus in Britain and the custom of giving gifts on his Feast Day, December 6th, has been transferred in many countries to Christmas Day. In Holland the Feast of St. Nicholas is still celebrated by the distribution of gifts to children and our photograph shows St. Nicholas riding on a white horse, on December 6th, through the streets of Amsterdam.

Will F. Taylor.

Here is a typical scene at a cheese market in Holland. The round pink cheeses are set up for inspection in pyramids, closely resembling piles of gigantic cricket balls. It takes 50 pints of milk to make a " cannon-ball " cheese weighing about 4¼ lbs.

What a blaze of colour can here be seen in springtime! And what a great area is covered by this important Dutch industry! Between Leiden and Haarlem alone there are some 16,000 acres devoted to bulb growing.

From these fertile acres, beautiful flowering bulbs are sent to most parts of the free world. To make sure that Dutch bulbs are free from pests and diseases, the Dutch have set up a special laboratory for bulb research at Lisse, in the heart of this colourful area. Near Lisse is the " Keukenhof," a wonderful park devoted to the permanent open-air display of Dutch bulbs. More than ten million bulbs are planted in the park and there are ten miles of footpaths.

South of The Hague is the fertile Westland district where there are literally acres of glasshouses. In these, market garden farmers produce fine, out-of-season vegetables and luscious grapes.

In Holland, as in Belgium, past and present rub shoulders. Not far from the busy centres of modern industry and commerce are picturesque old world towns and cities which people come to see from all parts of the world: Delft, the famous old china town that is as much the haunt of artists as is Belgian Bruges: Alkmaar, with its colourful cheese market: Middelburg, the fine old town on Walcheren. Holland has many such show-places.

Travelling through the Dutch country-side, you would notice that in many small towns and villages the people still wear their traditional costume. At Urk, for example, you might see an old fisherman wearing baggy breeches and wooden *klompen* (clogs). The headdresses of spotless white lace or linen worn by many Dutch country women, and the gold ornaments with which the headdresses are decorated, have remained the same for centuries.

Like the British, the Dutch have the tradition of being fine seamen and able colonists. Their colonies in the East Indies have now become the independent United States of Indonesia, a country which still has considerable trade and other links with Holland.

Other Dutch overseas territories include Surinam, or Dutch Guiana, on the north-east coast of South America; the Netherlands Antilles, in the Caribbean Sea, consisting of two groups of islands, the most important being Curaçao and Aruba, which have refineries for oil shipped from Venezuela; and Netherlands New Guinea.

Reece Winstone.

A GIRL OF SOUTHERN HOLLAND

The Dutch are proud of their national costume and wear it from day to day in the country towns and villages. The dress of this girl of s'Hertogenbosch is of sombre black, but her headdress is of spotless starched linen, with pins and spiral haircombs made of gold.

The Story
of the
World and
its Peoples

Farm, Forest,
and Fjord
in
North=East Europe

Will F. Taylor.

FASHIONED AFTER THE OLD NORSE LONGSHIPS

Ever since the days of the old Norsemen who set out in their longships on the " Viking path "
of plunder and conquest, the Norwegians have been fine seamen. The very fishing craft seen
lying peacefully in this Norwegian harbour are the lineal descendants of the old Norse galleys.

SCANDINAVIA AND THE BALTIC

SCANDINAVIA, the largest European peninsula, is the home of the Norwegians and Swedes. On the western shore, facing America and the North Atlantic, is Norway whose people are traditionally seafarers, living on the sea and by the sea. To the east, facing Russia and Continental Europe, is Sweden whose people, with advantages of land and climate, have become expert dairy-farmers.

The Norse Sea-Rovers

From the mountainous shores and winding fjords of this peninsula sailed the Norse sea-rovers who harried the shores of Western Europe, penetrated the Mediterranean, fought their way across Russia and down the Volga, and crossed the North Atlantic in their " long dragons " to discover America some 500 years before Columbus. The

Norsemen formed many settlements in our own country as we can see from the modern place names of towns and villages where they made their homes. Normandy got its name from the Norsemen whose leader, the redoubtable Rollo the Ganger, carved out a dukedom for himself at the mouth of the Seine. To this day, Norwegians are among the finest seamen in the world, and they can build ships with a skill that is the heritage of many centuries of ship-building.

Historically, the people of Denmark are of the same racial group, the Nordic branch, as the Norwegians and the Swedes. Their languages, though now different, originate from the same roots and they share common myths and legends of the times before history. Once Norway, Denmark, and Sweden were united under one crown. From 1397 until 1523, the sovereigns of

Denmark ruled all three countries. Then Sweden broke away to raise herself under Gustavus the First and his grandson Gustavus Adolphus to a pre-eminent position in the Baltic, becoming one of the great Powers of Europe. Later, squandering her resources in profitless war, Sweden lost her position though she retained her independence.

During the Napoleonic wars, Denmark and her satellite Norway, whom she still ruled, staked their fortunes with Napoleon. When peace came, the Allies punished Denmark by taking Norway from her and giving it to Sweden whose king, Bernadotte, a former marshal of France, had helped to defeat the Emperor who had lifted him to his throne. From 1814 until 1905, Norway and Sweden were jointly ruled, different though they were in interests and aspirations. In 1905 Sweden, wishing to avoid war, honourably gave Norway her independence, thus replacing a turbulent

and discontented subject people with a land of friendly neighbours.

The Mountain Backbone

Geographically, Norway and Sweden have a natural frontier in the mountain backbone of the Kiolen. This runs southwards to lose itself in great mountain masses whose peaks soar above wide snow-fields and whose upper valleys are filled with the long tongues of big glaciers reaching to points below the snowline. Part of this mountainous southern region is called the Jotunheim (Giants' Home), a name that reminds us of Thor and the giants of old Norse legends. The highest peak is Galdhöpiggen and the next is Glittertind; both are over 8,000 feet high.

What a country for winter sports! On winter Saturdays the railway station of Oslo, the Norwegian capital, is crowded with men, women and children waiting for the electric trains to

E.N.A.

THE SAWMILLS AT SANDVIKEN

Sweden's great timber industry lies mainly in the north of the country where millions of logs from the dark conifer forests are floated down the rivers to the sawmills and pulp-mills of the Baltic coast. The Sandviken mills shown here are situated on an island in the harbour of Umea.

WHERE SCOTT OF THE ANTARCTIC TRAINED

E.N.A.

Norway is a great land for winter sports, and since much of the country is above the snow line, winter sports are possible in many places during the summer. The skiers in this picture are at Finse, the highest point on the Oslo-Bergen railway, where our Antarctic hero, Captain Scott, did much of his training with his men and his motor sledges before setting out on his ill-fated journey to the South Pole. Notice the patterns cut by skis in the snow carpet beyond the buildings.

Norway is above the snow-line (which is lower in the Scandinavian Mountains than in the Swiss Alps), winter sports are possible in many parts of the country *in summer*. A great ski centre is at Finse, the highest point on the Oslo-Bergen railway, where there is a monument to our Antarctic hero, Captain Scott, who carried out much of his training there before setting out on his ill-fated journey to the South Pole.

The Kiolen axis is much nearer the Atlantic than the Baltic,

NORWAY'S " SEVEN SISTERS "

Norway is a narrow country of many mountains into which the hungry sea penetrates by long, deep channels known as " fjords." The fjords themselves are often fed by falls of water cascading down almost vertical hillsides, as is illustrated by the " Seven Sisters " waterfall. One fjord penetrates inland for a hundred and six miles.

take them out to the nearest toboggan slides and ski runs. Everyone skis in Norway, it seems. Great competitions are held at the ski-ing festivals, especially at Holmenkollen where extraordinary feats of leaping and swift turning are performed. Since much of

Will F. Taylor.

IN A NORWEGIAN FJORD

This picture shows a peaceful scene in the famous Hardanger Fjord, with its deep and placid waters from whose edge rugged mountains tower like giant walls. Like all fjords, Hardanger is deeper at its inland end than at its entrance, where a glacial sill of detritus from prehistoric glaciers accumulated ages ago.

Swedish Travel Association.

A HOME OF OLD SWEDEN

This picture shows the interior of a home in Sweden, furnished in the traditional style. In Stockholm, the capital, and other Swedish towns and cities, you will find fine examples of modern architecture and furnishings; but in the lovely countryside, traditional dress and the old way of life still linger.

giving Sweden a much longer and more gradual slope, but almost filling the long narrow country of Norway with mountains. Norway descends steeply into the sea in sheer precipices hundreds of feet high in many places, as tourists who visit the fjords in summer soon discover when they find their steamer in deep, smooth water close under towering walls of grey and black rock.

Scandinavian Rivers

Norwegian rivers are nearly all short and swift, except the south-flowing Glommen, which is the only river having a considerable area of land suitable for farming. Swedish rivers, on the other hand, are longer and slower, many coming down from large lakes that keep the rivers in full and regular flow, making them particularly useful in the northern half of the country for floating down the millions of logs from the dark conifer forests to the

saw-mills and pulp-mills at the Swedish ports on the Baltic Sea. But although Norway's rivers are too swift for transport purposes, and too full of swift rapids and high falls, they are the sources of abundant electrical power that runs everything—mills, factories, trains—and gives cheap lighting and heating, too, to tens of thousands of homes in town and country. Two very beautiful falls are the Laatefos and the Skarsfos (Fos means " Falls "). The Rjukanfos, 345 feet high, now drives the great power-stations of the famous Norwegian works where nitrates are made from the air to fertilise the fields of Europe.

Sweden's rivers supply abundant power, too. One of the most wonderful power-houses in the world is operated by the giant force of the Trolhätten Falls, a few miles north of Gothenburg (Göteborg), Sweden's sea-gate to the North Sea and the Atlantic Ocean.

Scandinavia has very little coal, but thanks to the abundant " white coal " supplied by the many falls and rapids, both Norway and Sweden can run transport and factories even more cheaply than other countries dependent on- coal can run theirs. Even tiny out-of-the-way villages have their electric light and their telephones in many parts of Scandinavia.

The Effects of the Kiolen Axis

This Kiolen axis, of which we have already said a good deal, has another very important effect. It shuts off Sweden from the warmth and moisture brought by the west winds from the Atlantic, and causes Sweden to tilt towards the Baltic and Eastern Europe. The result is that Sweden has a much more severe winter than Norway; its Baltic ports are sealed by ice, but the Atlantic ports and harbours of Norway are open all the year round. Sweden, too, has much less rain than Norway; Bergen in Norway has more than 80

inches of rain a year, but Stockholm, Sweden's beautiful capital, has fewer than 20 inches.

The winter difference between Baltic and Atlantic ports is well seen in relation to the great Swedish iron-mines of Gellivaare and Kiruna, huge open workings of very rich iron ore in Swedish Lapland. This ore must be taken to the sea coast, for a great deal of it is not used in Scandinavia, but is sent away to Britain and other countries of Western Europe. Electric trains driven by power from the great power-station at Porjus go down to the Baltic coast at Lulea, and also to the Atlantic coast at Narvik. But the ore can be shipped at Lulea only during the summer months, whereas Narvik is busy shipping ore all the year round.

Kiruna, ninety miles north of the Arctic Circle, produces about $8\frac{1}{2}$ million tons of iron ore each year, and within ten years this quantity may be doubled. This means that both the railway and the ports must be improved to handle

E.N.A.

A SAETER ON THE MOUNTAIN PASTURES OF NORWAY

When the winter snows have melted, the Norwegian farmers drive their cattle up to the high pastures, where the herd will live all the summer. The saeter, or mountain hut, provides accommodation for the farm-people and a place where cheese and butter can be made.

NORWAY'S SEA-GIRT OUTPOSTS

Dorien Leigh.

The Lofotens, rocky islands off the north-west coast of Norway, are the centre of a vast fishing industry which reaps the rich harvest of the sea—chiefly cod and herring—and processes them for home and international markets.

Keystone.

In 1920, the Svalbard group of islands in the North Arctic, which includes West Spitzbergen, came under Norwegian rule and were formally taken over by Norway five years later. The picture shows Longyear City, the main coal-mining camp of Svalbard.

the increase. New railway tunnels have been driven through the mountains and more powerful electric engines built to haul the ore to Narvik and Lulea. The latter port now has a large new Government steel works to use the Lapland ore, which means that Sweden will not have to rely so much on imported steel.

Northern Norway

Norway's largest iron ore mines are also in the north, at Kirkenes, near her frontier with Russia. Kirkenes stands on the new National Highway, which runs for nearly 2,000 miles from Oslo to the Arctic north.

Although Tromsö, the chief town of northernmost Norway, has a population of some 10,000 people, most of the inhabitants of these Arctic lands are fisherfolk and peasants living in small villages along the coast. For a long time their prosperity has depended upon the great cod fisheries; but this may in time be changed as a result of the North Norway Plan, which will build new power stations in the north, develop the timber and iron ore resources there, and modernise agriculture and the fishing industry.

The Norwegian Fjords

The greatest of all the many attractions of Scandinavia for summer visitors are the beautiful fjords, the longest of which, the Sogne Fjord, penetrates inland for a hundred and six miles from the sea. Another famous fjord is Hardanger Fjord, on a branch of which is Odda with its important chemical works.

The coast of Western Norway is cut up into a fringe of close tatters by the fjords, which are often much deeper at their landward ends than at their seaward entrances, so that quite large steamers can go right up, almost to their farthest shores.

These fjords are the result of the slow sinking of the Norwegian coast-

A. F. Kersting.

A GREAT FISHING PORT

Norwegians have been fine seamen ever since the days of the Norsemen. They are also great fishermen, and this picture shows Bergen, the fish market port of Norway, and headquarters of Norway's great fishing fleets. Bergen is also one of the western termini of the main cross-country railways.

NORWAY'S COUNTRYSIDE

Norwegian State Railways.

If you were touring in Norway you would bring home with you many impressions, like photographs on your mind, of which the above is a typical example. It shows a pleasant farm in the central part of the country, a valley homestead, above which on three sides the mountains pile.

A. F. Kersting.

When harvest time comes, the cut grass is hung on wires stretched between poles to dry and, from afar, the fields look as if small walls of green had been built within them. This picture was taken in Central Norway. In the background can be seen a part of the vast Jostedalsbreen glacier, which is one of the largest in Europe.

OSLO AND COPENHAGEN

Dorien Leigh.

This view of Oslo from the roof of the Parliament House shows (left background) the National Theatre and, beyond, the Royal Palace. The time to see Oslo is on May 17th every year, when the constitution of 1814 is commemorated in a national holiday.

E.N.A.

A sixth of the Danish people live in Copenhagen, Denmark's seaport capital on the island of Zealand. The picture shows the imposing Christiansborg Palace, which is occupied by the Rigsdag (Parliament) and the supreme Court of Justice. Copenhagen means " merchants' haven."

STOCKHOLM FROM THE AIR

This view of the Swedish capital shows (centre) the Royal Palace and, to the right, the Riksdagshus or Parliament building. The " granite capital " is built upon two groups of islands. Its name means Isle of Logs, which is appropriate, for Stockholm's prosperity has come from timber forests.

Stockholm's Town Hall adds beauty to Lake Mälaren. The tower supports a lantern above which are the three crowns of the Swedish coat of arms. Each of the small plates in the copper roof bears the name of a citizen who contributed to the cost of the building.

E.N.A.

STOCKHOLM'S WEST BRIDGE

The strong girders of the Vasterbron, or West Bridge, link the Kungsholmen and Soder districts of the island capital. Being a city built upon islands, Stockholm has many bridges and ferry steamers.

voyage home again, and even that, in summer, is rarely very bad for people who fear sea-sickness.

Another great attraction for tourists to the fjords is the Midnight Sun, which can be seen at midsummer at all places on and north of the Arctic Circle. Hammerfest is a favourite spot for Midnight Sun hunters, but the sun makes a much braver show at North Cape in the far north of Scandinavia.

The Lofoten Islands

The Lofoten Islands are the centre of Norway's greatest cod-fishing, and during the season the Lofoten banks, above which the swarming cod move in vast shoals that are from 100 to 160 feet deep from top to bottom, are thronged with fishing craft, and the harbours of the islands are packed with vessels that have come there to buy fish for the big markets, especially for Bergen. Tromsö and Hammerfest also are important centres of the fishing industry. The fish are split, cleaned, salted and dried on the rocks or spread on high platforms ready for export. The heads and other refuse are made into fish manure for gardeners and farmers. The chief centre for Norwegian sardine fisheries is Stavanger, where, it is said, 600 million sardines (brisling) are canned every year. Stavanger has gained new importance as a European airport. Developed during the German occupation, its airfield of Sola is one of the largest on the Continent.

The famous Maëlstrom, the dread whirlpool of Edgar Allen Poe's strange tale, " A Descent into the Maëlstrom," is between two of the islands at the

line, which allowed the sea to flood the deep valleys carved out in former ages by moving ice and running water. Outstanding peaks were surrounded, and now stand in the sea " up to their necks," appearing as the multitudes of islands that fringe the coast, creating behind them an " inner lead " of perfectly smooth water sheltered from the outer sea. The calm waters of the inner lead and the long, deep fjords make a trip to Norway particularly delightful for those who wish to take a voyage without the discomfort that results from rough weather. Once across the North Sea from Hull, or Newcastle, or Leith, the steamer is on an even keel for the rest of the trip, save for the southern tip of the Lofoten Archipelago. It is dangerous to small craft.

Just as Norway is famous for fish, so Sweden is famous for timber in the northern half and dairy produce in the south. Norway carries on dairy-farming, too, but farmers there are hard put to it to feed the cows during the long winter, when they must be kept indoors just as they are in Switzerland. Norwegian farmers treasure every little bit of grass, and even mow it on perilous slopes, sending it down to the valleys by wire ropes. They do not dry it in haycocks as we sometimes do, but hang it out to mellow over long rows of wire ropes supported on posts, so that the air and sun can quickly do their work.

The Scandinavian Capitals

The capital of Norway is Oslo, whence electric trains run to Bergen, the great fishmarket and timber port, to Trondhjem, the old capital, and to Gothenburg and other towns in Southern Sweden. Oslo's most famous street is the Karl-Johans-Gade, which runs from the railway station to the King's Palace on its low hill; along this street the chief places of interest are the Norwegian Houses of Parliament and the Stor-Torv or chief market-place of the city.

Sweden's capital is Stockholm, the "city of granite," built on many islands in Lake Mälaren, with its sea approaches from the Baltic guarded by multitudes of rocky "skerries" or islands.

You can travel by water from Stockholm in a fine little pleasure steamer along the Baltic coast to the entrance of the Göta Canal, which takes you right across Southern Sweden by way of the great lakes Vattern and Vänern and the Göta River to Göteborg (Gothenburg), facing the Atlantic, Sweden's

E.N.A.

FERRY BOATS LINK THE RAILWAYS OF DENMARK AND SWEDEN

This train ferry plying between Elsinore in Denmark and Hälsingborg in Sweden, links the railway systems of the two countries. In normal times Denmark's rail communications with Germany are similarly linked by the ferry from Gjedser to Warnemunde as well as by overland routes. In the background is the Kronborg Castle, famous as the place where Hamlet is supposed to have seen his father's ghost.

great commercial port that trades with the whole world.

It is on the Göta River that the famous Trolhätten Fall occurs, which we have already mentioned as the site of one of the greatest power-houses in Europe.

The Gates of the Baltic are commanded jointly by Sweden and Denmark. Danish islands bar the passage to the sea, limiting entry to three waterways—the Sound, between Sweden and the largest island, Zealand: the Great Belt, between Zealand and the island of Fünen: and the Little Belt, between Fünen and the Jutland Peninsula. Situated thus, Denmark is strategically important to any nation wishing to use the Baltic and, in times of war, has been courted by Powers mindful of her commanding position. Germany evaded the issue by cutting the Kiel Canal through the base of the Jutland Peninsula from Brunsbüttel to Holtenau, a great engineering feat which was completed during the reign of Kaiser Wilhelm II.

Denmark is a green, flat, pleasant land similar in type and climate to Scania, the southern part of Sweden, rich in cattle, and studded with dairy farms and neat towns and villages. Like Sweden, Denmark is a country famous for her progressive dairy-farming. Danish butter and bacon are justly world-renowned and a co-operative dairy is a feature of nearly every village in Denmark. Like the Norwegians, the Danes are also fishermen, but while the Norwegians fish chiefly for cod and herring, the Danish harvest of the sea is mainly plaice. In the north of Denmark, the Lijm Fjord has been made into a vast " fish pond " whither the Danes bring young plaice from the North Sea to keep in floating cages until they are needed at Esbjerg, the fish-market town of Denmark.

Over a quarter of the Danish people live in Copenhagen, on the island of Zealand, the city-seaport which is Denmark's capital. In some ways, Copenhagen reminds us of Holland's cities. It is without hills; it is near the sea; it has many canals.

Donald McLeish.

BUILT BY A SWEDISH KING

This castle, so different from the fortress homes we find in our own fair land, was erected in the sixteenth century by a Swedish King named Gustavus the First. It stands in the town of Vadstena, on the shores of Lake Vattern. Sweden possesses many lakes, and her rivers often widen into lakes. Canals are also used for transport and travel.

Copenhagen is where Tycho Brahe, the great sixteenth century astronomer, lived and worked. It is the city of Hans Andersen, one of the world's greatest tellers of children's tales, and of Thorwaldsen, one of northern Europe's great sculptors. Here, too, many a tourist gets his first taste of *smörrebröd*—an intriguing meal that is really a vast hors d'œuvres of endless and appetising variety.

Denmark has many show-places. Few visit her green and pleasant land without wanting to see Kronborg Castle at Elsinore, Hamlet's castle, as we at once think of it; Roskilde, the burial-place of the Danish kings; the castle of Frederiksborg; and the unusual open-air museum at Lyngby which is dedicated to the ancient art and crafts of the Danish countryside.

Iceland

Denmark includes the Faroe Islands, which rank as a Danish " county ", but her only colony is Greenland. Most of the people living in Greenland are Eskimo and much of the country is buried beneath a thick ice cap. Recently large quantities of lead were found there.

Iceland was once ruled by Denmark, but was acknowledged to be a sovereign state in 1918 and has been an independent republic since 1944. The capital, Reykjavik, is supplied with constant hot water by its natural hot springs. The next most important town is Akureyri, the northern port. Iceland has broad pastures where sheep, horses and cattle are reared,

Wide World Photos.

A TOWER OF DRAGON'S TAILS

The Royal Exchange, Copenhagen, was erected in the seventeenth century. The structure is surmounted by a tower upwards of 160 feet in height, at the top of which are four dragons. Their tails, intertwined, form the spire.

and around her shores the rich fisheries that bring seamen from many parts of north-western Europe. Iceland is mainly of volcanic origin and still has active volcanoes, the most famous being Hekla. When Hekla erupted in 1947, the noise of the eruption was heard 200 miles away. The name Iceland does not mean " land of ice," but simply " the island."

Northwards up the Baltic

The Baltic Sea, rich in the history of Hansa trading cities such as Danzig and Lübeck and the old walled island town of Wisby, becomes a sea of many islands as the coast of Finland is neared. There are literally thousands of them, some inhabited, some mere rock, others almost submerged in the dark salt waters. Presently, ahead, looms up the great lighthouse of Uto which is the outer guard of the Finnish skerries and is first seen as a tall pillar striped vertically in white and dark red. Among the islands, the boisterous waters

of the open sea give way to a magic lake calm. The islands grow larger; many are thickly covered with larch and spruce trees; some have villa residences used by the southern Finns in summer. Then, ahead, is the long wharf of Türkü abutting a deep and tideless river mouth and, above the dockside warehouses, an old castle. Türkü is where timber and wood-pulp from the forests inland are loaded and where tall-masted wood schooners come to take cargoes of birch and pine logs to the island-dwellers for storage for winter fuel. An equally important Finnish timber port is Pori, not far from which are paper and wood-pulp factories built of ferro-concrete and equipped with the most modern machinery. The raw timber for these factories is cut along the banks of the Kumo Elf and floated downstream to the mills in vast loose rafts.

Finland is a country of dark forests and innumerable lakes some of which are large enough to hold several English

E.N.A.

THE GREAT BRIDGE ACROSS THE LITTLE BELT

The entrances to the Baltic Sea are commanded by Denmark and Sweden. Danish islands limit entry to three waterways—the Sound, the Great Belt and the Little Belt. The Little Belt separates the island of Fünen from the Jutland Peninsula, but island and mainland are joined by this fine bridge which was built by a famous British engineering firm.

counties and have room to spare. Indeed, Finland is known as "The Land of a Thousand Lakes" and in the south-east, the lakes and their connecting rivers provide the most common way of getting about. The still lake waters and sombre greens of the vast forests give Finland a sad and lonely beauty that is so wonderfully expressed in the music of Finland's great composer Sibelius. Among the most impressive sights in this part of Europe is Imatra, the great

E.N.A.

THE SURGING RAPIDS OF MIGHTY IMATRA

The falls and rapids of Imatra, a few miles north of Viborg (Viipuri), provide an amazing spectacle for visitors. Like Niagara, Imatra is so tremendous that it can supply abundant power to nearby hydro-electric stations. Viborg is now in the Soviet Union.

Mondiale.

A FAMILY RE-UNION IN FINLAND

At this family re-union on a Finnish farm, dinner was served in the old style. "The Land of a Thousand Lakes," as Finland is sometimes called, has vast forests which have given her an important wood-pulp industry. But at such places as Tammerfors (Tampere) and Vasa, she has also important iron and steel works.

FROM FINLAND'S FORESTS

Camera Press.

Tiny tugs tow a huge raft of timber through the waters of a harbour in south-eastern Finland. Heavy beams chained round the edge of the raft keep the logs in place until they can be loaded on to the waiting ship. Finland does a great trade in forest products—timber, wood pulp and paper, matches, plywood and pit props.

E.N.A.

This fine building is the General Post Office at Helsinki. It was completed in 1939 and is typical of the many modern buildings erected in the Finnish capital. Helsinki is often called " the granite city " because, like Stockholm, it is founded upon granite. Many of its public buildings are made of this stone. Helsinki is sometimes called Helsingfors.

THE FINNISH CAPITAL

This aerial picture shows us the heart of the Finnish capital. In the background is the great square with its statue of Tsar Alexander II, who protected Finland's liberties when the country was part of old Russia, and the Lutheran Church of St. Nicholas, which is reached by forty wide steps. Nearer to us are government buildings and the waterfront.

Photos: E.N.A.

The imposing Parliament Building is constructed of Finnish granite and contains a thousand rooms. On the desk of each member in the Diet chamber are two buttons. Pressure on one electrically records a " yes " vote ; on the other, a " no " vote. It takes only a minute and a half for all the members of the Diet to vote.

falls a few miles north of Viipuri (Viborg), which is now Russian. Here, through a long narrow cleft between granite walls, the torrent fights its way, surging in foaming billows that wrestle and leap like struggling giants only to fall in clouds of spray as the swift river hurls itself onward. The hotel that stands within sight and sound of the Falls seems a frail and flimsy human toy compared with the mighty Imatra thundering by its very threshold. Like Niagara, Imatra is so tremendous that she can supply abundant power to the hydro-electric stations standing close by.

Türkü was once the Finnish capital and is still the religious centre of the country, for it was here that an early English missionary first brought Christianity to this northern land. But the political capital is now Helsinki which, like Stockholm, is a city of granite built upon granite itself. Tammerfors (Tampere) is the "Manchester" of Finland where cotton goods are woven from yarn imported from the United States. Tammerfors and Vasa also have iron and steel works. In the extreme north, in the Petsamo region, Finland once had important nickel mines, but the Petsamo region was ceded to Russia in 1944.

The loss of the Petsamo region robbed Finland of about 4,000 square miles of territory; at the same time, a further 13,000 square miles along the east and south-east were lost to Russia. From these lands came some 450,000 refugees, who sacrificed all they had rather than live under Russian rule. They were resettled in new communities set up by the government on triangular stretches of land, called by the Finns "Petsamo triangles," around Lake Inari in the north and along the river Kemi.

The Farms of Finland

The people of Finland call their country *Suomi*, which means "lake land" or "swamp land." Although the lakes cover about an eighth

Camera Press.

HOW THEY KEEP WARM IN FINLAND

In many homes in Finland nearly every room will have a large stove of the kind seen in this picture. The winters are bitterly cold and more than half the country is frost-bound for some six months of the year. But although much of the country is forest, farming is carried on, especially in the south-west, where it is warmer and wetter.

Mondiale.

LAPP CHILDREN TRAVEL BY REINDEER

The Lapp mother has pressed into service reindeer chosen for their tameness and docility. Baby is wrapped in a chequered rug on the leading reindeer; the older child is safe and sound in a basket. The weight of the youngsters is balanced by bundles.

of the surface of the country and although, as we have seen, much of the remainder is thickly forested, farming is one of the chief occupations. Half of Finland is frost-bound for six months of the year, but the fine weather and the great length of the summer days favour dairy farming and arable farming too, particularly on the rich lands of the south-west, where it is wetter and warmer.

Even so, Finnish farmers often have to cut their hay and harvest their grain before it is ripe, drying their crops in heaps mounted on tall stack-poles or in barns warmed by birch-wood fires. Birch-wood is favoured because it gives out more heat than pine and lasts longer. Rye, barley, wheat, oats and potatoes are the main crops, and considerable quantities of butter are produced.

If we visited the countryside of Fin-land we should notice that near each farm was a small house, or large hut, within which we should find tiers of benches and, at one end, a large pile of stones heated from below by a blazing fire. Here we might sample that famous institution of Finland, the *sauna* (steam bath), perhaps following it with a *piehtaroida* (roll in the snow).

Nomads of Arctic Lapland

In far northern Scandinavia, covering the Arctic lands of Finland, Sweden, and the north-western corner of the U.S.S.R., is the region known as Lap-land. Here dwell the Lapps, a wander-ing race of people about whose begin-nings little is known. Small and sturdy, and possessing wonderful endurance, they move from place to place getting a living from their herds of reindeer. Not all Lapps live nomad lives. Indeed, many of the settled Lapps are prosperous farmers with dairy herds.

The Lapps are of many tribes, each of which has caps of a distinctive shape and colour. Although many Lapps wear garments of heavy woollen cloth, reindeer skin is also used for trousers, tunics, coats and boots. Their clothing is often gaily decorated with ribbons and embroidery. The nomad Lapps live in small conical tents or build themselves huts of turf. When they move with their herds of reindeer from one feeding ground to another, every member of the family helps to carry some part of the tent, or *kata* as it is called.

Travelling Schools

In summer the Lapp boys and girls are taught by a teacher who travels with the family during their migration. But in winter, the children attend a permanent school in one of the Lapp villages.

In summer, the Lapps round up their reindeer so that each family can separate his herd from those belonging to others and make sure that his animals bear the correct mark or brand. Stockades are built at the place selected for the round-up, and into these dogs and beaters drive the herds. There are probably thousands of reindeer to be brought in, and the earth almost trembles under the pounding of their hooves as they are driven into the pens. The herdsmen shout, the dogs bark, and the Lapps gathered at the entrance to the pens wave their arms to keep the thundering dust-cloud that is the herd on its proper course. When the stragglers have been rounded up and driven in, and the birch-pole barriers secured across the entrance, the herdsmen will be glad to rest for a while. They have probably been several days without proper sleep or food, intent only on mustering the herds and getting them to the stockades.

The Lapps go with their herds to the highland pastures in summer, but when winter comes they return to their villages of wooden huts and turf dwellings, there to stay until the warmer season returns.

Swedish Tourist Traffic Association.

REINDEER HERDS IN SWEDISH LAPLAND

The Lapps are a race of nomads who live in northern Scandinavia and who move from place to place with their herds of reindeer. The picture shows one of the regular round-ups, made so that the owners can pick out their animals and brand them with their marks.

The Story
of the
World and
its Peoples

Among
Mountains, Lakes,
Winter Sports
and Thriving Industries

Mondiale.

LINED UP AND ALL READY FOR THE SKI-RACE

During her long but dry winter Switzerland is a country of ice and snow with most invigorating air, and there are opportunities for many kinds of sport over the white wastes. In this scene a group of girls and boys are lined up on their skis, eager for a thrilling race down a snow-clad slope at Adelboden. The word " ski " is of Norwegian origin, and its real meaning is nothing more than " snow-shoe." Some skis have blades 90 inches in length, made from the wood of ash.

SWITZERLAND, THE PLAYGROUND OF EUROPE

LITTLE SWITZERLAND, a sanctuary of freedom and one of the most prosperous of modern states, is more than a Republic. Switzerland is a Confederation, a union of peoples formed to protect themselves from cruel overlords and greedy neighbours. Small though Switzerland is—the whole country is only about twice the size of Wales—she has French, German, and Italian as official languages. In some parts, her people speak dialect or patois or the ancient Romansch tongue. These differences in language show the diversity of the people who live in the twenty-two cantons which make up the Swiss Confederation and who now number over 4,700,000. Common ideals of justice and freedom, nurtured by the fertile valleys and majestic mountains, brought these people together in the political unit that is called Switzerland.

The Fight for Freedom

Like most of the great little nations of the world, the Swiss have had to fight for their liberty. Their story is a long one that dates back to the days of primitive lake settlements of a thousand years before Christ, models of which

SCENES AND SIGHTS FAMILIAR TO—

The city of Berne is the capital of the Swiss Confederation, and contains the Federal Palace or Parliament House here depicted. The river in the foreground is the Aar.

During the summer months cows are taken to pasture on the mountains, both milk and cheese being sent to the towns in the valleys. Girls often mind the cows, as seen above.

Photos: Donald McLeish.

The Lake of Geneva, situated between Switzerland and France, is upwards of forty miles in length; and on the eastern shore stands the entrancing Castle of Chillon, seen above. The Castle occupies a small island and is connected with the mainland by a bridge. There has been a castle on this site for more than seven hundred years.

E. Gyger.

This is the Jungfrau, one of the peaks of the Bernese Oberland, which can be visited from such centres as Interlaken, Grindelwald and Wengen.

Donald McLeish.

This photograph shows the Market Street of Berne and the city's famous clock in its spired tower. The fountain is surmounted by the " Armoured Bear."

Donald McLeish.

Geneva, the third largest city in Switzerland, has long been regarded as one of Europe's great centres. It has played a large part in religious affairs, and this monument, over 100 yards in length, depicts scenes and persons intimately connected with the Reformation, when the faiths of so many countries were remodelled.

can still be seen in the museum of Berne. Then came the Celts: then the conquering Romans who drove roads across the Alps at the Passes of St. Bernard and Julier. Remains of Roman occupation can be seen to-day along the shores of Lake Geneva.

Rome never conquered eastern Switzerland where tribes of Germanic stock developed very differently from those who had settled in the west and who were influenced by Roman civilisation. In the east, Germanic law, language, and culture prevailed; in the west, Roman influence told and blended the Bur-

gundians with the native Celts, producing a people essentially French in outlook and language.

For many decades, east and west fought each other, but both were eventually absorbed into the empire of the great Charlemagne, only to fall apart once more when Charlemagne died. There followed times of desperate struggle to maintain rights and liberties against local lords and princes, and against the Hapsburgs whose oppression brought the first league of Swiss cantons. In 1291, the men of the cantons of Uri, Schwyz, and Lower Unterwalden, all cantons bordering the lovely lake of Lucerne, banded together in a defensive League. Their spirit of resistance lives to-day in the still-told story of the patriots of Ruetli who first raised the standard of revolt and in the epic of William Tell who is still commemorated in an annual festival at Altdorf where he defied the tyrant Gessler.

At Europe's Crossroads

Gradually the League grew and gained its independence from the Holy Roman Empire at the end of the Thirty Years War. Over a hundred years later, when Napoleon's mailclad hand clutched at Europe, Switzerland was formed into the unified Helvetic Republic. After Napoleon's downfall the nations of Europe guaranteed Swiss neutrality and accepted the Federal Pact which had been prepared at Zürich and which brought the

Paul Popper.

EVERYONE HELPS IN HAYMAKING

When haymaking time comes in Switzerland, the whole family goes out to the meadows. Wide-pronged forks for lifting the hay, and baskets of food are brought to keep everyone busy and contented during the day. Even the St. Bernard dog apparently does not want to miss the fun.

number of cantons in the Swiss Confederation to twenty-two. But all this had been arranged by foreign powers, and it was not until 1848 that the Swiss were able to draw up their own constitution without foreign intervention. The country to-day is ruled under the Constitution of 1874. Switzerland has a President, Vice-President, and a Parliament of two chambers—a State Council in which each canton has two seats, and a National Council of representatives chosen in direct election. Because of her widely democratic system and the law which requires every male Swiss to have a period of service in the army, Switzerland is sometimes spoken of as the land of "one man, one vote, one gun."

Situated as she is at the main cross-roads of Middle Europe, Switzerland is the most important of European "buffer states" between powerful rivals who as yet have never dared to challenge the natural defences of the country and the resolute independence of its free citizens.

Paul Popper.

BRINGING HOME THE HAY

This Swiss farmer is almost hidden by the bulky load of hay that he is carrying. His wooden farmhouse, with its overhanging eaves, is typical of northern Switzerland, and of parts of Austria and southern Germany.

A Happy Republic

Switzerland is admired to-day for her democracy, for the humanity which characterises her conduct of affairs, for the kindness and generosity which have made themselves felt in her work as a neutral during two world wars and which make her so hospitable a host to

the countless thousands who visit her.

For Switzerland is the Playground of Europe. No other country in Europe is so much visited by tourists, for no other land can give in the same measure the things for which Switzerland is famous. Her tourist business is the greatest in the world, and many of her people get their living by hotel-keeping, or by providing visitors with things they need on holiday or things to take back home. But apart from all this, Switzerland is a busy farming country and a thriving manufacturing country.

Farming in Switzerland is chiefly dairy-farming, for there is little land for agriculture, except in the valley plains. The cows are kept on the high pastures during the summer, tended by the farmers' sons and daughters who live up there in their châlets during the summer months, making cheeses or sending down the milk to the towns in tall wooden containers that fit snugly to the carrier's back as he descends the steep slopes. In winter the cows are " stall fed "—kept in their cowsheds which, as often as not, are beneath the living-room of the farm. The Swiss farmer saves every bit of fodder he can for winter use; that is why you may often see men cutting hay on perilous and lofty slopes, gathering it in a wide-meshed net and taking it down to the valley by paths which seem almost too

difficult for any living thing but the mountain goats.

Some of the Swiss are foresters and wood-cutters, for many mountain slopes are covered with dense conifer forests whose soft timber is useful not only for building, but also for wood-carving and the making of wooden trinkets, implements, vessels and toys—work that occupies the long evenings of the dark, cold winter when all the world seems mantled in deep snow.

Swiss Manufactures

Switzerland is a manufacturing country, too, although she has little or no coal, and no raw materials to speak of. She has plenty of " white coal," however, in her many waterfalls and rushing streams, and no other land in Europe, except perhaps Scandinavia and Northern Italy, is so well and so cheaply supplied with electric power, light and heat. Her trains are practically all electrically drawn; even small

Donald McLeish.

WHERE CALVIN AND JOHN KNOX PREACHED

This vaulted building in Geneva is known as the Auditoire and dates from the thirteenth century. It is famous as the place where Calvin, the great religious reformer, explained his doctrines, and it was here also that John Knox, the famous Scottish reformer, preached.

SNOWS OF THE MATTERHORN

Donald McLeish.

This peak is known as the " tooth " of the Matterhorn, one of Switzerland's mightiest mountains, which rears its snow-capped summit nearly 15,000 feet above sea level. The mountain is
notorious for its terrific precipices. It has been mastered by intrepid climbers, but many of
those who have attempted the feat are sleeping their last sleep in the churchyard of the little
town far below.

villages have electric light and the telephone, and her mills and factories are mainly electrically driven.

North-eastern Switzerland is busiest in manufactures and textile and metal goods, especially in and around the towns of Zürich, St. Gall and Winterthur. Geneva, the beautiful city at the western end of the lake, and the towns of Le Locle, La Chaux de Fonds and Bienne are all famous centres of the Swiss watch and clock manufacture. Basle, the great frontier town and railway centre, makes fine silks.

But the Switzerland we love is the Switzerland of the towering peaks, of the beautiful lakes and waterfalls, and of the deep and mysterious valleys. Lucerne is usually the starting-place of those who are visiting the country for the first time; they can voyage on its deep, winding lake, they can ascend the Rigi and Pilatus, which any good walker can manage, and which even people who cannot walk at all can climb in the mountain railways.

The High Alps

But later they go over into the Grindelwald to see the fine snow-clad peaks of the Bernese Oberland—the Eiger, the Monch and the Jungfrau, staying either at Grindelwald or at Interlaken, or perhaps at Murren, high perched at its cliff edge above the valley. Mighty glaciers extend their icy tongues down the upper valleys of these mountains of the Oberland, and they and the towering peaks above present fine sport to climbers—and not a little risk. A mountain railway has been made to enable non-climbers to ascend the Jungfrau and get the wonderful views which are to be seen up there.

The highest and most difficult peaks, however, lie to the south-west on the other side of the great deep trench of the Rhône valley. Zermatt is the chief centre there; above it towers the grim tooth of the Matterhorn, whose icy slopes and terrific precipices have been responsible for the untimely end

Donald McLeish.

A CANINE SAVIOUR OF HUMAN LIFE

Among the Alps of Switzerland, high above the snow line, is the Hospice of St. Bernard, famous for the strong intelligent dogs who go out into the white wastes seeking for lost human beings. The faithful St. Bernard dog here shown with the prior is named " Turc." He has made no fewer than thirty-five gallant rescues.

IN SCHEIDEGG'S WINTER SNOWS

Mention of winter sports makes us think at once of Switzerland where scenes such as this may be witnessed at any of the many famous centres. Casting up foamy clouds of snow, the experts turn with an ease that makes ski-ing seem all too simple.

Photos: Topical Press.

Every year, "Avalanche Dogs" are trained on the Grosse Scheidegg, in the Bernese Oberland. They are police, Army, or Customs' dogs, and are usually Alsatian wolfhounds. Each dog has its own master, and dog and master work together in learning how to find casualties which may be buried under six feet of snow.

of many of those who now lie sleeping in the little churchyard in the town below. To the east of the Matterhorn is the great knife-edge of Monte Rosa, across which runs the boundary between Switzerland and Italy, and far to the west is the French peak of Mont Blanc, " monarch of mountains " in Europe.

This mighty mountain knot of the Alps long proved a serious obstacle to man, though he crossed the barrier by many passes. To-day he has driven giant tunnels through it—the St. Gotthard Tunnel between Goeschenen and Airolo; the Simplon (the longest, 12½ miles), between Brig and Domodossola, the Lötschberg between Kandersteg and Brig, and the Mont Cenis which links France with Italy. Splendid motor roads, too, follow the passes.

Because Switzerland has such imposing mountains and because many of her mighty peaks are snow-capped all the year round, we are tempted to think of this country as a land mainly of winter sports and snow. But in speaking of Switzerland we must not forget the warm sunshine which comes to the mountain slopes and valleys and gives Switzerland those remarkably hot summers that are so enjoyed by her visitors from colder climes. Even in the spring, the Swiss sunshine has remarkable warmth.

South of the St. Gotthard

Travel in Maytime, southwards from Zürich and south of the St. Gotthard to the valley of the Ticino. Here we are in that part of Switzerland where Italian is the first language, where

Central Press.

ALP-HORN PLAYERS REQUIRE GOOD LUNGS

These curious instruments are Swiss alp-horns. They are about twelve feet long and are made of wood, and need considerable skill and wind-power if they are to be played well. The three players seen dressed in their national costume in this picture are all members of the same family and were photographed with their instruments outside London's Albert Hall when they visited England for an international festival of folk songs and dancing.

Mirror Features.

THE SPRING FESTIVAL IN ZÜRICH

Zürich, the largest town in Switzerland and an important textile manufacturing centre, still has its trade Guilds such as were common throughout Europe during the Middle Ages. On the third Sunday in every April, members of the Guilds celebrate the coming of spring with processions through the city and the burning of winter (represented by a cotton wool " snowman ") at the stake. In this picture we see members of the Guild of Saint Nicholas.

buildings are more in the Italian than the Germanic style, and where—even though it is early in the year by British standards—we are greeted with brilliant sunshine.

Tunnels through the Mountains

In our train journey from Zürich to the canton of the Ticino we should have come through the St. Gotthard tunnel, which runs for $9\frac{1}{4}$ miles between Goeschenen and Airolo. In winter, when the St. Gotthard pass (6,935 feet) is blocked by snow, a special train service is provided to get motor vehicles past the mountain barrier by taking them through the railway tunnel. Before long, however, a new tunnel may be bored to carry a road that would be open at all times of the year. Even in the depth of winter, snow ploughs can keep the road clear to a height of more than 4,500 feet. The new tunnel has therefore been planned to run for about $6\frac{1}{4}$ miles from Motto Bartola in the south to Hospental in the north. It has been said that the cost of building the tunnel will amount to some £4,250,000.

Another new Alpine tunnel may eventually be bored through Mont Blanc, linking Chamonix with Courmayeur and shortening the journey from Rome to Paris by about a hundred miles.

The river Ticino, whose course we have followed southward, gives its name to this canton of Italian-speaking Swiss. It flows past the old city of Bellinzona, where three castles dominate the heights of the town, and empties into the northern end of Lake Maggiore not far from the charming resort of Locarno. The difference in temperature is most striking. To the north, there has been sunshine naturally: but here, it is really hot; it is so hot, in fact, that if we are going to Locarno on Lake Maggiore, or to Lugano on Lake Lugano we shall be glad of light summer clothing. Here,

we are on the very threshold of Italy, and a short trip by steamer on Lake Maggiore would actually take us across the frontier, as indeed would a similar trip upon Lake Lugano. A trip by lake steamer, visiting the small lakeside villages, is one of the nicest ways of enjoying oneself in this part of Switzerland.

From Lugano we might cross the lake to Capolago and then climb by funicular railway to the summit of Monte Generoso (5,581 feet), where we might stay the night in the comfortable hotel and be called early next morning to see the splendid spectacle of dawn breaking across the snow-covered peaks of the Alps. From Locarno, we might travel by a Swiss Federal Postal bus up any number of colourful mountain valleys, or take the single-track electric train up the Centovalli to Domodossola in Italy. This valley of a hundred valleys,

Graphic Photo Union.

AN ALPINE GIANT

The Wetterhorn, seen in all its majesty in this picture, is an Alpine giant more than 12,100 feet high. Near its summit, steep precipices shoot up to an immense height; these sudden heights and the enormously deep and narrow valleys are the result of extreme compression and mountain folding which took place in past ages.

BY MOUNTAIN AND LAKE

A party of climbers pause to check their route on the map as they make their way down to Adelboden, a popular resort which lies in the valley below them.

Lucerne, which we see in this picture from St. Niklausen, is often said to be the most beautiful lake in Switzerland. On its shores began the Swiss struggle for freedom.

Photos : Kenneth Scowen.

This cobbled street is part of the village of Brissago, on the shores of Lake Maggiore. Although small, Brissago is known all over Switzerland for its cigars.

In many Swiss towns and villages the walls of the houses and other buildings are decorated with designs and figures. The example shown in this picture may be found in Lucerne.

with its crags, clefts, dells, mountain pastures and fir trees, is the loveliest of this Swiss-Italian borderland.

At Domodossola, we are on the main Simplon line by which we might travel farther into Italy or through the long Simplon Tunnel, 7,000 feet below the Alpine peaks, to Brig and the canton of Valais. Here the valley of the upper Rhône provides the grapes for the noted white wine of the canton. This wine is known as Fendant du Valais, the French verb *fendre* meaning " to split "; if the grapes from which this wine is made are pressed, they will split lengthwise. Eighteen of the Swiss cantons produce wine.

Following the Rhône, we come to the Lake of Geneva, at the eastern end of which is Montreux. Not far distant is the famous Castle of Chillon, known to poetry lovers through Byron's poem *The Prisoner of Chillon*. Lausanne, a city built upon steep hills, might also beckon us: Geneva, too, long the home of the ill-fated League of Nations, whose buildings are now used by various United Nations' organisations.

Some Swiss Festivals

Every country has its holidays and festivals, and Switzerland is no exception. Many of the festivals are centuries old and in many districts they are associated with the wine harvest. Zürich has its famous Spring festival, the *Sechseläuten*, or " six o'clock " festival, when the members of the city's guilds ride through the streets wearing their traditional uniforms and mark the end of winter by burning the effigy of a snowman. At Zürich, also, there is the autumn *Knabenschiessen*, which is really a shooting festival for the boys of the city. The prize goes to the best shot, who is also declared the " king " of the festival. But the greatest holiday is August 1st, the birthday of Swiss independence, which is kept as a day of thanksgiving throughout the country.

Kenneth Scowen.

EARLY MORNING ON THE MOUNTAIN SLOPES

The Bernese Oberland is one of the most popular tourist regions of Switzerland. The Oberland lies almost entirely in the Alps and forms the southern part of the canton of Berne. This picture of the mountain slopes above Grindelwald shows how the great snow peaks, conifer trees and high pastures combine to make a landscape of striking beauty.

The Story
of the
World and
its Peoples

Yesterday and
To=day
in Divided
Germany

E.N.A.

ONE OF THE MANY CASTLES ALONG THE RHINE

The Rhine, the most important river in Europe, rises in Switzerland, flows between France and Germany, through the latter country and then across Holland. Along its banks are many ancient towns and castles. Here, for example, is the castle of Deurenburg, also known as the Maus (mouse), with the townships of St. Goar and St. Goarshausen beyond.

GERMANY AND THE RHINE

IN the very heart of Switzerland a great glacier protrudes its icy tongue down a high valley. As it melts, a stream of water runs away in a turbid creamy flood down the valley, past tiny villages of wooden houses, until it is joined by another stream that has come from the Adula group of mountains farther south.

A Mighty River

You would never think, to look at them, that either of these mountain streams was of any great importance ; and even after they have joined their insignificant floods near the small town of Tamins, the river thus formed is just like hundreds of others in this beautiful mountain land.

Yet if you follow this river from its wild home among the mountains to the sea, you will find that your respect and admiration for it grow as the river increases in beauty and importance.

For this river is the Rhine, the most important river in Europe, with many great cities in its basin, which is rich in most of the things that go to make a land the home of large numbers of people. It turns the great turbines of monster power-stations in Switzerland and South Germany, it carries down the timber in great rafts from the forests that clothe the mountains, it bears an incredible number of big barges—thousand-ton and even two-thousand-ton barges in strings of two or three towed by powerful tugs—and gives large steamers passage inland for hundreds of miles from the sea. In normal times, 76 million tons of shipping travels this way each year to the great port of Rotterdam.

One of the tributaries which join it in the lower half of its course has in its basin the richest coal-field in Europe, and a number of giant town-clusters whose industries produce iron and steel goods of all kinds, dyes, and chemicals, and textile goods of every sort, to supply the markets of the whole world. That tributary is the Ruhr. We must look at it more closely presently.

Rhine Scenery

Along its banks the Rhine has some of the most magnificent scenery in Europe, especially in the middle course, where during long ages it has sawn a deep gorge through the block of old hard plateaux known as the Rhine Highlands, and where it flows in a deep and mighty flood between high, steep banks terraced to their very crests with orderly vineyards, and crowned on the topmost crags with the ruins of great castles that were the strongholds of robber barons who in the Middle Ages defied kings and emperors and took toll of all who passed, whether on land or water.

This part of the Rhine is much visited by tourists, not only from every part of Europe, but also from America, for its fine scenery is worth coming half across the world to see.

The Dutch Rhine

When you reach the rich meadow-lands of Holland, where the two arms of the great Rhine wind placidly under its Dutch names of Lek and Waal, you realise that all this rich densely-peopled country has been built up through the long ages from the silt brought down by the Rhine. For Holland is made largely of soil torn from its parent rock among the mountains of Switzerland, ground into fine sand, and carried for hundreds of miles by this great river, to be deposited on its mouth in the delta that forms most of Holland.

If you follow the Lek, the chief mouth of the Rhine, you come at length through many neat Dutch towns surrounded by their pasture-lands and flower-fields to the great seaport of Rotterdam, whose fine docks shelter the ships of the nations, and whose works, factories and mills gather their raw materials from all parts of the world, but especially from the East Indies and from Dutch Guiana. Cocoa and chocolate factories, sugar refineries, rubber factories, oil works, margarine factories and ship-building yards are Rotterdam's chief business enterprises.

The long, deep, straight waterway from Rotterdam to the sea has been made partly by the Dutch themselves, who have dredged out and straightened the bed of the Lek to admit the largest ships afloat. They call it "The New Waterway." At its seaward end is the packet-station of the Hook of Holland, the port for the steamers that run from Harwich, carrying passengers and the mails from Britain to all parts of Middle Europe.

The Rhine on the Map

If we now turn to our atlases and look at the Rhine and the Rhineland, we shall see clearly how the river is divided. First, there is the *Mountain Rhine* rising in Switzerland, flowing through the large Lake Constance (over which Count Zeppelin flew his first zeppelins, and where great experiments with aircraft were carried on), and on past the beautiful Falls of Schaffhausen to the important Swiss frontier station of Basle—perhaps the biggest railway station in Europe.

At Basle the Rhine turns northwards, flowing through a deep but wide and flat valley, between the dark mountain forests of the French Vosges on the left and of the German Black Forest on the right, until you come to Mainz, where the Main flows in from Bavaria and the German Jura. Before reaching Mainz you would see the big river port

SNAPSHOTS OF BEAUTY AND ROMANCE

Some of the castles along the Rhine are in ruins, others have been restored. Among the latter is Sooneck, seen in this picture with Toteninsel beyond. In the Middle Ages, many of the castles were the strongholds of robber barons who levied toll on all who passed by road or by river.

Photos: E.N.A.

This view is taken from the level of the Rhine and shows the town of Königswinter. The mountain beyond is the Drachenfels, with a castle as its crown. In the story of the great opera, "Siegfried," the hero slays a dragon who lives in a cavern on the Drachenfels, the word meaning "Dragon's Rock." The district is described also in Byron's "Childe Harold's Pilgrimage."

of Mannheim, where the river Neckar that has come from the Black Forest past the beautiful old university town of Heidelberg, joins the Rhine. The third division is the *Rhine Gorge*, which the river has cut deeply through the Rhine Highlands between Bingen and Bonn. At Bingen you can still see the mouse tower in which Bishop Hatto, the profiteer in grain of his day, according to an old legend, took refuge against a swarm of advancing rats. On the way down to Bonn you pass the high rocks where the Lorelei—the sirens of German fairy tales—sang to lure voyagers to destruction. Legend says that the Nibelungen treasure lies hidden beneath the rock.

Coblenz and Cologne

Soon after, you see the great commercial city of the Middle Rhine, Coblenz, with its fortress of Ehrenbreitstein frowning down from the heights on the opposite side of the river. But the best-known of all the castles of the Rhine Gorge is Drachenfels, high perched upon the " castled crag of Drachenfels," famed in old song and story.

Beyond Bonn the valley opens out into a wide and fertile plain in which sit Cologne and other great cities where great industries flourish. All of them suffered heavily during the Second World War, but rebuilding has been rapid. The fifth part of the Rhine is the delta, which is Southern Holland. Each of these parts of the Rhine has its own distinctive features and its own people living in the ways best suited to their homeland.

What countries belong to the Rhineland ? Switzerland is the home of the Rhine ; from Basle for many miles northward the Rhine forms the boundary between France and Germany; some little distance north of Strasbourg, the capital and cathedral city of Alsace, which was restored to France as a result of the Great War of 1914–18, the Rhine becomes entirely German for hundreds of miles to Emmerich, near the Dutch frontier.

For centuries the Germans have looked upon the Rhine as their own national river and have exalted its legends in verse and song and immortalised them in great music by such masters as Wagner whose operas *Der Ring des Nibelungen* and *Das Rheingold* draw exclusively upon Rhine legendry.

A Barrier River

More significant is the part the Rhine has played in history as a barrier and the importance which such nations as France attach to keeping the German people east of their mighty river. Almost without exception, since the times of the chieftain Arminius (Hermann), German leaders have been men of " blood and iron " whose ambitions led to conquest and domination.

In the days of Roman greatness, it was along the Rhine that the Romans made contact with the barbaric tribes of Germany. For many years the Romans advanced along the Rhine valley, building forts and cities and more than once attempting to subdue the tribes without success. To this day Germans remember the valour of their early ancestors in opposing the might of Rome, especially that of Arminius who destroyed three Roman legions in the *Saltus Teutobergensis* in A.D. 9.

From such tribes as that of Arminius came the rovers who crossed the North Sea to settle in our own country, and it was a Germanic tribe, the Goths, who marched southwards, driving through to Rome and sacking the Imperial city. Later, Christianity spread its humanising influence. Missionaries penetrated barbaric Germany, turning the tribes from the hammer of Thor to the Cross of Christ. Their work was made easier by the rule of Charlemagne whose dominions included nearly all of what we call Germany. The great emperor took up arms to save the Pope from the assaults of his enemies and for this devotion was rewarded with the crown of the Holy Roman Empire.

ALONG THE BANKS OF THE RHINE

Here is a bend of the Rhine in the spring season, with fruit trees in the full splendour of their blossom. The hard, high bluff on the farther bank is the Lorelei Rock, which figures in one of the many legends and songs connected with the Rhine. On this rock the Lorelei sang to lure passing travellers to their doom.

Photos: E.N.A.

Here is another magnificent view, this time of a considerable stretch of the River Rhine, showing how it winds placidly along its appointed course from the icy tongue of a glacier in a Swiss mountain to the sea off the coast of Holland. The building in the foreground of this delightful panorama is the Schloss Stolzenfels.

When Charlemagne died, his empire fell apart. France, as we have seen, went her own way. In Germany, there rose numbers of small independent states, each owing nominal allegiance to the Holy Roman Emperor whom they themselves elected. But the Emperors found it hard to keep order in a Germany full of ambitious princes and at the same time rule in Italy where they were loathed by their subjects and often in conflict with the Pope. The German monarch, Henry the Fourth, actually defied Pope Gregory the Seventh, but submitted after he had been excommunicated, and went to Canossa, where the Pope was staying, to sue for pardon.

Conflict with the Pope

The Emperor Barbarossa also opposed the Pope and crossed the Alps on five occasions to assert his rule. But even-

tually he also had to yield and at Venice knelt to kiss the Papal toe and to receive in return the Papal kiss of peace. Barbarossa was renowned for his courage and feats of arms, and German legend tells that he is not really dead, but sleeps in a vast subterranean cave ready to gird his sword and armour and come forth when his people should need him.

The Hanseatic League

The Germans have been not only great fighters, but great traders. Trade has characterised the progress of the German people to modern times. As early as 1241, the towns of Lübeck and Hamburg had made a pact to safeguard the road route from the Baltic to the North Sea. For two hundred years, from the eleventh to the thirteenth centuries, German influence was extending eastwards from

E.N.A

WHERE LUTHER WORKED ON HIS TRANSLATION OF THE BIBLE

One of the finest old castles in Germany is the Wartburg, near Eisenach, at the north-western end of the Thuringian Forest. Once the seat of the Landgraves of Thuringia, and completely restored in 1889, it is famous as the place where Martin Luther worked on his translation of the Bible. This view of one of the courtyards shows the Vogtei (steward's house) and the window of Luther's room.

E.N.A.

LUTHER'S STUDY IN THE WARTBURG

At the castle of the Wartburg in Thuringia, Martin Luther, the great German religious reformer, found shelter from his enemies and worked on his translation of the Bible. This picture shows the interior of his study in the castle where he worked from May, 1521 until March, 1522. From the protest against Papal authority made by Luther and his followers comes our modern word " Protestant."

the Elbe, and where colonies and settlements arose, merchants and traders followed. Soon there were German trading posts in all parts of the Baltic, and one of the earliest trading associations, formed at Wisby on the isle of Gothland, extended from Cologne and Utrecht in the west to Reval (Tallinn) in the east.

Gradually these associations fell into the hands of German home towns and there came into being the Hanseatic League, with Lübeck, Hamburg and Bremen as its leading towns. The Hansa merchants had special privileges where they had trading posts and virtually controlled commerce in the Baltic. So powerful were the Hansa cities that they could even make war, defying German princelings and other rulers. Their power fell as it was challenged by the rising trade of other nations which, unlike the League, were backed by strong and unified states. By the seventeenth century, only Lübeck, Hamburg and Bremen kept the Hansa name alive, and these three maintained trading posts at Bergen until 1775, at London until 1852, and at Antwerp until 1863.

Germany, during the period of the Hanseatic League, was very loosely-knit and a stage for the rivalries of states and princes and for wars and disturbances that flared across the land. These were particularly violent during the reign of Emperor Charles the Fifth, when the Reformation reached its peak in Germany.

The long conflict between Popes and

Emperors made Germany ripe for the Reformation. In many parts of the country, the Pope, and Christianity as taught and practised by Rome were attacked, and popular feeling was behind Martin Luther when in 1517, two years before the accession of Charles the Fifth, he nailed to a church door in Wittenberg, a denunciation of Papal practice, later (1520) burning publicly the Papal Bull which excommunicated him for his teaching. Luther found himself opposed by his Emperor, but supported by many of the German princes.

Hardly had this thorny religious issue arisen when the new Emperor, Charles, found himself faced with the Peasants' War. The grievances of the German peasants were much the same as those which later brought the people of France to revolution. They had lost their old privileges, were sorely op-pressed, and were taxed beyond the limit of endurance. Already there had been peasant risings in protest at these wrongs, and discontent finally came to a head at Stühlingen in 1522 with an insurrection that flared rapidly across central and southern Germany.

Meanwhile, the religious problem had still to be solved. The princes who supported Luther prepared a protest against Papal authority, whence comes the modern name of Protestant for those who do not conform to the teachings of Rome. For thirty years, Germans waged war for the right to worship God in the way they felt nearest to His Word. Not until Germany lay prostrate did peace come, and with it, religious freedom. But though the countryside was devastated and people were in want and poverty, it was not long before war came again.

Associated Press.

The quaint old town of Rothenburg stands on the steep rim of the valley of the River Tauber. The town has changed but little in appearance since the days of the Thirty Years' War (1618–48). This picture shows us a street junction known as the Plönlein and (left) the Siebers Tower and its gateway.

CATTLE GRAZING BENEATH THE SNOW-CLAD PEAKS OF THE BERNINA ALPS

The herdsmen tending their cattle on this sunlit mountain pasture have beyond them one of the snow-crested mountain giants which have made Switzerland famous. It is Piz Roseg, nearly 13,000 feet high and fourth highest peak of the Bernina Alps of the frontier region of south-eastern Switzerland and northern Italy.

A. C. K. Ware Ltd.

A RIVERSIDE SCENE AT ZÜRICH

Where primitive lake-dwellers once had a settlement there now stands the prosperous and important commercial town of Zürich. It is the largest town in Switzerland and the seat of a leading university. Zürich stands at the northern end of the lake of the same name. Flowing swiftly through the city is the River Limmat, or Linth, one of the tributaries of the River Aar. The houses of the Limmatquai, seen in this picture are typical of this part of Switzerland.

N.P.K. IV, p. 81.

The Holy Roman Empire was dying, and the future of Germany resolved itself into a struggle between Austria, home of the Hapsburg Emperors, and the new and martial state of Prussia, one of the few German states which did not indulge in the luxury and extravagance that Louis the Fourteenth of France had made fashionable through the Courts of Europe.

The Rise of Prussia

At the beginning of the eighteenth century Prussia was ruled by King Frederick William the First, a monarch whose greatest joy was his army to which went every penny that his royal treasury could spare. Under his stern, but popular rule, Prussia rose to be the third military power in Europe, its army famed and feared in all quarters. The Prussian army was the best-equipped and best trained of the day.

Associated Press.

MEDIEVAL ROTHENBURG

When ruthless General Tilly captured Rothenburg during the Thirty Years' War, he threatened to execute the town councillors unless one of them could empty the Pokal, a huge goblet holding three quarts of wine, at a draught. The seemingly impossible was done, and the councillors' lives were spared.

Its reputation was as formidable as was the appearance of the Regiment of Potsdam Guards, the élite of Frederick's troops, of which each member was giant in stature, bribed, lured, or even kidnapped into the service of the martial monarch. Frederick's successor, Frederick William the Second, named the Great, was not slow to use the weapon he had inherited from his father. By force of arms, he wrested Silesia from Queen Maria Theresa of Austria, making Prussia a great Power.

The French Revolution seemed to explode the myth of the invincible Prussian army, for Prussia was defeated by Napoleon and, after the battle of Jena, was stripped of half her dominions. This humiliation was erased with the defeat of Napoleon at the Battle of Nations, fought near Leipzig, which freed German soil from the French.

Bismarck, Man of Blood and Iron

In the early nineteenth century Germany was a confederation of states of which the most powerful were the

Empire of Austria and the Kingdom of Prussia. This was an age when the peoples of Europe were clamouring, not only for freedom, but for national unity, and in Germany the lead was taken by Prussia, who used all means to extend her influence over the other German states. For Prussia, the man of the hour was Bismarck who, with a reorganised and strengthened army as his weapon, won the provinces of Holstein and Schleswig from Denmark, rounded on his ally, Austria, and defeated her within seven days.

France came next and in the war of 1870–71 tasted defeat, German troops marched into Paris and in the Hall of Mirrors at Versailles Bismarck asked his king to become emperor of the new Germany he had created.

Guided by Bismarck, Germany became a centrally governed state which soon began to reap the rewards of its ruthless conquests. After Kaiser Wil-

helm II came to the throne, Germany's mineral resources and shipping developed enormously, and in all fields she strode forward at a terrific pace as if striving to make up for all the years she had been disunited.

The First World War

But Kaiser Wilhelm II was as much an ambitious militarist as any of his predecessors. His vision was fixed upon an overseas empire and the establishment of German supremacy. In 1914 Germany again drew the sword and plunged Europe into a terrible war that went on for four years, until Germany was defeated and her Emperor a fugitive. The peace treaty, marking her absolute defeat, was drawn up in that same Hall of Mirrors where not many decades earlier she had humbled France.

Germany had been beaten to the ground, but except for the narrow strip of Rhineland, she did not suffer

Reece Winstone.

IN THE OLD HANSA TOWN OF LÜBECK

Lübeck was founded in 1143 and is the oldest of the German towns on the Baltic. It soon became a leading city of the Hanseatic League, the great trading association of the ports and cities of north Germany. Building in brick began here in medieval times, and you can see (left centre) the towers of the thirteenth-century brick-built Marienkirche.

Aerofilms Library.

SHIPPING IN THE RHINE DELTA NEAR ROTTERDAM

The Rhine flows through Holland in two broad arms, the Lek and the Waal. The Lek, which reaches the sea by way of Rotterdam, is the chief mouth of the Rhine. The picture shows large seagoing barges anchored in the river not far from the great Dutch port.

the humiliation of an occupying army. So terrible had been the ruin and loss of life in the war of 1914–18 that people were only too ready to forget and to forgive. The world hardly bothered when German troops reoccupied the Rhineland or when the rich industrial region of the Saar returned to Germany. More concern was shown when Hitler forcibly welded Austria into his Greater Germany, and when he demanded the Czech Sudetenland, people were at last alive to the danger in their midst. But then it was too late. Elated by his Czech success, Hitler turned on Poland.

Germany in Defeat

For a fateful time, Germany bestrode Europe. Then came her defeat, more ruthless and utter in its modern form than it could ever have been in 1918. War with all its horrors reached into the heart of Germany. Towns and cities were razed to the ground by aerial bombardment. Germany became a

land of ruin and devastation and felt in her own streets and homes some of the suffering and misery which she herself had brought on much of Europe. Her land was divided into four Zones of Occupation by the very nations she would herself have destroyed.

At the Potsdam Conference of 1945 Britain, the U.S.A., France and Russia decided to work together in arranging the future of defeated Germany. But it soon became clear that Russia had very different ideas from those of her Western Allies and, as a result, certain important decisions taken at the Conference were never carried out. Russia and the Western nations could not agree and before long Germany emerged as two sharply divided territories. Controlled by an Allied High Commission (Britain, the U.S.A. and France), the western zones have now become the Federal Republic of Germany. By the Convention signed in Bonn in May, 1952, the Federal Republic is allowed

6—2

to conduct its own home affairs and business with other countries, while the Western Allies have rights covering the presence of Allied troops in the Federal Republic and the future of Germany as a whole. The first parliament of the Republic, the Federal Diet, was elected in August, 1949, and there was a further election in 1953. Capital of the Republic is *Bonn*, on the river Rhine.

What about Eastern Germany, the zone occupied by Russia ? When the Federal Republic was set up, the Soviet zone of Germany was converted into the " German Democratic Republic," which is ruled on Communist lines.

Berlin, former capital of all Germany, has really been similarly divided. As there are now two Germanys, so there are now two Berlins. " West Berlin " (British, American and French sectors) looks towards the Federal Republic, even though it thus becomes an island outpost of the West surrounded by Eastern German territory. East (Russian) Berlin is the seat of government of the Communist " German Democratic Republic."

Lands Lost to Germany

The frontiers of Germany to-day differ greatly from those she had before the Second World War. She has lost the province of East Prussia, of which the northern part (including the capital, Königsberg, now renamed Kaliningrad) went to Russia, the remainder going to Poland. She has also lost to Poland her territories east of a line running along the rivers Oder and Neisse.

The loss of these lands involved the expulsion of the millions of Germans living in them. As refugees, they had to trek westwards, leaving behind practically everything they had. It is said that

E.N.A.

THE KIEL CANAL FROM THE AIR

In the days of the Hanseatic League, the only sea routes into the Baltic were those commanded by Denmark and Sweden. So it remained until the year 1895, when the great Kiel Canal was opened to link the North Sea and the Baltic. The canal was constructed during the period 1887–95 and is about sixty-one miles long. Its locks are among the largest ever made.

UNDER THE WATZMANN'S SHADOW

The little town clustering at the foot of the Bavarian Alps is Berchtesgaden, which has been visited by tourists from all parts of the world. The peak behind the town is known as the "Watzmann," and there are lovely lakes in the vicinity. Though from the photograph you might think the town was in a low situation, it actually stands 1,700 feet above sea level. The mighty Alpine peaks separate Bavaria from the district known as the Austrian Tyrol, and the country is to a considerable extent covered with dense forest-land, in the glades of which animals of many kinds still roam. Further, these widespread wooded tracts offer scope for game-hunting on a particularly large scale, the wild boar being the most frequent object of the chase. Berchtesgaden has a place in history as Hitler's mountain home and fortress. At the "Eagle's Nest" the German Fuehrer made holiday and received his friends. The residence as well as the barracks near it were destroyed during and after the war.

during the period 1945–46, no fewer than eight million refugee Germans arrived in western Germany from east of the Oder-Neisse line and from the Sudetenland (which Germany also lost).

In addition, the Federal Republic has had to accommodate refugees from the eastern zone, who could endure no longer the tyranny of Communist rule. Refugees are still making their way westwards, although the journey is perilous because the Communists keep stern guard along the frontier. Most refugees now reach the west by way of Berlin, where it is easier to escape from the eastern zone. During 1952 and the first six months of 1953, over 360,000 refugees reached the west *via* Berlin. Special reception camps were set up in western Berlin and in the Federal Republic to help these refugees to find new homes and new jobs. It is all part of the heavy price Germany has had to pay for the misery and destruction she brought upon Europe during the Second World War.

Germany Rebuilds

These terrible conditions have made it all the harder for Germany to rebuild her shattered towns and industries. While it is true that this suffering and destruction are, in a sense, just punishment for the hideous wrongs Germany herself has wrought, no good would come from preventing the recovery of this divided country or her eventual return to the family of European nations. Once Germany has learned the lesson that only defeat could teach, she can contribute in good measure to the progress of mankind. Her people are hardworking, thorough and inventive, and have already added much to the store of human knowledge. Germans first made paper out of rags. Germans invented modern methods of printing. Germans have led the world in optical work and in the use of chemicals and dyes. Germans have made great contributions to European literature and music.

In her days of greatness, before the war of 1914–18, Germany was the commercial heart of Central Europe and supplied her neighbours with manufactured goods and raw materials; even in recent times many of her cities, such as Leipzig and Hamburg, have retained an international reputation as trading centres, while tourists once more come from far and wide to see the beauties of the Rhine, the Black Forest, and the Bavarian Alps, and the glorious architectural heritage of the past in such towns as Nuremberg, Munich, Frankfurt and Stuttgart. Many of these famous towns and cities had their wonderful old buildings destroyed in the fighting and bombing of the war; others escaped large-scale destruction or even emerged quite unscathed. Now that these terrible days are past, tourists are again visiting Germany. For we must realise that if the German people can follow the paths of peace and recovery, Europe will again welcome German skill and genius, and the Rhine will once more be a river of legend and romance rather than a frontier of people outlawed for their crimes against humanity.

The Recovery of the Ruhr

The Germans are among the most hard-working people in the world and, despite their refugee and other problems, have lost little time in rebuilding their towns and industries. One of the areas where recovery has been most rapid is the Ruhr, a great industrial district which is based on the most important coal-field in Europe.

The Ruhr is a right-bank tributary of the Rhine, which it joins at *Duisburg*, one of the largest river ports in the world. The Ruhr basin is the most thickly peopled and busiest part of Germany, containing at least twelve great towns each with a population of more than a hundred thousand. Before the Second World War more than two million men were employed in the coal-mines and iron and steel works of the

LIFE RETURNS TO THE RUHR

Before the Second World War, Germany produced more than 11 million metric tons of finished iron and steel products every year, much of this output coming from the Ruhr. Recovery has been so rapid that in 1951 the production of Western Germany amounted to over 9 million metric tons.

Photos: Topical Press.

The Ruhr produces over 600,000 tons of steel each month. Here slag is being tipped into specially constructed railway wagons at Duisburg.

The largest steel plant in the British Zone is the Huckingen-Huttenwerk at Duisburg where this picture of a Thomas Converter plant was taken.

Ruhr. Here also are important chemical works and textile factories.

Largest of the Ruhr towns is *Essen*, with a population (1950) of over 600,000, where the Krupp family had their great steel works. Krupp's works was said to be the largest steel works in Europe and from it came guns and other war material as well as railway plant, locomotives, industrial and farm machinery and many other goods in metal. Other important towns in the Ruhr are *Solingen*, famous as the " Sheffield " of Germany, *Wuppertal* (really the twin town of Elberfeld-Barmen), *Bochum* and *Dortmund*.

From Dortmund runs the Dortmund–Ems Canal, linking the Ruhr coalfield with the river Ems, which enters the North Sea at *Emden*. Barges from the Ruhr can thus reach a German outport and do not have to rely on the Dutch port of Rotterdam.

Essen and other Ruhr centres, including Hamm and its huge railway marshalling yards, had to be bombed repeatedly during the Second World War, for Germany's power to wage war had to be destroyed. But when the war was over, it became important to revive the great industries of the Ruhr, for traditionally they supplied many parts of Europe. Ruhr coal was used by France, Switzerland, Belgium and Holland; manufactured goods from the Ruhr were sent not only to German towns and cities, but to all parts of Central Europe.

If we wished, we might go to see for ourselves how this revival is proceeding, for the Federal Republic (the old western zones) of Germany is open to tourists. What should we find ? Firstly, there would still be plenty of evidence of war damage, but even more should we notice that the forest of factory chimneys is again smoking busily ; that the mines, furnaces, foundries and rolling mills are once more working hard. In 1938, finished iron and steel products from Germany amounted to over $11\frac{3}{4}$

ON THE RIVER MAIN AT FRANKFURT

Associated Press.

These large barges are anchored in the docks on the river Main at Frankfurt. Frankfurt-on-Main, an important commercial and industrial city, has a population of over 532,000. The river Main flows through southern central Germany to join the Rhine at Mainz.

A NEW ERA OF PEACEFUL INDUSTRY

These cloth mills at Kettwig were once used by the notorious armament concern of Krupps for gun experimental work. To-day, 15,000 workers are employed here to produce much-needed textiles. This picture shows some of their products in the examination and mending room.

Photos: Topical Press.

After the Second World War, a large part of the great Krupps plant at Essen was dismantled. This was part of the Allied plan to make it impossible for Germany to equip herself for another war. Among the sections of the works which were brought into production again were these large shops for the building and repair of railway engines.

million metric tons, of which the over-whelming part came from the Ruhr. Just after the end of the war the Ruhr was producing little more than million metric tons a year. Since then the recovery has been so rapid that in 1951 the Federal Republic produced over 9¼ million metric tons. By the end of 1953, the Ruhr was again producing more coal than was needed by its own industry.

There is, however, this important difference. The works and factories that once made guns and tanks and other war material are to-day turning out much-needed industrial or railway equipment. Some factories which once made armaments or munitions have been dismantled ; others have been transformed and are now used for the manufacture of textiles. For while it is right that the Ruhr should recover, the western Allies do not intend this great industrial district to become once again a threatening war arsenal.

The Saar Basin

Another important industrial area which was formerly part of Germany, but which is now self-governing under the supervision of France, is the Saarland. Its important coal-mines feed the iron and steel works of Lorraine, and it is from Lorraine that supplies of iron ore come for the iron and steel works of the Saarland. *Saarbrücken* is the chief town and German the official language. We thus have in the Saar a territory with a German way of life which is inevitably linked industrially with France. The nations know that the present strange position of the Saar territory

Pictorial Press.

A VOLKSWAGEN (" PEOPLE'S CAR ") GETS ITS COAT OF PAINT

One of the most modern car-manufacturing plants in Europe is at Wolfsburg. In 1948, the factory was making only twenty cars a day; now nearly a thousand a day are produced and a new town has been built to house the 20,000 workpeople employed at the factory. Cars from the Volkswagen factory are now exported to every continent.

THE CITY WHERE GOETHE WAS BORN

Goethe, the great German poet, was born at Frankfurt-on-Main in 1749, but there is little to suggest those far-off times in this modern aerial view of a district of the city. The large building is a Congress Hall, erected when Frankfurt and Bonn were rivals for the title of capital of West Germany. It is now part of the state broadcasting organisation.

cannot continue for ever, and it has been suggested that the Saar should become a self-ruling " European territory." Whether this will come about, and in what form, has still to be seen.

The Elbe

The second great river of Germany is the Elbe, which rises in the Czecho-Slovakian plateau called the " Bohemian diamond " and flows through the deep gorge of the Elbe Gate to *Dresden*, capital of Saxony and famous for its art galleries and porcelain. This is the region of the Saxon coalfield whence came the fuel for smelting the ores of the Harz Mountains farther north. Industry is centred in the towns of *Chemnitz* and *Zwickau*, which produce cotton and woollen goods, hosiery, and heavy railway machinery. From Annaberg, in the mountain range of the Erzgebirge, to Aue are important uranium mines which have been worked since 1945 under Soviet supervision.

North of the coalfield is Leipzig, whose trade fairs have been held annually for centuries; Leipzig is famous for its printing and book-binding.

The Elbe flows on through rich farmland which gives, among other crops, sugar-beet for the refineries of Magdeburg and other towns. Much of the lower Elbe is now in the nature of a frontier, for it divides eastern and western Germany. *Hamburg* is the second city of Germany, with a population of over 1,600,000. Its waterfront reaches for ten miles along the banks of the river, and in the years before the war some of the world's finest liners came from its shipyards.

Westwards lie the river Weser and *Bremen*, another old Hanseatic city and port, second only to Hamburg as a sea gateway. Most of us will remember the river Weser in connection with Hamelin and the Pied Piper. Well up-river from Bremen—south-east of Minden—lies Hamelin itself, which the

Germans know as Hameln. There, on the seventeenth-century " rat-catcher's house," visitors would see an inscription commemorating the famous Pied Piper.

The Beautiful South

In sharp contrast to the low North German Plain is beautiful southern Germany, whose uplands include rich and fertile valleys, much forest and some of the finest old German towns. Many of these towns grew up at river crossings or at other places where routes met from several directions. At one time many of these old cities relied on products from the nearby farms and forests for their crafts and industries. Then roads and railways enabled them to overcome the local lack of coal and raw materials, and finally large-scale industry was developed when the considerable water resources of the south were harnessed to provide hydro-electric power. Although southern Germany draws power from the Ruhr generating stations, she has considerable hydro-electric production of her own.

Among the places we should want to see, if we visited this part of Germany, would be the old " Free Imperial Town " of *Nuremberg*, which stands on the Pegnitz river. Famous as the home of toymakers, as the town of Wagner's Mastersingers and as a picture-book place of medieval houses, ancient walls and towers, Nuremberg was heavily bombed during the war because munition and aircraft factories had been built upon its outskirts.

Munich, a university city and the capital of the old kingdom of Bavaria, grew up on the river Isar where a river-island made bridging easy. With the coming of the railways, Munich's importance as a commercial and industrial centre grew still more, because it commanded the routes from the Alps to the Rhine.

The Bavarian farmlands with their picturesque villages, each with its own

Camera Press

THE INNER AND OUTER ALSTER AT HAMBURG

At Hamburg, the Elbe is joined by two small rivers, the Alster and the Bille. This basin, which is actually within the city, is formed by the Alster and is divided into the *Aussen* (Outer)-Alster and *Binnen* (Inner)-Alster by the embankment and Lombard Bridge seen in this picture.

HAMBURG TO-DAY

Camera Press.

Much of Hamburg was destroyed during the Second World War, but has now been rebuilt. Through the arcade, we see the new tower of the Town Hall.

Camera Press.

From the top of the Town Hall we get this view of the Mönckeberg-Strasse, the main thoroughfare of the " Old Town," with St. Peter's Church.

Associated Press.

Hamburg is one of the chief German ports and has long been a centre of the shipbuilding industry. Its water-front stretches for ten miles along the banks of the river Elbe. This view shows us one of the principal shipyards, with an 18,000-ton tanker under construction.

NEW BRIDGES AT COLOGNE

Cologne was noted for its fine bridges. But like many other Rhine centres, the city suffered heavily from air bombardment during the Second World War, when its bridges were almost completely destroyed. Among the new bridges since built is the Deutzer Bridge, which links the city with Deutz, one of its industrial suburbs.

Photos: Camera Press.

Dusk reveals the gracefully modern lines of another new bridge across the Rhine at Cologne. In this case, the bridge links Cologne with Mülheim, another of the city's industrial suburbs, and takes the place of the old Mülheim suspension bridge. Cologne is one of the chief commercial, manufacturing and railway centres of Germany.

GERMAN INDUSTRY REBUILT

This skyline composed of smoking chimneys, cooling towers and pylons carrying electric power lines at once suggests to us the busy industrial region of the Ruhr. Here, since the war, German heavy industry has been reborn. Taken in December, 1953, the picture shows us the giant soft-coal power plant near Cologne.

Photos: Camera Press.

A symbol of the growing strength of German industry is this modern rubber factory, which was opened in August, 1953. It looks out over the Königsworther Platz at Hanover, an important city in north-west Germany. It is sometimes said that the purest German is spoken at Hanover.

wonderfully carved *Maibaum*, or May-pole, and clusters of chalet-type houses, can have changed but little since the days when Bavaria was the realm of Ludwig II. The " Swan King," as he is called, loved to roam the countryside and had little liking for his capital of Munich and the cares of kingship. He was far more interested in building castles than in politics and statecraft. He was also the friend and patron of Richard Wagner, and at Neuschwanstein, per-haps the most incredible of his castles, the walls are covered with murals portraying scenes from Wagnerian opera.

The Bavarian Alps are the highest part of Germany. Their highest peak is the famous Zugspitze which rears its snowy crest to nearly 10,000 feet above sea level. Not far away is Oberammer-gau, the small village which has become world-famous for its Passion Play.

More scenic beauties are to be found in another German mountain range, the Harz Mountains which protrude in a natural bastion into the plains of northern Germany about midway between Co-logne and Berlin. The highest moun-tain of the range is the 3,419 feet high Brocken, a sinister barren peak, often hidden by clouds, which legend says is the meeting place of witches and war-locks on Walpurgis Night (April 30th). Nestling by the wooded slopes of the mountains is the old town of Goslar which still has its walls, timbered houses, and the Kaiserpfalz, the Romanesque palace built by Emperor Henry the Third (1039–1056). Iron and copper are mined in the Harz, and at Clausthal-Zellerfeld there is a famous Mining Academy, which was founded in the eighteenth century.

Berlin

Although divided, as we have already seen, Berlin is still the largest city in Germany and has a population (1950) of over $3\frac{1}{4}$ millions. It stands astride the river Spree and until it became the capital of all Germany in 1871, was the capital of Prussia.

E.N.A.

THE ROLLING LANDSCAPE OF THE BLACK FOREST

One of the most romantic and legended parts of Germany is the Black Forest region where mountains, rolling highlands, and great expanses of dark evergreen forest provide some of the finest scenery in Europe. This view shows the small townlet of Hinterzarten in the distance.

A. F. Kersting.

A MINARET RISES ABOVE THE MARKET PLACE OF OLD SARAJEVO

At one time the Turks ruled over all the lands that now form the republic of Yugoslavia. Reminders of their rule, and of the fact that there are still many Moslems in the Balkans can be found in many places. An example is the old market place at Sarajevo, dominated by a mosque and its slender minaret. Sarajevo is the capital of Bosnia-Hercegovina, which is one of the six republics making up Yugoslavia. It was at Sarajevo, in 1914, that the Austrian Archduke Franz Ferdinand was assassinated—a deed which eventually led to the First World War.

SEVILLE, WHERE THE MOORS ONCE RULED

Seville, the chief city of Andalusia, was ruled for several centuries by the Moors. A beautiful reminder of those distant times is the Alcazar, a palace which was begun by the Moors in 1181 and later altered extensively by the Spanish kings. This picture shows us the courtyard of the Alcazar and, in the background, the cathedral and Giralda Tower. The tower was once a minaret, but now contains the bells of the cathedral. There are twenty-five of them and each is named after a saint. The ramp by which visitors reach the top of the tower is wide enough for a horseman to climb.

NORTHERN CITY AND ALPINE VILLAGE

Camera Press.

Like many other German towns and cities, Hanover was heavily bombed during the Second World War. The Germans have rebuilt very rapidly, however, as witness these new dwelling houses gathered round the ancient Kreuzkirche (Church of the Cross). Hanover stands in a fertile plain and on the river Leine.

E.N.A.

Oberammergau is one of the most famous villages in the Bavarian Alps. It is a village of wood-carvers and a winter sports centre, but it is best known for its Passion Plays. These began in 1633 and were held regularly from 1680 onwards, at ten year intervals. The performers in the Passion Plays are all natives of the village.

Associated Press.

BAVARIAN DANCERS ENTERTAIN

This beer garden in the Bavarian Alps has dancers wearing local costume to entertain its customers.
In more modest form, their dress is worn from day to day on Bavarian farms and in the villages. The
feathered hats are green; the shorts are of leather and have gaily-embroidered bib braces. Look
carefully and you will see that the socks finish long before they reach the ankle.

Berlin suffered terrible damage during the Second World War, for there was severe fighting within the city before it surrendered. But the task of rebuilding is being handled energetically—in the western sectors, at any rate. The Kurfürsten Damm, a fashionable shopping street, now has new shops and other buildings and in the famous park, the Tiergarten, two million new trees have been planted. Everywhere old buildings are being repaired and new ones built.

Rebuilding is the keynote of life in the Federal Republic of Germany to-day. On all sides there is evidence of the immense effort that is being made— the building by day and night of new houses and public buildings, the rising of new shops and offices where before

there were ruins, the building of new bridges on the *autobahnen* (great trunk roads) to replace those destroyed or damaged in the war. Of course, there are still terrible ruins to be seen in many places and life is difficult, but Germany is now firmly on the path to recovery. Whether east and west will be re-united, and under what conditions, only time will tell.

Forest and Farm

Although Germany is one of the great industrial nations of Europe, many of her people get their living in the forests or on the farms. There are large forest areas, especially in the highlands of the south, and from these comes the timber that is floated down both the Rhine and

IN DIVIDED BERLIN

Berlin, the former capital of all Germany, became a divided city after the war. The sectors occupied by the western Allies became an island of the Western way of life within the Soviet Zone. The Soviet sector (East Berlin) became capital of the Communist " German Democratic Republic." The picture shows part of the Stalinallee.

Photos: Planet News.

The Stalinallee, with its newly-built blocks of flats, is the show street of East Berlin. The workmen seen in this picture are using salamanders to thaw the frozen pavements. Behind them is a board bearing a Communist slogan. Notice that there is practically no traffic in the streets of East Berlin.

7—2

the Elbe to the busy places of the north. Naturally enough, there are all kinds of forest industries in these areas—paper-mills and saw-mills, the carving of wooden toys and cuckoo clocks, the making of guitars, zithers and other instruments. Some villages and country towns where the peasant craftsmen work have become famous for their products. An example is Mittenwald in Bavaria, which has been the home of violin-makers since the early eighteenth century and which has a special school to teach this skilled craft.

Hillside Vineyards

The farmers of northern Germany breed cattle and horses and grow rye, flax, oats and potatoes. In the south of the German Plain, sheep and pigs are reared also, and wheat, hops and sugar-beet are important crops. Farther south are the warm valleys clothed in vineyards. The most important vineyards are found along the Rhine and its tributaries from Lake Constance to the Bonn district. The vines have to be tended carefully throughout the year. In the early spring they are pruned and then, later, are fastened to stakes. Spraying takes place during the summer. In September, when the harvest has been gathered from the terraced slopes, the chief centres hold their wine festivals. The German word for " vineyard " is *weinberg*, which means " wine hill "—a good name, indeed, for the vinelands of the Rhine which climb in their terraces to the very tops of the river valleys. *Hock*, the word used in England to describe many German wines, is derived from Hochheim, a Rhineland town noted for its vintages.

Associated Press.

BERLIN, A WAR-DAMAGED AND DIVIDED CITY

Once the capital of the powerful German Reich, and ranking in 1939 as the fourth largest city in the world, Berlin became by 1945 a war-devastated ruin, divided against itself between the Western Allies and Russia. This aerial photograph shows part of the American sector with the Anhalter railway station; in the centre background, the Reichstag building stands in the British sector, and in the right background is the Russian sector. The boundaries of the three sectors meet just beyond the railway station.

FROM BLACK FOREST TO BLACK SEA

E.N.A.

A BLACK FOREST HAMLET

The thickly-wooded mountain range of the Black Forest in south-western Germany contains many such little communities as well as old medieval towns and modern health resorts. The people of the region are foresters and timber workers, and clock- and watch-making are also important.

IN south-west Germany, within the elbow of the Rhine, is an uplift of rolling highlands and mountains that from the air seem carpeted with dark-green velvet and sprinkled with towns and villages that might have come from the illustrations of some fairy story. This region, the ancient crustblock of the Black Forest, is as richly endowed with romance and legend as either the Rhine or the Harz and challenges them with its own scenic wonders and historic places.

This is a countryside of forestry and timber workers, of clock- and watch-makers, where can be seen the Schwarz-wald cottages with their thatched or shingled roofs. Countless thousands visit the Black Forest, some to take the cure at the famous health resorts of Baden-Baden, Freudenstadt or Baden-weiler, others to hike or motor through the forest depths and visit the ancient cities.

Those who visited the small town of Donaueschingen would most certainly see the twin-towered Stadt-Kirche, where there is the *Donau-Quelle*, the source of the mighty river Danube.

The " Blue " Danube

The Danube, immortalised in music by Johann Strauss (although its waters are green or grey in colour, and not blue), links western and eastern Europe. From its source as far as the Iron Gate, the Danube flows among western peoples with western customs. Thence, to its mouth on the Black Sea, the great river travels through lands whose Moslem mosques and Moslem customs speak plainly of the East.

A look at the map shows the Danube to be more than double the length of the

Rhine; the only river in Europe that is longer is the Volga. The Volga flows through one country, but the Danube serves many lands and many different peoples on its 1,800 mile journey from Donaueschingen in the Black Forest to Sulina on the Black Sea. Germany, Austria. Czecho-Slovakia, Hungary, Yugoslavia, Bulgaria and Rumania are all vitally interested in this great waterway. For them it provides the best and cheapest means of transport for the things they sell and the goods they buy; for them it is a natural highway because it can be navigated by barges and small steamers for 1,600 miles of its length.

Which of these nations is to rule the Danube, to maintain its waterway and ensure free and safe navigation upon its broad bosom? There was only one way to settle this important question, and that was to make the Danube an international highway—everybody's river, but nobody's in particular! To ensure that the river was kept in order, with its wharves and quays, its lights and buoys and canals all in proper working condition, and to make certain that all who wished should have freedom of navigation along its course, a great committee of the nations, called the European Commission of the Danube, was appointed, and in 1921 special laws and regulations were drawn up to guarantee freedom of navigation to all nations living in the Danube basin. After the War, the Soviet Union and other nations of eastern Europe virtually took control of the Danube and set up their own new River Administration. The shipping that had belonged to the European Commission of the Danube was handed over to Rumania, which country also assumed many of the powers of the Commission, including control of sea-going shipping on the river from Braila to the sea. Rumania now operates the largest fleet, comprising hundreds of tugs and barges, on the river.

The Flying Tailor

From Donaueschingen until it reaches the "Austrian Gate" guarded by the fortress-city of Passau, the Danube flows through Germany. The first great city through which it passes is Ulm, a great medieval trading centre and the Villa Rigea of

Moult.

TYROLEAN HOUSES NEAR INNSBRUCK

These houses at Lans, near Innsbruck, are typical of the homes in small towns and villages in the Austrian Tyrol. They are sturdily built to withstand the rigours of the winter. The lower part is made of thick concrete; the upper, of stout wooden beams and timbering. Notice the overhanging eaves.

THE GATEWAY TO AUSTRIA

Standing on the banks of the river Inn, where the Brenner and Arlberg passes join, Innsbruck is built on the site of an ancient Roman camp. This view shows the Maria-Theresienstrasse with the majestic mountains in the background. The monument is the Pillar of St. Anne which commemorates the defeat of the French and Bavarians in 1703.

This picture was taken at St. Anton and shows part of the procession of the Corpus Christi festival. The Feast of Corpus Christi, which falls upon the first Thursday after Trinity Sunday, is one of the great festivals of the Roman Catholic Church and is the occasion for a procession of the Sacrament in every Roman Catholic community.

Charlemagne's days, which is still a noted industrial and commercial town. At Ulm they still tell the old legend of the Flying Tailor who made himself wings and leapt off the city walls in an attempt to fly, only to land himself in the sanity-restoring waters of the Danube. Ulm, too, has given Germany one of her best known tongue-twisters: " *Um Ulm und in Ulm, und um und in Ulm,*"—" Round Ulm and in Ulm and round and in Ulm."

Ulm is the point at which navigation of the river begins, although the highest and westernmost of the river-ports is Regensburg, a wonderful old thirteenth century town whose fine old bridge has seen the Danube help to make history ever since those boats crammed with eager Crusaders floated beneath it on their way to fight the battles of the Cross in distant Palestine. An old legend tells us how Satan would not let the builders finish the bridge until they promised him the souls of the first three living beings who should cross it, and how the master builder foiled the Evil One by sending across the newly-completed bridge a dog, a cock and a hen!

Not far from Regensburg is Ludwig's Canal which cuts across Bavaria to join the Danube with Bamberg on the upper Main, the big tributary of the Rhine flowing past the historic city of Frankfurt. This link provides a great water highway right across Europe from the North Sea to the Black Sea.

From Regensburg, the Danube flows on to the " Austrian Gate " where the Inn adds its waters from the snow peaks and dark forests of the Tyrol to the main stream, and where the Danube enters Austria, which is once more a free and independent nation.

Austria's Past Empire

From the thirteenth century until the fall of the Austro-Hungarian Monarchy in 1918, the story of Austria is the story of her ruling house of Hapsburg. At the time of her greatest power, Austria held sway over the Magyar peoples of Hungary, the Czechs of Moravia and Bohemia, the Poles and Ukrainians of Galicia, the Rumanians of the Transylvanian Highlands, the Italians of the South Tyrol, and the Slavs of Croatia, Slavonia and Dalmatia as well.

These loose-knit subject peoples broke away when the Germanic Powers were defeated in 1918. Bohemia and Moravia became the republic of Czecho-slovakia; Serbia and the southern Slavs united to form the Kingdom of Yugoslavia; Austria and Hungary, hither-to a Dual Monarchy (for Emperor Francis Joseph of Austria had been crowned King of Hungary with the iron crown of St. Stephen), became separate and independent. The Treaty of Versailles and the demands of her neighbours took from defeated Austria further slices of her territory, leaving the once proud heart of an Empire a small inland State.

Vienna, the City of Song

Germany had never forgotten that Austria was Germanic and that only her defeat by Prussia had excluded her from the Germany created by Bismarck, and it was not long after Hitler came to power that he brought Austria by force into the Greater Germany which, he boasted, would last a thousand years.

Although the Second World War freed Austria from German rule, she had to accept occupation by the Allies, and her land is still (1954) divided into four zones (French, American, Russian and British), with all four powers sharing in the occupation of *Vienna*, the capital, which lies well within the Russian zone. More than a third of her 7 million people live within the Russian zone, but her way of life belongs to the free western world. Regarded as a liberated nation, Austria again has her own Federal Government and, like any other state, conducts her own affairs with foreign countries. The end of occupation depends on agreement between the Western Powers and Russia.

IN THE TYROL OF AUSTRIA

In winter a carpet of thick snow covers the mountains and slopes, making the Tyrol an ideal playground for skiers. There are comfortable hotels, cable cars and ski lifts to bear the skiers up the
slopes, and rest huts such as the hut seen here, which is near the Arlberg Pass.

Mondiale.

The jagged Nordkette (North Chain) peak dwarfs the railway station at Innsbruck, the chief
town of the Austrian Tyrol. Notice the large electric locomotive, which draws its power from
overhead cables.

Look at the map and see how far *Vienna*, the Austrian capital, is from Istanbul and it becomes hard to realise that a Turkish army once encamped round the walls of the old Imperial city. That is what happened in 1683, when Vienna was saved from the Turks only by the arrival of a Polish army under John Sobieski, the warrior King of Poland whose name alone was enough to fill any Turkish Janissary with terror. For centuries Vienna was a fortress of the " west " holding at bay invaders from the east. As a meeting-place of many routes and many peoples, Vienna is famous; commanding the " Austrian Gate " (the gap between the Alps and the Bohmer Wald), the city has been rightly called " The Key to the Danube."

Most of us think of Vienna as the city of song, as the home of tuneful operettas and lilting Strauss waltzes. We think fondly of Vienna as a town of luxury and temple of the arts, a city of splendid buildings, parks and palaces.

Many of its splendours were destroyed during the War, but since then the Viennese have worked hard to make good the destruction. St. Stephen's Cathedral, which was a burnt-out shell, has been restored and is once again the city's most famous landmark; a new Opera house has sprung from the ruins of the old; and the fashionable shopping streets are once more lined by smart stores and salons.

There is so much to be seen in and around Vienna: the Schönbrunn Palace, a vast building containing 1,500 rooms, that was the summer residence of the Hapsburg emperors; the Vienna Woods, immortalised by Johann Strauss, and the city's famous amusement park, the Prater; the houses where Mozart, Bach, Beethoven, Schubert, Haydn and other famous composers lived and worked; and the Art History Museum, with

Dorien Leigh.

THE " HUNDRED-SPIRED, GOLDEN CITY " OF PRAGUE

Standing astride the river Vlatava, Prague has been called " the Rome of the North." Besides being a beautiful city, the Czech capital is an important textile and glassware manufacturing centre, and contains the chief refineries for the Czech sugar-beet crop.

BRATISLAVA, WHERE THREE FRONTIERS MEET

Once the capital of Hungary, Bratislava is now Czechoslovakia's Danube port, handling goods from Austria and Hungary as well as Czechoslovakia. The picture shows the ancient St. Michael's gateway.

THE CATHEDRAL FOUNDED BY KING WENCESLAS

Rising from an immense courtyard in Prague Castle are the Gothic spires and pinnacles of the Cathedral of Saint Vitus. The Cathedral is said to have been founded by the " Good King Wenceslas " of our Christmas carol.

those priceless collections of art treasures built up by the Hapsburg emperors over four hundred years.

Before the War Vienna was noted also for the large, modern blocks of flats built as homes for families of moderate income. Although war destroyed many of these, the ruins have been cleared and new blocks built. Some contain as many as 3,000 separate flats and have their own schools, playgrounds, central kitchens, laundries, shopping centres and the like, as if they were independent little communities within the great city of Vienna.

The Austrian Countryside

The Vienna basin, through which flows the middle Danube, has much fertile land where grain crops, potatoes and other foodstuffs are grown. Cereals, fruit and vines flourish around Klagen-furt in the province of Carinthia, in southern Austria, and the valley lowlands and terraces of the river Inn, which flows through the western provinces of Vorarlberg and Tyrol, are intensively cultivated. But not enough food is produced to supply the whole population, and Austria has therefore to import foodstuffs. Over 70 per cent. of her land is mountainous and much is covered by forests, in which Austria has her greatest wealth.

A Mountain of Iron

Not that Austria is entirely without industry. She has steel mills at *Donawitz* and *Linz*, which are fed with crude iron from the Erzberg, a mountain of iron 5,033 feet high. Man has mined iron from the Erzberg for centuries, yet this remarkable mountain still has over 300 million tons of valuable ore. Worked into terraces by huge electric shovels, it now resembles some vast fantastic pyramid.

Another important industrial region is the province of Vorarlberg. Here a few large, and many small, factories produce lace, cotton, worsted and other textiles, using electric power from dams in the Montafon valley.

It is by harnessing the mountain rivers to produce electric power that Austrian industry can be made modern and more productive. Her greatest hydro-electric project is the new dam at Kaprun. Sealing a steep and rugged valley, Kaprun will use the unruly waters pouring from the melting glaciers of Hohe Tauern to make electricity for Austrian industry. The dam is said to be one of the largest in Central Europe and was largely brought into being through funds granted to Austria under the Marshall Plan. Not far from the dam is the Gross Glockner ("Great Bellringer") Alpine road, on which stands the small town of Heiligenblut. The road climbs to a height of nearly 8,500 ft. and is considered one of the highest in Europe. The Gross Glockner itself (12,461 ft.) is the highest peak in Austria. Heiligenblut (Holy Blood) gets its name from the phial of blood which is still carefully kept in its church. It is said that the phial was brought from Constantinople (Istanbul) many hundreds of years ago and that the blood is some taken from Our Lord.

Like Klagenfurt, *Graz* is an important manufacturing centre. Here, also, iron-ore is smelted. Graz stands on the river Mur and is the second city of Austria and capital of the province of Styria. The city is rich in art treasures and is noted for its music and its drama. Another industrial centre is Zistersdorf, which stands well to the north of Vienna in the part of Austria occupied by the Russians. Zistersdorf is said to produce a million tons of oil every year. Most of its output goes to eastern Europe.

Dorien Leigh.

"GOLDEN" PRAGUE'S FINE OLD BRIDGE

Built by King Charles IV of Bohemia 600 years ago, the Charles Bridge at Prague is only one of the architectural beauties which the Czech capital owes to that monarch. Beyond, on the Hradčany hill, rise the castle buildings and the spires of St. Vitus Cathedral.

Keystone.

WHEN PRAGUE GOES GAY

On national holidays and times of national thanksgiving, the streets of the Czech capital are coloured by the national costumes of people who have come in from the villages and farms. Notice the knee-high boots and great puffed sleeves of lace worn by the girl on the left.

Coal, zinc ore, copper and other minerals also are produced in Austria. She is, too, one of the world's largest producers of graphite.

Holidays in the Tyrol

But for many people, Austria is first and foremost a country for holidays. *Innsbruck*, capital of the Tyrol and an important route-centre commanding the Brenner Pass, is one of her loveliest places and a favourite tourist centre. Many of its fine old buildings date from the time of the emperor Maximilian I, whose splendid tomb can still be seen in the Hofburg Church. *Salzkammergut*, the lake district of Austria, contains beauty spots famous all over the world; its name comes, as you may guess, from

the salt mines in the district. The largest of these is at Hallstatt and is said to have been first worked three thousand years ago. Another famous centre is *Salzburg*, a small but lovely city of palaces and churches dominated by the ancient castle of Hohensalzburg. The birthplace of Mozart, Salzburg is most famous for its music festival.

Czechoslovakia and its Industries

From Vienna the Danube flows on to Bratislava, the river-port of Czechoslovakia, whose massive castle overtopping the town was built to guard it in the old days when the Danube valley was infested by pirates. *Bratislava* is at the meeting place of three frontiers and is the port for the coal and metals,

A SON OF THE PUSZTA

Calling for comparison with the pampas of the Argentine and the vast prairies of Canada, the puszta, or plain, of Hungary is a region where horses and cattle are reared by the thousand. The Hungarian cowboys, or *čsikos*, who tend the cattle are wonderful riders who spend long, lonely days in the saddle. Here is one of them wearing traditional dress and riding the fine steed that carries him across the plain.

THE WOMAN AT THE WELL

Will F. Taylor.

Upon the widespread Hungarian plains and in many parts of Slovakia wells at the roadside are
as plentiful as milestones, providing refreshing drink not only for human beings, but also for
cattle and sheep. Though the buckets themselves are heavy, the load is lightened by means of
a cross-piece of heavily weighted wood, so that even women can draw water without undue effort.

glass and sugar of Czechoslovakia, for the timber and salt of Austria, and for the grain, cattle and sheep of Hungary.

Czechoslovakia, the land of the Czech peoples of Bohemia, Moravia and Silesia, and of the Slovak people of Slovakia, is the most densely populated of the Danube countries. In 1949, her population was estimated at over 12½ millions. In getting her freedom from the old Empire, Czechoslovakia was lucky to acquire the richest industrial region of old Austria-Hungary as well as some of Central Europe's finest farm and forest lands. *Prague* (Praha), the capital, shares Brno's importance as a textile and glassware manufacturing centre and is the chief refinery centre

for the Czech sugar-beet crop. Czechoslovakia is one of Europe's largest producers of beet sugar. Her other main crops include wheat and similar cereals, and potatoes. She also breeds large numbers of cattle, pigs and other livestock. Her thriving timber industry is based upon some of the finest forests in Europe which are, like all her industry, controlled by the Government. Paper, furniture, matches, and rayon are among the products which begin in her rich forestlands.

About seven out of every nine people in Czechoslovakia live in the western part of the country (Bohemia and Moravia), for here are found most of the important industrial towns. Among

E.N.A.

PEASANTS SELL EMBROIDERY IN THE HUNGARIAN CAPITAL

You have only to see the elaborate national dress worn by Hungarian peasants to realise how skilled with the needle their womenfolk are. These peasant women have brought some of their work to market in Budapest, the Hungarian capital, where visitors and townspeople are glad to buy such beautiful embroidery.

E.N.A.

NATIONAL COSTUMES SWIRL AS HUNGARIAN PEASANTS DANCE THE CSÁRDAS

Sad and troubled though their history has been, the people of Hungary's plains and villages still enjoy dancing to the fierce rhythms of the *csárdas*, their most famous national dance. The dance originated in the nineteenth century and takes its name from the word *csárda*, meaning tavern.

these towns are *Pilsen*, with its huge iron and steel works, its world-famous breweries, its important textile mills, its chemical, pottery, glass and fertiliser factories; *Brno*, mentioned previously; *Gottwaldov* (formerly known as Zlin), which has one of the largest shoe factories in Europe; and *Ceske Budejovice* (Budweis), where lead pencils are made. Coal is mined at such centres as Most, Chomutov, Teplice, Moravska, Ostava and Sokolov. Iron, silver, copper and other metals are mined also.

Although Czechoslovakia is an inland country without seaports, she is well served by waterways for carrying on a busy trade. Bratislava, as we have seen, is her Danube port and outlet for the Black Sea and the Mediterranean, but she can also use the Elbe waterway as an outlet to the North Sea or the Oder waterway as an outlet to the Baltic.

From Prague, moreover, spreads a great network of railways, linking Czechoslovakia with all parts of Europe. But nowadays Czechoslovakia looks mainly eastwards for trade; in 1952, some 70 per cent. of her trade was with Russia and the other sovietised countries, including China.

Hungary of the Great Plains

On flows the Danube, a highway for great timber rafts from the now-distant Black Forest, each with its little hut for the raftsmen, and for tugs towing empty oil barges back to Rumania for another load. The banks are lined by floating grain-mills, whose huge wheels are worked by the rushing current that here has a speed of about five miles an hour. This land through which the river courses is the Little Hungarian Plain. Presently, the river reaches *Budapest*, the Hungarian capital that is really two cities in one. On the high western bank of the river is the old city of Buda, nestling round its castle. On the eastern bank is the newer city of Pest built upon lower ground and joined to Buda by five bridges.

Hungary is the land of the plain where the Magyar people live. The Hungarian plains are almost treeless, their level expanse reaching to the rim of the world, it seems. Great herds of long-horned cattle and sheep roam over these wide natural grasslands, where peasants dressed in wide linen trousers, loose shirts, and wonderfully embroidered sleeveless jackets, lean on their long staffs and watch their grazing animals from beneath wide brimmed hats. In winter they wear thick sheep-skin coats; in summer, on high days and holidays, they fling over their shoulders, like capes, magnificently embroidered overcoats whose sleeves they never use. Here and there in the Hungarian plains are wells from which water for the sheep and cattle is drawn by a bucket from a great pole slung across a stout upright.

The great Hortobagy plains, where fine horses and cattle are reared, are the home of the *čsikos*, or cowboys, who are just as skilful with the lasso as the cowboys of America. In the villages of white-walled, heavily thatched houses, richly adorned headdresses and costumes are worn on holidays by the women, some of whom wear as many as a dozen skirts at a time, the whole standing out stiffly in a wide circle around their white stockings.

Like other eastern European countries where Communism or something very like it has come to power, Hungary has undergone great changes in recent years. Many of her peasants now work on State farms and the large estates have been

Copyright.

HARVESTING WATER MELONS

These Hungarian farmers and their womenfolk are gathering a fine crop of water melons. Until recently much of the land in Hungary formed large estates, but these have now been broken up into smallholdings or have been formed into collective farms after the soviet pattern.

VILLAGE SCENES IN YUGOSLAVIA

Here is a street in a typical mountain village and it is evidently the shopping centre. Before the open-fronted shops are bags of vegetables and grain, baskets of fruit, beans, onions and paprika and many other things for sale. Beyond the village are the mountains, barren and rugged.

Photos: Will F. Taylor.

Wearing their everyday dress, two peasant women pause for a chat in the village street. The dress worn and the language spoken vary from place to place in Yugoslavia, because the republic embraces Serbs, Croats and Slovenes. But most people in Yugoslavia understand the Serbo-Croat tongue.

broken up. Similarly, all industries in Hungary have been taken over by the State. Most industries are based on farming; for example, distilling, flour-milling, making farm machinery, and manufacturing beet sugar. The main Hungarian coalfields are at *Pecs* and *Komlo*. Some iron and steel, manganese and petroleum are produced also. Thirty-five miles south of Budapest, on the west bank of the Danube, the new iron and steel town of *Sztalinvaros* (Stalin town) is being built.

Yugoslavia and the Balkans

Belgrade, where the Danube next takes us, is the capital of Yugoslavia, and is perched high on a rocky hill at a point where the Sava comes down from the Alps to join the Danube. This key hill has been fought over by many peoples in history: Celts, Romans, Byzantines, Hungarians, Turks and others. But few old buildings remain. One building in every five in Belgrade was destroyed during the Second World War. New offices, shops and public buildings have now been erected not only within the city, but upon its outskirts, where volunteer youth brigades have played their part in raising a new Belgrade. New homes were an urgent need; in 1939, Belgrade had a population of about 100,000, but in 1948 nearly 400,000 people were living in the capital.

If we were to walk down the main street of the city, which is called the Terazije, we should at once notice what a variety of peoples Belgrade contains. Here can be found representatives of all parts of the republic; some dressed in European clothes such as we wear,

A. F. Kersting.

MODERN BUILDINGS IN YUGOSLAVIA

Much rebuilding and development have taken place in Yugoslavia since the end of the war. At Belgrade, the capital, a new city is rising on the outskirts of the old; and at Zagreb, the chief city of Croatia, a " university city " is being built by youth brigades like those that made the new, straight 240-mile motor road from Zagreb to the capital. Typical of Yugoslavia's new buildings is this civic centre at the Bosnian town of Banja Luka.

others with baggy breeches, sheepskin waistcoats and fezzes, which remind us that we are in eastern Europe, in the Balkan Peninsula.

The Balkan Peninsula is the home of a number of widely-different peoples some of whom, such as the Greeks, settled here in early times, while others, such as the Turks, came to the Balkans as invaders.

"Field of the Black-birds"

If you visit the desolate Kosovo plain in the Serbian part of Yugoslavia, you may perhaps hear the story of this "Field of the Blackbirds." It was here, in 1389, that the Turks defeated the Serbs under Prince Lazar, killing the Prince and bringing Serbia under Turkish rule. Soon after that fateful battle, the Turks spread their power over all that now forms the republic of Yugoslavia.

A. F. Kersting.

ST. MARK'S CHURCH, ZAGREB

On the roof of St. Mark's Church in Zagreb are the coats of arms of Croatia and Zagreb. Croatia is one of the Republics which form Yugoslavia ; Zagreb is the chief town of this, the most thickly populated part of the country.

Later, the north and west were occupied by the Austrians and Hungarians, while along the Adriatic shore the republic of Venice had established its rule.

From such events have come sharp differences in outlook, language and religion. And in more recent times the mixture of peoples in the Balkan Peninsula has created problems of national frontiers which are still not entirely solved. But let us see how problems of race and outlook have been faced in Yugoslavia, which is the home of several different peoples.

Once a kingdom, Yugoslavia is now a "Federal People's Republic" organised on Communist lines, but independent of other sovietised countries in Europe. Her President is Marshal Josip Broz-Tito, who emerged as a vigorous partisan leader during the Second World War.

The country is really a union of several federated republics—Serbia, Croatia, Slovenia, Bosnia-Hercegovina, Macedonia and Montenegro—and has three officially recognised languages: Slovene, Macedonian and Serbo-Croat.

The most thickly peopled part of Yugoslavia, and the most fertile, is the northern plain where the Danube flows. This is the home of the Croats and Slovenes, and is probably the best farming region in the country. Maize is the chief grain crop, and wheat, sugar beet and tobacco are also grown. Dairy farming is also important in this part of Yugoslavia. The chief town is *Zagreb*, on the river Sava, which is linked with Belgrade by a new motor road and, of course, by rail. The new road linking the cities is 240 miles long and runs so straight that it is almost an " as-the-crow-flies " route from one city to the other. Zagreb is the site of a new " university city " which will accommodate some 12,000 students when it is complete.

The southern highlands are part of the " core " of the Balkan peninsula. They have valuable forests of oak and beech, and sheltered valleys where vines, tobacco, sugar beet and maize are grown. Northern Serbia is noted for its plum orchards. Much of the plum crop is dried for export as prunes or used to make the famous *sljivovica* (plum brandy).

But much of Yugoslavia is rugged, almost inhospitable country with sparse upland pastures that provide a precarious living for shepherds with their flocks of sheep and goats. The barren western mountains are the best example of this. They form what geographers call *karst-land;* that is, they are mainly formed of limestone, which has little surface water and does not support much vegetation. In such regions, the limestone is often weathered into strange forms, and below ground there are caverns and streams. The Peak District of Derbyshire is really a karst region on a small scale.

Yugoslavia also has coastlands along

A. F. Kersting.

YUGOSLAVIA REMEMBERS ITS WAR HEROES

When Yugoslavia was overrun during the Second World War, resistance was carried on by partisans operating from hide-outs in the mountains and forests. This monument at Titova Korencia, near Gospic, is a memorial to the local partisan leader and stands outside the new school buildings.

A. F. Kersting.

A NEW DAM IN THE VALLEY OF THE SAVA

The river Sava, which flows down from the Alps to join the Danube at Belgrade, is now being tamed by such dams as this. The picture was taken at Most and shows the dam nearing completion.

the Adriatic. These enjoy a Mediterranean climate and support typical Mediterranean crops (vines, olives, mulberries) and interests (tunny and sardine fishing and canning). We shall see more of these coastlands when we visit the Mediterranean and Adriatic.

Through the Iron Gate

Yugoslavia has much mineral wealth, but her resources have still to be fully developed. Her important mining centres include Vares and Ljubija, in Bosnia (iron); Bor, in Serbia (copper); and Trepca, in Montenegro (lead). Coal, gold and chrome also are mined. Ljubljana, the capital of Slovenia, is a growing centre of heavy industry.

From Belgrade the Danube, wide and strong, plunges through the fortified defile of the Iron Gate where passage for river craft is made possible only by the walled channels that have been constructed in the bed of the stream. On either side of these fairways the turbulent waters rush madly so as to make navigation there impossible. In the old days boats had to be dragged by main force by gangs of men, the vessels hugging the shore as closely as they dared. In 1878, the rapids were subdued, partly by blowing up the rocks in the river, but chiefly by building the walled channels. The gorge itself is shut in by high rugged walls of rock on which, at one point, there is a deeply-cut inscription in Latin recording the passage of the armies of the Emperor Trajan through this stupendous cleft—a passage made by building great platforms supported by wooden beams sunk in the rock face above the swirling flood.

Further downstream are the remains of Trajan's wall between Constanta (the Rumanian oil and passenger port on the Black Sea) and the Danube which shows how hard a fight he must have had to keep out the Visigoths, who in his time were hammering at the outer defences of the Roman Empire.

For two hundred miles, as far as Giurgevo, the Danube is a frontier river dividing Bulgaria and Rumania. Bulgaria is a land of farmers whose richest lands lie between the Balkan Mountains and the forested crustblock of the Rhodope in the plain of Rumelia.

Bulgaria's Road of Conquest

But though they are a peasant people, the Bulgars were once strong enough to control the whole Balkan Peninsula. Standing athwart the Turkish road of western conquest, however, they became a subject people and had Turkish overlords until the nineteenth century. To this day there is abundant evidence of the long period of Turkish rule; even from the waters of the frontier river you can see the slender minarets of Mohammedan mosques which show many of the Bulgars to be Moslems.

Bulgaria stands on the road of migration and conquest. The routes from Istanbul to Central Europe pass over her plains. That is why *Sofia*, the capital, stands where it does.

Sofia's history is that of a fortress town built to dominate the Dragoman Pass leading from old Serbia into Bulgaria and to command the way from the Danube to the Aegean Sea.

Bulgaria is a poor country. Her most fertile lands are along the upper Striema and Tunja, both tributaries of the Maritza which flows through the plain of Rumelia. This region is called " The Garden of Bulgaria " and it is here that the age-old skill of Bulgar rose-growers produces the famous " attar of roses."

In the " Valley of Roses "

If you went to Bulgaria's sheltered " Valley of Roses," you would find it inhabited not only by Bulgars, but by people whose customs and dress would proclaim their descent from the Turks who long ago conquered Bulgaria. In May and June, roses are picked every day in the early morning and sent off by the sackful to be distilled, ox-carts and lorries being used for their transport. This rose oil industry is now controlled

T. Weir.

IN THE JULIAN ALPS

These lofty crags are peaks of the Julian Alps in the extreme north-west of Yugoslavia. They are said to be the home of many chamois. Below the peaks are the pine forests and mountain pastures.

E.N.A.

HARVESTING IN THE VALLEY OF THE PRAHOVA

One of the most important industrial regions of Rumania is around Ploesti, the centre of the oilfields of the Prahova valley. In this picture the gaunt outlines of the Ploesti oil refineries make a stark background to the peaceful harvest scene.

by the Government, which also maintains a number of state farms, animal-breeding farms and tractor stations. Since 1951, the great coastal area of the Bulgarian part of the Dobrudja—the home of some 300,000 people—has been transformed into one vast collective farm based on the port of Varna (now called Stalin) and the inland town of Dobric (now called Tolbukhin after the Russian Marshal of the same name). It has been said that this area is largely under Russian direction.

Fruit, especially grapes, is grown in great quantities in Bulgaria, particularly in the Kustendil and Plovdiv districts. The plain of Plovdiv is one of the regions irrigated by water from the new Vassil Kolarov dam in the Rhodope mountains. Electric power trains from Russia have also been used to increase the irrigation area in Bulgaria.

Although Bulgaria has rich deposits of coal, they lie mostly in mountainous parts of the country where they cannot be easily worked. Industry is being developed, particularly at the new town of Dimitrovgrad (founded in 1947), with its " Stalin " chemical works and thermo-electric station.

A Land of Contrasts

North from the high steep bank of the Danube that is Bulgarian is the low marshy ground of Rumania, speckled with lake-like expanses that are really the old cut-off loops of the river.

Like Bulgaria, Rumania is a land of peasant farmers, most of whom raise maize, wheat and cattle in the plain of Wallachia. Formerly, Rumania had another fertile region in Bessarabia which has now, however, returned to Russia. In Transylvania, Rumania has a rich industrial region of mineral ores where new industries are being set up, and even more important are her oilfields of Prahova, Dambovitza, Bacau and Buzau. Pipe-lines link the oil refineries with the port of Constanta, on the Black Sea, and with the port of

Giurgiu, on the Danube. Oil is piped also from the refineries to *Bucharest*, the Rumanian capital. Oil, coal and much other Rumanian industry is now controlled by " Sovroms." These are joint Rumanian-Russian companies set up by the governments of the two countries. By 1953, fifteen " Sovroms " had been established, each with a Russian managing director.

The Rumanian landscape contains many contrasts. There are the farm-lands, the industrial and oil-producing regions, and the thickly forested Car-pathian mountains which are the centre of her timber industry. Some distance east of Giurgiu, where the mighty Danube turns abruptly northwards, the river is entirely Rumanian, crossing the low dry plateau of limestone called the Dobrudja—the home of countless sheep and goats. North of the Dobrudja are the big grain and timber river-ports of Galatz and Braila, crowded with barges and steamers of all kinds, rafts of timber, oil tankers and grain boats, which all tell of the way in which Rumania earns her keep in the world.

The Danube is now linked by canal with the Black Sea. The canal crosses the Dobrudja and enters the sea some miles to the north of Constanta. At its mouth the large new port of Midia has been built.   Like the Bulgarian Dobrudja, Midia and the coastlands on either side are said to be largely con-trolled by Russia.

Peasant Songs and Dances

From Czechoslovakia onwards our journey from the Black Forest to the Black Sea has been through lands of peasant peoples where we have seen beautifully worked national costumes and heard gypsy music that strikes our western ears quite strangely. We have seen the *csárdas* danced in Hungary, and heard in Bulgaria melodies sugges-tive of the East; in Rumania, *tzigani* (gypsy) bands have played the *hora* for us.

No one can say how old the *hora* is; it is a dance whose beginnings are lost in antiquity and it is intended to be danced on what we would call the village green. Everyone joins in, form-ing a circle, with the musicians in the middle.

The songs we should hear, too, in the homes of these peasant people would remind us of the great heroes of the past and tell by word and note of the happiness and sadness of days gone by.

The Sulina Delta

But now we have almost reached the end of our long journey down the great river Danube, and its source—the *Donau-Quelle* at the small town of Donaueschingen—is far behind us. After Galatz the Danube turns east again, fanning out into the wide marshes of the Sulina delta. At Sulina itself, two long jetties have been built to con-fine the Danube flood and make a well-scoured channel deep enough for ships to enter from the Black Sea. Here we are 1,800 miles from Donaueschingen where our armchair journey down the Danube began.

Fishing for Sturgeon

Fish of many kinds are found in the waters of the lower Danube. The most prized is the sturgeon, whose roe is known to us as that highly-priced delicacy, caviare. The sturgeon come up river from the Black Sea, seeking spawning grounds, and are caught by hook, net and trap. In a prize catch the roe may be as much as a fifth of the total weight of the fish. When the roe has been removed, it is strained and washed, then treated with salt and packed in tins or barrels. To the Rumanians of the Danube delta caviare is part of their everyday food, but in Britain and other Western countries it is an expensive luxury. Carp, burbot (a member of the cod family), plaice, perch and herring are among the other fish caught.

The Story
of the
World and
its Peoples

Russia, mighty
in two
Continents—and
Poland

THE DNIEPER DAM

Society for Cultural Relations.

The giant dam and hydro-electric station on the river Dnieper are probably the best-known of
Russian engineering achievements. Designed by Americans, the dam was wrecked when German
armies swept into the Ukraine; but it has now been rebuilt and once more harnesses the Dnieper
as it flows on its 1,300-mile journey to the Black Sea.

RUSSIA: U.S.S.R. IN EUROPE AND ASIA

SOVIET RUSSIA covers about one-sixth of the land surface of the globe, for it includes vast territories in Asia as well as those which form Eastern Europe. It extends from the Baltic to the Pacific, along the longest railway in the world. Much of the northern part of Russia lies within the Arctic Circle.

A Union of Republics

This enormous land is really a union of republics, each managing its own affairs by its " soviet " or council, but looking to the great council at Moscow as its leader and supreme authority. For this reason Russia is usually referred to as the U.S.S.R.— the Union of Socialist Soviet Republics.

How did this enormous system of interlocked republics all owing allegiance to a central government at Moscow come about? The story of Russia covers over a thousand years of history and reaches back into the days of primitive tribes and early legends. It is a story of the rivalries of different princes, of invasion by Tartars and Mongols, of such ruthless rulers as Ivan the Terrible who, in 1547, took the title of Tsar of all the Russias and carved out an empire stretching from the Caspian Sea to the White Sea. It is a story of the expansion of a central power across the greatest plain in the old world which offers few obstacles to such domination.

Peter the Great

One of the most famous of Russian Tsars was Peter the Great who travelled widely in Holland, England and other western lands and strove to bring his

backward country into line with western progress. So determined was he
that his people should shake off their
old barbarism that he ordered his
nobles to shave off their beards and
made them wear the western dress of the
time. From his reign on, Russia grew as
a European Power, particularly under
the Empress Catherine the Second who
added the Crimea, Lithuania, Odessa
and much of Poland to her dominions.

The Russian people, however,
remained oppressed and the enlightened
ideas which the writers of the French
Revolution spread across cultured
Europe reached Russia only through
secret societies whose members went in
constant fear of their lives and liberties.
So backward was Imperial Russia that
serfdom was not abolished until 1861.
Even such long overdue reforms did
little to improve the condition of the
people. Tsar Alexander the Third, an
extreme autocrat, virtually ruled
through his secret police, who sent thousands of his opponents to exile or
imprisonment in Siberia.

When the First World War began in
1914, Russia was still among the most
backward of European Powers. Her
great natural wealth was undeveloped,
her farming was primitive, her roads and
railways out of date. Apart from the
cultured and rich-living ruling classes,
her people were poor and illiterate.
Only 30 per cent. of her population
could read and write. Most Russians
were pitifully poor peasants, but there
were also, in the few manufacturing
towns, an increasing number of industrial workers whose conditions were as
bad as, if not worse than, those of the
peasants. There had already been one
revolt in October 1905, which had
induced the Tsar to give Russia a *Duma*
or parliament. But the *Duma* did not
solve the Empire's troubles. Its power
was rigorously limited and it was safely
controlled by the nobility who were as
autocratic as their Tsar.

For Russia, the war of 1914–18 was a
titanic conflict for which she could not
have been worse equipped. Brave
though her soldiers were, they had
not the arms, supplies or industrial
power which any country needs to make
war. Defeat followed defeat, and her
soldiers, lacking weapons, ammunition
and other equipment, began to desert.
At home, conditions were chaotic. Food
was short and there were bread riots,
strikes, and demonstrations. In 1917,
Tsar Nicholas the Second abdicated and
a Provisional Government was formed of
statesmen who had led the opposition in
the *Duma*.

The Revolutionary Soviets

Already, in various parts of Russia,
revolutionary Soviets (Councils) had
sprung up among the peasants, industrial
workers and soldiers. All these had sent
delegates to a Congress of Soviets at
Moscow which had helped to organise
the strikes and demonstrations leading
to the abdication of the Tsar. Lenin
returned from exile where his revolutionary ideas had driven him, gained the
leadership of this Congress with his
Bolshevik party, and compelled the
Provisional Government to surrender
power to the Soviets.

Such was the " October Revolution "
of 1917. It was the second revolution in
Russia within eight months—and she
was still at war with Germany.

Lenin's first need was time; time in
which he could rebuild, in his own
manner, the life and industry of the
country which had almost completely
collapsed. Peace with Germany was
essential, and in March, 1918, Russia
accepted her terms in the Treaty of
Brest-Litovsk. Hardly had this happened when civil war broke out in
Russia between those who opposed Lenin
and his Bolsheviks (the " White " armies)
and the " Red " armies of Bolshevism.
In this war, the " White " armies were
helped by several foreign governments
and two years of bitter fighting passed
before Lenin knew victory. Even then,
fighting continued in some places and
it was not until 1922, with the departure

THE RED SQUARE, MOSCOW

The capital of the vast Soviet Union has a splendid stage for its parades and celebrations in its Red Square, once no more than the market-place of a twelfth-century trading town. The fantastically-coloured, onion-shaped domes of St. Basil's Cathedral rise in the background. On the right are the walls of the Kremlin and the granite mausoleum of Lenin, the father of the Soviet Union, and of Stalin, his successor. Moscow is the fourth largest city in Europe and is a great manufacturing centre.

of the Japanese from the Pacific port of Vladivostok, that the last was seen in Russia of organised forces hostile to Bolshevism. Lenin was now master of the vast, exhausted country.

He believed in the Communist system proposed by a German socialist named Karl Marx (1818–1883), whose large book *Das Kapital* is still the basis of Communist beliefs; and as soon as he could, he set Russia on the path to Communism.

At that time, most Russians were simple peasants who knew little about Communism, or even Socialism, and probably cared less. According to Karl Marx, the first stage in making a country Communist was to set up a " dictatorship of the proletariat," that is, a dictatorship of the industrial workers. So Lenin began by giving Russia more industry, reasoning that with more factories, Russia would have more factory workers and fewer peasants.

First, there was a fifteen-year plan for providing electricity in all parts of the country. Dams were constructed across great rivers such as the Dnieper, power stations were built, and new lines and cables carried electricity even to the farms and villages, where the new lighting was called " Lenin's lamps." By 1928, Russia had almost twenty times as much electric power as there had been in 1913. But Lenin himself never lived to see the full development of his hopes. He died in 1924 and the massive granite mausoleum in the Red Square at Moscow where his embalmed body lies is to this day a place of pilgrimage. For he was the father of the Soviet Union.

The Rise of Stalin

Lenin's successor was a man who had been a revolutionary from youth and had been general secretary of the Communist party since 1922. Born with the name of Josef Vissarionovich Djugashvili in the village of Gori, in Georgia (1879), he became better known as Stalin, meaning " man of steel," and after the

E.N.A.

RIGA, CAPITAL OF THE LATVIAN S.S.R.

Here we are looking across the river Dvina, or Daugava, at Riga, the capital and port of Latvia, which is one of the Baltic republics of the Soviet Union. In winter, the river is frozen so hard that you could drive a horse and cart across the ice.

Paul Popper.

IN A MOSCOW PARK

This fine avenue is part of a large park in Moscow, the capital of the Soviet Union. Best known of Moscow's parks and open spaces is the Central Park, commemorating Maxim Gorky, the great Russian writer, which stretches for four and a half miles along the Moscow River.

death of Lenin he removed or defeated his opponents and became the virtual ruler of Russia, where he came to be called the *Vozhd*, or leader. He did not openly acknowledge his power for several years. His only official post was party secretary until 1941, when he became official head of the government as Chairman of the Council of People's Commissars (since 1946 this body has been called the Council of Ministers of the U.S.S.R.). As Generalissimo Stalin, he remained Chairman until his death in 1953, when he was succeeded by Mr. Malenkov.

New Industries

From 1928 onwards, Russia's industries were developed and made modern by a series of Five Year Plans, which paid particular attention to heavy industry. Great new iron and steel works, factories and engineering plants, mines and railways came into being. The Third Five Year Plan had still two years to run when, in 1941, Russia was attacked by Nazi Germany. The German invasion laid much of European Russia in ruin and Russian casualties during the fierce fighting were enormous. When the Second World War ended in 1945, the rulers of the country were once more faced with rebuilding a shattered land.

During the War, the formerly independent republics of Estonia, Latvia and Lithuania were brought within the Soviet Union, which has also acquired most of East Prussia, Petsamo (formerly a province of Finland), and the southern half of the island of Sakhalin and the Kurile Islands (previously ruled by Japan). Poland also had to give considerable territories to the U.S.S.R. Other areas added to the Soviet Union in our own times include Bessarabia (ceded by Rumania in 1940), Karelia (handed over by Finland in 1940), and Ruthenia, which was obtained from Czechoslovakia by treaty in 1945. Some of the territories mentioned in this paragraph had previously been part of Russia, but had been lost by her as a result of the First World War.

After the defeat of Germany, Russia was one of the Allies who had the task of maintaining an occupying army in the territories of the defeated nations. In her zone of Germany, which included part of Berlin, the Communist " German Democratic Republic " (sometimes loosely called the East German Republic) was established. She also had charge of the north-eastern (Soviet) zone of Austria and a part of Vienna, the Austrian capital.

A Different Way of Life

We must remember that the Communist way of life that Russia and several of her neighbours follow is very different from that of the western nations. These sovietised countries follow the teaching of Lenin and Karl Marx, and in Russia a new generation has been reared and educated in Communism and probably knows much less about the western world than we know about the Soviet Union. The Russians have beliefs and values very different from our own; and although they may use the same words as we use, they often attach quite different meanings to these words. These are some of the reasons why the western nations have found it difficult to reach agreement with the Soviet Union over many of the world's problems. So the world seems to be divided and people speak of an " Iron Curtain " separating Russia and her friends from the nations of the west. Only time can tell whether we of the western world shall succeed in getting the curtain lifted.

Peoples of the U.S.S.R.

There are about 212,700,000 people living in the U.S.S.R. and they belong to nearly 200 different nationalities. The most numerous are the Russians themselves. Then come the Ukrainians, followed by the White Russians (not to be confused with the " Whites " who opposed the Bolsheviks). Other peoples of the Soviet Union include the Nentsi and Evenki, and other primitive hunters, fishers and reindeer herdsmen of the far North; the Uzbeks and Turcomans of Central Asia; the Mongolian peoples of eastern Siberia; the people of Karelia, who are much like the Finns, and many other groups and races. So it is not surprising that in some parts of the Soviet Union the natural language of the people is not Russian but some other tongue or dialect.

As we shall see, some of these peoples are simple folk with primitive ways of life. Others are highly-cultured and have made important contributions to the world's store of scientific knowledge and to music, art and literature. But all are subjects of the Soviet Union.

The U.S.S.R. covers about a third of Asia and almost half of Europe. Its climate ranges from the arctic cold of the north to the almost tropical heat of the Central Asian deserts of the far south. Although the summers generally may be hot (in July, it is almost as warm in Archangel as it is in London), the winters are bitterly cold. Thick ice seals the rivers and the waters of the White Sea are frozen over. For five months of the year the temperature in Moscow stays below freezing-point and even in some parts of the south—Astrakhan, on the shores of the Caspian Sea, for example —the average January temperature is much lower than it is in London during the same month.

The People of the North

Across the north of the U.S.S.R. stretch two great vegetation belts through which several large rivers flow to the Arctic. The northernmost belt covers the Arctic shore and is called the *tundra*. South of this lies the *taiga*, or forest belt.

On the tundra, the winters are long and harsh, the summers short and cool. The soil is perpetually frozen not very far beneath the surface and there is little plant life. Mosses and lichens are the most common form of growth, but in the southern tundra there are also dwarf

THE CONTINENT OF EUROPE

E.N.A.

Holland, the land of dykes, canals, windmills, is one of Britain's nearest neighbours. Flat though the Dutch countryside is, there is unique charm in the trim and often gaily-painted houses and windmills and in the national costume that is worn in many parts of the country, and which you see in this picture. The sombre black dresses are relieved by bright aprons, spotless white headdress, and pins and ear-rings that are often of gold and have been handed down from generation to generation.

SCENES IN THE LOW COUNTRIES

Scattered across Belgium and Holland are many wonderful old towns and buildings recalling the days of the powerful trading cities. Here, for example, is the old east gate of the Dutch city of Delft, whose name is still linked with fine pottery.

This is Dinant, the chief centre for visitors to the beautiful Ardennes country in Belgium. High on its crag overlooking the river Meuse is the citadel which, like the thirteenth-century church (right), received damage during the Second World War.

ON THE SEINE AND THE RHÔNE

More than 2,000 years ago a small tribe called the Parisii settled on the Ile de la Cité on the Seine, and the history of Paris had begun. Here we see the Champs Elysées, one of the most famous avenues in the French capital. In the distance is the Arc de Triomphe.

The Rhône is a great French river on whose banks rises many an ancient town. Here we are looking down from the walls of Avignon to the ruined bridge of St. Bénézet, widely known through the famous song "Sur le pont d'Avignon". On the bridge is a tiny chapel.

The beautiful lake of Lucerne is one of the most popular centres for visitors to Switzerland. The lake is more than twenty-three miles long. At its northern end is Lucerne itself, seen here with Mount Pilatus in the background.

Photos: E.N.A.

In Berne, the capital of the Swiss Confederation, you can see this unusual fountain. On top of the fluted column is a representation of Moses holding the Ten Commandments.

Here is another beautiful fountain, the Samson fountain in the main square at Budejovice, in Czechoslovakia. This town is famous as a centre for the manufacture of lead pencils.

LAND OF THE ETERNAL CITY

Along the Swiss-Italian border there are several remarkable lakes whose natural loveliness has made them renowned throughout the world. Lake Como is one of them, and here you see the south-eastern end of the lake with the town of Lecco.

Photos: E.N.A.

Rome, the Eternal City that is the capital of Italy, stands on the banks of the river Tiber. In this view of the historic city we look across towards the bridge of St. Angelo and the great Cathedral of St. Peter whose dome rises on the horizon to remind us that Rome is a Papal city. The bridge leads (right) to the ancient castle of St. Angelo.

SEAPORTS OLD AND NEW

Naples, in southern Italy, is not only a busy seaport; it is a city in an unrivalled setting of imperishable beauty. This panorama shows part of the famous Bay, the ancient, islanded Castel dell'Ovo, and beyond, the majestic bulk of Vesuvius.

Venice, once "Queen of the Adriatic" and a great maritime republic of the eastern Mediterranean, is still an architectural treasure-house. Here is part of the Piazza San Marco with (left) the Doge's Palace. Gondolas are moored at the water's edge.

BUILT BY MOOR AND MONARCH

Paul Popper

The fortified palace of Alhambra at Granada in Spain stands as a monument to the Moorish empire, of which that country was once part. Built more than seven hundred years ago, Alhambra's walls and towers are dwarfed by the distant peaks of the Sierra Nevada.

E.N.A.

The Castle of Neuschwanstein, in the Bavarian Alps in southern Germany, was built by King Ludwig II, friend and patron of the composer Wagner. It was begun in 1884, and was planned as an exact copy of a medieval Ritterburg, or knight's castle.

Hungary, land of the great Hortobagy plain, still sings and dances in traditional fashion. Dressed in peasant finery this young man performs the Shepherd's Crook dance.

These jagged peaks are part of the mountains known as the Dolomites, in the Trentino region of Italy. Their ruggedness and harshness are typical of this particular range.

Photos: Paul Popper

This is Istanbul, once the capital of Turkey and centre of a mighty empire. From the mosque of Ahmed we look towards Saint Sophia, the church of the Byzantine Emperors that became a mosque when the Turks took the city in 1454.

PREPARING FOR THE WINTER

Planet News.

The iron hand of winter closes very heavily upon most parts of the great Soviet Union and there are not many districts which escape lengthy periods of intense frost and deep, long-lasting snow. Much of Russia is densely wooded and it is for this reason that picturesque timber houses, like the one seen above, are so common except in large cities, where reinforced concrete is freely employed. In this scene the women of the homestead are making their preparations to meet the onslaught of winter by applying moist clay to every joint and crevice in the woodwork so that, aided by the log-burning stove inside the house, Jack Frost can be defied.

blackberry, bilberry and other bushes, and dwarf birch trees. During the brief summer, many small flowers appear in clusters on the higher ground.

The people of the tundra hunt, fish, and keep reindeer and until the Soviet government began to develop the Arctic lands, knew no other life. Their food was meat and fish, and what wild berries they could gather during the summer. Their clothing was mostly made of reindeer skin, which they also used for their *choums*, or summer tents. Some made rough, brushwood shelters built round a framework of poles as homes in the summer. But when winter came, both tents and shelters would be discarded in favour of crude, but warmer, dugout dwellings that had been prepared during the autumn. These were partly below ground and were protected by wooden frames covered with earth and mud frozen into a solid roof. Under such conditions, life was often a desperate struggle, especially if food supplies failed

or there was illness. While there are still people with such primitive ways of life in these Arctic lands, many changes have taken place in this part of the Soviet Union, as we shall see.

By Canoe and Sledge

To travel in the far North you need either a canoe or a sledge, depending on whether your trip is made in summer or in winter. Dogs or reindeer will draw your sledge, which may well have been made without the use of a single nail. The various parts of the sledge will be bound together by leather thongs, for these are the only " nails " known to the more simple peoples of the North. If you are visiting the Yakut people, you may travel on the back of a reindeer; the Yakuts ride them as we ride horses.

Transport has always been one of the problems of the North, where there are vast areas without roads or railways. The great rivers, of course, can be used for north-south travel, at least during

Society for Cultural Relations.

HUNTERS OF THE SIBERIAN TAIGA

The U.S.S.R. is so vast that many widely different peoples and types of country are included within its frontiers. Here, for example, are hunters of the Siberian Taiga, or great forest, on their way to a hunters' post in sledges drawn by reindeer.

PEOPLES OF THE SOVIET UNION

These workers inspecting a maize crop on the Kirov Collective Farm in the Ukraine are members of a team or brigade and may receive a prize if their work surpasses that of other teams.

The traditional dress worn by this collective farmer from the Buriat-Mongol Soviet republic makes a strange contrast with the modern motor cycle on which he is mounted.

Photos: Society for Cultural Relations.

Painting on wood is a traditional Russian folk art. This girl from the Gorki region uses black, gold, and red colours in a flower design and is a member of a co-operative factory.

Here we see a pupil of the Ulan-Ude trade school in the locomotive works. Ulan-Ude is an important town on the trans-Siberian railway about 100 miles east of Lake Baikal.

the summer months, but east-west travel was extremely difficult until regular air services were introduced and the northern sea route opened up for the transport of heavy goods. The first voyage from Archangel to Vladivostok in one season was made in 1932 by the icebreaker *Sibiriakov*. Since 1936 there have been regular shipping services along this route, which is the responsibility of the Northern Sea Route Board. As a result, the Arctic shores of the Soviet Union now have their radio and weather stations, air bases, and new ports such as Novi Port on the estuary of the river Ob, and Igarka on the lower Yenisei. The old route from Archangel to Vladivostok (by the Atlantic, Mediterranean, Indian Ocean and Pacific) was a voyage of 14,000 miles. By the northern sea route it is only 6,000 miles.

Polar Agriculture

At one time it was considered impossible for there to be any agriculture in these northern lands. But the Soviet government has encouraged what is called " Polar agriculture " and maintains a number of research stations where scientists study the growing of vegetables and other crops.

The results can be seen at such towns as Igarka, which is almost seventy miles within the Arctic Circle. Here vegetables and grain crops are now grown from special seed; special strains of grasses have been developed and yield fodder crops for cattle. About a million acres of land in the Far North are now under cultivation. Grain crops, potatoes and other vegetables are now raised on Kamchatka, and market garden crops in the Anadir basin and on the northern shore of the Okhotsk Sea, while flax, sugar-beet and the Kok-sagyz rubber plant have been grown successfully.

The North also has its State cattle, fox and reindeer collective farms, fish canneries, sawmills and power stations. Schools and hospitals have been built, and the people encouraged to forsake their precarious nomad life and settle down in proper houses. In some places, coal and other minerals are mined.

In the south, the tundra slowly blends into the *taiga*, or forest belt which stretches from the Pacific to the Baltic. In the north of the belt, most of the trees are conifers, e.g. fir, pine, larch and spruce, but there are broad-leaved trees such as birch and aspen in the southern part. The taiga is widest and most dense in central and eastern Siberia.

The Great Forests

In European Russia the people of the great forest belt cut timber or labour in the saw-mills, pulp-mills and paper-mills which eat up the lumber as fast as it can be cut; or they have little farms in forest clearings around their gaily-painted wooden houses. The most important thing in every house is the monster stove which keeps the family snug during the long and bitter winters, and which is fed by short logs from the great stack piled just outside the door.

Other people in this part of European Russia are trappers who catch animals for their furs. In Karelia, some may work on the waterways that connect the many lakes of this region, while in the Kola peninsula many will be employed in the bauxite, nickel, copper and other mines.

Timber from European Russia can be shipped from *Archangel*, which is closed during the winter; from *Murmansk*, which, although it is farther north, is warmer and is open all the year round; and from *Leningrad*, at the head of the Gulf of Finland. A further outlet is the great river Volga, down which timber can be carried to the lands of the south.

The Siberian forests are not so well served, as we have seen, and it is much more difficult to get timber away to places where it can be sold. There is to the south of the forests the great railway known as the T.S.R. (Trans-Siberian Railway), whose steel rails run in an unbroken line from Moscow in Europe to the shores of the Pacific; but carriage

ON THE LONGEST EUROPEAN RIVER

" Little Mother Volga " (*Matushka Volga*) is how the Russians often speak of the great waterway which flows for nearly 2,400 miles from its source in the Valdai Hills to the Caspian Sea. The picture shows us a typical Volga barge disembarking passengers near a riverside village.

The Volga is an important commercial waterway and is now linked by canal with the river Don and, by another canal, with Moscow. Timber from the northern forests is floated south down the river in giant rafts. From the south come grain, coal and other products.

of timber all that way by rail is an expensive business.

Even those mighty rivers—Ob, Yenesei and Lena—are not as useful as you might think, because they flow to the Arctic and have their mouths sealed by ice for nearly ten months of the year. These rivers, however, and their ports such as *Igarka* are—with the Northern Sea Route—the main outlet for timber from the Siberian forests. It sometimes takes two years for the timber to reach the ports, but the cost is half that of bringing it out by river and rail.

On small-scale maps Igarka sometimes looks as if it is at the mouth of the great Yenesei river. Actually, it is as far from the sea as London is from Glasgow and the voyage upstream takes ships three or four days. The lumber camps served by Igarka are mostly hundreds of miles up-river; indeed, some of the huge rafts of timber brought down to Igarka may have started their river journey a thousand miles away and two and a half

months before they reach the port. All through the winter, the Igarka saw-mills prepare timber for the loading season, which starts with the arrival of the first ships towards the end of July. Stacked timber is loaded throughout August and September—but no later, for the timber ships must be clear of the Arctic before the ice closes in.

In the Siberian forests, fur trappers hunt lynx, sable, fox, wolf, ermine and other fur-bearing animals, sending their pelts to the market centres such as *Irbit*, in the Sverdlovsk area of the Urals. Important fur markets in European Russia include *Gorki*, on the Volga, and *Moscow*.

The Baltic Republics

Much of the three Baltic republics of the Soviet Union (Estonia, Latvia and Lithuania) is forestland, but many of the Ests, Letts and Lithuanians work on the collective farms. The Ests are successful cattle-breeders and dairy far-

Society for Cultural Relations.

REBUILDING A BIG INDUSTRIAL CITY

During the Second World War the city of Stalingrad, on the river Volga, suffered terrible damage during its long siege. Among the new buildings which have now been erected is this school at the important tractor factory.

IN TWO SOVIET REPUBLICS

An interesting fact about the Soviet Union is the way in which its government has brought Western ways and industry to peoples who once lived the simple lives of peasant farmers. Here is the Farkhad dam in Uzbekistan which provides hydro-electric power.

Society for Cultural Relations.

In Soviet Russia, the womenfolk do many jobs which we in Britain would consider quite outside their province. These women, for example, are helping in building part of a residential estate for workers at the Minsk motor-car factory in Byelorussia.

mers; butter from the co-operative dairies is among the products exported from *Tallinn*, the capital and chief port.

Since their return to Russia these Baltic lands have become more industrialised. In Estonia, increasing quantities of liquid fuel and gas are being produced from the rich shale deposits, and the gas is now piped to both Tallinn and Leningrad. The swift-flowing rivers are being harnessed for electric power, which is used by the important textile industry and, of course, the towns and other industries. But farming and forestry are still the main activities.

Riga is the capital and chief port of Latvia, and is second only to Leningrad as a Baltic port. Lithuania has *Vilnius* (*Vilna*) as its capital and chief city, and *Klaiped* (*Memel*) as its main port.

The Rich Steppe Farms

South of the great forest belt lies a rich farming land stretching from the shores of the Black Sea to Western Siberia. Its fertile black earth is suitable for grain. Seeing these fertile lands makes it easy to accept Russia as one of the world's greatest growers of wheat.

The people who live in the European parts of this rich farming land are not all Europeans; some are Asiatics who came to Russia long ago, and who now have their own soviet republics in the Union.

Ukraine

The richest land of all the farming country of European Russia is Ukraine, where wheat and maize, tobacco and fruits, sugar beet and other crops are raised. Before the War, 20 per cent. of Russia's grain and nearly 70 per cent. of her sugar beet were grown in the Ukraine. The farmlands of the eastern Ukraine are scourged each year by the *Sukoveyi*, dry winds that blow from the Caspian and from Central Asia. A forest-belt 3,000 miles long has therefore been planted to protect the land from the ravages of the *Sukoveyi*.

Press Cliche.

YOUNG MEN AND WOMEN FROM KAZAKHSTAN

Kazakhstan is the largest of the Soviet Republics in Central Asia. It stretches from the Caspian in the west to China in the east. The Kazakhs are noted breeders of cattle and sheep. They also grow large crops of rice, wheat, fruit and cotton. Kazakhstan has extremely rich mineral deposits, especially copper, lead and zinc.

LUNCH=TIME ON A COLLECTIVE FARM

Under the Collective Farm system entire villages provide the labour for the farm which itself is managed by a board elected by the farmworkers. Machinery, fertilisers and seeds are supplied by the State. When the harvest is gathered part goes to the State, part to the tractor station which has loaned machinery to the farm, part to store for next year's sowing, and part to the farmworkers. At harvest-time, everyone helps to gather the yield of the enormous cornfields. It was in one of these that our photograph was taken showing groups of workers gathered together for their mid-day meal. Besides the Collective Farms, there are State Farms, and these are very large and may cover as much as a million acres.

The Ukraine has good rail and water communications to handle the products of her rich Black Earth farmland and to serve her important heavy industries, of which we shall see more presently. *Odessa*, on the shores of the Black Sea, is the chief grain port of the Soviet Union.

The Black Sea Coast, especially in the Southern Crimea, is very like the Mediterranean coast of France in both appearance and climate. Cork-oaks, cypresses, laurels and other typically Mediterranean trees cover the hillsides where the ground has not been taken for orchards, vineyards, olive groves or tobacco plantations. All along the coast are health and holiday resorts visited by people from all parts of the Soviet Union. For the Black Sea coast is " the Russian Riviera."

In Western Siberia, the Black Earth belt contains rich natural pastures as well as grainlands, and dairy-farming is important. Butter, cheese, eggs, pig-products and poultry are produced for *Omsk*, *Novosibirsk* and other cities of the region and for dispatch in large quantities to European Russia by the Trans-Siberian Railway.

The Steppe Nomads

As one goes south from the grain-lands and the dairy farms of Western Siberia the land grows drier and drier, and the grass-lands become the steppes on which herdsmen live in their felt " yurta " or tents, moving from place to place with the seasons in search of pasture for their sheep, horses and camels. The Kirghiz and the Kalmucks are the best known of these nomads. They are very fine horsemen, and live almost entirely on what they get from their flocks and herds. Their " yurta " are of grey felt faced with leather and bound by long ropes of horsehair over a beehive-shaped latticework of poles, which meet in a ring at the top forming a hole for the smoke from their small fires.

Paul Popper.

AN AUCTION SALE IN BOKHARA

The men offering goods for sale stand in the background, above the crowd. Behind them is the *madrasah*, or Moslem religious college of Shir Arab. Bokhara is one of the chief cities of the Uzbek S.S.R. It stands in a region of fertile, irrigated farmlands and has long been a centre of Moslem learning.

A HOME MADE OF FELT

Paul Popper.

Felt-making is an important job for nomad people such as the Kirghiz, who live in tents (*yurta*). This picture taken on the shores of the Issyk-kul lake in Kirghizia shows a group busily " matting " the felt which may later become the walls of their home.

E.N.A.

This is a " yurt." It is made from a framework of poles covered with leather-faced grey felt, which is secured by ropes of horsehair. It is used on the steppes by herdsmen, who move from place to place with their animals.

Such dwellings can be set up or taken down by the womenfolk in an hour or so, and packed on the backs of camels or horses ready for the next journey in search of fresh pastures. Many of these people, however, are now settled in villages as farmers, while others work in the new industries which have sprung up in this part of the U.S.S.R.

The Desert and the Town

Farther south the steppes gradually change to the dry desert country of Soviet Central Asia, where people are desert men who keep sheep and camels, and who wear tall sheepskin hats and thick sheepskin coats; or dwellers in the oasis cities, or in the towns by the rivers that flow down from the high mountains of the heart of Asia. The cities—Bokhara, Khiva, Samarkand and Tashkent, for examples—are older than London and Paris; they are vivid with the strange life of the East; in their bazaars are spoken all the languages of Asia, and

above their mazes of narrow streets of flat-roofed houses of sun-dried brick, rise the great domes and the slender minarets of many mosques. But although we can still find colourful scenes and old customs in Soviet Central Asia, many of the towns and cities have been modernised and are growing industrial centres. Presently, we shall look more closely at Soviet Central Asia to see some of the many great changes that have taken place in recent years.

Our quick journey from north to south has taken us through many of the Soviet Socialist Republics which together make up the U.S.S.R. It is important to remember that all the peoples we have seen—the Yakuts, Tungus, Chukchi and other peoples of the north; the peoples of Karelia and other parts of European Russia; the Kirghiz and Kalmuck horsemen; and the peoples of the desert lands—look to Moscow as the head centre of government, for all are members of the U.S.S.R.

Paul Popper.

THE DYNAMO STADIUM, MOSCOW, DURING A FOOTBALL MATCH

This stadium, which can accommodate 75,000 spectators, is claimed to be one of the largest in Europe. Football and many other sports are very popular in the Soviet Union, whose picked Dynamo team has played with great success in Britain and other countries.

A CITY IN SIBERIA

Russians are great lovers of music, drama and ballet, and the people of Novosibirsk are no exception to this rule. Among the finest buildings in the city is this imposing theatre, which is one of the largest in the Soviet Union.

Photos: Pictorial Press.

The sign on top of this building means " Central Hotel," while that over the entrance doors means " Universal Shop " (State co-operative store). Novosibirsk, where the picture was taken, is a modern industrial city in south central Siberia, and the junction for the Turk-Siberian and Trans-Siberian railways.

Moscow, the capital of all Russia, is a very ancient city standing on the banks of the Moskva.   It was founded in the twelfth century or even before that.

The Kremlin

The most famous place in Moscow is the Kremlin, enclosed by a great wall with nineteen green-tiled towers and containing many palaces and churches. Once upon a time it was a mighty fortress as well as the home of emperors and archbishops, but now within its walls are most of the offices of the Soviet Government. Here distinguished visitors are received.   Near at hand is the renowned Red Square, the forum of the city and site of Lenin's tomb, where gatherings and parades of national importance are held.   The Kremlin formed the heart of Moscow.   From such beginnings the city has become the home of some five million people; it is a city with many fine buildings, an underground railway whose stations are made beautiful with glistening marble, theatres and cinemas, and well laid-out parks and open spaces.   Many of its citizens live in flats, paying a rent which is fixed according to the income of the family and enjoying such new services as the natural gas supply piped to Moscow from the Saratov oilfields 527 miles away.

In replanning the city, the Soviet architects sometimes found that certain buildings were in the wrong places. But instead of pulling them down, the architects had them moved, using steel girders and rollers put under each building to make a mobile platform for shifting it, under power, to its new site.   Whole blocks of flats have apparently been moved in this fashion, water and other supplies being maintained through flexible pipes whilst the move was in progress.

Moscow now has a number of "sky-scrapers," including spacious new University buildings, but the highest building

Markov.

THE GORKI DAIRY AT MOSCOW

Moscow is a great manufacturing centre and has a population of some five millions. Among the establishments providing food for all these people is the Gorki Dairy, one of several dairies supplying the capital with milk products of various kinds.   In this picture we see the automatic process used for pasteurising milk.

Copyright.

A RUSSIAN IRON AND STEEL WORKS

The Ural mountains are rich in minerals, which have given rise to important centres of heavy industry, such as Magnitogorsk and Sverdlovsk. In this picture we see part of the huge iron and steel works of Magnitogorsk, which can produce iron and steel at the rate of three million tons each year. Coal for the industries of the Urals comes from the Kuznetz Basin.

planned has still to be constructed. This is the " Palace of the Soviets " which, with a height of 1,300 feet, will dwarf every other building in Moscow. On top of the palace will be a statue of Lenin made in stainless steel and 280 feet high.

Moscow is not only the first city of the U.S.S.R.; it is a great manufacturing centre with large motor factories and the most important electrical-engineering and machine-tool plants in the Soviet Union. These industries are supplied with local brown coal and, more important, coal from the Donetz basin. In the region round the capital are other industrial towns—Rybinsk, Gorki, Vladimir, Tula and Kaluga—whose working populations are fed from neighbouring mixed farming areas.

A Centre for Many Routes

Roads, waterways, railways and air routes converge on Moscow. From the capital a vast communications network stretches out in all directions: northwards to the Arctic, southwards to the Black Sea and the Caspian, eastwards to the Pacific and westwards to the Baltic. Moreover, since the opening of the Moscow-Volga Canal in 1937, Moscow has been an inland port with a water outlet to the Caspian, Baltic and White Seas.

In the Soviet Union generally, much use is made of rivers and waterways for getting goods and materials—and passengers—from one place to another. One of the most recent additions to Soviet waterways was the V. I. Lenin Volga-Don Ship Canal, which was opened in July, 1952. The completion of this canal meant that the five seas of European Russia (White, Baltic, Caspian, Azov and Black Seas) were linked by a single waterways system. The coal, grain and other products of the Ukraine could be taken by water transport into the very heart of European Russia, whilst timber and other products of the north could be sent southwards by the same system.

Another important new waterway is the Turkmenian Canal, which was planned in 1950 to run 650 miles across the Kara Kum desert from the Amu Darya river to Krasnovodsk. A South Ukrainian Canal also is to be built from Zaporozhe on the river Dnieper to the river Molochnaya and thence to Sivash. Schemes have been approved also for using the waters of the Ob, Yenesei and Lena rivers of Siberia. Many of these projects include the building of dams for hydro-electric power and the irrigation of dry lands with water from the canals and reservoirs.

After Peter the Great

Leningrad, once known as St. Petersburg, after Peter the Great, and then as Petrograd, was given its present name in honoured memory of Vladimir Ilyich Lenin (1870–1924), the founder of the Soviet Union and its first President. From 1713 until 1927 it was Russia's capital and now ranks as the second city.

Here we can find a State university, St. Isaac's Cathedral with its gilded dome, and a notable State library.

Leningrad stands at the mouth of the Neva and although the river is icebound for six months of the year, the important harbour of Leningrad is kept open by icebreakers except for the period mid-December–February. Waterways connect the port with the Volga, Dnieper and other rivers; and with Lake Ladoga, which is almost as large as Lake Ontario in North America, and with Lakes Ilmen and Onega. The last named is connected with the White Sea by the Stalin Canal.

Leningrad is more than an outlet for Russian timber and other products. Many of its population of over 3 millions work in factories in and around the city. Engineering, the making of paper and cellulose, the manufacture of chemicals and fertilisers, the building of cars and tractors, the production of cloth and synthetic rubber, and, of course, shipbuilding—all these are carried on at Leningrad.

Modern Russian Industry

In Tsarist Russia, there were few factories to supply the needs of this vast country and some of the most striking developments in Russia since the Revolution have been in industry and manufacture. Whole new cities came into being—Stalingrad on the Volga, the steel town famous for its resistance to the Germans: Magnitogorsk in the Urals, another great iron and steel centre, and other such places. Magnitogorsk and Sverdlovsk were developed as a result of the Second Five Year Plan which began the move of Soviet heavy industry from the west to behind the low range of the Urals where development is still going on.

In the past the Ural Mountains, which run for about 1,500 miles in a north-south direction, were regarded as a land frontier dividing Europe from Asia; but to-day their importance springs from the central position which they occupy within the Soviet Union and from their immense mineral wealth. First and foremost there is iron ore— whole mountains of it; recently the deposits of Mount Magnetnaya were estimated at 450 million tons, and there are several others like it. Iron mined in the Urals is used in the great iron and steel works of *Magnitogorsk*. Other important industrial centres in this region are: the tractor-building town of *Chelyabinsk*, whose iron and steel works are said to be the largest in Europe ; *Sverdlovsk*, which supplies all parts of the Soviet Union with machinery and machine-tools; and *Nizhne Tagil*, whose railway wagon-building plant is said to be the biggest in the world. Gold, copper, zinc, manganese and nickel are mined in the Urals area, which also contains a rich oilfield whose reserves

TRACTORS AND TEXTILES

Chelyabinsk is an important town in the Urals industrial region. Its iron and steel works is one of the largest in Europe and its huge tractor factory produces more than 40,000 heavy tractors a year. This picture shows us part of a tractor assembly line.

Photos: Society for Cultural Relations.

Tashkent, the capital of the Uzbek S.S.R. and one of the largest cities in Soviet Central Asia, is an important centre of the textile industry, where both silk and cotton are made. This picture shows us part of the hosiery and knitwear factory. Yet within the city can still be seen old buildings made with sunbaked bricks, and camel caravans on their way to the grain market.

were estimated in 1938 to be 2,700 million tons. The main oil centres of this " second Baku " are Samarska Luka (Kuibyshev), Molotov (Perm), and Tuymazy and Ishimbaev (Bashkiria).

Serving the big industrial cities of the Urals are the coalmines of the " Kuzbass "—the Kuznetz Basin coalfield near Novosibirsk—and the Karaganda coalfield of the Kazakh S.S.R. The Kuzbass also has its own iron and steel works at such centres as *Stalinsk* and *Guryevsk* and is grouped with the south Urals area in what the Russians call a " Combine." Although they are a thousand miles apart, the two units in the Urals-Kuzbass Combine work together, mineral ores from the Urals going to the big works and plants of the Kuzbass, and coal from the Kuzbass going to the Urals.

Russia's " Black Country "

An older industrial area, and a more important coal-producing region is the Donbass, or Donetz Basin, which lies mostly in the eastern Ukraine. About 60 per cent. of the Soviet Union's coal comes from this area. Here again there is much mineral wealth, including iron, manganese, aluminium. Some of the highest-grade iron ore comes from *Krivoi Rog*. Among the important iron and steel centres are *Stalino, Makeyevka, Dniepropetrovsk* and *Zaporozhe*.

The Dnieper area draws power from the great dam across the river and its hydro-electric station, and is organised as a " Combine." A pipe-line from the Caucasus supplies the Donbass with oil.

There are now rich oilfields in several parts of the Soviet Union but before the war, the Caucasus fields were the source of nearly all Soviet oil. The Caucasus Mountains rise between the Caspian and Black Seas and are said to be more beautiful than any European mountain range. Among the high peaks are Mount Elbruz (18,471 feet), and Kazbek (16,541 feet). The oilfields lie mostly on the northern flanks; the *Grozny* and *Maikop* fields are the most important. Another impor-

tant field is at *Baku*, whence oil is piped to *Batum*, on the Black Sea. Oil is also piped from the Caucasian fields to *Tuapse*, on the Black Sea, and to *Trudovaya*, in the eastern Ukraine.

Lands of the Caucasus

This rich oil region falls within the Azerbaijan S.S.R., which, like the neighbouring Soviet republics of Georgia and Armenia, is the homeland of both European and Asiatic peoples. All these republics have important industries: Azerbaijan, its oil; Georgia, its Chiatura manganese mines, hydro-electric power, Kutais motor works, and iron and steel industry; Armenia, its rich deposits of copper, aluminium, zinc and other metals. The Soviet Union as a whole is so vast and so rich in natural resources that it is impossible to mention all her industrial centres within these few pages.

But the southern republics do not live from industry alone. The valleys and lowlands of the rivers Rion and Kura contain fertile soil which is farmed collectively. Even in the fields, however, oil plays its part; gumbrin, a waste material from the oil refineries, is used as a fertiliser for the irrigated cotton-fields of Azerbaijan.

Cotton and fruit thrive on the irrigated lands of Armenia, which, like Azerbaijan and Georgia, has large flocks of goats and sheep, and valuable herds of cattle.

Central Asia and the Far East

The old name for Soviet Central Asia was Turkestan. It contains five Soviet republics: Kazakhstan, Turkmenistan, Uzbekistan, Tadzhikistan and Kirghizia. The heart of Soviet Central Asia is the lowland around the Aral Sea, to which flow the Syr Darya and Amu Darya rivers from the Tien Shan and Pamir mountains. Their courses run through dry and desert country, but there are fertile upper valleys, such as the plain of Ferghana, where cotton, vines and grapes thrive in well-watered soil.

In these dry parts of the Soviet Union, irrigation is most important and it has

A HUGE BOOK REST

In the courtyard of the Bibi-Khanum, a Moslem religious college in the city of Samarkand, in the Uzbek S.S.R., stands this carved marble support for a huge copy of the Koran. The Koran is the sacred book of Islam, the religion of the Moslems, or Mahommedans. Samarkand was the capital of the empire of Tamerlaine (1336–1405), the fierce conqueror.

Photos: Paul Popper.

This Kirghiz blacksmith is fitting a pony with special shoes rather like a mountaineer's crampons so that he will not slip on the icy mountain tracks. Kirghizia is one of the republics of Soviet Central Asia and its people are great breeders of cattle, sheep, goats and horses.

been particularly developed in Uzbekistan, where lies the plain of Ferghana. With water supplies assured by reservoirs and canals, the Uzbek people can farm their land intensively. They produce half the rice, and more than half the cotton grown in the Soviet Union. Although much of the cotton is sent away to other parts of the U.S.S.R., mills and factories have been built in the cotton-growing areas. At *Tashkent*, the capital of Uzbekistan, are some of the largest cotton mills in the Soviet Union. They are said to be larger than any in Europe and are capable of producing over 67 million yards of cloth in a year.

The largest of the Central Asian soviet republics is Kazakhstan, which stretches from the Caspian Sea in the west to China in the east. It is larger than all the other Central Asian soviet republics combined. Most of its people are Kazakhs, but in the grain-growing areas of the north there are Russians and Ukrainians. Although much of Kazakhstan is dry land or desert, especially in the west and centre of the republic, irrigation canals have transformed many arid districts into fertile farmlands. An example of this can be seen on the Syr Darya river, where, in the Kzyl Orda district, stands one of the largest dams in the Soviet Union, its purpose being to hold back water for irrigating the rice fields. Wheat, cotton, sugar beet, tobacco and other crops are also cultivated, and there are splendid vineyards and orchards. But the Kazakhs have always been noted for their livestock, and the rearing of cattle and sheep is still very important.

Nearly all these Central Asian lands have rich mineral resources. Kazakhstan contains about half the Soviet deposits of copper, lead and zinc, as well as large deposits of coal, tungsten, manganese, iron ore and oil. Copper is smelted at the Balkhash, Irtysh and Karsakpai works, while the chief centres for lead are Leninogorsk and Chimkent. Emba and Aktyubinsk are important for their oil. During the last ten years, valuable new coalfields have been discovered in Central Asia, especially near Tashkent. Tadzhikistan is one of the chief sources of uranium and other rare substances.

Asia's Largest Lake

In south-eastern Siberia, near the Mongolian frontier, is the largest freshwater lake in Asia—Lake Baikal, which has a volume of water greater than that of even the Caspian Sea. It is also the deepest lake in the world, for at the centre its waters go down to over 5,700 feet. Although most of the area around the lake is thickly forested with pines, there are steppes too where the Buriat people raise cattle. The Buriats and Mongols were once nomad herdsmen, living in *yurta*, or tents, but nowadays most of them inhabit wooden houses and keep their herds of cattle, horses, sheep and goats on the collective system.

The great river of the Soviet Far East is the Amur, which flows into the Pacific Ocean and which is frozen up during the winter months. *Nikolayevsk*, at the mouth of the river, would be icebound for seven months of the year if icebreakers were not used to keep the port open for part of the time; *Vladivostok*, the main port of the Soviet Far East, is icebound for more than three months of the year.

Because of the vast distances separating the Far East from the western U.S.S.R., the Soviet Government has tried to make the Far East able to provide for itself. Settlers were encouraged to leave the more thickly peopled parts of the U.S.S.R. to establish farms there and special communities such as the self-governing Jewish colony of Birobidjan founded. The main city of the Soviet Far East is *Khabarovsk*, which stands where the Trans-Siberian Railway crosses the Amur, and here a river port is being developed. Among the products of the Khabarovsk district is uranium ore, which is also mined at *Komsomolsk*, another new city of the Far East. Like Khabarovsk, Komsomolsk stands on the Amur. Its shipyards and steelworks are among the largest in this part of the

IN THE WARM SOUTH

Paul Popper.

The picture shows a typical landscape on the southern slopes of the Caucasus mountains. These mountains lie between the Black and Caspian Seas, the highest peak being Mount Elbruz (18,471 feet).

Pictorial Press.

Sheltered by the mountains, Yalta is the largest health and holiday resort of the Crimea. Palm trees grow along the Lenin Waterfront, and other Mediterranean type trees and crops flourish in this region. Mild winters and sunny, rainless summers make Yalta a favourite holiday resort.

Soviet Union. Railways link it with the ports of Nicolayevsk, Soviet Haven and Vladivostok.

Vladivostok and Khabarovsk grow in importance as heavy industry develops in this region. The raw materials are all to hand: iron ore can be mined in the valley of the Amur, in the Little Khingan Mountains and south of Lake Hanka; oil is obtained from the island of Sakhalin; and coal from the valley of the River Buryea.

Owned by the State

You will have noticed how often the word " collective," or the phrase " collective farm," has appeared when we have been describing Soviet industry and agriculture. What do these words mean ? How does the Soviet Government direct work in its factories and on its farms ?

It is a rule of the Soviet system that the main resources such as minerals, foodstuffs and raw materials, are owned and operated by the State and not by individuals. Land, for example, is the property of the State and is farmed under Collective and State systems.

The Collective Farms (*kolkhozy*) are groupings of former smallholdings into one unit sufficiently large to allow the use of labour-saving machinery and scientifically prepared fertilisers and seeds supplied by the State. The farm land, machinery, implements and horses, the barns, stables, and farm-buildings are for collective use; but the farmworkers' houses, domestic animals such as pigs, and their personal property remain their own. Moreover, each farmworker has a small plot of land where he may grow vegetables or what he pleases for his family. If he wants to, he may own one or two cows.

Each Collective Farm is managed by a board elected by the farmworkers. The workers are formed into brigades and teams, each team having a

Planet News.

A NEWSPAPER PRINTED IN THE FIELDS

Workers on Collective Farms are organised in brigades and teams, and work is hardest at harvest-time. On this Collective Farm, the district newspaper is actually produced in the fields as the harvest is gathered in. On the larger Farms, harvesting sometimes goes on at night under electric flood lamps.

Society for Cultural Relations.

HARVEST-TIME IN THE UKRAINE

These broad acres of golden grain are part of a Collective Farm in the Zaporozhe region of the Ukraine. The Ukraine contains the richest of European Russia's farmlands and produces large crops of wheat, maize, fruits and sugar beet. Land, of course, is the property of the State.

particular job to do at a particular time of the year. Competitions are held between brigades and teams, with prizes for the best. The peasant teams and brigades have to work hard, especially at harvest time when, on the larger farms, they will often work at night by the light of electrically-powered flood lamps. When the harvest is gathered part goes to the State, part to the tractor station which has loaned machines to the farm, part to store for next year's sowing, and part to the farmworkers.

What sort of homes have Collective Farmworkers? Trim cottages mostly, each with its radio set. Amusement is provided in the communal buildings of the farm which will include a theatre or entertainment hall. Children on the farms have to attend school when they are eight years old, and before that they will almost certainly be put in kindergartens or crèches, for their mothers have to work as hard on the farms as their fathers.

The State Farms (*Sovkhozy*) are very large indeed. The " Gigantic " State Farm near Rostov, for example, covers a million acres. These immense farms are usually devoted to specialist purposes such as wheat-growing, vine-growing, tea-planting, or experimental farming, and are limited in number.

What the farms shall produce is decided by the State Planning Commission or *Gosplan*, whose proposals can be altered by discussion at the various Collective and State Farms.

This system of trying to get everyone interested in the plan for their work is applied also to industry. Thus the economic plans for the whole of the Soviet Union are discussed in farm and factory before their final draft is presented to the chief governing organ, the Council of Ministers. A Fourth Five-Year Plan covering all industrial and agricultural output was issued in 1946, and a Fifth in 1951.

Apart from the farms and factories,

every village, town, city, district and region has its own soviet or form of local government. In each individual republic there is a supreme soviet which rules that republic, with guidance and direction from the Supreme Soviet of the U.S.S.R. at Moscow.

The Supreme Soviet comprises a Soviet of the Union and a Soviet of Nationalities, the former having 700 deputies and the latter, 631 deputies. The way in which the deputies are elected is very different from the way in which we elect our Members of Parliament. Candidates are nominated chiefly by trade unions, collective farms and other organised groups. There is only one political party — the Communist Party; and although non-party candidates are permitted, they are rarely elected to the Supreme Soviet. In 1950, eighty-three out of every hundred deputies were members of the Communist Party. At elections everything is done

to ensure that each Soviet citizen records his vote, no matter how remote the district in which he lives. The Supreme Soviet does not have the same functions as our Parliament. It meets only twice a year, and then only to approve measures taken by the Council of Ministers.

Going to School

The State also controls all education. Very young children may be cared for in a kindergarten or infant school, which is attached perhaps to the factory where mother works. School proper does not begin until children are about seven or eight years old. There are three types of school : the Four Year School, which the children attend until they are twelve years old : the Seven Year School, which children leave when they are fifteen years old, going on perhaps to a technical school or factory apprentice-school ; and the Ten Year School, at which the pupils remain until they are seventeen or eighteen years of age. Anyone who does well at the latter has the opportunity to go on to one of the universities.

Science, current affairs as seen through Communist eyes, mathematics and Russian literature are among the subjects taught, and the senior children are also trained in military subjects.

Russia has made many great contributions to the arts and her peoples are great lovers of the theatre, the cinema, music and literature. Russian ballet is world-famous, and Russian producers and directors have done much to develop the art of making films. Besides the great theatres, such as the Moscow Art Theatre, there are companies catering for the peoples of other races within the Soviet Union. For example, there are Georgian and Tartar theatres. There are also touring companies which visit the collective farms and factory institutes. Most of the plays and films deal with present-day matters of life in the Soviet Union, or with incidents in the Revolution, for even in their leisure hours the people are encouraged to keep their minds to the Soviet system.

Society for Cultural Relations.
GRAIN FROM THE COLLECTIVE FARMS
At harvest-time, each day sees truckloads of grain brought to central collecting points such as these Voroshilovgrad grain elevators. Voroshilovgrad is in the Ukraine.

POLAND—PAST AND PRESENT

Z. Kociuba.

THE ANCIENT TOWN HALL AT TORUN

Torun, the birthplace of Copernicus, the great Polish astronomer, stands on the right bank of the river Vistula in north-west Poland. It was founded in the year 1213 by the Teutonic Order of knights and was a prosperous Hanseatic town. Among its fine old buildings is the thirteenth-century town hall, seen in this picture.

POLAND'S history is of the misfortune and courage of a "buffer state" hemmed in by powerful and aggressive neighbours. Until the middle of the eighteenth century, Poland was a strong and healthy country of much greater size than she is to-day. Internal dissensions made her weak and she fell a victim to the ambitions of her neighbours —Russia, Austria, and Prussia, who on three occasions, in 1772, in 1793, and in 1795, helped themselves to large portions of Poland, despite the gallant resistance of the great Polish patriot Kosciuszko.

Kosciuszko was too far-sighted a man to be deceived by the Grand Duchy of Warsaw which Napoleon subsequently created. He knew that the French Emperor merely wanted another recruiting ground for his armies and that the Grand Duchy was not Poland reborn, but a French puppet state which would disappear—as it did —when the French retreated from Moscow.

The Fight for Polish Freedom

The Congress of Vienna confirmed the division of Poland among Austria, Russia and Prussia, but although Russian Poland received a Constitution from Tsar Alexander, the Poles revolted in 1830. The rising was suppressed and Poland was reduced to the status of a Russian province, which she remained until the various parts of Poland—in Russia, in Austria and in Prussia— were united into a single state at the end of the 1914-18 war by General Pilsudski. Pilsudski was not the only Pole to fight hard for his country's freedom. Another great patriot,

Paderewski, worked tirelessly to rouse public sympathy, particularly in America where his friendship with President Wilson served the Polish cause well.

Despite the enmity of its neighbours, the Polish State established itself, but with frontiers that held the seeds of future war. Westwards there was defeated Germany, separated from her province of East Prussia by the Polish Corridor and the Free Port of Danzig. Eastwards there was Russia, until recently Poland's overlord, and smouldering at the part which Pilsudski's troops had taken in efforts to strangle young Soviet Russia.

When war came again in 1939, Poland was invaded from both east and west and divided between Russia and Nazi Germany. The Polish State, it was declared, had ceased to exist. At the end of the Second World War, Poland was freed again, but with considerable changes in her frontiers as the map shows. A large part of her former eastern territories remained in Russian hands. In compensation she received Germany's rich eastern province of Silesia, the Free Port of Danzig and over half the former German province of East Prussia.

Poland To-day

By the end of the war, nearly all Poland was in ruins, for the country had been a vast battlefield. *Warsaw*, the Polish capital, had been ruthlessly bombed and then systematically destroyed by the invaders; when peace came, little more than a quarter of its buildings were standing. Large parts of Danzig and other cities also had been reduced to rubble.

But the Poles worked hard to restore their land. New towns and cities are rising from the ruins of the old. At Warsaw, where a special government department called the Office of Metropolitan Reconstruction was set up to direct the rebuilding of the city, there are now new offices and shops and homes. Before the war, the city had a population of nearly 1,500,000; to-day, some 600,000 people live in Warsaw, which is Poland's largest city.

The site on the banks of the Vistula which Warsaw has occupied since 1224 is a strategic crossing-point of the river, where routes from the North German Plain meet those from Russia. Lying between the lowlands and marshes of the north and the highlands of the south, it is the natural bridging-place for these routes. The Vistula is Poland's great river; indeed, much of the country

E.N.A.

IN THE WORLD'S MOST AMAZING SALT MINES

Wieliczka, a town near Cracow, has deep salt mines that run for miles underground at seven different levels. The mines were being worked as long ago as the eleventh century and contain wonderful rooms and statuary carved out of the salt. The picture shows the waiting and refreshment rooms in the underground railway station.

SPRING-TIME IN POLAND

Film Polski.

To compensate for war losses, Poland received, among other territories, the rich German province of Silesia. These new Western Territories of Poland include the holiday resort of Karpacz, near Hirschberg, which you see in this picture.

Copyright.

The model village of Liskow is near Kalisz in the Poznan district. Long noted for its pioneer experiments in co-operative work, its present-day enterprises, among which weaving and mixed farming are prominent, are all conducted on co-operative lines.

consists of the basin of this river. Although the Vistula's exit to the Baltic is blocked by ice in winter, and although the spring and summer floods are often serious, the river is an important waterway for cargoes of coal, petroleum and other products of the Carpathian lands; of timber from the great forests, which cover almost a quarter of the country; and of farm produce and hides from central Poland.

New Lands and New Industries

Before the war Poland was chiefly a farming country, but to-day only 46 per cent. of her population of nearly 25 millions get their living from the land. The richest and most densely peopled part of the country is in the south, where there are good coalfields, oil-wells, and iron, copper and lead mines. *Cracow*, where the kings of Poland used to be crowned, is an important centre of the iron and steel industry. Nowa Huta, the huge new steel works near Cracow, was designed and planned in the Soviet Union. To the north, *Lodz* is important for its textiles, especially cotton; like Warsaw, which is also an important textile centre, Lodz gets its coal and iron from the plateau region of the south.

The Wonders of Wieliczka

A few miles from Cracow is Wieliczka, a town which has the most remarkable salt mines in the world. These mines were being worked as long ago as the eleventh century and they run for miles underground at seven different levels. They are a maze of corridors, rooms and halls, many of which are adorned with statuary and carvings in the natural rock-salt. There are actually two chapels in the mine with altars and ornaments that have, like the chapels themselves, been hewn from the rock-salt.

If you look at a map of modern Poland, you will see that her western frontier follows the rivers Oder and

Associated Press.

HOUSING THE HOMELESS OF WARSAW

These pre-fabricated Finnish chalets were erected in the Ujazdowski Park, Warsaw, to house the homeless citizens of the capital. Made in Finland, they were sent to Russia as part of Finland's war reparations; Russia sent two hundred such homes to Warsaw to help satisfy Warsaw's urgent housing needs.

IN POLAND TO-DAY

Copyright.

For over 700 years, the *hejnal*—a trumpet call—has been sounded from the tower of St. Mary's Church, Cracow.

Polish Photo News.

National costume such as this is found in many places. Lowicz, between Warsaw and Lodz, is especially famous for its costumes.

Film Polski.

When the time came for rebuilding Warsaw, schools were among the many urgent needs of the Polish capital. This picture shows us the library of a modern school in Warsaw. Notice that some of the Polish boys favour much more severe haircuts than we have in Britain.

Neisse. This Oder-Neisse line, as it is often called, was agreed by the Allies at the Potsdam Conference (1945) and meant the transfer to Poland of a large slice of former German territory, including the rich province of Silesia. This province has valuable deposits of coal, iron, lead and other ores. Among the manufacturing centres of this part of Poland are *Wroclaw* (Breslau), the chief city of Silesia, and *Lignica* (Liegnitz), which are both important woollen manufacturing places. Most of the German population has now gone from the German territories handed over to Poland and its place has been taken by Poles from the areas which Poland lost to the Soviet Union.

Another effect of the transfer was to give Poland additional seaports. Before the war, Poland's outlets to the Baltic were limited to the Polish Corridor and Gdynia, a port which the Poles built not far from Gdansk (Danzig). To-day, Poland has not only *Gdynia* and the old Hansa city of *Danzig*, but even more important, *Szczecin* (Stettin), formerly Germany's greatest Baltic seaport.

Besides these, there is the port of *Kolobrzeg* (formerly known as Kolberg) and the port of *Elblag* (which used to be called Elbing). The latter, however, is of lesser importance as it is an inland river harbour. Notice how the change of national frontiers has brought about a change in the names of many places.

Farms and Forests

Although fewer people are now employed on the land in Poland, agriculture is still very important. The most fertile land lies in the great middle plain, where wheat, rye, oats and barley are grown; and from this same region come heavy crops of potatoes and sugar beet. Horse-breeding and dairy-farming are carried on by the farmers of the northern lands; while in the south, where the plateau country rises up to the lofty, forested Carpathians, sheep are reared on the hill and mountain pastures.

Besides providing food, Polish farmers supply raw materials for industry. For example, part of the potato crop is used for making starch and alcohol, flax is supplied for the linen mills of Warsaw and Lodz, hides for the leather factories and tanneries. The forest lands yield raw material for the many pulp- and paper-mills of the country.

Before the war, Poland was one of the chief European exporters of farm produce. But her farmlands were so laid waste that when peace came, she had to import foodstuffs for several years from the Soviet Union.

E.N.A.

CARVINGS FROM NATURAL ROCK-SALT

The salt mines at Wieliczka contain two chapels in which everything has been carved from the natural rock-salt. Here we see one of the entrances to St. Anthony's Chapel which has been a place of worship since 1698.

The Story
of the
World and
its Peoples

Through the
'Great Sea'
of Ancient
Civilisation

E.N.A

TANGIER'S SPACIOUS PROMENADE

Tangier, at the western gateway of the Mediterranean, has this pleasant promenade known as the Avenue of Spain because its palms were the gift of the Spanish Government. The Garden of the Hesperides was supposed to have been near the city. The golden fruit which Hercules sought there are thought to have been the oranges known to us as Tangerines.

THROUGH THE BLUE MEDITERRANEAN

DIRECTLY we enter the Strait of Gibraltar and turn eastward into the Mediterranean past the great Rock that has been a British stronghold since 1704 in spite of many efforts on the part of other nations to take it, we feel that we have come to a new world.

For the Mediterranean is very different from all other European seas, and the lands on its shores are different from any other countries of Europe— the trees and plants are different, the people are different, and so are their homes and their ways of living.

The Mediterranean can be very unpleasant on rough, stormy days; but on the fine days which come more often than they do in our seas, it is bright and sunny and its waters are an unbelievable and beautiful blue. The towns along its shores and the people who live in them are bright with colour that seems very strange and wonderful to folks from Britain who see it for the first time. The trees and plants are those of warm Southern Europe. Graceful palms, tall and mournful cypresses, olive groves with their thin grey-green leaves, orange groves of a darker green filled in the autumn with the glowing gold of ripening fruit, and dark forests of evergreen trees all make the shores look very different from those of Western Europe.

This great sea is as long from end to end as the North Atlantic is wide. It is very deep, and its waters are very salt.

The long peninsula of Italy, with the triangular island of Sicily at its toe, divides the Mediterranean into two great basins. The shores of Tunisia in Africa are not very far from those of Sicily, and commanding the gap between is the island group of Malta, which belongs to the British Commonwealth.

Between Europe and Africa

Around the western basin of the Mediterranean lie the most important countries; Spain, France and Italy have shorelands there, and so have the lands of the French Union in Northern Africa—Tunisia, Algeria and adjacent Morocco. The beautiful Balearic Isles are Spanish, Corsica is French, and Sardinia and Sicily, Italian.

The eastern basin has not such important shorelands as the western basin. The Balkan lands of Yugoslavia, Greece and European Turkey, of Asiatic Turkey (Asia Minor), Syria and Palestine, and lower Egypt, lie on the shores of this part of the Mediterranean. Just as France has lands in North Africa on the opposite shores of the Western Mediterranean, so Italy had her North African lands prior to the Second World War. These former Italian colonies have now gained independence; in 1951, they were brought together to form the United Kingdom of Libya.

On the whole, the lands fringing this eastern basin are drier, less productive and much more thinly populated than those along the shores of the western basin.

There is a great difference, too, between the lands of Southern Europe and those of Northern Africa on the other side of this great sea. The African lands are much drier, and in Algeria we need not travel far to the south by train or motor car before we find ourselves in the Sahara, the greatest desert in the world. In Tripolitania, which is now part of the kingdom of Libya, the desert is nearer the sea, and camel caravans come down to its very shores.

The Great Sea of the Ancients

The Mediterranean was the " Great Sea " around whose shores arose the mighty empires of the ancient world. Egypt, oldest of them all, had her ships upon it; and the Phœnicians, world traders of their day, ploughed its waters with the keels of their merchant vessels and planted their trading colonies around its coasts. Greek galleys flashed across its blue in the days when Greece was the greatest country in the world; and Roman triremes and biremes thrashed its waters into foam with their great banks of oars on their way to attack the Carthaginians in their great city port of Carthage.

Along its southern shores the Arabs fought their way in later days, overcoming all resistance and carrying the green banner of their prophet to the shores of the Atlantic, and even across the Strait of Gibraltar into Spain, where the Moors (of Arab blood) ruled for over seven centuries until the fall of Granada, their last stronghold, put an end to their power in the very year in which Columbus sailed from Palos in Spain to find the New World.

All around the shores of the Mediterranean we can still see reminders of its glorious past, which alone make the " Great Sea " still the most wonderful in the world. The pyramids and temples of Egypt, the ruins of Carthage near Tunis, the wonderful ruined city of Timgad in Algeria, the Acropolis and the remains of other glorious buildings of ancient Greece, the old Forum at Rome, the Roman amphitheatres and aqueducts of Southern France and

ON THE ISLAND OF MAJORCA

You will know of the beautiful Balearic Isles, set like gems in the blue waters of the Mediterranean Sea to the east of Spain. Majorca and Minorca form the two largest islands of the group, and the entrancing view shown above is but typical of "Mollorca," as the Spaniards call Majorca. The island is some sixty miles in length and nearly fifty miles across.

Photos: Mondiale.

Salamanca, one of the chief cities of Spain, famous for its wonderful buildings, was once one of the greatest centres of learning in Europe. On the right of the picture is the Cathedral, seen across the River Tormes, partly through the arch of a bridge. Salamanca was a place of considerable importance in the times before the coming of Jesus Christ.

Spain, and the beautiful Moorish palace of Alhambra at Granada, all remind us of the rise and fall of the mighty empires of the ancient world, and make a voyage through the Mediterranean a never-to-be-forgotten experience.

The Iberian Peninsula

The great western Peninsula of the Mediterranean Region is called Iberia from the name which ancient Greek traders gave to the inhabitants. The Peninsula is the land of Spain and Portugal, both formerly great sea powers from whose ports sailed intrepid discoverers such as Diaz, Columbus, Da Gama, Balboa, Magellan and Orellana, to reveal to the world the riches of the Americas and to build great empires for their homelands. Of these empires little or nothing remains save the Spanish and

Portuguese tongues, manners and customs which still rule the life of Latin America.

It has been said that " Africa begins beyond the Pyrenees " and certainly when the traveller has left France and crosses the tableland of the Meseta he finds himself in lands more like Africa which lies ahead than France which he has left behind. Since the Meseta, deep-gorged by the Douro and Tagus on their way to the Atlantic, has an average height of three or four thousand feet above sea level and mountain ranges that are very much higher, its extremes of heat in summer are matched by extremes of cold in winter. Even in Madrid, the treacherous bite of the Meseta wind is dreaded, and Spaniards have a proverb, " *El airé de Madrid es tan sutíl, que mata a un hombre y no*

Mondiale.

THE ESCORIAL, SYMBOL OF SPAIN'S PAST GREATNESS

The Escorial, built by King Philip II of grey granite from the Guadarramas on whose south-western slopes it stands, is one of the most remarkable buildings in Europe. It is palace, convent, church, and mausoleum in one, and is dedicated to Saint Laurence, on whose day in 1557, King Philip defeated the French at the battle of Saint Quentin.

FARMING IN SPAIN

Spain is chiefly a land of farmers. Its Meseta is a region where sheep and cattle are reared, but there are irrigated lands—in Castile, for example—which provide the best Spanish crops of wheat. Our picture shows a typical new Castilian farmhouse. It is plain and simple by our standards, but much better than the farmhouses of yesterday.

The fertile plain of Andalusia and the basin of the Guadalquivir river in southern Spain produce crops of maize, sugar-cane and citrus fruits. Vines also flourish. The picture shows seven ploughmen cultivating a maize crop on a large estate. Most of the land is owned by big proprietors.

apago un candil," " the air of Madrid is shrewd enough to kill a man, though not strong enough to blow out a candle."

The Meseta is a land of herdsmen and shepherds who rear Merino sheep, famous for their fine wool, long-haired goats, and cattle. Round the old city of Valladolid there is a favoured basin where golden grain covers the earth in summer and ripe fruits hang from the trees and vines. *Madrid*, the Spanish capital, is in the very heart of the Meseta, and is a focal point for the Spanish railways and motor roads.

Spain is a land of contrasts, in climate and in people. In the far north dwell the Basques of the French borderland, fiercely independent and very aware of their separate language and race. Here also, we find the Navarrese and the proud Castilians. To the east, around the sea-port city of Barcelona, capital city of the province of Catalonia, live the frugal Catalans who speak a tongue of their own and have more than once revolted to claim independence. Once we leave Madrid and go south of the ancient city Toledo, famous in older days for the fine temper of its swords and the skill of its metalworkers, we are in the warm, gentle lands of Andalusia where both climate and people are again very different from those in the north. Andalusia is a true Mediterranean land with hot dry summers and mild winters. Here are the orange groves of Seville, the vines of Jerez de la Frontera from which sherry takes its name, the tanneries of Córdova, and the green crops, bordering the Guadalquivir, watered by a maze of irrigation channels.

Harvesting the Olives

It is said that nearly half the world's supply of olive oil comes from Spain. Much of the oil comes from Andalusia, especially from the provinces of Jaén, Córdova and Seville. Jaén alone has no fewer than 32 million olive trees! Olive trees produce good crops for a hundred years or even more. Green olives, which are the eating olives, are carefully picked by hand and then perhaps bottled, either in their natural state or stuffed with pimentos or anchovies. But the black olives, from which olive oil is extracted, are harvested by men with long poles, who "beat" the olives from the trees. At the refinery, the olives are first pulped into a paste, which is then spread on circular mats of esparto grass. The paste-coated mats are then put through a

Paul Popper.

WHERE THE MOORS ONCE RULED

This is a typical Andalusian valley. The ruined buildings in the foreground date from the times of the Moors, who ruled large parts of southern Spain for some 700 years. Although 450 years have passed since their final defeat, the influence of their rule can still be noticed in Andalusia.

Picture Post Library.

AN EASTER PROCESSION

Great religious fervour characterises Holy Week in Spain. In such great centres as Seville, this time of happiness and yet of sorrow brings solemn processions of penitents and of members of the religious Brotherhoods who, as the picture shows, wear the rather fearsome garb that reminds us of the days of the Spanish Inquisition.

hydraulic press, which forces out the oil into a line of vats. The best oil is that which comes from the first pressing. As it flows from vat to vat, water and impurities are extracted from the oil, which eventually emerges as a clear, yellow-green liquid ready for bottling and selling as a cooking oil. Or it may be refined further until it is quite colourless and tasteless and pure enough for medicinal uses.

Spaniards make all sorts of things from the tough esparto grass—from mats for their olive oil presses to harness, baskets and sandals. We should probably see men wearing esparto grass sandals treading the grapes, if we visited the famous wine district of Valdepeñas at harvest time. Valdepeñas is not in Andalusia but in La Mancha, where grape vines thrive in the loose, stony soil of the level plains. Even if you know little of Spain, you will probably have heard of La Mancha, for it is the country of Cervantes' famous characters, Don Quixote and Sancho Panza.

Watering the Dry Lands

From the early seventh century until 1492, the Moors held the greater part of Spain and it was their industry that made these southern provinces so fruitful. They showed the Spaniards how to water their parched lands, and how to rear the luxuriant crops of grapes, oranges, mulberries, sugar-cane and even rice that can be seen in southern Spain; and the Moors left behind them stately palaces and towns whose beauties draw tourists from all parts of the world. Most famous of these is Alhambra at *Granada*, the ancient Moorish capital in the foothills of the Sierra Nevada.

Irrigation canals cut by the Moors still water the fertile land around Murcia, a town that has been famous for its silk since medieval times. At Valencia, to the north-east, a " Water Tribunal " meets regularly to supervise the irrigation of the farmlands and to punish those who disobey its rules, for in eastern Spain are the *huertas* which are irrigated gardens yielding crops of luscious oranges and other fruits, nuts, grapes, rice and sugar-cane.

A Storehouse of Metal Ores

Like all old block-mountains in Europe, the Spanish Meseta has rich deposits of metal ores around its rims. The iron ore of the Cantabrian Mountains, in the north, is shipped from *Bilbao* and *Santander*, although the coalfield near *Oviedo*, with its port of *Gijon*, uses Cantabrian iron in local iron and steel works; the iron ore of the Sierra Nevada, the highest range in the

peninsula, is shipped from Malaga, which is a Mediterranean port better known for its rich wines, its raisins and its oranges. The well-known copper-mines of *Rio Tinto*, the lead- and silver-mines of *Linares*, and the quick-silver-mines of *Almaden* (said to be the richest in the world), all lie near the southern edges of this old tableland.

Spanish Ports

The ports of *Malaga*, *Almeria*, *Alicante* and *Valencia* are the fruit-ports which send us heavy cargoes of oranges and lemons, almonds and raisins, pomegranates and grapes for our Christmas tables. At Valencia are big silk-mills to which the silk from millions of cocoons spun by Spanish silkworms is sent, and from millions of others in Japan, China and Asia Minor, too.

Mondiale.

THE CATHEDRAL OF OLD SEVILLE

The name of Seville reminds us of the oranges so extensively used for the making of marmalade, but the word is taken from the large Spanish province of that name, which has as its capital the ancient city of Seville. Above we see the majestic cathedral of this city, in which much Moorish architecture is featured. The tall structure on the right is the Giralda tower built by the Moors.

Barcelona is a fine up-to-date port and a manufacturing town (noted especially for its textiles), for it has the advantage of electrical power from the rushing streams of the Pyrenees, and rich salt mines not far away supply the chemical works with some of their raw material.

In rugged north-west Spain, which is very different from the Meseta and the Mediterranean shorelands, there are ports such as *Vigo* and *Corunna* which are bases for the tunny and sardine fleets that gather their sea harvests in the Bay of Biscay and the Atlantic and bring them to port for handling by the fish canneries.

Will F. Taylor.

COLUMBUS PEERS OUT TO SEA

Barcelona, standing on the Mediterranean shore, is the second city in Spain and the seaport-capital of the province of Catalonia. Overlooking the busy harbour is this 200-foot high statue of Christopher Columbus. Although the great discoverer was of Italian birth, he was much helped in his voyages by Spain. The Catalan people speak a tongue of their own and have more than once revolted in attempts to win independence.

Do you know why the north-west is so different from the rest of Spain? One reason is that it looks towards the westerly winds from the Atlantic; its climate is very like that of other parts of north-western Europe, and in summer the north-west is cooler than any other part of Spain.

The beautiful Balearic Isles, renowned for their ancient towns, their lovely flowers, and the skill of their potters, are popular winter holiday resorts. The largest is Majorca, which has the ancient sea-port of Palma as its capital.

Portugal

In the west of the Iberian Peninsula is Britain's oldest ally, Portugal. Though small in size, Portugal led the world in the search for new lands and continents that made the fifteenth and sixteenth centuries "The Great Age of Discovery." From his lonely study at

Sagres near Cape St. Vincent, Prince Henry the Navigator directed the Portuguese discoveries of the fifteenth century.

Portugal is also known to us in history as the base from which Wellington fought his battles against the French in the Peninsula War. Not far from Lisbon, there are still standing parts of his famous Lines of Torres Vedras.

Portugal is a land of corkwoods and vineyards watered by two great rivers, the Tagus and the Douro, that tumble down canyons and deep valleys from the Spanish Meseta to cross the Portuguese lowlands to the sea, the Douro at Oporto, and the Tagus at Lisbon. *Oporto* is world-renowned for the shipments of wine which come from its outport of *Leixões*, and the most famous of her vineyards are in the Pais de Vinho (wine country) on the slopes of the lower Douro valley. As in all winegrowing regions, harvest time is the busiest season of the year and, if the harvest is good, the happiest. The sound of a drum calls the men and women together and they march out briskly into the vineyards, singing as they go. Picking the grapes continues for many months, the harvesters working their way methodically up the steep slopes; grapes on the lower slopes are ready for picking when those higher up are hardly coloured. Stout wicker baskets, each as tall as a man, are loaded with grapes and carried in to the rhythmical blowing of a whistle. Day and night, men with their trousers rolled up to their thighs tread the grapes to extract the precious juice, while in the villages there is dancing and merrymaking. When at last the harvest is all gathered in, there is the biggest celebration of all; everyone joins in, from the vineyard owner to the most humble labourer. As for the wine, that is stored in huge oaken vats to mature.

Cork oak grows mainly in the hill country of eastern Portugal. Not until the trees are over fifteen years old are they stripped for the first time. They are then stripped about every eight or ten years, the best cork coming from the third stripping onwards. Stripping does not kill the trees, which may live for more than a hundred and fifty years. This is because the cork tree does not have its sap under the bark.

The time to see cork gathered is July or August. Everyone in the family helps with this strange harvest, living in the cork forests until the work is done. The cork bark must be taken from the tree with care, for if the cuts are made too deep the next crop will suffer. The bark is light, and huge loads can be piled on the ox-carts that carry the harvest away from the forests.

The Atlantic ports of Portugal— Lisbon, Matozinhos, Setubal and many smaller ports—are bases for the sardine and tunny fishermen whose boats bring their harvest to wharves and slipways at

Will F. Taylor.

BUILT BY THE ROMANS

When Rome's power was at its height, both Spain and Portugal were part of the Roman Empire. This aqueduct at Segovia dates from Trajan's day. It is ten miles long and is the most important Roman relic in Spain.

OLD WAYS AND NEW BUILDINGS

These peasant farmers of the Minho district of Portugal are threshing rye. The team of horses is driven round and round so that the grain is crushed by their hooves. Standing to one side are men armed with forks to remove the threshed rye when the horses have done their work.

Photos : Paul Popper.

This spacious thoroughfare, with its tree-lined walks, gardens and large blocks of flats is the Avenue Alfonso Henriques. It forms part of the most modern quarter of Lisbon, the great city-port that is the capital of Portugal. More than 790,000 people inhabit the city.

the canneries which clean and pack and send to all parts of the world.

Lisbon, the Portuguese capital, is a fine modern city that is not only an important seaport for shipping bound to South America, but a focal point in the airways of the world. Lisbon airport is a meeting place for air liners and freight planes from Europe, Africa and the Americas. Half an hour from Lisbon by electric train is Estoril, a fashionable winter holiday resort.

Atlantic Outposts

Both Spain and Portugal have their outposts in the Atlantic, Spain in the Canary Islands, and Portugal in Madeira and the Azores.

The *Canaries*, sixty miles off the west coast of Africa, are old volcanic islands whose peaks rear sharply upwards from the Atlantic deeps. Their finest city is Las Palmas, on the island of Grand Canary, which is an important coaling and oiling station for ships bound for the Americas and for South Africa. The people of the islands live chiefly by growing tomatoes and bananas for export.

Madeira, like the Canaries, is a favourite winter resort for tourists, for it, too, has a warm Mediterranean climate. Funchal, its chief town, is the centre of the famous wine industry and here you can ride about the cobbled streets in sledges drawn by bullocks or skid precariously down the cobbled slopes on sledges held in check by their owners who run beside them during their erratic descent.

The *Azores* might be called a half-way house of the Atlantic, although the islands are much nearer Europe than they are to the Americas. The Azores are an important link in the airways of the world. Santa Maria, an island of the group, is a refuelling point on the trans-Atlantic air route.

E.N.A.

BEAUTIFUL CINTRA

The Portuguese have a proverb: " To leave out Cintra in seeing the world is no better than travelling blindfold." The famous beauty spot, seventeen miles from Lisbon, has four palaces, a castle, and a convent, as well as magnificent gardens. The picture shows Pena Palace, built in the Moorish style in 1840. King Manoel II spent his last days here before his abdication in 1910.

The French Mediterranean

French Mediterranean lands in Europe are the lower Rhône Valley, the Riviera and the mountainous island of Corsica, at whose capital *Ajaccio*, "the little corporal," who after-

HISTORY ALONG THE TAGUS

Looking out over the estuary of the Tagus is the Tower of Belem. From this spot, Vasco da Gama set sail in 1497 on his voyage around Africa to India. The tower was completed in 1521 and was then surrounded by water. Once a fortress, it now serves as a lighthouse for shipping sailing to and from Lisbon.

Photos : Paul Popper.

At Belem, which is a suburb of Lisbon, the capital of Portugal, is the Monastery of Jeronymos, where King Manoel I and his brave navigator, Vasco da Gama, are buried. The cloisters, seen in this picture, are enriched by delicate stonework. The Monastery is now a national monument.

E.N.A.

THE PONTE VECCHIO, FLORENCE

Said to have existed in Roman times, this famous bridge over the River Arno was rebuilt by Taddeo Gaddi in 1345. Since the days of the Medici, the bridge has been flanked with goldsmiths' shops and on it is a bust of Benvenuto Cellini, the most famous Florentine of that trade. Florence took a leading part in the Renaissance that was, perhaps, Italy's finest hour.

wards became Napoleon, Emperor of France, was born.

These are lands of the vine and the olive, of oranges and lemons, of wonderful flowers and gorgeous scenery. Both the lower Rhône Valley and the Riviera are favourite haunts of the tourists. The Rhône Valley has fine old Roman remains, such as those at Nîmes and Arles, and, around its delta, is the home of the *gardiens de la Camargue*. The Camargue is a cattle-rearing region where the *gardiens*, mounted on sturdy ponies and carrying long stave-like goads, and wearing wide-brimmed hats, ride with their herds in much the same way as the cowboys of America and the *čsikos* of Hungary.

Of increasing importance in this part of France is the growing of rice. And in the years to come there may be many changes in the way of life in the Rhône Valley and delta. For the whole of this great river is being harnessed to provide electric power and to irrigate the dry lands. The Riviera is favoured by tourists because of its lovely scenery and its mild winter climate. Cannes, Nice, Monte Carlo and Mentone, are only four of the many pleasant places with which this magic strip between the mountains and the sea is studded.

The Riviera extends eastward into Italy to the great seaport of *Genoa*, where Christopher Columbus was born, and where you will see large ships from all parts of the world.

Italy is one of the youngest, yet one

ALONG THE FRENCH RIVIERA

Nice is one of the famous pleasure resorts of the French Riviera. In this view of the town from the slopes of the Château Rock, we see the palm-fringed Promenade des Anglais. Nice is the home of the world-famous Carnivals and Battles of Flowers which are among the most popular of Riviera attractions.

From the small harbour at Nice, a steamer will take you to Corsica, the " scented isle " where Napoleon was born. This picture shows us the old port of Bastia in the north of the island. Above the waterside buildings rise the domed towers of the church of St. John the Baptist.

of the oldest, of European countries: young because she did not win unity and independence until 1870: old because her towns were once the very heart of the Roman Empire whose influence remains to-day in lands where Roman legions marched.

The Renaissance

Italy, too, was the country of the Renaissance, the Revival of Learning, that great resurgence of culture and the arts, thought and literature that revivified the Western world. The wonders and beauties of those times have made Italy a land of pilgrimage for lovers of art and enlightenment. Her ancient ruins, beautiful palaces and churches, and her unique art treasures are the heritage, not only of Italy, but of civilisation itself. Florence, home of the Medici family, of Dante, Giotto, Michael Angelo and Leonardo da Vinci, led the great intellectual and artistic revival, although it was at Rome that most of the genius of the age subsequently gathered. Italian love of the things of art and intellect found expression in every town and city, each wishing to surpass the others in the splendour of its churches, the beauty of its paintings, or the grace of its statues. The Renaissance was, perhaps, Italy's finest hour.

A great poet of the Renaissance, Dante, sowed, in those distant times, the seed of Italian unity, giving the peninsula its common language and writing words that were themselves a call to unity. But his seed did not bear fruit until the nineteenth century which was an age of great Italian patriots — Victor Emmanuel, the brave King of Piedmont and Sardinia: Cavour, his able Prime Minister: Mazzini, whose writings roused Italy against foreign

A. F. Kersting.

THE CHURCH OF AN ITALIAN MONASTERY

The Monastery of Certosa di Pavia, about twenty miles from Milan, was begun in 1396 by a member of the great Visconti family to fulfil a vow made by his wife. This picture shows the North Transept of the church of the monastery and (right) the screen and entrance to the Choir.

RICEFIELDS IN LOMBARDY

E.N.A.

The North Italian Plain, or Plain of Lombardy, lies between the Alps and the Apennines. The central part of the Plain is well irrigated and has rice as its most important crop. In this picture, oxen are drawing a harrow through an irrigated rice field.

Italian State Tourist Office.

At the busiest times of the year many workers are needed in the flooded rice-fields. They come from the towns and cities to special camps set up by the rice growers and work hard at the crop. The poplar trees, seen in this picture, are very common in this part of Italy.

domination: and Garibaldi, the valiant soldier of fortune. These leaders, aided by Emperor Napoleon the Third of France and public opinion in the western world, drove out the Austrians and the Bourbon King of Naples and welded the peninsula into a unified Kingdom of Italy. Since 1946 Italy has been a republic.

Italy has long been an over-populated country. Her great problem is how to provide enough food, shelter and clothing for her 47 millions of people. The most densely peopled part of the country is the Plain of Lombardy, which is not truly Mediterranean in character. Its summer rains and colder winters are more like those of Central Europe and, because frosts often follow the rain, it cannot support that typically Mediterranean fruit, the olive. Mediterranean Italy is Peninsular Italy and its shore-lands.

The Plain of Lombardy lies between the Alps and the Apennines, watered by the River Po and its tributaries as they flow towards the Adriatic, where the marshlands of the Po delta are being reclaimed. Large crops of wheat, maize, sugar-beet and hemp are grown, and in the irrigated lands of the eastern part of the Plain the most important crop is rice. The Plain also has its rich pastures where cattle and horses are raised.

On the Plain are three of Italy's five largest cities, each with a population of over half a million: the sea-gate city of *Genoa*, and the engineering and textile (silk and cotton) cities of *Milan* and *Turin*, whose hydro-electric power comes from both the Alps and the Apennines. And there are many other large towns in the Plain: *Verona*, a centre for the fruit-growers of the Adige river; the old university towns of *Padua* and *Bologna*; and *Venice*, " Queen of the Adriatic," the wonderful island-city that is the eastern sea-gate of the Plain.

North of the Lombardy Plain is Alpine Italy, a land of lovely lakes, snowy peaks and deep valleys. Silkworms are reared in the warm valleys

E.N.A.

LOOKING ACROSS THE PLAIN OF LOMBARDY

The picture shows us part of the great Plain of Lombardy, which is one of the most intensively cultivated parts of Italy. Wheat, rye and maize are among the crops produced by the farmers of the Plain, who also cultivate vines and mulberry trees.

ST. MARK'S CATHEDRAL AND CAMPANILE, VENICE

Few cities in the world are more lovely or remarkable than the city and seaport of Venice, the Italian "Queen of the Adriatic." For the most part the city is built on piles and its three main thoroughfares are waterways, connected by over 150 smaller canals. Built in the fourth and fifth centuries it became a republic and a great maritime city-state. Its famous cathedral of St. Mark's, seen in this picture, is a wonderful example of Byzantine architecture and was built in the tenth and eleventh centuries. On the right is the great campanile, built about the same time, but this bell tower collapsed in 1902 and was rebuilt on stronger foundations.

A. F. Kersting.

ON THE SHORES OF LAKE MAGGIORE

Fishing boats and yachts moored in the calm lake waters, houses clustered round the church, green terraced slopes rising swiftly to the mountains—these are typical of beautiful Lake Maggiore. This famous lake is partly in Switzerland and partly in Italy. As its name suggests, it is the most extensive of the several delightful lakes which lie at the foot of the Alps in this part of Europe. The Swiss town of Locarno, at the northern end of the lake, and the Italian town of Stresa, on the south-western shore, are among the many popular tourist resorts.

E.N.A.

THE WONDERFUL CATHEDRAL AT MILAN

Built upon the site of an earlier church and begun in 1386, Milan Cathedral is one of the largest and most beautiful in the world. Architects from Italy, France, and Germany worked on this masterpiece which was not completed until 1815. There are more than 4,000 marble statues upon the roof, which is supported by massive pillars, each 11 feet in diameter. Forty thousand people can be accommodated in the cathedral, which is the major glory of this rich industrial town of northern Italy.

to supply silk for the factories of Milan and other centres, which, however, get most of their silk from the Far East, Turkey and elsewhere. Vines and mulberries are cultivated on the lower slopes; higher up are the chestnut forests, and higher still the conifers and mountain pastures. Roads wind their way through the mountain passes and railways run through tunnels that are wonderful feats of engineering to link Italy with middle and western Europe.

Quarries of Carrara

The backbone of the long Italian peninsula is the Apennines, on either side of which are broad and fertile plains with many beautiful old cities. The plain of the Arno is part of Tuscany, and the most famous of its

towns is *Florence*, one of the homes of Italian art. In this plain, too, are the leaning tower of Pisa, the olive groves of Lucca, and the rich wheatfields that supply the Leghorn strawplait, which was once famous all over the civilised world. Among the hills by the sea to the north are the great quarries of Carrara, where the finest marble is obtained.

Rome and its Ruined Forum

Rome sits upon her seven hills with a marshy plain between them and the sea. All who are lucky enough to go there visit the ruins of the old Forum, where the mighty Emperors of ancient days showed themselves to the Roman crowd, and where famous orators and senators, poets and musicians, patricians and plebeians thronged when Rome ruled the world, and the Colosseum where gladiators fought in the arena.

In Rome, too, are the papal palace of the Vatican and the great Cathedral of Saint Peter, which remind all who come that this city is the home of the head of the Roman Catholic Church throughout the world.

On the shorelands south of Rome are the Pontine Marshes, which were once no more than thousands of acres of mosquito-infested swamp that were a breeding ground for malaria. These have been reclaimed and now yield fine harvests of wheat and other crops. Among the new towns which have been built on the marshes are Littoria and Pomezia.

Beautiful Naples

Farther south is the plain of *Naples*, which is another well-populated part of Italy. Naples, with over a million inhabitants, is the third largest city in Italy. It stands on a lovely bay, with the volcano of Vesuvius as a strange and wonderful background behind a rich and fertile land of orange and lemon groves, vineyards and flowers. This is the land of macaroni, made from the paste of fine wheat grown in the plain of Naples, or in that of Apulia on the other side of the Apennines. You can see miles of macaroni drying on frames in the yards of Naples, Amalfi and other towns in the neighbourhood.

No one can visit Naples without being tempted to do two things: first, to ascend by the mountain railway to a point high on Vesuvius to go on to view its panting cone in the midst of its old crater; and second, to see the once buried cities of Pompeii and Herculaneum, which were overwhelmed in the great Vesuvian eruptions of A.D. 79, and whose uncovered remains enable us to form a good idea of what life was like in a prosperous Roman city over eighteen hundred years ago.

Paul Popper.

A FAMOUS OPERA HOUSE

La Scala, at Milan, is one of the largest and most famous opera houses in the world. It can accommodate an audience of more than 3,000 people. It was built in 1776 on the site of the ancient church and convent of Santa Maria alla Scala and has seen the first performances of many great operas.

BUILT BY A ROMAN EMPEROR

E.N.A.

With triumphant parades and noble arches the Roman Emperors celebrated their victories. The Arch of Titus, shown here, was built by the emperor Domitian in A.D. 81 to commemorate the capture of Jerusalem by Titus, who was his predecessor. Through the arch, we get a glimpse of the Colosseum which was completed in the reign of Titus and opened with gladiatorial contests that went on for a hundred days.

Alinari.

The main Forum of ancient Rome is now but an assembly of majestic ruins, but in olden times this spot and the buildings centred round it constituted the very heart of the great city. Here we see, through a beautiful arch which has well withstood the passing of time, the remnants of what was once a mighty temple

OUTSIDE THE PANTHEON AT ROME

The picture above gives us a view of one of Rome's most wonderful buildings, the Pantheon of Agrippa. The word " pantheon " means a temple for all the gods, and the structure here illustrated is perfectly circular, the entrance being supported by massive columns.

In this illustration we see the ruins of the Forum of Augustus at Rome, with the remains of a temple in the background. The term " forum " was in the days of ancient Rome applied to a market-place, or centre, where different kinds of business were transacted. In connection with a forum there was usually a court of justice.

THE LEANING TOWER OF PISA

Will F. Taylor.

In the city of Pisa, in Italy, there towers a building that is of outstanding interest even in a country possessed of so much that is wonderful in architecture. The Campanile, or Leaning Tower of Pisa, is 179 feet high. Owing, it is thought, to a sinking of the ground on the south side, the tower is now $16\frac{1}{2}$ feet out of the perpendicular, but yet stands firm.

VESUVIUS AND POMPEII

Pompeian holiday-makers once crowded the ruined tiers of the amphitheatre to enjoy the cruel gladiatorial contests that took place in the arena, one of whose main entrances is shown here. In the distance, smoke pours from the crater of Vesuvius which has still the power to erupt and destroy.

No one goes to Naples without seeing the once buried cities of Pompeii and Herculaneum, proud cities that were overwhelmed in the Vesuvian eruptions of A.D. 79. Herculaneum is thought to have been the summer resort of rich Romans; Pompeii, part of which is seen here, was chiefly employed in wine-making. The greater part of the buried town has now been unearthed.

Harnessing a Volcano

Italian engineers have now found a way of using volcano energy. To see what has been done, we must leave Naples and Vesuvius and return northwards to the ancient town of Siena, in Tuscany, where we can see the Larderello power station, which is said to be the only volcanic power plant in the world. To bring this about, wells have been drilled to tap the steam rising from the underground lava beds. This steam is used to drive the turbines that operate the generators and is then fed to a chemical plant where boric acid and borax are produced.

Towns of the Hilltop

There are many wonderful old hilltop towns in Southern Italy. One of the best known is Orvieto, perched on a volcanic rock overlooking a fertile valley, and crowned with an ancient castle and a beautiful old Gothic cathedral.

Sicily, "the island of lemons," is dominated at early morn by the huge triangular shadow of Etna, its giant volcano, which rears its mighty nest of cones nearly 11,000 feet above the blue waters of the Mediterranean. Messina, its port on the straits, Palermo, its capital, and the old ruins at Taormina and Syracuse remind us of its ancient glories when the Greeks made their homes there, and of later days when Rome was the ruler of the world.

North of Sicily is another volcanic island, Stromboli, which belongs to the Lipari group. Seen at night, Stromboli's mysterious peak rearing sharply from the sea resembles the fires of some celestial furnace as vivid orange smoke and fierce tongues of flame leap upwards from its crater.

Not far away are Elba, where Napoleon was imprisoned before his last battle at Waterloo, and the island of Sardinia, of very much greater size, with important lead and zinc mines, but few people. Its chief town is *Cagliari*. Carbonia is the industrial centre of the Sardinian coalfield.

G. L. Blake.

A STREET MARKET IN APULIA

The Plain of Apulia, in south-east Italy, is noted for its fine wheat. In the small towns you will find colourful street markets, where the country folk can buy everything that they need for their day-to-day life.

Alinari.

A CITY CONSTRUCTED IN THE SEA

Venice is one of the most fascinating cities in Europe, for it has many waterways instead of streets, and is a treasure-house of old and beautiful buildings. Notice both the gondoliers and mooring posts for their craft in this view of the famous Grand Canal. Some of the mooring posts are illuminated at night with lanterns. The domes are those of the church of Santa Maria della Salute erected three centuries ago.

Up the Adriatic

The long thumb-shaped Adriatic lies between the Italian and Balkan peninsulas. As we enter the sea through the Straits of Otranto, to our left is the long stilt-like Apulian heel of Italy where there are still people who speak a curious dialect of mixed Greek, Latin and Arabic and where there are the three ports of Otranto, Bari and Brindisi—the last-named famous as the terminal city of the Via Appia, the great highway of Roman Italy. Forty-seven miles away to our right, is the blue haze of the Albanian coastline, and behind rise the snow-clad peaks of the Epirus.

Albania is a wild and undeveloped

country whose warlike people belong to "the most ancient existing race in Europe." Its capital is *Tirana*. Its port is Durazzo, behind which is the small Albanian oilfield.

These deep blue waters of the Adriatic were once dominated by Venice whose long-oared galleys would sweep down majestically from the lagoon city at the northern end of the sea to trade with her dominions elsewhere in the Mediterranean or to fight the Turk. Venice was not the only republic on Adriatic shores. For five centuries, Slav Dubrovnik was independent. It was at Dubrovnik that Richard Coeur de Lion, returning by ship in 1192 from the Holy Land, took shelter from a storm. Dubrovnik was once called Ragusa, and her power and importance in those times is shown in our modern word "Argosy" which was first applied to any Ragusan vessel, but has come to mean "treasure ship." Dubrovnik is

the most picturesque of Dalmatian towns containing many fine old buildings and girdled by walls built in the fifteenth century. A little way south of Dubrovnik is the fjord-like Gulf of Kotor. Kotor is also a walled town and from here a road zigzags sharply for 3,000 feet up the precipitous mountain-side to Cetinje, which was once the capital of Montenegro.

North along the Dalmatian coast are *Fiume*, which was seized by the Italians after the war of 1914–18 and has now returned to Yugoslavia: Pola, a former Italian naval base, which is now Yugoslav: and Trieste, the newly-created Free Territory, which, formerly Italian and still claimed by Yugoslavia, is independent of these countries much as Danzig was independent of Germany and Poland before the war. Trieste is important as an Adriatic trade outlet, not only for Italy and Yugoslavia, but for all the countries of Central and Eastern Europe.

E.N.A.

ON THE GRAND CANAL, VENICE

There is only one way to see the Grand Canal, and that is by gondola. As the picture shows, these are still used, despite the competition of motor launches. Flanked by magnificent palaces and stately churches, the Grand Canal is one of the most beautiful sights in Europe. The picture shows the famous Rialto bridge, built between 1588 and 1592, and flanked by shops.

At the mouth of the Adriatic, on the eastern side, is the island of Corfu, once a stronghold of the Venetians, and once ruled by Britain.

Greece

Greece comprises not only the mainland forming the south-eastern tip of the Balkan peninsula, but also the islands forming the Archipelago of the Aegean and bounded in the south by the island of Crete. These are lands of ancient culture whose early history and immeasurable contributions to world civilisation are recorded elsewhere. The tragedy of Greek history is that, despite her glorious past, she had to endure centuries of foreign rule. When Moslem Turkey swept westwards, Greece was overrun and remained a part of the Turkish Empire until the nineteenth century when her bid for liberty won the sympathy and support of Russia and the western powers. It was to fight for Greek liberty that Lord Byron went to Greece, only to die at Missolonghi.

Modern Greece

Greek freedom was assured by the destruction of the Egyptian fleet at the battle of Navarino in 1827. Since then, Greece has recovered most of her lands from Turkey and other powers, her most recent acquisition being the Dodecanese Islands.

As in Themistocles' days, the Piræus

Paul Popper.

IN A MACARONI FACTORY IN MILAN

Macaroni, spaghetti and similar cereals are made from a special variety of wheat. The wheat flour is mixed with boiling water into a *pasta*, or dough, which is then forced through the pierced end of a steam-jacketed cylinder. In the case of macaroni, the long sticks or pipes which result are hung on wooden frames, which are wheeled into the drying chamber.

is still the port for *Athens*, the Greek capital. As one drives up the straight road from the port to the capital, the sharp contrast between ancient glory and striking modernity is seen in the fine modern buildings of the new city and the noble relics of the " glory that was Greece " that draw one's gaze to the age-old Acropolis.

Much of Greece is mountainous, with extremes of heat and cold. Dominating all are the lofty peaks of Olympus,

Parnassus and Helicon, mountains which appear time and again in the myths and legends of ancient Greece. But Greece has sheltered valleys for her farmers and fruit-growers and her hillsides provide pasture for sheep, goats and mountain cattle. Along her rugged shore with its many coves and inlets live hardy fishermen.

Southwards is one of the great engineering feats of the country, the Corinth Canal, first planned by the Emperor Nero and not completed until recent times. This canal cuts the Morea, the Peloponnesus of ancient time, from the Greek mainland. The Morea is the home of the currant vine-yards which are directed by the " Central Currant Office " which is an association of currant growers and merchants. The chief currant port is *Patras.*

To the north, in Macedonia, Thessaly and Thrace, tobacco is grown to be shipped from Salonica, which was a British base in the First World War.

Many of the Greek islands are rich in history. Patmos has associations with St. John the Divine. Rhodes, chief island of the Dodecanese, was the site of the famous Colossus, a hundred-foot-high statue of the Sun God which bestrode the harbour entrance. Rhodes, too, once had a renowned school of oratory whose pupils included Cicero, Julius Caesar, Augustus and Tiberius. Much later Rhodes became the fortress city of the Knights of St. John whose lofty towers and massive walls, dungeons and palaces, can still be seen.

Another island rich in history is Crete where King Minos' vast palace at Knossos, once the centre of his Aegean empire, has been excavated from the island's cornfields by British archæologists. The Minoans are thought to have been the first people to navigate upon the Mediterranean.

Dorien Leigh.

MOUNTAIN GRANDEUR IN THE DOLOMITES

The Dolomites, a chain of lofty peaks of limestone rock, form a natural frontier region between Italy and Austria. Passes, such as the one shown here, cleave the majestic mountains where snow and rock combine in untamed beauty, and where—at such centres as Cortina—climbing and winter sports attract the holiday-maker.

Turkey

Northwards once more to the barren beaches of Gallipoli where the British homeland and

WHERE VENICE ONCE RULED

A. F. Kersting.

One of the loveliest parts of Yugoslavia is the Dalmatian Coast, where many years ago the city-state of Venice ruled. As this picture of a small Dalmatian fishing village shows, the Venetian influence can be seen in the ancient cities and small ports of this beautiful Adriatic shoreland.

E.N.A.

Canea, the political capital of Crete, was laid in ruins during the Second World War. The harbour, which is seen in this picture, was fortified many centuries ago by the Venetians, whose galley slipways could still be seen there in our own times.

KNIGHTS AND LEGENDS

The island of Rhodes has been ruled by Greeks, Romans, Turks and Italians. With the other Dodecanese islands, it has now returned to Greece. During the period 1308–1522, Rhodes was
the Crusader headquarters of the Knights of St. John of Jerusalem. Their palaces and fortifications
have been carefully restored and make Rhodes a wonderful showplace.

Photos: E.N.A.

This Greek peasant looks towards the lofty peaks of Olympus, which rise to heights of almost
10,000 feet. The name Olympus is borne by many mountains in Greece and Asia, but the most
famous are those seen in this picture, which form a high range bordering Thessaly and Macedonia.
The Greeks of early times believed Olympus to be the home of the gods.

WHERE ST. PAUL LANDED

Nearly forty miles from the town of Rhodes is Lindos, where St. Paul landed on his journey to Rome. Perched high on a rock above the village is the 2,000-year-old citadel, with its Temple of Athene, which was later made into a fortress by the Knights of St. John. On the promontory (left) is the tomb of Cleobulus, tyrant of Lindos and one of the Seven Sages of Greece.

Photos: E.N.A.

At Knossos, just outside Heraklion (Candia) in Crete, archæologists have uncovered the great Palace of King Minos, parts of which date back to the period 3400 to 2100 B.C. This picture shows the throne room decorated with frescoes of sacred animals and equipped with stone benches for the royal councillors. A cast of the throne itself may be seen in the British Museum.

Dominions lost so much fine manhood in the grim, vain assaults of the First World War. These quiet waters are the entrance to the Dardanelles and Bosporus, third gateway to the Mediterranean and link with the Black Sea. This great waterway separates Europe from Asia Minor and Asiatic Turkey from her European lowlands between Adrianople and Istanbul (Constantinople). At Istanbul the waterway is less than a mile wide and may one day be bridged. A plan for a suspension bridge across the Bosporus was submitted to the Turkish Government in 1953 and was almost certainly not the first of its kind. It is said that the great Leonardo da Vinci proposed such a bridge to the ruling Sultan of his day.

Istanbul's greatest glories lie in the past. She was the proud capital of the Byzantine Emperors whose richly decorated churches and powerful fortifications still stand, and later the capital of the Ottoman Empire which in its heyday reached from the Danube in the north to the Euphrates in the south, and from the Caspian Sea in the east to Gibraltar in the west. Although Istanbul is no longer the capital, she remains the largest city and chief trading centre.

Modern Turkey

The modern Turkish State owes its existence to a great national leader, Kemal Ataturk, first president of the Turkish Republic which came into being after the last of the Sultans had been dethroned. Kemal Ataturk knew that his country was backward and, like Peter the Great of Russia, devoted his energies to high-speed westernisation. He even changed age-old customs of the country, introducing western dress and the western alphabet, curbing the power of the priesthood, and freeing Turkish women from the subjection of the harem. *Ankara*, a much smaller town than Istanbul, became the capital of the new Turkey, with fine buildings such as those along the Ataturk Boulevard.

If you look at a map of Turkey, you will see that European Turkey forms quite a small part of the country. Most of Turkey is Asiatic and occupies the mountainous tableland of Anatolia, with coastal strips along the Mediterranean, Aegean and Black Seas.

E.N.A.

TWO FISHERMEN OF THESSALY

These hardy fishermen ply their trade in the salt lagoons along a narrow coastal strip of Thessaly. Much of the Greek coast is gaunt and rugged, but it has many coves and inlets where you will find the gaily painted boats and humble homes of Greeks who get their living from the sea.

A. F. Kersting.

BEAUTIFUL MADEIRA, " FLOWER GARDEN OF THE ATLANTIC "

This delightful coastline forms part of Madeira, the chief island of the Madeira group in the north-east Atlantic. The town partly hidden by the headland in the foreground is Funchal, the capital, where most of the islanders live. When winter envelops Britain, Madeira enjoys warm sunshine and clear skies. Fortunate indeed are those who can escape to this island of wonderful gardens and fine villas and hotels. From the fertile hillside vineyards come Malmsey and other types of Madeira wine. In Funchal, the many visitors to Madeira can buy the hand embroideries, inlaid woodwork and wickerware for which the island is also noted. Madeira and the other islands of the group belong to Portugal.

Specially painted for this work.

COALING AT PORT SAID

Though oil fuel has been adopted on many of our warships and on most of the great modern liners, large numbers of the world's merchant ships use coal. On the great ocean trade routes there are many coaling stations, the majority of which are under British control. In the picture above is depicted a night scene at Port Said, the town at the Northern entrance to the Suez Canal and a great shipping centre on the route to the East. Under the ship's searchlight the coal drifters are being brought alongside to enable the coal to be taken aboard until the ship's bunkers are again filled.

IN ANCIENT ATHENS TO=DAY

Capital of ancient Attica before 700 B.C. and of modern Greece since 1834, the antiquities of the city of Athens are unequalled in the world. The original site of the city was the fortified hill, the Acropolis, seen in the background. The old Athens is connected with the modern city by two main thoroughfares which meet at Constitution Square, seen in this photograph.

Photos: Associated Press.

One of the problems that has faced Athens since its earliest days has been an adequate water supply, and history records the city's efforts to obtain more water as long ago as the time of Christ. The Roman Emperor Hadrian built the city's first aqueduct some 18 centuries ago, and it is still in use. In 1926–30 this Marathon Dam, near Athens, was built; it is the only marble-faced dam in the world.

Once a very backward country, Turkey has worked hard to develop her industry and agriculture, especially since the Second World War. She is now producing double the amount of iron, chrome and copper that she produced in 1948, while her production of manganese is more than thirteen times as great. Her most important export crops were once tobacco, figs and raisins, but these were surpassed by wheat in 1952, and by cotton in 1951. At Kaiseriyeh, she now has the largest cotton mill in the Middle East as well as an aircraft assembly factory: at Adana and Malatya, a flourishing textile industry: at Istanbul, paper, glass and pottery manufactures: and at Izmit a paper mill which supplies half the needs of the country. The main development centres for heavy industry are at Zonguldak on the shores of the Black Sea and Karabuk. Zonguldak has a large anthracite works, and Karabuk, an iron and steel plant, built by a British firm.

Turkey, however, is predominantly an agricultural country. Four-fifths of her population of nearly 21 millions are farmers or live from the land. Kemal Ataturk did much to modernise Turkish agriculture, setting up an experimental farm at Ankara, and inaugurating the Cubbuk Barrage Scheme which, since 1935, has supplied the capital's water. *Kombinates* were also set up to lend farm machinery to the villages, especially in the Cilician Plain, where much of the cotton crop is grown. After the War, more machinery was obtained for the farms. In 1950 Turkey had only 6,000 tractors; to-day she has over 35,000.

What crops besides wheat and cotton do Turkish farmers grow? In the Mediterranean-type lands, which include the Black Sea coastlands, olives and figs, vines and pomegranates, opium poppies, liquorice, tobacco and mulberries are grown. *Samsun* is the most important tobacco-growing

Paul Popper.

THE FOUNDER OF MODERN TURKEY

This statue of Kemal Ataturk (1881–1938), the founder of modern Turkey and first President of the republic, stands in the National Square at Ankara, the Turkish capital. The modern building in the background is a bank and department store, and is typical of those built in the city.

Associated Press.

THE LAST RESTING-PLACE OF KEMAL ATATURK

November 10th, 1953, was the fifteenth anniversary of the death of Kemal Ataturk, and on that day his remains were brought, in solemn state, to the imposing mausoleum that had been built on a hill overlooking Ankara, the Turkish capital. Taken during the ceremony, the picture shows just a few of the tens of thousands of Turks who paid a final tribute to the founder of the republic.

district, and *Bursa* the chief centre of silk production. *Aydin* is important for its olive oil.

The City of Byzantine Emperors

But most Mediterranean sightseers will prefer to forsake modern, westernised Turkey for the Turkey of old that is to be found at Istanbul, the city of the Byzantine Emperors; so let us return there and linger awhile amidst its wonders. This wonderful city of the ancient world has four main districts— Scutari, on the Asia Minor side of the Bosporus: Pera, which is the foreign quarter: Galata, the business centre: and—across the Golden Horn—the Stamboul quarter which occupies the site of ancient Byzantium.

It is in Stamboul that we find the greatest glory of Constantinople's rich past—the church of San Sofia. Built over fourteen hundred years ago, this beautiful building is said to have cost the equivalent of 64 million pounds. When the Turks converted it into a mosque in 1454, they covered the walls with plaster; but this has now been removed and the wonderful Byzantine mosaics are once more visible.

The Blue Mosque

It is amazing how great a span of the past is covered by the relics to be seen in Constantinople, or Istanbul, to use its modern name. The Snake Column from Delphi, which can be seen in the ruins of the Roman Hippodrome, recalls the Greek cities which participated in the victory of Plataea in 479 B.C. Of much more recent date is the Mosque of Sultan Ahmed I which is better known as the Blue Mosque from the delightful coloured tiles which adorn its interior. Even lovelier is the Suleimanieh Mosque built during the sixteenth century for Suleiman the Magnificent. Out on the Seraglio Point, overlooking the Golden Horn and the Bosporus, is the Seraglio Palace that was the home of the Sultans in the heyday of the Turkish Empire. Here can be seen the richly jewelled golden throne of Shah Ismail which, in size, compares with a large double bed.

Beyond the Bazaars and minarets to the north-west of the Seraglio Palace are the Byzantine walls which run down to the Golden Gate and the Castle of the Seven Towers at the edge of the Bosporus. At Istanbul we have reached the north-easternmost limit of our journey and we return through the Sea of Marmora and the Dardanelles to the Aegean.

Volcanic Islands

You will remember that our visit to Italy showed us three famous volcanoes —Vesuvius, Etna, and Stromboli. Volcanic activity in the Mediterranean is not limited to these three giants. As we journey across this sea of ancient civilisation towards the north African shore we come to one of the most unusual volcanic islands known to man.

That island is *Santorin*, which is also called Thera. Where it now stands there was a mighty volcano some three thousand five hundred years ago. At some time in that distant past there must have been a tremendous eruption in which the head of the volcano was destroyed. So complete was that destruction that the sea poured in, flooding the crater to a great depth and making strange, precipitous islands of its surviving sides. Those islands are Santorin and its attendant isles as we know them now. They form a wide arc round a deep harbour that is the very heart of the old volcano where the waters still seethe and boil, and where black smoking masses rise mysteriously from the depths

to prove that the volcano is still active beneath the surface.

Thera, the chief town of the island, stands apparently aloof, its white, barrel-roofed buildings perched high on sooty-brown cliffs a thousand feet above the jet waters of its volcanic harbour. Long acquaintance with this amazing place has accustomed the islanders to its marvels and resigned them to its terrors. Many of them are miners of pumice; some produce sandpaper; others are humble fishermen. Their strange home has no timber trees or vines, although in ancient times it must have had both, for then it was called Kalliste, which means " Most Beautiful."

The Southern Shores

From Alexandria in the east to Tangier in the west, we are in coast lands that were once ruled by Turkish Sultans, lands which also bear traces of earlier empires. A hundred miles south of the Algerian port of Philippeville is Timgad, the " African Pompeii," one of the finest ruined cities of Imperial Rome. Not far from Tunis are the ruins of ancient Carthage; and about sixty miles east of Tripoli are the ruins of Leptis Magna, a great Phœnician seaport. These southern shores of the Mediterranean were once used by the dreaded corsairs—Kheyr-ed-dīn, the Scourge of Christendom, Urūj of the Red Beard, and many others. The badge of modern Tripoli is a corsair ship.

The Kingdom of Libya

Libya, which consists of Cyrenaica, Tripolitania and the Fezzan, was once an Italian colony. After the War, Cyrenaica was granted its independence by the Allies, and in 1951 was joined with Tripolitania and the Fezzan to form the independent kingdom of Libya. The sovereign is Sayyid Muhammad Idris El Senussi, the Emir of Cyrenaica. *Tripoli* and *Benghazi* have equal status as the capital.

Libya is a very poor country. Its most

SHIPS AND SOLDIERS

E.N.A.

Outward bound through the pillared entrance to the old harbour at Rhodes is this caïque. In the background is the former guardian of the harbour, Fort St. Nicholas. This type of sailing vessel is very common in eastern Mediterranean waters. Some caïques have auxiliary motors, but many depend upon their sails.

Oscar Marcus.

Many years ago, Greek mountaineers took to wearing the *fustenella*, a kilt-like garment which first came to Greece from Albania, because it gave them greater freedom for clambering about the crags. In time it became an item of national costume. The *fustenella* is still worn by the Evzones, who mount guard at the Royal Palace and at the Tomb of the Unknown Soldier in Athens.

ANCIENT ISTANBUL

One of the great festivals in the year for Mohammedans is the Feast of Ramazan, which lasts for thirty days, the actual celebrations being always held after midnight. Above we see the Mosque of Fatih at Istanbul during the progress of one of these festivals. Ramazan, known also as Ramadan in certain countries, is the month in which the Koran was revealed to the Prophet.

E.N.A.

In this picture of the Theodosian walls of Istanbul, we see the Golden Gate which, in the time of the Byzantine Emperors, was opened only for triumphal processions. Legend says that Christians will one day pass through the gate to recapture the city lost so long ago. That is why it has been kept shut ever since. Following the line of the walls is an old Turkish cemetery.

THE NORTH AFRICAN SHORE

E.N.A.

Along the North African shore of the Mediterranean are coast lands once ruled by Turkish Sultans. To-day, many of the old towns and palaces can still be seen there. Here, for example, is the palace of the Sultan of Morocco at Tangier.

Pictorial Press.

Casablanca is a seaport town and the chief trading centre of Morocco, with regular steamers to Europe as well as air services. During the Second World War it was the scene in 1943 of a famous meeting between President Roosevelt and Mr. Churchill. Our picture shows a story-teller and his audience in the town.

fertile land lies along the coast and produces dates, olives, and citrus fruits.

One of the most important crops is esparto grass, which grows wild, especially in the Jebel mountains.

West of Libya is the French Protectorate of Tunisia, once provider of grain and oil to ancient Rome and still important for these products. For Tunisia is predominantly an agricultural country. In the Cape Bon peninsula and the north-east citrus fruits, such as lemons and oranges, are grown; olive trees are plentiful in the Sahel region, while dates come from the famous oases of the south. *Tunis* is the capital and largest city.

The Barbary Coast

Westwards we come to yet another part of the French Union—Algeria.

Algeria is a Barbary State, one of the historic homes of the Berber people, although her population now contains many nationalities and mixtures. *Algiers*, her chief city, is the most important town of the Barbary coast — and with its *Kasbah* or citadel, and *souks* or markets, one of the most typical. From Algiers the fruit, olives and wheat of the fertile *El Tell*, or coastal plain, are shipped. South of *El Tell* are the Little Atlas mountains, and still farther south, the barren plateau of the *Shotts*, or salt lakes. South again is the desert where date-palms flourish round fertile oases, their crops being shipped from Biskra in Algeria or Tafilet in Morocco.

French Morocco is a Protectorate whose capital is *Rabat*, while the sacred city of Fez is one of the old Muslim capitals. *Casablanca* is the chief trading centre and port. Spain also has a foothold in Morocco, with a capital at *Tetuan*, for which the port is *Ceuta*. To the west is the international city of *Tangier*.

Camera Press.

THE GREAT MOSQUE AT TUNIS

This scene, taken from the roof-garden of a wealthy merchant, shows the tower of the Great Mosque in Tunis, capital of Tunisia, a French Protectorate in North Africa. Within the Great Mosque is a Mahommedan university. Tunis is a walled town, and in the centre is the Medina, built partly from the ruins of ancient Carthage, some three miles away. Nearly all the houses are built of stone.

EUROPE'S LITTLE STATES

E.N.A.

A TOWN'S MEETING IN ANDORRA-LA-VELLA

The tiny State of Andorra nestles in the Pyrenees between France and Spain. It is ruled as it was ruled 600 years ago, by a Council, two " Princes " and a President. The picture shows a meeting in the square of Andorra-the-Ancient, which is the capital.

SANDWICHED among the great nations of Europe and almost over-looked in the march of history are a number of tiny States which have some-how preserved their individuality and remained independent. One at least, the Republic of Andorra, has altered little with the passing of the centuries.

Valleys of Andorra

Andorra or, to give it its proper name, the Valleys of Andorra, nestles in the Pyrenees between France and Spain. There are just a hundred and ninety-one square miles of it. We speak loosely of it as a Republic, but it is not. Andorra is ruled as it was ruled six hundred years ago, by a triumvirate of a President and two " Princes," and a Council which sits in the House of the Valleys. The members of the Council are called " Notables " and are required to wear cocked hats, black ties, and black gowns like those of schoolmasters.

The Andorrans are mountain people living in very primitive conditions. They have no towns as we know them, only crude stone houses, even in the capital, Andorra-the-Ancient.

Even smaller is the Principality of Liechtenstein, wedged between Swit-zerland and Austria, which has an area of sixty-one square miles. Liechten-stein has been a sovereign state and has enjoyed freedom since 1342, even though she has had no army since 1868. Her last soldier died in 1943 at the ripe age of ninety-one. Liechtenstein is a peaceful farming country, and nearly a quarter of its annual revenue comes from the sale of stamps.

Less fortunate were the people of the Duchy of Luxemburg who were as much in the Second World War as any of their neighbours. Luxemburg, bor-dered by Germany, Belgium and France, was occupied by Germany and was our ally during the battles of liberation.

THE CASTLE OF LIECHTENSTEIN

Wedged between Austria and Switzerland is the tiny Principality of Liechtenstein, which has been a sovereign State since 1342. The chief centre is Vaduz and nearby is the 500-year-old castle of the Prince which rises on the crags like some fairy-tale stronghold against the imposing backcloth of the Swiss mountains.

MOUNTAINOUS SAN MARINO

Legend says that Serbian fugitives from the advancing Huns were led across the Adriatic to a high Apennine peak by a Christian missionary to found the tiny Republic of San Marino. The old volcanic mountain shown in this picture is the very heart of the little State, which covers only thirty-eight square miles.

Photos: E.N.A.

San Marino is ruled by a Grand Council and two *Capitani reggenti*, or Regents. The two Regents are elected on April 1st and October 1st every year and hold office for six months. Once a councillor has been Regent, he cannot again hold this office for three years. Notice the traditional dress of the Regents, who are here shown with their predecessors.

MONACO, JEWEL OF THE RIVIERA

Monaco, one of Europe's little States, consists of three towns that are really one, for where one ends the next begins. In the background, on a rocky headland, is Monaco, the capital; next is La Condamine, while in the foreground is Monte Carlo, famous for its Casino and its gardens.

Photos: E.N.A.

Monte Carlo's flood-lit Casino is as much a lure to gamblers as a candle is to moths. Here, at the green baize gaming tables, fortunes are lost and—more rarely—made. Virtual capital of the French Riviera, Monte Carlo has beautiful gardens and an unrivalled setting that have made it one of the world's most famous pleasure resorts.

IN ANCIENT LUXEMBURG

Spanning the gorge of the Petrusse is the Pont Adolphe which links streets at the southern end of the public park on the site of the old city walls of Luxemburg town, which was once one of the strongest fortresses in Europe and has weathered many invasions in its long history.

Photos : E.N.A.

For over a thousand years dancing pilgrims have annually visited the tomb of St. Willibrord at the small Luxemburg town of Echternach on the River Sure. Linked with handkerchiefs, the pilgrims move through the streets leading to the tomb of the saint, an English missionary who founded an abbey in Echternach.

But this was not the first invasion of the Duchy, which has weathered many such aggressions in its long history. Luxemburg has an area of 999 square miles. It is a prosperous little country, whose iron mines and iron and steel works are among the most important in Europe. *Esch-Alzette* is the chief mining town.

One of the oldest of Europe's little States is San Marino which, so tradition tells us, is a still-existing fragment of the

Central Press.

ON GUARD AT THE VATICAN

In 1505, Zurich and Lucerne supplied a bodyguard for Pope Julius II. Since that time, the guards at the Vatican have always been Swiss and still wear the traditional sixteenth-century uniform. On State occasions, the Swiss guards wear plumed helmets and shining breastplates and carry halberds.

Roman Empire. When the Huns were advancing down the Danube, Serbian fugitives led by a Christian missionary are believed to have crossed the Adriatic and reached a high peak in the Apennines where they were safe from the invaders and where they founded the Republic of San Marino. The thirty-eight square miles of the Republic are ruled by a Grand Council and two *Capitani reggenti*, or Regents, who are appointed every six months. The old volcanic mountain which is the very heart of San Marino is crowned by the administrative buildings beneath which is a gigantic water reservoir which supplies all the needs of the Republic. An electric railway connects San Marino to the Italian town of Rimini.

Also in Italy is the Papal territory of the Vatican, the *Città del Vaticano*, which is the independent territory of the Holy See and Church of Rome. Its extent is little over 100 acres, but it has its own coinage, judicial power, newspaper, and railway and broadcasting stations. It is the seat of the Supreme Pontiff of the Roman Catholic Church who, small in area though the Vatican is, exerts world-wide power and influence as one of the highest leaders of Christian thought and ethics.

Last, but not least, there is the picturesque Principality of Monaco, whose brilliantly uniformed soldiers are known to every visitor to the French Riviera. The rugged rock on which Monaco itself stands juts out into the blue Mediterranean not far from the frontier between France and Italy. Across the small harbour is Monte Carlo, renowned for its Casino. The Casino and the famous international car races, as well as its favoured position on the Riviera coast, have made Monaco one of the greatest pleasure resorts of the world. But people also visit Monaco to see the fine Oceanographical Museum in which the rulers of the Principality have taken a personal interest and which has increased our knowledge of life in the ocean deeps.

The Story
of the
World and
its Peoples

Through the
Storied Lands
of the
Middle East

THE NEW ISRAEL IN THE HOLY LAND

E.N.A.

Since 1922, large numbers of Jews have settled in Palestine, there to make their " National Home."
The modern city of Tel Aviv, with its tree-lined boulevards and pleasant squares and places, is the
largest city of their new state of Israel. The picture shows Zina Dizengoff Place, which is named
after the wife of the founder and first Mayor of the city.

THE HOLY LAND

PALESTINE, the " Holy Land," where Christ walked and taught nearly two thousand years ago, was placed under the care of Britain by the League of Nations in 1922. From 1922 until 1948, when the last British troops were withdrawn, Britain had the difficult and unenviable task of preserving order in a land of bitterly opposed Arabs and Jews. For to the Arabs, the efforts of the Jews to build a National Home in Palestine seemed nothing but an invasion of land that had been Arab for over a thousand years. With the end of the British mandate in May, 1948, the Jewish National Council in Palestine proclaimed the establishment of the State of Israel. Fighting with the Arabs and their supporters had already broken out, and despite an uneasy truce, the problem of reconciling Jew and Arab in Palestine and of defining the boundaries of their respective areas has been one of the most difficult questions the United Nations has been called upon to handle.

Although armistice agreements had been arranged in 1949 between Israel and the countries of Egypt, Jordan, Lebanon and Syria, no one looking at Palestine in January, 1954, could have said that the problem had been solved. The country had been divided, but in a way very different from that originally proposed by the United Nations. A large eastern sector, including part of Jerusalem itself, was administered by Jordan and had, indeed, been formally incorporated in that state in April, 1950. In the south-west, a coastal strip and the town of Gaza were held by Egypt. Along the boundaries both sides stood guard and, despite the presence of United Nations' observers and a Mixed Armistice Commission, border incidents, raids and reprisals were still occurring.

This rending apart of Palestine was not merely a matter of land and frontiers, but of homes and families. Many thousands of Arabs fled from Israeli territory. In 1953 the number of Arab refugees in Jordan was said to be 467,000.

New Ways and Old Ways

Palestine is small. You could go from one end of it to the other by motor car in a morning, and you could cross it from the Mediterranean Sea to the River Jordan in about half that time, if the road was good. It is amazing to think that the wonderful things which are recorded in the Bible—events that changed the whole history of the world and made it a better place in which to live—happened in a tiny country like this. The Holy Land of the Bible was not as large as Wales; Palestine is smaller still.

Although along the coastal plain you find ports and towns in close touch by steamers and telegraph, by wireless and the aeroplane, with the busy world outside, and although there are places where modern engineers have built great bridges to carry the railways and dams to hold back water for irrigation or for power-stations, there are some parts of Palestine where people live their lives in the old way.

The little villages on the hilltops and in the fertile valleys are still in the same old spots, and the peasants live there in much the same simple fashion as their forefathers did in the days of King David. Many still bear the ancient names as well as their Arab ones, and look much as they must have appeared thousands of years ago. The world's rapid progress seems to have passed them by.

Lebanon and the Jordan

To understand Palestine you must look at it on the map in relation to the nearby independent Republics of Syria and Lebanon. Large parts of what is now called Syria were included in the Holy Land of ancient days. In the north are the mountains of Lebanon, where you will still find some of the

A. F. Kersting.

A MODERN SHIP OF THE DESERT

Although camel caravans still travel the desert lands of the Middle East, air and bus services now cover many of these vast sandy wastes. Here, for example, is the comfortable coach which operates between Damascus and Baghdad.

A. F. Kersting.

LEBANON LANDSCAPE

Though once a granary of the Roman Empire, Syria now embraces large tracts of desert. To the south-west is the rocky and mountainous Lebanon. Here we see the mountain resort of Zahle which nestles between the Lebanon and Anti-Lebanon mountains, nearly thirty miles east of Beirut.

descendants of those wonderful cedars which Hiram, King of Tyre, felled to send in great rafts along the sea coast to be used by King Solomon in the building of the Temple at Jerusalem. Mount Hermon still lifts its snowy crest into the blue, and the clear streams still flow down from Lebanon to water the oasis city of Damascus and the cities of the plain.

The Oldest City in the World

Damascus is the chief centre in Syria, and is said to be the oldest city in the world. It is an important meeting-place of road, rail and air routes. But Syria's largest city is *Aleppo*, another ancient trading centre, long famous for the skill of its weavers.

Syria is mostly a country of farmers and cattle-breeders. To her small fishing port of *Banias* runs the new pipe-line from the Kirkuk oil-field in north Iraq. This pipe-line came into use in April, 1952.

Beirut is the chief city and port of Lebanon. The second seaport, *Tripoli*, is a terminal for one of the pipe-lines bringing oil from Iraq. *Saida* (the old Sidon) is the terminal of a pipe-line bringing oil from Saudi Arabia.

From Lebanon the great River Jordan flows southwards between " the desert and the sown," first through the Sea of Galilee on whose shores are the places where Christ lived and taught, and on whose waters He and His disciples often went in a fishing boat ; and then, after a long and winding course at the bottom of a deep and hot valley-trench, the river enters the Dead Sea, a sea so salt that people bathing in it find it difficult to swim because so much of their bodies is buoyed up out of the water. Its shores look " dead," indeed, for hardly a living thing is to be seen there ; it seems like a great salt lake in the heart of a desert. Beyond those high shores on its eastern side, indeed, there *is* real desert—the Syrian Desert that stretches in an arid stony waste all the way from the Jordan to the great twin rivers of Mesopotamia, which in these days is called Iraq.

Part of the Syrian Desert comes within the Hashemite Kingdom of the Jordan, which at present administers part of Palestine, including the Old City area of Jerusalem. *Amman* is the busy, and unexpectedly modern, capital of Jordan. It was once known as Rabbath Ammon and was a stronghold of the Ammonites. Later it was called Philadelphia, after its rebuilder, Ptolemy Philadelphus of Egypt. Its Roman arena is still to be seen.

The Hill Country

Between the Jordan and the Mediterranean Sea, Palestine rises in a long ridge of limestone hills, which have been carved by the weather of the ages and by running water into deep valleys, leaving heights outstanding many of which are crowned with villages, some with towns. The city of Jerusalem, indeed, stands on just such a height; the Crusaders found it hard to take because on three sides it was defended by deep valleys from which the hillside rose steeply almost like the walls of a castle.

At Jericho

The limestone hills look dry and barren. You find it hard to believe that even goats could obtain a living there, yet on their grey slopes there are not only goats but flocks of sheep which still follow their shepherds as they did in the days of the Bible

Will F. Taylor.

" THE STREET WHICH IS CALLED STRAIGHT "

One of the chief main streets of Damascus is covered for part of its course by an arched roof, so forming what is known as the " covered street," here shown. The portion beneath the roof is used as a bazaar, and presents a most animated scene during business hours.

A VIEW IN "ROYAL DAVID'S CITY"

American Colony, Jerusalem.

Some five miles from Jerusalem is the little town of Bethlehem, known to Christians the world over as the birthplace of Jesus Christ, the Saviour who was born in a manger in " Royal David's City." It is to this ancient place, whose name means " house of bread," and to the wonders of the Bible story that our thoughts go every Christmastide.

14—2

story. There are fertile spots, too, where the toiling peasants till the stony soil, still ploughing it with the old primitive ploughs and scattering the seed broadcast, reaping the thin harvest with the sickle, and winnowing out the grain by the old-fashioned threshing floors made in open places, so that the wind can blow away the chaff when the grain trodden out by the oxen is cast up into the breeze by the wooden shovels of the harvesters.

The hill country is nearer the Jordan than it is to the Mediterranean. From the sea you go up a long slope to the hills and Jerusalem, but from the hilltops there is a steep descent to Jericho and the Jordan valley. Jericho is one of the lowest-lying towns in the world; it is 840 feet below sea-level.

Excavations at Jericho have revealed the aged walls of the city of Old Testament times; like those streets of Jerusalem along which Christ and His disciples walked, they are buried deep beneath the earth which has collected there through the ages. These, and more recent excavations, have taken place at the site of the oldest of the three Jerichos, which lies to the north-west of modern Jericho and to the north-east of the Jericho of New Testament times. Archæologists consider that the walls of the city were repaired or entirely rebuilt at least sixteen times during the period 3100–2100 B.C. Their destruction by the Israelites is thought to

Topical Press.

AN OLD CUSTOM IN MODERN PALESTINE

Should you feel thirsty, what better drink than a cup of coffee from this picturesque street merchant? You can hear him approaching because he jingles two brass cups together to advertise his wares. The coffee he sells is very black, very thick, and very sweet and has a delightful flavour that you will remember long after he has gone on his way.

Dorien Leigh.

WHERE CHRIST WAS BORN

This picture shows us the main entrance to the Church of Nativity in Bethlehem, a church built over the very spot where Christ was born. Notice the dress of the people in this picture. The old man (right) wears clothes much like those worn long ago at the first Christmas of all time.

have taken place at some time between 1400 B.C. and 1250 B.C.

The State of Israel

As we have seen, much of Palestine now forms the state of Israel, the National Home of the Jews. In 1950 the Knesset (parliament) of Israel passed a law which says that " every Jew has the right to immigrate to Israel." Jews have come to their homeland from many countries: from Germany and the countries of Central Europe, from Rumania, Yugoslavia and Poland, from Arabia, Iraq, Persia, Turkey and Syria, and from the lands of the Far East. In 1952, of a total population of over 1,600,000, more than 1,400,000 were Jews.

Many Israelis are farmers, working on mixed farms, or growing olives, vines or tobacco, or cultivating oranges and grapefruit. Oranges are often said to be Israel's most valuable crop. They are grown, with other fruits and crops, in the rich plains of Sharon and Esdraelon along the shores of the Mediterranean. Water is important and wells have been dug and pipe-lines laid to irrigate the orchards. Jaffa (the ancient Joppa) has given its name to the oranges grown along Israel's Mediterranean shorelands.

The Rich Plains

Jaffa oranges are ready just in time for Christmas. Numbers of people are engaged in the orange groves, picking, grading and packing the golden fruit, which is then taken by motor lorries to large sheds for inspection.

The cases of oranges are next taken out to the steamers anchored off shore. Over two million cases of Jaffa oranges per season come to Britain in normal times.

There are many other fertile regions: the Emek, or Valley of Jezreel, which is one of the chief farming districts ; the plains of Jordan and Beisan, where bananas and other fruits are grown ; the Hills of Ephraim, with their vineyards; and Galilee, with its tobacco and olive plantations and its mixed farms.

Much of the work of the countryside is carried out by the farming settlements. There are several types, and some are rather like the collective farms of the Soviet Union. There are *Kibbutz* and *Kvutza*, settlements where all property is collectively owned, where work is organised collectively and where the profits go not to individuals but to the settlement; *Moshvei Ovdim*, settlements of smallholders working co-operatively; and *Moshav Shitufi*, collective farming settlements which often operate indus-

trial enterprises as well. By the end of 1951 there were nearly 700 rural settlements of one kind or another. The oldest communal settlement in Israel is Deganya B, on the shores of Galilee, which was founded in 1909.

Aided by Jews in all parts of the world, the Palestine settlers have had the money to develop their land and their new towns on an impressive scale. They have brought modern machinery to their farms, made their land fertile by irrigation schemes and harnessed river waters to provide electric power. On the river Jordan, where it is joined by the Yarmuk a few miles south of the Sea of Galilee, is Palestine's greatest hydro-electric station. On the southern shores of the Dead Sea there are great salt pans from which come such valuable products as chlorine, sulphuric acid, caustic soda, and the potash which fertilises the fruitful fields and orchards. One of the most recent and most important development projects concerns

J. Allan Cash.

A STREET IN MODERN JERUSALEM

Jerusalem is a city where old and new meet. The Old City and its holy places turn our minds from the present to the far-off days of the Bible story. The New City has risen outside the ancient walls and is a place of modern streets and buildings, as the picture shows.

A. F. Kersting.

THE TEMPLE AREA, JERUSALEM

To the east of modern Jerusalem, where the Great Temple of Solomon is supposed to have stood on Mount Moriah, is the Haram-el-Sherif, or Temple Area. This picture shows the principal building, the Kubbet-es-Sakhra or Dome of the Rock which, in both Jewish and Mohammedan tradition, is the centre of the world. Within its walls is the sacred boulder, said to be the altar where burnt offerings were made.

the Negev, a large triangular area of southern Israel which has its apex on the Gulf of Akaba, on the Red Sea. Here has been built the Red Sea port of Elath, which is now connected by trunk road to Beersheba. New roads and water-pipelines are being laid as part of the plan to bring a new prosperity to this region.

Pipe-lines

At the seaward end of the plain of Esdraelon is Haifa which is the port terminal of one of the great pipe-lines, which in normal times brings oil from the rich Iraqi fields at Kirkuk and other places east of the Tigris. A branch of this pipe-line carries oil from Iraq to the Syrian port of Tripoli.

Haifa harbour is the largest in Palestine and has plant for refining the crude oil before it is pumped on board the tankers. To Haifa also come ships for the oranges which have made Jaffa famous, even though more of them are shipped from Haifa than from Jaffa. While the massive artificial break-waters of Haifa harbour were being built, caverns were discovered on the slopes of Mount Carmel in which were found skeletons of the earliest humans to have inhabited Palestine. The Palestine Man, as these humans are now called, lived in the Holy Land over 50,000 years ago.

Tel Aviv

Although Jerusalem was proclaimed the capital of Israel, the largest city is Tel Aviv, which with Jaffa (to which Tel Aviv is joined) has a population of 400,000. Tel Aviv was begun as a Jewish suburb of the ancient Arab city of Jaffa. To-day it has completely out-grown Jaffa and is a thoroughly modern city, where people mostly live in

BY THE SHORES OF THE DEAD SEA

The Dead Sea is about 1,300 feet below the level of the Mediterranean and is so salt that people bathing in it find it difficult to swim because so much of their bodies is buoyed-up out of the water. The Sea receives the waters of the Jordan and other rivers, and there is no outlet, so the fluid evaporates. The crystals (top left) are salt and were found by the shores of the Dead Sea.

SCENES IN THE HOLY LAND

E.N.A.

To Jew, Christian and Mahommedan alike Jerusalem is the Holy City. Outside the city walls in the days of old stood Mount Calvary, and it was on His journey to Calvary that Christ, bearing the Cross upon His shoulders, struggled along the street seen in the photograph above, the Via Dolorosa, or Street of Pain. In the Middle Ages the Crusaders fought to free the Holy City but later it passed under Islam's domination, and was finally recovered when General Allenby entered in December 1917. Britain became responsible for the government of Palestine under mandate from the League of Nations but relinquished this in 1948.

DAMASCUS GATE AND THE WAILING WALL

The Damascus Gate, one of the four main gateways to and from Jerusalem, stands to the north of the City. Here, within the Gate, is a group of Arabs taking refreshment before they set forth upon their journeys. This scene must have been enacted over and over again for many centuries.

Photos: E.N.A.

The Wailing Wall, or the Wall of Prayer, is sacred to the Jews and has been so from the earliest days since it was here that many of their ancestors were slain. The Christian sacred places, associated with the life of Christ, have also been preserved, and there are mementoes of Roman, Crusader and Islamic occupation.

THE MOUNT OF OLIVES TODAY

The Mount of Olives is one of the Holy Places which has been preserved through the centuries. In this photograph is seen the Mount, viewed from the West. Here, too, can be seen the Garden of Gethsemane and the road by which Our Lord made His triumphal entry into Jerusalem.

Photos: E.N.A.

In this photograph we have a view of the city of Bethlehem from the North. Bethlehem was the birthplace of King David and here Our Lord was born. It is some five miles distant from Jerusalem and is a centre of religious interests of many kinds. The meaning of the word Bethlehem is "house of bread."

"UNTO YOU IS BORN THIS DAY"

Dorien Leigh

In Bethlehem the Church of the Nativity is built on the site where Christ was born. It is probably the oldest Christian church in the world and is surrounded by chapels and convents.

Topical

In this photograph we see the building which is regarded as the most sacred in Christendom, the ancient Church of the Holy Sepulchre. It stands over the burial place of Christ in Jerusalem.

E.N.A.

The River Jordan is often mentioned in the Bible. It is a river of Palestine, nearly 200 miles in length, which runs a zig-zag course through the Waters of Merom to the Sea of Galilee from which it descends into the Dead Sea. Our photograph shows the scene at the ford of the Jordan.

WORKING WITH HANDS AND TOES

The tools used by this Arab carpenter may be primitive, but he certainly seems happy enough in his work. The whip-like object he holds with his right hand rotates a drill by means of a strap attachment. The piece of olive wood on which he is working is held firmly on the block that serves him as a bench by his toes. His methods must be very similar to those used in the Holy Land of ancient times when Jesus Christ himself was known as a carpenter.

co-operatively owned blocks of flats : and when it is viewed from the air, it can be seen as a pattern of spacious tree-lined boulevards and squares flanked by tall buildings in the most modern architectural styles.

The Older Villages

But the development of Israel does not mean that the Palestine of old has vanished completely. Villages where the way of life has changed but little with the passing of the years can still be found. You can see them in the plains. Their houses are of stone or of sun-baked brick, with flat roofs of rolled clay or beaten earth. It is not uncommon for such house roofs to be covered with a thin growth of herbage upon which enterprising goats may graze. Many housetops provide space for drying and storing grain, fuel and fruits, as well as for the inhabitants to " take the air in the cool of the evening."

The rooftop is reached from the ground by a flight of steps outside. Inside, most large village houses have a platform or *mastabeh* raised well above the lower part or *rowyeh* in which animals are kept, and where the people may sleep if the upper part, which is really the living-room, is too crowded. Light and air come through one or two tiny windows high in the wall and without glass in them. Warmth in winter and opportunities of cooking are provided by the little fire in the stone fireplace. There is scanty furniture ; these peasant folk live very simply and their needs are few.

Hill villages are built of stone taken from the hill itself ; the houses huddle closely together on the slopes or even on the very hilltop, their dusty, crooked and unpaved streets making things difficult for people on foot if a laden camel comes that way. The backs of the houses face the street ; there are no such things as " front gardens "

Paul Popper

FERTILISER FROM THE DEAD SEA

Nearly three thousand people are employed in producing potash, a valuable soil enricher, from the salts of the Dead Sea in these large evaporating pans. The pans, which extend over 500 acres at the southern end of the Dead Sea, also produce other valuable chemicals.

JAFFA AND GAZA

Once known as Joppa, Jaffa is a seaport which has given its name to the oranges which come from the Holy Land. The oranges, and other fruits also, grow in well-irrigated gardens and are ready just in time for Christmas. In a normal season, more than two million cases of Jaffa oranges may come to Britain.

Photos: E.N.A.

Gaza (also known as Guzzeh) was once a city of the Philistines and was known to Alexander the Great long before the time of Christ. The town and a coastal strip of southern Palestine, including the railway junction of Rafah, are now held by Egypt as a result of the armistice made with Israel in 1949.

JERUSALEM TO-DAY

We have climbed the tower of the Franciscan church of St. Sauveur and are looking eastwards towards the Mount of Olives. Within our view are the three chief religious centres of the city—the Dome of the Rock (left centre), the Church of the Holy Sepulchre, and the Jewish Synagogue.

Not all Jerusalem is given up to ancient and revered buildings of Bible days. Buildings in the new style have been erected in this city which remains the cultural centre of the Palestine Jews whose Hebrew University is upon Mount Scopus.

THE HARBOUR AT HAIFA

Central Press.

Haifa, seen in this picture, has the argest harbour in Palestine and is normally the port terminal of one of the great pipe-lines bringing oil from the fields at Kirkuk and other places east of the Tigris river. From Haifa, too, Jaffa oranges are shipped—in greater quantities than they are from Jaffa itself.

Topical Press.

Despite the passing of time, camel caravans are still the chief means of long distance transport in the remoter parts of the Holy Land. Here, within sight of the walls of an Arab town, a caravan loaded with grain is seen resting after its long journey.

here. Stone sheepfolds are attached to many of these houses, for the chief wealth of these simple villagers is in sheep and goats which browse on the thin pastures of the grey hillsides. Lower down there may be little patches of fertile soil in which the peasants manage to grow grain, fruits and vegetables.

The Changing Seasons

Winters are cold in the open hill country, bringing chilly rains and sometimes snow, and the peasants and shepherds are glad of their thick woollen robes and their coats of sheep-skin. When spring comes, it brings with it a magic change, for green things grow up in all sorts of unexpected places as well as in the fertile spots, and for a time the hillside is gay with flowers. But the summer sun soon withers the flowers and burns up the grass, and the land becomes parched and dry, except in those fortunate places supplied by water from wells or irrigation channels.

Grain is sown just after the rains, and beans and lentils are also sown in the moist red soil. Camels and asses as well as oxen are yoked to the rough wooden ploughs, which plough shallow furrows so that the precious moisture shall not be lost. The grain is reaped with toothed sickles and carried to the threshing floors of hard earth, where oxen tied side by side tread out the grain with their wide iron shoes. The grain is winnowed by throwing it up so that the chaff may blow aside, leaving the wheat in a heap by itself. The grain is then carefully sifted in big sieves to make sure that it is quite clean.

Most of the hill-folk spin wool from their sheep, and the yarn is woven on

Photos: E.N.A.

A FORMER GUARDIAN OF THE CRUSADER ROAD

The road of the Crusaders to Jerusalem, the Holy City, is signposted by such mighty castles as the Krak des Chevaliers shown in this picture. These ruined walls were once manned by two thousand soldiers, and a thousand horsemen stood ready to sally forth against the crescent banner of Islam. To-day the moat is empty and the once-proud towers have no other company than the lonely Syrian desert hills.

WHEN ROME RULED THE WORLD

A. F. Kersting.

When ancient Rome was struggling to dominate the Middle East, the citizens of desert Palmyra were adding to their wealth and power. To-day, the ruins of their once-great city rise from the desert sands midway between the upper reaches of the Euphrates and the Syrian coast. In the background we see a hilltop crowned by a Moslem castle built with stones taken from the ancient city that fell to Rome in A.D. 273.

E.N.A.

About midway between Tripoli and Damascus are the remarkable ruins of Baalbek, a city of the past. The present ruins are mainly Roman, and we can see from this picture of the Great Court of the Temple of Jupiter how fine a city Baalbek must have been in the days when Rome was mistress of the world.

CRUSADER FORTRESSES

Large parts of what is now Syria were included in the Holy Land of ancient days. Through Syria, too, ran the *Via Dei*, or " Road of God," by which the Crusaders travelled to Jerusalem, a fact which accounts for such ruined castles as the " Kadifekalasi " shown in this picture.

Photos : E.N.A.

Aleppo, in northern Syria, is another town which has links in history with the Crusaders. Foremost in this picture of the town is the ruined gateway of the ancient citadel built by one of the sons of the great Saladin.

HEWN IN THE LIVING ROCK

American Colony, Jerusalem.

Petra is a city of the desert long since vanished except for its remains of rock-hewn temples and tombs, of which the " Corinthian " tomb above is an example.

American Colony, Jerusalem.

These tombs were hewn out of the living rock 2,000 years ago, and the one above towers 120 feet in height. It is known as the Temple of El Khazneh.

American Colony, Jerusalem.

Petra can be reached only through this *sik*, or narrow gorge. The ravine is a mile in length, lined on either side with tombs, niches and inscriptions.

Will F. Taylor.

In this picture we see the Temple of El-Deir, and there are hundreds of tombs in the sandstone rock. Egyptians, Greeks and Romans knew Petra.

hand-looms in many districts to make the woollen stuffs so widely used for clothing.

Road of God

Via Dei, " Road of God," was the name given by the Crusaders to the desert trails leading to Jerusalem. Among the many splendid monuments of the Holy Land are the castles and citadels built by crusading kings and knights. At Aleppo, high on a barren hill above the city, is the double-barbicaned fortress of one of the sons of the great Saladin ; in the hills south of Antioch are the ruins of Sahyun, the thirteenth century fortress of the crusading lords of Soane ; Syrian plains and ravines are overlooked by the mighty Krak des Chevaliers whose walls were once manned by two thousand soldiers and whose stables could take a thousand horses.

The Wonders of Petra

In the Hashemite kingdom of the Jordan, but fairly near the long railway that links Damascus with the Holy City of Medina in Arabia, are the wonderful ruins of *Petra*, "the rose-red city half as old as Time." Petra's rock-hewn temples and tombs and its theatres and terraces carved in the red rock by master-masons two thousand years ago stand in a place that was easily defended for its only approaches were by narrow defiles which a handful of men could have held against an army.

Among the wonders of Petra are the beautiful front of the Temple of Isis, and the great amphitheatre which could seat three thousand people.

Will F. Taylor.

IN THE VANISHED CITY OF PETRA

Here we have a view of the front of the great High Place at Petra. Among the ruins of this lost city are those of an amphitheatre which could provide seating accommodation so that 3,000 spectators might view the sights in the arena below.

EGYPT, THE SUDAN AND THE NILE

Will F. Taylor.

A GATEWAY TO THE SUEZ CANAL

The wonderful canal joining the blue Mediterranean with the Red Sea has Port Said as its Mediterranean gateway. Here, at the end of the mole, stands a statue of Vicomte Ferdinand de Lesseps, the famous French engineer who built the great waterway. Eleven years' difficult work went to the making of the canal which was opened in 1869.

"EGYPT," said the ancients, "is the gift of the Nile." It is not until we visit Egypt that we realise how exactly true this is. The real Egypt is the narrow valley of the Lower Nile and its rich fan-shaped delta. It was in the Nile Valley that the wonderful civilisation of Ancient Egypt arose thousands of years before the Cæsars of Rome set their iron rule upon the Mediterranean world of their day. Only a river like the Nile, with its yearly flood that enriches the valley and gives life to everything in it, could have made an almost rainless country like Egypt, land of the Pharaohs who at one time held sway over nearly the whole of the known world.

The Nile

The Nile, whose steady flow is maintained by the great lakes of the East African plateau, begins to rise about the middle of July—soon after the heavy rains have begun to fall in the Abyssinian highlands, and it is this heavy summer rain brought down by the Atbara and the Blue Nile tributaries that is the real cause of the regular Nile flood that reaches its highest level in Egypt in September. To control this flow, and to make it serve greater areas than it used to do in ancient times, great dams or barrages have been constructed by British engineers. The most famous of these barrages in Egypt is the Assuan Dam (built 1898–1902) at the first of the six great cataracts of the Nile; and there are others, at Asyut and at Zifta (below Cairo), for example.

The Nile waters are lifeblood to the fields of Egypt which give a precarious livelihood to three-quarters of the population. Over half the farms are less than an acre in extent. In fields that sometimes literally border desert expanses the Egyptian farmers, or *fellahin*, grow cotton, sugar, rice, millet, maize and garden crops. Not far distant are the villages where they live —huddled mud-walled places whose flat-roofed buildings are made of sun-baked bricks. The villages are often built on raised mounds as a safeguard against the floods, and village is connected to village by causeways above the level of the fields. Thanks to the Nile dams and the irrigation schemes, most farmland yields crops both in summer and in winter, and the *fellahin* no longer have to rely entirely on such primitive devices as *sakiehs*, or

water wheels, or *shadufs*, which are lifting contrivances for drawing water from the river. The green belt of farmlands that hugs the course of the Nile gives Egypt its greatest crop and export—cotton, which is shipped from Alexandria.

Cairo and the Pyramids

It is only recently that Egypt ceased to be a kingdom. In July, 1952, King Farouk abdicated and his baby son, Prince Ahmed Fuad, was proclaimed king. But in June, 1953, Egypt was declared to be a republic, the powers of President being conferred on General Mohammed Neguib.

The pleasantest time for us to visit Egypt is between October and April, especially during November or December, when the weather is at its best for people coming from Europe; and the only way to see Egypt and its wonderful monuments of a mighty and glorious past is by Nile steamer.

Cairo, the capital of Egypt, will be our starting point—an amazing city that is both old and new. The new Cairo has fine buildings, great modern hotels, and broad, shady avenues along which are shops, theatres and cafés as good as any in Paris or Vienna. The old Cairo still has its crooked, narrow streets, its balconied houses with windows discreetly covered with screens of pierced woodwork or with metal grilles, its mosques with tall, slender minarets and

Mansell Collection.

RAISING WATER FROM THE NILE WITH A SHADUF

The shaduf (pronounced " shadoof ") used by this peasant farmer is one of the oldest ways of drawing water from the Nile to irrigate the fields. As the picture shows, a shaduf consists of a pole, hinged on two uprights. At one end of the pole is a bucket; at the other, a weight. The pole can be swung round so that the bucket can be emptied into one of the small irrigation channels.

A. F. Kersting.

TWO MOSQUES OF CAIRO

In this picture we are looking over Cairo from the Citadel. Immediately before us rise the fairy-tale minarets and domes of the mosques of Sultan Hassan and Er Rifai. The minaret of the mosque of Sultan Hassan (left) is over 250 feet high and is the tallest in Cairo. Cairo has many such wonderful buildings as these; the Citadel itself was built by the great Saladin.

long glazed tiles, its bazaars, and its seething day-to-day life.

Cairo is the largest city in Africa; the population numbers more than two millions. The city has a long history as a meeting place for caravans from Palestine, from Arabia, and from the Sahara, and is still a focal point in Middle East communications. Cairo has railway links with Ismailia on the Suez Canal and with the Mediterranean ports of Alexandria, Rosetta, and Damietta and Port Said, and with the Nile valley as far south as Assuan and Shellal. Cairo is an important centre for air routes and has two busy airports: Almaza, and the International Airport.

Across the Nile from Cairo is Gizeh, where the famous Pyramids and the Sphinx are within easy reach by car, tram or carriage—only nine miles from Cairo itself. Whilst at Cairo, we should certainly visit the ancient city port of Alexandria, founded by Alexander the Great in 332 B.C., and site of the famous lighthouse, or Pharos, that was one of the Wonders of the Ancient World. Alexander is said to have been buried there in a golden casket. Even in recent years archæologists have been searching for his tomb, mostly beneath old mosques in the city, but so far no discovery has been made in this connection. We might also visit Sakkara, about sixteen miles south of Cairo, to see the 6,500-years-old pyramid and avenue of sphinxes, the discovery of which was announced in December, 1953.

IN THE LAND OF THE PHARAOHS

Seen from the Mokattam Hills, with the dismounted rider in the foreground, Cairo might be some city of the Arabian Nights.

Every visitor to Egypt knows the donkey boys, who are seen in this picture on the banks of the Lower Nile.

Photos: H. J. Shepstone.

Peoples of many races and religions can be found in Cairo. Here, for example, is a Bisharin boy, short and slight, and dressed in the age-old manner of his people.

This Bisharin girl is not so sad as her brother as she faces the camera. The Bisharin people, living between the Red Sea and the Nile, are typical Nubian desert Arabs.

H. J. Shepstone.

These are some of the columns of the Great Temple of Luxor. Luxor, upon the banks of the Nile in Upper Egypt, is virtually the ancient city of Thebes and has been the scene of much excavation. It is a favourite place of call for tourists.

Wonders of Ancient Egypt

Leaving Cairo by Nile steamer, we view the city in its real setting—the green Nile with splendid buildings on both banks, the bold Mokattam Hills with the Citadel almost at their feet, and away to the westward the three Pyramids of Gizeh at the desert's edge. Two or three hours' travel brings us to a point whence we set out on donkey back with our gorgeously-clad *dragomans* (guides) to see all that is left of ancient Memphis, the old capital of the Pharaohs, and its vast Necropolis in which the great ones of old time were buried with all that care and religious ceremonial which was observed in Ancient Egypt by a people who believed in preserving their bodies for use in the life beyond the grave.

Vivid pictures of life in Ancient Egypt are to be seen in the marvellous paintings on the walls of tombs near Beni Hassan, which we visit after about two days' journey upstream from Cairo on the broad Nile that here flows between red sandstone cliffs, with the green of cultivated fields between them and the river.

On the seventh day after leaving Cairo the tall temple pylons of Karnak appear, and the beautiful colonnades of the temple of Luxor—both worthy of their place among the wonders of the world. It was on the opposite (western) bank that the Egyptians built their capital of Thebes, which we shall visit to see the Tombs of the Kings and the tomb of Tutankhamen, which revealed to an astonished world buried secrets of the Egypt of long ago.

Twelve days' journey from Cairo we reach Assuan and cross the mighty dam by trolley car. From Assuan we can go by boat to see the lovely Temple of Philæ, and the famous Nilometer on Elephantine Island. If we continue southwards up the river, we enter the *Sudan* whose capital, Khartoum, stands at the

A. F. Kersting.

OLD HOUSES NEAR CAIRO'S ZOUEILA GATE

In the older parts of Cairo there are houses like these that have survived the passing of the centuries. Notice the *mushrabia* screen windows round what were evidently the women's quarters. Through these windows the womenfolk of the family could see, yet remain unseen.

A. F. Kersting.

THE PYRAMIDS OF GIZEH

The pyramids were built as tombs for the royal rulers of Ancient Egypt. The three at Gizeh, of which only two are seen here, are the greatest and most famous. To the left is the Pyramid of Chephren, which still has some of its granite casing; to the right is the Great Pyramid of Cheops, built 5,000 years ago and originally nearly 500 feet high, which was one of the Seven Wonders of the Ancient World.

junction of the White Nile and the Blue Nile.

In the Sudan

In 1899, after a troubled history of war and famine, the Sudan became a condominium; that is to say, it came under the rule of two countries acting together—in this case, Britain and Egypt. A Sudanese Executive Council and Legislative Assembly were set up in 1948, and in 1952 a constitution was approved which provided for Sudanese control of all matters except defence and foreign affairs. The elections for the first national Parliament of the Sudan took place towards the end of 1953.

In many ways these elections were very different from those of our own country. There were candidates to be voted for, of course, and the people voted in secrecy as we do. But in some places the voting had to be carried out by a system of tokens. Each candidate was given a symbol—a spear, perhaps, or a leopard—and this symbol was marked on his ballot box at the thatched hut that was the polling station. The simple tribesmen, who had never before experienced an election, voted for the man of their choice by dropping their tokens in the ballot box marked with his symbol.

The Gezira Scheme

The Sudan is about eleven times as large as the United Kingdom. The north is dry scrubland or desert where there is very little rain. The people here —Muslims, Nubians and others—are often nomad herdsmen, who with their camels share the dry lands with wild antelopes, lions, giraffes and zebra. South of Khartoum, between the White and Blue Niles, are the fertile cotton fields of the plain of Gezira. Gezira cotton is by far the most valuable crop of the Sudan. Millet and a fodder crop called *lubia* are also grown in the Gezira, whose fields are irrigated by waters from the Sennar Dam across the Blue Nile. More land was brought under irrigation in 1952, and in time some two million acres may be irrigated.

There is direct railway communication from the cotton fields to *Port Sudan*, whence the cotton is shipped, most of it to Great Britain. What water has done for cotton, it has done also for the mixed farmers and market gardeners of the northern Sudan. Irrigation and deep wells have turned many people from a nomad life to the more settled existence of the farmer.

Gum arabic comes from the Sudan. It is tapped from the *talh* and *hashab* trees of the gum gardens of Kassala and Kordofan. Hides and oil seeds also are produced.

The southern Sudan is the home of primitive tribes, some of which raise cattle. But certain areas of the south are haunts of the tsetse fly, and in these areas cattle breeding is not possible.

The Sudd

As we go on, we may see boats at work clearing the *Sudd* of the thick vegetation, from the river. We are now in a region where the rain is more plentiful in the summer and where and tall grasses grow. The nearer we get to the Great Lakes, the more the vegetation thickens, until we are in country of dense forests and rich farmlands. If we wanted, we could continue by steamer to Rejaf and from there travel by car to Nimule on the borders of Uganda, a journey which would take us nineteen days in all from Cairo, the Egyptian capital.

Such is the Nile, whose waters mean

A. F. Kersting.

THE " GULLI-GULLI " MAN

There is plenty to attract the interest in the byways and side-streets of Cairo. But the " gulli-gulli " man, or street conjurer shown here, does not seem to have got the full attention of his small audience which has perhaps already guessed how he does the trick.

THE SUDAN GOES TO THE POLLS

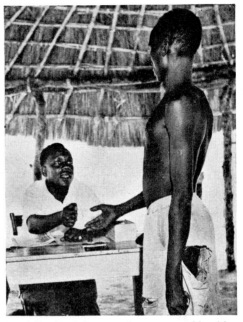

The elections for the first national Parliament of the Sudan were held towards the end of 1953. This picture shows voting in progress on polling day.

In some places, because the voters could neither read nor write, voting had to be carried out with the help of tokens. Here we see a tribesman at Juba receiving his token.

Photos: Copyright.

The result of the election is declared. This picture was taken in Equatoria and shows a southern Sudanese announcing to his compatriots the name of the successful candidate. The board against the tree shows the various symbols adopted by the candidates to guide those who voted by putting their tokens in the box marked with the symbol of their candidate.

fertility or starvation to the people who live along its course. The problem of how Egypt is to provide food for her people may be answered by a big international scheme which will build new dams on the upper Nile. The first of these is the dam on the White Nile at Owen Falls controlling the outlet from Lake Victoria, and making the lake the biggest reservoir in the world. A second dam will control the waters of Lake Albert. On the Blue Nile, Lake Tana will be dammed. The waters lost by the White Nile as it passes through the Sudd region will flow through the by-pass Jonglei Canal. When complete, the scheme will provide an assured water supply to thirsty Egypt and increase her areas of cultivation by some million and a half acres. This great scheme may take twenty-five years to complete.

Borderlands of the Upper Nile

East of the Upper Nile is the ancient Empire of *Ethiopia* (*Abyssinia*) which was conquered by Italy, but regained its independence during the Second World War and saw its Emperor, Haile Selassie, restored to his capital of Addis Ababa. The people are mostly farmers, and the main route of trade is the railway linking Addis Ababa with Djibouti in French Somaliland.

In 1952 Eritrea was federated with Ethiopia as a self-governing unit. Massawa is the chief port of Eritrea.

South-east of French Somaliland lies the protectorate of *British Somaliland*. Berbera is the chief port, and Hargeisa the seat of government. Bordering the protectorate is *Somalia* (formerly known as Italian Somaliland), which Italy holds under United Nations' trusteeship.

H. E. Watterson.

THE SPHINX AT GIZEH

No one can estimate the age of this gigantic figure, carved in rock and partly buried in the sand. It is to be found in Lower Egypt, and is a man-headed lion. The figure is nearly 200 feet in length, and the face of the monster 14 feet wide. Between the paws are the remains of an open air temple. The Sphinx in various forms appears in other parts of Egypt.

MESOPOTAMIA AND BEYOND

A. F. Kersting.

RELICS OF A PROUD PARTHIAN CITY

From 250 B.C. until A.D. 266 most of Mesopotamia was ruled by a Parthian dynasty. In the desert, south-west of Mosul, at El Hadhr or Hatra, as it is called, you can see these remains of one of their cities. The crumbling pillars and arches of the sun temple speak of a once prosperous city, whose walls and defenders defied the Emperor Trajan in A.D. 116.

THE valley of the Tigris-Euphrates which the Greeks named Mesopotamia, "the land between the Rivers," and which to-day we call Iraq, was, like Egypt of old, one of the first cradles of civilisation; and, like Egypt of to-day, it is a wonderful storehouse of history. Yellow mounds, long barren amid the fertility of the plain, were proved to contain the ruins of mighty cities of the past—of Babylon and Nineveh; and eager excavators soon revealed the walls of temples and palaces that Nebuchadnezzar knew, and the very streets along which the exiled Israelites must have walked in the days of the Captivity.

Ur of the Chaldees

More wonderful even than these in some ways were the discoveries made at Ur of the Chaldees, the city of the plains whence Abraham started on his long journey to the west, where he founded a nation in the Land of Israel. Here modern scientists discovered in the ancient burial grounds of the city relics of remote antiquity dating back beyond 3200 B.C., reaching far into times that are prehistoric.

Like Egypt, Mesopotamia is hemmed in by the desert, which is never very far from "the sown"—the cultivated field. Summer heat is so great in many places as to be unbearable; flies, mosquitoes and the fevers they carry render life uncomfortable to human beings; and the winter half-year brings days that are as chill and raw as summer days are hot and stifling.

Tradition says that the Garden of Eden was in the lower Tigris-Euphrates Valley. Tigris is the river Hiddekel of the book of Genesis, and the plain was the Plain of Shinar, upon which the Tower of Babel was upreared like one of

237

those huge ziggurats whose foundations archæologists have uncovered at Babylon and other places in the broad, sand-strewn valley.

The City of the Arabian Nights

Iraq was freed from Turkey during the war of 1914–18, but was under Britain's care for some years. Not until 1932 did Iraq become a sovereign independent state. Modern Iraq occupies more than " the land between the rivers." Eastwards her frontier runs about half-way between the Tigris and the Zagros Mountains in Iran; to the west her territory protrudes, in the shape of a pig's snout, towards the Hashemite kingdom of the Jordan, with Syria to the north and Saudi Arabia to the south.

The centre of modern Iraq is the famous old city of *Baghdad* on the Tigris—the city of the " Arabian Nights " where the great Caliph Harun al-Rashid once held sway. Baghdad is a junction of Middle East communications and can be reached overland from Europe by the Baghdad Railway.

You leave the station of Haidar Pasha in Uskudar, also known as Scutari (the Asiatic suburb of Constantinople across the Bosporus), cross the high and dry plateau of Turkey, and go down again to the ancient caravan centre of *Aleppo*. Then the train goes east to the old city of *Mosul* on the upper Tigris, which has there emerged from the terrific gorges through which it has cut a way from the northern mountains to the plain.

The Lower Basin

From Mosul you travel south to Baghdad, the City of the Caliphs, and on, if you like, down the Euphrates Valley to the port of *Basra*, near which are the greatest date groves in the world.

Basra is built on the Shatt-el-Arab, the river formed by the union of Tigris and Euphrates. Into the Shatt-el-Arab flows the Karun River from the Persian oilfields, whence crude oil is piped to the huge refinery at *Abadan*. Abadan is in Persia and we shall see more of it

when we visit that country presently.

Caravans still converge on Baghdad from all points of the compass, as they have done, doubtless, almost since the beginning of history; but two and a half miles from the city is the Baghdad West Airport for air liners serving the route to India; and arriving there, too, are the fine " desert cars " of the regular motor service from Damascus and the Mediterranean port of Beirut in Syria.

As in Olden Days

Yet on the bosom of the Tigris you can still see peasants crossing the river swimming on inflated sheepskins, just as you see men doing so on the famous Assyrian bas-reliefs at the British Museum. You can cross the river in a *goufa*—one of those strange, circular boats which are exactly like those used in Abraham's time; or you can voyage up and down in a *bellem*, or in a *mahaila*, with eyes at the prow and a tall, triangular sail; or you can take a comfortable and up-to-date motor launch—whichever you please.

Nowhere else in the world is the remote past closer to the present than in this age-old land of Mesopotamia, where the days of the book of Genesis are linked with the twentieth century in which we live.

Land and Water

Despite Iraq's importance as an oil-producing country, most of her people get their living from the land. Their country has long dry summers and it is then very hot and dusty. But in the winter Iraq is cold and has rains which turn the parched land into mud. More than 80 per cent. of the world's dates come from Iraq. Grain, cotton and fruits are grown and wool is exported. In many areas canals and pumps are used to keep the land fertile, for irrigation is as important to modern Iraq as it was to the ancient empires of Babylon and Assyria. Irrigation schemes are vital and the Iraq Irrigation Development Commission has already set about

BAGHDAD'S BLUE MOSQUE

E.N.A.

The Great Mosque, with its beautifully decorated blue dome, is but one of many in this old city of the Arabian Nights. In the days of the great Harun al-Rashid, Baghdad was virtually the capital of Islam, both in matters of religion and politics. Its power and splendour did not decline until about the time of the death of the caliph Mamun in A.D. 833. To-day, Baghdad is the chief city of Iraq and an important communications centre.

controlling the flood waters of the Tigris and Euphrates and diverting them to make the desert areas fertile. Lake Habbaniya is the key point of these schemes, and progress has been made with the Bekhme Dam on the Great Zab river which is a tributary of the Tigris. The most ambitious part of the scheme reached its final plan in 1947. A dam is to be built at the Wadi Tharthar, which is between the Tigris and the Euphrates between Baghdad and Mosul. This dam will create a vast artificial lake nearly twice the size of Lake Meade at the famous Boulder Dam in the United States. When completed, this project will open to agriculture vast areas of fertile soil which the Iraqi Government intends to farm by the most modern methods. If these and the other sweeping plans for education and social services which were recently announced come into being, Iraq will be one of the most progressive countries throughout the Middle East.

Iraq is one of the world's great oil-producing countries. Her main oilfield at Kirkuk is linked by great pipe-lines to certain east Mediterranean ports. The oil is first piped to Haditha and then either westwards across Syria to the port of Tripoli or south-west across Palestine to Haifa. The Haifa pipe-line, however, ceased to operate when trouble broke out in Palestine, and in 1952 the oil company began to use a newly built line to Banias, in the Lebanon.

New Oilfields

Oil also comes from the Mosul region. A pipe-line is being built from Ain Zalah, a recently discovered field, to Baiji, on the Kirkuk-Haditha pipe-line. Oil has been found recently also in the Basra district. Much of the oil used in Iraq itself comes from Khanaqin, which has its own refinery. This refinery also handles oil from Kermanshah, in Persia.

Iraq's eastern neighbour is Persia,

Iraq Petroleum Company

AN OIL PROCESSING PLANT AT KIRKUK

This processing plant at Kirkuk handles some twenty million tons of crude oil every year. At this plant the corrosive gases are removed from the oil before it is piped to the Mediterranean sea terminals at Tripoli (Syria) and Banias (Lebanon).

THE GREAT SPHINX OF GIZEH STILL GUARDS THE NILE VALLEY

Every visitor to Egypt makes a point of seeing at least some of the remarkable relics of its ancient civilisation. Among the best known is the Great Sphinx at Gizeh, or El Giza. More than four thousand years old, this strange creature, half lion and half man, was carved from the living rock, probably at the command of King Chephren (Khá-ef-Rē). The heads of sphinxes were usually likenesses of the kings, and the Great Sphinx may well portray, therefore, Chephren himself. Behind the Sphinx is one of the three pyramids of Gizeh.

Specially painted for this work.

A BAZAAR IN THE MIDDLE EAST

All the ancient cities of the countries of the Middle East have their bazaar quarter where time seems to have stood still. In such places as Cairo, or Baghdad, or Damascus, we shall find old and narrow streets in which the buildings and the people seem to have stepped from the pages of the *Arabian Nights*. We shall find, too, dust and dirt, and intolerable heat, with swarms of flies and other insects, all part of a world that is strangely different from more Northern lands.

known for a time as Iran, linked with such famed warriors of ancient history as Cyrus and Darius, Xenophon and Alexander, who raised to imperial greatness the Aryan tribes from which Iran takes her modern name.

Persia's days of glory were buried in the past and the country was weak and disorganised until a strong national leader came to lift his country to a place in the modern world. What Kemal Ataturk did for Turkey, Rheza Khan did for Persia. From the time of his march upon Tehran in 1921, his personality dominated this backward country which, after he became Shah in 1926, was hurried forward to catch up with the outside world. He abdicated in 1941 and left the country. His place on the throne was taken by his son, Muhammed Rheza.

A. F. Kersting.

A GATEWAY OF KADHIMAN'S SACRED MOSQUE

Through this ornate gateway lie the four minarets and twin domes of the sacred mosque of Kadhiman, a place of pilgrimage just outside Baghdad to the north. Domes and minarets are overlaid with gold and beckon on the pilgrim from afar to what is one of the four major shrines of the Shi'ite Moslems. The mosque is said to be the most beautiful Shiah monument in Iraq.

Persia To-day

Two things make Persia of importance: *firstly*, its geographical position as a crossroads country of the Middle East whose routes link India with Egypt and the whole Middle East with Russia; *secondly*, the rich oil wells of the Karun valley and the more recent wells of Kermanshah.

In Tehran, the capital, the modern flat-roofed buildings of Rheza Khan's University contrast with the mosaic-ed minarets of ancient mosques and the snow-tipped grandeur of the nearby Elburz Mountains. The highest peak in the country, Mount Demavend, can be seen from the capital. Camel caravans have given way to airlines, bus services, and motor lorries. The important rail connections via Dzhulfa to Tiflis and Baku in the Soviet Union were augmented during the war by the completion of the Trans-Iranian Railway at a cost of £28,500,000. This railway runs from Bandar Shah on the Caspian Sea, via Tehran, to Bandar Shahpur on the Persian Gulf.

A new railway line is now being built from Tehran to Tabriz, where it will link up with the existing line from the Soviet Union. Another new line to link Tehran with Meshed had reached Shahrud, 300 miles from the capital, by April, 1953. A third new line will eventually link Tehran with Kerman and in time run on to Chahbar, on the shores of the Indian Ocean, where there is a fine natural harbour.

But although there have been these striking developments, we still find, in out-of-the-way towns and villages, the mud-built fortified houses of old, and tribesmen, such as the Bakhtiari, who combine traditional pantaloons of brightly coloured silk with the loudest of check jackets from some modern clothing factory.

The age-old Persian carpet industry still thrives in such towns as Isfahan (an important textile centre), Shiraz, Hamadan, Tabriz, and Kerman, where beautifully patterned weaves are made from wool and silk.

If you look at a map of Persia, you will notice that most of the country is dry

A. F. Kersting.

THE TOGRUL TOWER, RHAGES

This strange tower stands at Rhages, to the south-east of Tehran. Similar towers in other parts of Persia have domes or conical roofs. Rhages is an ancient town mentioned in the Book of Tobias, and was sacked by Genghis Khan in the early thirteenth century. Harun al-Rashid, the Caliph of the *Arabian Nights*, was born at this place.

A. F. Kersting.

THE MASJID-I-SHAH MOSQUE AT ISFAHAN

Probably the finest specimen of Iranian art, the Masjid-i-Shah or Royal Mosque was built during the reign of Shah Abbas (1586–1628), who was one of Persia's most enlightened rulers. Of Isfahan, his capital, it was said " Isfahan is half the world," so many and wonderful were the beauties of the city. Tehran is the modern capital.

plateau which is hemmed in by the Elburz Mountains in the north and by the Zagros Mountains in the west and south-west. Most parts of the plateau have less than 10 inches of rain in a year, and life there depends upon irrigation. But you will notice also that Persia has few rivers and even fewer lakes. Where, then, is the water found for irrigating the land ?

Most of it comes from beneath the surface. Wells are dug by hand and, if water is found, an underground tunnel is made to carry it to the villages and fields. At intervals along the tunnel the diggers have to make holes to extract the soil. So if you go to Persia and see a line of holes running across the countryside, you will know that below is an irrigation tunnel. *Kanats*, as these water systems are called, are a way of irrigation that has been used in Persia for hundreds of years. *Kanat*-digging is still a trade that is handed down from father to son. But Persia also uses modern methods; in 1953, the Shah

16—2

opened the Kohrang Dam, which has made possible the cultivation of thousands of acres of barren land.

The farmers of the irrigated lands grow grain crops, sugar-beet, cotton, opium and vegetables. Shepherds and herdsmen feed their flocks and herds on the pastures. Fruits, tobacco and grain crops flourish on the coastlands of the Caspian, which, unlike the rest of the country, have a heavy rainfall. From here too comes the greater part of Persia's rice and silk.

The Arab States

The million square miles of desert land between the Persian Gulf and the Red Sea which we call Arabia are the home of nomad people who were roused by Lawrence of Arabia to fight on the Allied side during the war of 1914–18. Lawrence, a scholar and archæologist as well as a guerrilla leader and friend of the Arab peoples, championed their cause at the peace conference after the war. Much of the political organisation of modern Arabia is the work of Lawrence and the Arab leaders whom he inspired and brought together. But it is not easy to understand the make-up of Arabia because few of the boundaries have been fixed with exactness.

Greatest of the Arab States is the Kingdom of *Saudi Arabia*, which includes the Kingdom of Hedjaz and has twin capitals at Mecca (Hejaz) and at Riyadh (Nejd) which are connected by a motor road.

Saudi Arabia has some of the richest oilfields in the world, but it is only in recent years that they have been extensively developed. The chief centre of the oil industry is Dhahran, in the province of Hasa, on the shores of the Persian Gulf. Abqaiq, Ain Dar and Damman (where the first Saudi Arabian oil was discovered in 1936) are the main

E.N.A.

PILGRIMS ROUND THE KA'ABA, MECCA

Mecca is a centre of pilgrimage for tens of thousands of Mohammedans every year. The centre of their devotions is the Ka'aba, the sacred Black Stone, hidden from our gaze in this picture by heavy black curtains on which texts from the Koran have been woven in gold. The Ka'aba stands in the courtyard of the Great Mosque at Mecca. Beyond are the lodging houses where the pilgrims stay.

Camera Press.

THE CAPITAL OF A NEW OIL CENTRE

Kuwait on the Persian Gulf is one of the Arab states, a small sheikdom of 6,000 square miles in which fresh water is scarcely known and where no trees grow. Until recent years it was little more than a desert land; to-day houses, offices, schools and hospitals are being built rapidly from the wealth produced from oil. The photograph shows Sabat Square, the centre of Kuwait town.

fields, but there are others which have still to be developed. Some of the crude oil is piped to Bahrein Island for refining and some is processed at the new refinery at Ras Tanura, which is now linked by a railway to the oilfields and Riyadh. But in 1950 a new pipeline was also brought into use. It is over a thousand miles long and links the oilfields with the east Mediterranean port of Sidon. This Trans-Arabian Pipe-line system (TAPline) now carries some 15,000,000 metric tons of crude oil every year.

Kuwait, at the northernmost end of the Persian Gulf, is another Arabian state which has recently developed oilfields. Its Burgan oilfield is connected by pipe-line with the rapidly developing port of Mina al Ahmadi.

In the southern corner of Arabia is the *Yemen*, which is ruled by an Imam. This is the most fertile of Arab lands and is renowned for its Mocha coffee, which takes the name of the port whence it is shipped. Eastwards round the coast past Aden is the *Hadhramaut*, a fertile region which is ruled by

Sultans of the house of Qa'aiti and the house of Kathiri and is included in the Aden protectorate.

Adjoining this are the coastal territories of the Sultanate of *Muscat and Oman*, and to the north, along the shore of the Persian Gulf, the island state of *Bahrein* which is important for its oil refineries and its pearl-fisheries. Manamah is the capital. In addition to all these, Arabia has seven Trucial Sheikhs who rule along a small coastal strip of the Gulf of Oman and whose relationship with Britain dates back to 1820 when they first made treaties with the East India Company. Another Arabian territory is *Qatar*, a sheikhdom on the Persian Gulf south of the Saudi Arabian province of Hasa. Its Dukhan oilfield began production in 1949. Until this happened, Qatar relied almost entirely upon pearl fishing, but to-day the sheikhdom grows rich from the four million tons of oil which are produced annually. Exploration for fresh oilfields continues, even off the coast where the oil companies hope to find workable supplies below the sea bed. As a result of its new-found wealth, Qatar is rapidly modernising Doha, its capital, in which at least half the population of 20,000 live.

Arabia is a land, not only of nomad tribes living in the deserts and desert pastures, but of well-educated and cultured Arabs who dwell in towns which modern progress has reached. An example is the way in which Arabia is using modern scientific methods to fight the locusts which constantly menace Middle East agriculture. Not far from Jidda, the Red Sea port for the thousands of pilgrims who annually visit the holy Moslem cities of Mecca and Medina, there is the headquarters of the Middle East Locust Mission.

Another example is the way in which the oil-producing countries, such as Saudi Arabia and Kuwait, are being modernised with the help of the oil companies. Schools, hospitals and houses are being built, ports and roads and railways constructed, and supplies of electric power and pure water provided.

Pilgrimage to Mecca

Christians and other " unbelievers " are not welcome at the holy city of Mecca where Mohammedan pilgrims go to kiss the sacred Black Stone and perform other acts of devotion. The stone reposes behind the black hangings of the huge Ka'aba and is said to have been given by Gabriel to Abraham. To it come pilgrims from near and far, for all Mohammedans who are fit enough to travel and can afford the journey must pay at least one visit to Mecca.

The pilgrims come in the last month of the Mohammedan year (which is a lunar year). They travel on foot, by camel caravan, by bus or railway (if these are available): or across the sea in sambuks and dhows, packing the decks and providing the captains with a good profit for their voyage. On the journey they will pray, read the Koran and tell the beads of their rosaries. The cramped quarters, poor food and other discomforts of the voyage do not perturb these pilgrims to the holy city of Mecca, which was a place of pilgrimage long before the rise of Islam. It was at Mecca, about the year 570 A.D., that the Prophet was born and it was at Mecca that he formed his belief in the unity of God.

The sacred Black Stone

On arrival at the holy city, the pilgrim runs around the Ka'aba seven times. Another duty to be performed is to enter the white building near the sacred Black Stone and drink from the holy well of Zemzem, from which, it is said, Hagar obtained water for her son, Ishmael. He will also pass within the heavy, embroidered curtains shrouding the Stone, sink down on to the marble floor and offer up prayers, and perhaps kiss the Stone itself. The Stone, which was probably of meteoric origin, has rested here for centuries.

LANDS OF SOUTH-EAST ASIA

E.N.A.

RAMA THE FIRST BRIDGE, BANGKOK

This fine modern bridge was built to commemorate the 150th anniversary of the founding of Bangkok as the Siamese capital and the accession of the Chakkri dynasty to the throne. During the war its central span was destroyed by bombing but the gap was spanned by a Bailey bridge.

WHEN we speak of " Siam," we are giving this country, one of the lands of south-east Asia, a name that has been in use for over a thousand years. But the Siamese often speak of their country as *Prades Thai*, or *Muang-Thai*, " the land of the free people," and since 1949 the official name of the country has been Thailand.

The kingdom of Siam is more than three times the size of England. The population numbers over 17½ millions, and just under a fifth of these are Chinese, who take an important part in trade, rice export and rubber and tin production. The most thickly peopled part of the country is the central fertile valley of the Menam river, where large crops of rice, sugar-cane and millet are grown. The eastern part of the country, which has the Mekong river as its boundary for many miles, is another fertile region. But in the north and west highlands the land is mostly covered by forest; fewer people live there, and it is difficult to travel from one place to another. Teak from the northern forests is floated down to the south by river: by the Menam to Bangkok, or by the Mekong into Indo-China, or by the Salween into Burma. Elephants help to get the heavy logs to the rivers.

Large Rice Crops

Before the Second World War Siam was the second largest rice exporter in the world and, although there was a serious rice shortage in Siam immediately after the war, the production during 1950–51 was well above the pre-war average. The British-sponsored Rice Organisation, which was set up at Bangkok in 1946, helped to bring the crop back to its former high figure. It was Britain, too, that helped the Siamese rice-growers by producing machines that could cultivate the flooded rice fields.

Improved irrigation also will help to increase the yield of the rice fields of the Central Plain. The plan prepared in 1950 provides for the building of a barrage across the Chao P'ya river at

247

Chainat, about a hundred miles upstream from Bangkok. This barrage and its system of canals will provide a reliable water supply for over $2\frac{1}{4}$ million acres.

Besides rice, Siam produces sugar, coco-nuts, tobacco, cotton, pepper and rubber. Although farm machinery, some of it from Britain, is now used in the fields, most Siamese farmers still rely on simple implements drawn by water buffaloes. The water buffalo can stand up to the heat and the wet and the insects—but he must have his daily mud-bath!

Siam has mineral wealth of many kinds, including gold, copper, manganese and precious stones. Her most important minerals are tin and wolfram; the island of Pukit is probably her most famous source of tin.

Bangkok, Capital and Seaport

The Siamese are practically all Buddhists; every town and village has at least one *wat*, or pagoda, and there are Buddhist monasteries all over the country.

One great landmark of Bangkok, the capital, is *Wat Arun Rajavararam*, "the Temple of Dawn," whose obelisk-like towers are crowned with the many-forked trident of Siva. In Bangkok alone there are over three hundred *wats*, and of these the richest and most ornate is the royal temple of the Grand Palace, where the Emerald Buddha, guardian of capital and country, is enshrined.

Bangkok has narrow oriental streets and fine old palaces and temples, but side by side with these are broad, modern avenues, and imposing administrative buildings many of which were completed just before the war. Western ways of life, too, are found in the Siamese capital which has air-conditioned cinemas as fine as any in the western world. In Bangkok, traditional Siamese dress—the brilliant *panung*

By courtesy of Rotary Hoes Ltd.

OLD AND NEW WAYS OF GROWING RICE IN SIAM

In the background, water buffaloes and wooden ploughs prepare the flooded land for the planting off young rice. Nearer the camera, a girl uses a power-driven rotary cultivator. This machine, which was invented by an Australian agricultural engineer, does the work much more quickly and efficiently.

Fox Photos.

A TEMPLE GUARDIAN

The figure of the glaring giant shown here mounts guard, with his companion, at the entrance to the Wat Arun. He represents a character from the *Ramayana*, an Indian epic story over twenty centuries old. The pattern on his armour is made from pieces of broken crockery.

In the older parts and along the upstream tributaries of the river, the banks are mooring places for small houseboats or sites for humble houses built on piles over the water. Native craft, punted or paddled and loaded with merchandise of many kinds move busily about, Buddhist priests in yellow robes go by canoe on their daily rounds of gift collecting, and in some places there are floating markets where merchant and customer sell and buy from boat to boat. The waters of the mainstream are cleft by the bows of small steamers, tugs, barges and sampans, and are a highway for the great teak rafts which come downstream to join in the ceaseless activity of this great seaport capital.

and *pasin*—is becoming a rarity, and European clothes are more and more the rule.

Bangkok is not only the capital; it is Siam's great seaport whence rice, teak, tin, and pepper are shipped. The port has railway links with Rangoon, in Burma, via Moulmein ; with Singapore, at the foot of the Malay Peninsula ; and with Chieng Mai, in northern Siam.

Standing a few miles from the mouth of the Menam river, Bangkok is almost an eastern equivalent of Venice or Amsterdam, for its waterways and canals, which the Siamese call *klongs*, are almost as numerous as its streets. In the modern parts of the city, these canals are lined with trees and spanned by graceful bridges.

Fox Photos.

THE SHRINE OF THE EMERALD BUDDHA

Within this temple, high on the many-tiered altar, reposes the Emerald Buddha, the protecting deity of the Siamese capital. The figure of the god is carved from a single piece of jasper and is thought to have come from Ceylon many years ago, first to northern Siam and then to Bangkok, where it was brought by King Rama I.

East of Siam is Indo-China, which consists of the Viet-Nam Republic (Annam, Tonkin and Cochin-China), and the states of Cambodia and Laos. Until 1946 Indo-China, which is larger than France herself, ranked as part of the French colonial empire ; Cochin-China was a French colony and the other states were protectorates. All were overrun by Japan during the war, and when the French returned they found that the revolutionary movement known as Viet-Minh ("Association of the People "), which was led by Ho Chi Minh, had obtained control of much of the country. Although an agreement was made between the French and Ho Chi Minh, it was not long before his followers took up arms again.

War-torn Indo-China

The bitter struggle was still in progress in 1954, with France using half her regular army to preserve Viet-Nam ("People of the South "), Cambodia and Laos as associate states within the French Union and to keep Indo-China free from Communism.

The total population of Indo-China is estimated at over 27 millions, of which some 22 millions live in Viet-Nam. The most numerous are the Annamites, but the total also includes about 43,000 French and 600,000 other foreigners. In their appearance and their ways of life, the peoples of Indo-China are very like the Burmese and the Siamese.

Mysteries of the Past

In normal times, Indo-China is the fourth largest rice-producer of the world. Her two great rice areas—Tonkin in the north and Cambodia and Cochin-China in the south—seem on the map to be suspended from the " pole " of the Annamite mountains which range along the eastern coast. That is why this part of Asia is sometimes described as " a pole balanced by two rice baskets." The northern " basket " is made fertile by the Red river and exports its rice via the port of *Haiphong*, which also handles coal and other products of northern

E.N.A.

MYSTERIOUS ANGKOR VAT

Angkor Vat is the greatest of the age-old temples of Indo-China. Hidden for many years by the thick jungle, this twelfth-century moated temple stands as a monument to the Khmer people whose capital, Angkor Thom, must have been the finest city in Asia in its time. Little is known of the Khmers and no one has been able to explain why they should have deserted their great city.

OLD AND NEW IN BANGKOK

Fox Photos.

The most modern street in Bangkok is Rajadamneon Avenue which is flanked by shops, restaurants and office blocks, built of brick and concrete in the western style. Half-way down the avenue is this amazingly modernistic monument to democracy.

E.N.A.

In some places pleasant gardens fringe Bangkok's waterways, but for the most part they are bordered by houseboats and humble dwellings on piles. The waterways are busy and in places there are floating markets where merchant and customer sell and buy from boat to boat.

E.N.A.

GRACEFUL CAMBODIAN DANCERS

Dressed in rich costumes, these dancing girls perform a sacred ballet in one of Angkor Vat's ruined courtyards. No one who has seen Cambodian dancers perform can forget the sinuous grace of their movements. Notice the dancer on the right who wears the triple-headed mask of a Demon and carries in her right hand an emblem representing a thunderbolt.

Viet-Nam and which has one of the largest cement works in the Far East. The southern " basket " is irrigated by the Mekong river and exports its rice by way of *Saigon*.

Cotton, sugar, groundnuts, coffee, arrowroot and tobacco are produced. Maize, grown chiefly in Cambodia, is probably second only to rice in its importance.   Rubber, which is cultivated chiefly in Cambodia and southern Viet-Nam, is produced in such quantity that, in normal times, Indo-China ranks third on the list of the world's sources. Coal, zinc and iron ore are mined, the most important coal-mines being in northern Viet-Nam.

The largest city and port is *Saigon*, the " Paris of the Orient," which is now the capital of Viet-Nam.   Other important centres are *Hanoi*, the chief town of Tonkin and until recently the capital of Indo-China ; *Hué*, the chief port of Annam and her old imperial capital ; and *Phnom Penh*, the capital and river port of Cambodia.

Indo-China is a land of age-old temples many of which have only recently been cleared from the thick jungle which concealed them and made them mysteries.   Greatest of these temples is the moated twelfth-century Angkor Vat, a unique, vast and complete relic of the Khmer people whose capital was Angkor Thom, a great walled city that must have been the finest in Asia in its day.

A New Republic

Among the best seafarers and colonisers in the world are the Dutch. Their East India Company, founded in 1602, two years after our Queen Elizabeth I had established the British East India Company, brought under Dutch rule the Netherlands Indies.   These island territories in south-east Asia remained Dutch colonies until after the

UNUSUAL THATCHED HOUSES

Paul Popper.

This is a village of the Batak tribe in the forests of northern Sumatra. The high, thatched huts are built upon stilts and the only way to enter them is by ladder. Sumatra is one of the chief islands of Indonesia and is important for its tin mines and petroleum wells.

H. Armstrong Roberts.

Over half a million Moros inhabit southern Mindanao and the Sulu islands in the republic of the Philippines. The Spaniards called them Moros (" Moors ") because they were Mohammedans, but they are actually of Malayan origin. They are expert weavers and silversmiths, but the owner of this palm-thatched seaside home is probably a fisherman.

Second World War. Then, in 1949, they became the independent *Republic of Indonesia*. A Netherlands-Indonesian Union was formed to provide for future friendly co-operation between Holland and the new republic.

Indonesia consists of four large islands (Java, Sumatra, Borneo—except for Sarawak and North Borneo—and Celebes), about fifteen lesser islands and literally thousands of small islands. Said to number about 3,000 in all, these islands are fertile and volcanic ; their total population is estimated at about 80 millions and is made up of many different races—Achinese, Javanese, Madurese, Balinese, Dyaks and many others. About twenty-five main languages are spoken, but the official language of the Republic, which is understood everywhere, is *Bahasa Indonesia* (the Indonesian language). The capital of Indonesia, and chief sea- and air-port of the East Indies, is *Djakarta* (formerly known as Batavia), on the island of Java.

Notice that Indonesia does not include the Netherlands New Guinea (West Irian); the future of this territory has still to be decided.

Java is the richest and most thickly populated island in the Republic. Although there are many large agricultural estates on the island, most of the rich soil is owned and cultivated by Indonesian smallholders. Rubber, spices, tea, tobacco, rice, cassava, coffee, sugar and coco-nuts are among the many crops grown. Before the War, Java supplied nearly all the world's pepper, but the Japanese destroyed the pepper vines and less than a tenth of the normal supply has been produced in recent years. Similarly, the present yield of cinchona, from which quinine is made, is low, although in normal times more cinchona is cultivated in Java than in any other part of the world.

In the towns and villages of Java many of the old arts and crafts survive. Silversmiths beat and hammer out intricate designs, model makers and wood carvers fashion fans, and puppets for the shadow plays and small figures and statues. Best known of all are the batik makers. Using metal stamps, wax and vegetable dyes, they transform plain cotton material into beautifully coloured cloth alive with gay designs and ready to be made into scarves and sarongs. Indonesia also has its dancers ; wearing elaborate costumes and headdresses of scarlet, blue and gold, they perform to the music of the *gamelan*, an orchestra whose instruments are gongs, drums, cymbals and strange instruments—rather like xylophones—with keys made of brass.

Copyright.

WORKERS IN A COCHIN-CHINA RICEFIELD

Working in a line in the water-sodden field, they plant young rice shoots. Rice is as important to these people as wheat is to us. The crops of flooded paddy fields, such as the one seen in this picture, provide both food and drink.

CHURCH AND TEMPLE

Fox Photos.

The Philippines were ruled by Spain until 1899. In their city of Manila, the Spaniards built many fine churches, such as the one seen here.

Fox Photos.

This statue at Manila commemorates the founding of the city in 1571, by Legaspi, the conqueror of the Philippines. The group shows Legaspi and Urdaneta.

By courtesy of Christmas Humphreys, Esq.

Here we see one of the entrances to the Temple of the Dawn, Bangkok, along whose many gables run plaster serpents, their heads rearing upwards from the eaves.

By courtesy of Christmas Humphreys, Esq.

The building at the back contains statues of Siam's Chakkri kings. To the left is a corner of the Temple of the Emerald Buddha (Wat Phra Heo), Bangkok's chief temple.

The dancers of Java and Bali begin their training almost as soon as they can walk. They have to learn the difficult, angular postures of the dances and the many graceful movements of arms, legs and hands which are made in rhythm with the music of the gamelan. By the time they are ten years of age, the young performers will be accomplished professionals wearing rich brocade cloth, gold ornaments and high headdresses. Some of their dances tell stories from Indian epics; some, like the popular *legong* of Bali, are stories from legend-history and are enacted by the dancers while a narrator chants the words.

A Wonderful Shrine

Java possesses one of the most wonderful ancient Buddhist shrines in south-east Asia, an amazing pyramid of stone dating from the ninth century and one of the world's architectural marvels. This huge, fantastically-carved structure is called Boroboedoer and it stands on a low hill on the Kedu plateau north-west of Djokjakarta, the old capital of the sultans and the former headquarters of the Indonesian independence movement.

The shrine rises in carved terraces to a height of about 150 feet and is crowned by a dagoba, or dome, 52 feet in diameter, in which some sacred relic was enshrined. Two miles of sculptures and panels in relief portray episodes from the life of Buddha and other sacred subjects. On the upper terraces are countless small dagobas, each containing a statue of the seated Buddha. It is said that anyone touching the upraised palm of the Buddha will have his dearest wish granted him. Crowning the great structure is the largest dagoba. When the Dutch began excavation and restoring the shrine some hundred and fifty years ago, they found the chambers of this great dagoba empty. None can say with certainty what this innermost shrine contained. But the whole vast edifice is thought to have been built as a resting-place for the ashes of some great Buddhist saint, perhaps for those of Gautama Buddha himself.

Oil and Tin

Sumatra is a large island with a backbone of rugged mountains and thickly-forested plains, but although it is about

Fox Photos.

MANILA, CAPITAL OF THE PHILIPPINES

Here we are looking across the waters of the Pasig River at Manila, capital of the republic of the Philippines, towards Jones Bridge which spans the river where once the historic Bridge of Spain stood. The building on the right is the Bureau of Posts and the Public Works department.

Photo : Ella K. Maillart.

A DESERT CARAVAN STARTING AT DAWN

In this picture is shown the start at dawn of a long-distance desert caravan ; notice the long morning shadows on the eternal sands, the blue of the sky and the purple hills shrouded in the mists of sunrise. Some years ago the English writer, Peter Fleming, and the Swiss traveller, Ella K. Maillart, set out together to win their way westward from Peking to the borders of Russian Turkestan, along a route much the same as that covered by Sir Francis Younghusband nearly fifty years before. Mme. Maillart secured a large collection of photographs during the journey and one of these is reproduced above.

H. Armstrong Roberts.

THE GRAND CANYON OF ARIZONA

If you ever visit the United States of America and go to the Grand Canyon National Park in Arizona, you will be able to see views such as this. The Grand Canyon is one of the great natural wonders of the world. It is a fantastic trough more than a mile deep, hundreds of miles in length, and between ten and twenty miles wide. Winding its way along the bottom of the trough is the Colorado River, which with its tributaries has slowly eaten away the rock of the dry plateau to form this amazing canyon.

E.N.A.

TERRACED HILLSIDES IN THE PHILIPPINES

Terraced hillsides like these are common enough in northern Luzon, for example, where for hundreds of years the mountain people have worked to build and irrigate their rice fields on the steep slopes. The vegetation is a vivid green; the terraces themselves are covered by muddy coloured water from which arise the quickly-growing rice shoots.

three and a half times the size of Java, it has less than six million inhabitants. Java, including Madura, is a crowded island, the home of nearly forty million Indonesians.

If you went to Palembang, on the Mœsi river in Sumatra, you would almost certainly find oil tankers anchored in the river estuary waiting to take on cargoes from the refineries near the town. The oilfields in Java, Kalimantan (Borneo) and Sumatra make Indonesia the chief producer of this liquid black gold in the Far East. Sumatra also has tin mines, and this same mineral is worked on the islands of Bangka and Billiton, between Sumatra and Borneo. Bauxite and coal are among the other minerals produced in Indonesia.

Many Islands of the Philippines

To the north-east of Borneo lie the seven thousand islands of the Republic of the Philippines, which was given its independence by America on July 4th, 1946. Largest of the islands are Luzon, on which *Manila* the capital stands, and Mindanao. A new capital, to be called Quezon City, is being built to the north-east of Manila.

Manila is also the chief port of the Republic from which come Manila hemp or Abaca, copra, sugar, tobacco from such centres as the Cagayan Valley, rubber and maize. The mountainous parts of the Philippines are thickly forested and contain great mineral wealth. Gold is mined in the Benguet region of Luzon, and the Philippines yield more gold than the famous fields of Alaska. Mindanao is relatively unexplored and has resources which as yet are largely undeveloped. The iron mines of the Surigao peninsula are some of the largest known deposits of iron ore in Asia.

The Filipinos are Malayan in origin, but as a result of the long period of foreign rule, first by Spain and then by America, they differ greatly from other East Asiatic peoples. Of the 19¼ millions of people in the Republic, nearly 90 per cent. are Christians. Mindanao, however, is the home of the Moros, who are Mohammedans, and in the mountainous regions of central Luzon there are primitive pagan peoples.

Strange Animal Life

Several unusual creatures live in the Philippines. There is the tarsier, a strange bulging-eyed creature smaller than a squirrel. Its body is no more than five inches from the tip of the nose to the base of the tail and is covered by greyish-brown fur. The tail is ten inches long and its base is stiff so that the tarsier can prop itself up on the branch of a tree by this means. Another unusual creature is the flying lemur, which uses its membranes as wings and can so glide from tree to tree.

Paul Popper.

A BALINESE ORCHESTRA

The dancers of the island of Bali are famous. Music for their graceful movements is provided by a *gamelan*, or Balinese orchestra. As the picture shows, the instruments are all of the percussion variety. There are drums, gongs, and richly decorated " xylophones ". The keys of the latter are made of brass and the notes are obtained by striking them with hammers.

The Story of
the World
and its Peoples

Lands and Places
of the
River Irrawaddy

Topical Press.

IN A RANGOON MARKET-PLACE

Burma is only about four times the size of England and Wales, but some 128 different tongues
are spoken in the country which is now independent of the Commonwealth. Here we see part
of a Rangoon market where men and women alike wear cotton skirts called *lungyi*.

BURMA, THE LAND OF PAGODAS

BURMA, which some say is the *Chryse Regio* of Claudius Ptolemy the famous geographer of the second century A.D. and which long ago was ruled by kings descended from the Buddhist rulers of India, was once the most extensive Province of British India. In 1937, Burma was divorced from India and ruled by its own elected government under a British Governor. Since then, as a result of the Anglo-Burmese Treaty of October, 1947, Burma has achieved complete independence and now is the Republic of the Union of Burma. Burma is no longer a part of the British Common-

wealth, although she receives help from Britain in the organisation and training of her armed forces.

Burma's Lands

Burma's most wonderful natural feature is the river Irrawaddy which runs from north to south almost throughout the whole length of the country—a water highway for 1,000 miles that has served the Burmese since the beginning of their history and is still, with its regular service of river steamers, a very important and cheap means of getting about in Burma.

Because Burma is divided by densely

forested mountain ranges running from north to south, it is not easy to travel from east to west or vice versa. During the war the famous *Burma Road* from Lashio in Burma to Kunming in China was of vital importance. Another road, the *Ledo*, or *Stillwell*, *Road*, was built by American soldiers through the jungles and mountains of the north-west, providing a link between the upper Irrawaddy and India.

Despite these new routes, most travel in Burma is between north and south and uses the main railway (Rangoon–Mandalay–Myitkyina) or the Irrawaddy, which can be navigated for 900 miles up to Bhamo. The Chindwin, a tributary of the Irrawaddy, can also be navigated for nearly 400 miles of its course.

The great parallel ranges of high mountains, thickly covered with forests, shut in the deep valleys of the Irrawaddy, the Salween, its smaller sister-river, and their tributaries. The forests, which are still the haunts of the tiger, the leopard and the wild elephant, come down to the rivers in thick jungles or deep elephant grass, or marshes, except where Burmese farmers have made their paddy fields around their little villages of brown houses on stilts. Towards the south and in the wider valleys the country is more open and the people more in touch with European people and European ideas, which enter Burma, as we do, by way of the great port of *Rangoon*, which is the Burmese capital.

Topical Press.

A SAMPAN ROWER OF BURMA

The dusky toiler seen above is characteristic of the great River Irrawaddy, which runs from north to south almost throughout the whole length of Burma, forming a water highway a thousand miles in length. Sampans are the native boats, often elaborately carved, and this rower handles his oars in a manner that seems very strange to western eyes.

Rangoon is Burmese enough, but its European quarter, its up-to-date rice-mills and saw-mills and factories, and a hundred and one other things made it a "city of the world," like other great sea-gates of the Far East. In a single street, for instance, we could see a Christian church, a Jewish synagogue, a Hindu temple, and a Chinese joss-house, as well as the inevitable Buddhist pagoda : for Buddhism is the chief religion.

The Water-front

Along the Rangoon water - front we meet people of all the trading nations under the sun from farthest East to farthest West; and in Rangoon itself we are likely to come across representatives of all Burma's peoples, except, perhaps, the wildest and most remote of the tribes, who never leave the depths of the great forests and jungles of the far north.

For although Burma is only about four times the size of England and Wales, with an estimated population of just under 18¾ millions, there are 128 different languages spoken in the country —and this is not counting those of the foreigners living in the land. (Remember that *we* are foreigners, too, when we go to Burma!)

Burma's Peoples

The *Burmese*, whose cheery, happy-go-lucky ways and whose habit of speaking with tremendous politeness about quite ordinary things has caused travellers to nickname them "The

Will F. Taylor.

LOADING THE RICE BOATS

Rice provides more foodstuff for the support of human beings the world over than any other crop grown. In eastern lands especially is it a staple crop, and Burma is no exception. This picture shows rice being loaded at Rangoon, one of the great sea-gates of the Far East.

Irish of the East," make up at least three-quarters of the population. They are dwellers in the valleys and plains along the rivers, villagers, and growers of rice and fruits, living easily in that fertile land where the hot sun and the heavy summer rains between May and October ensure good crops without much labour.

The Hill people have a much harder life, for they must clear forest or jungle away if they want to grow crops, and fight it all the time to prevent it overgrowing their little fields again. Elephants may come when there are no bamboo shoots for them in the jungle, and trample down more than they eat. And there is always the danger of the tiger, the leopard and other wild beasts.

A BURMESE TOMB

The last resting-place of a Burmese is marked by an ornate tombstone such as the one seen here. The number of tiers in the roof indicates the rank of the deceased.

as inferiors because of their belief in evil spirits which must be kept happy and well fed by strange offerings in lonely places. The Karen lives in a poor land, where farming is hard, and where he must use his *dah* (heavy knife) to clear away the cane and bamboo growths, and to make the simple farming tools he uses.

Along the North-eastern Frontier live the wild *Was* in a region about which little is known. The Wa resents the intrusion of strangers, and waylays them when he finds opportunity. In some parts the Wa is a head-hunter, and sets up skulls on poles at the entrance to his village, so that the ghosts of the former owners of the skulls may keep others out!

Other Peoples in Burma

But besides these different peoples— that is to say, the Burmans, the Karens, the Shans, the Chins and the

The *Shans* are the best known of the hill-folk. There was a time when there were Shan kings in Burma; but nowa- days the Shans are the labourers of the hill country, and the raftsmen who bring down to Rangoon the mighty rafts of teak from the forests up- country during the time of the rains. Many are tattooed from waist to knee. They wear few clothes when working, but all have wide hats of cane or straw to protect their heads from the hot sun.

Among the mountains of the middle and north live the *Chins* and the *Kachins*. The Kachins, or Jingpaws, as they call themselves, live in villages on the hillsides, and are not Buddhists, but worship the spirits of Nature.

The *Karens* are quite different from all other Burmese people. They are as solemn and dour, timid and silent as the Burmese are jolly, outspoken and high-spirited. In past times Karens were constantly raided and persecuted by the Burmese, who looked on them

Photos: E. H. Davey.

A STONE ELEPHANT

This white elephant in stone performs the same task as the Chin-thé. He mounts guard at a Burmese monastery to ward off evil spirits, but to western eyes he seems more friendly than ferocious.

Kachins, and the wild Was—there are other races living in Burma. Of these other races, Indians are the most numerous; in fact, there are nearly a million of them; and besides Europeans and Anglo-Indians, there are Indo-Burmans and Chinese, and others less important as well.

Burma, we see, has peoples in every stage of civilisation, from primitive savage head-hunters and folks who are still in the Stone Age, to highly-educated Burmese, some of whom have attended British universities and are doing much to introduce European systems of education among their countrymen.

As we steam up the Rangoon River, past the tall-pointed pagoda on a hill to starboard, we pass ships of all the seafaring nations of the world, it seems. When we come to the Rangoon water-front we can see the gilded spire of the splendid Shwe Dagon pagoda, the wonder of Burma, and a sacred

Photos: E. H. Davey.

A DAGOBA

This is a typical Burmese pagoda, a Dagoba or Stupa as it is called. Beneath such monuments there is often a reputed relic of Gautama Buddha.

A TEMPLE GUARDIAN

Pagodas and monasteries in Burma often have such stone guardians as the Chin-thé shown here. They are believed to frighten away evil spirits from the precincts of the holy place.

place to all Buddhists, for within its shrine are eight hairs from the head of Gautama Buddha himself.

Rangoon was only a village sixty or seventy years ago: but by 1939 it had become a great modern city-port, with its wharves fronting the Strand for several miles along the river. Teak yards, rice-mills and oil refineries showed plainly whence came the wealth to which Rangoon owed its growth and prosperity; for teak, rice and petroleum, with tin and rubies, are the chief products of this country which has now ceased to be part of the British Commonwealth. Downstream come the great teak rafts, the laden rice boats, and the little steamers with all kinds of produce to the port.

Teak Yards at Rangoon

Teak yards are among the sights of Rangoon, for there we can see the wise elephants hauling the great logs across the black squelchy mud to pile them up in neat heaps in the yard. The male elephant is strong and picks up a great log between trunk and tusks and carries it to its place; the female drags or pushes, but rarely lifts. The elephants feed on the tall grasses cut from the riverside upstream. We are a little sorry in some ways to see in up-to-date teak yards modern hauling and lifting machinery that may in due time do away with the help of elephants altogether.

Cutting Teak

The teak is cut in the hot, wet forests, and got out in the rainy season. European supervisors have a most unpleasant time of it up there in the wet weather, what with the water and the rain, the mud and the leeches, the fevers and the hordes of stinging and biting insects. Only the elephant with his strength and intelligence can move the huge logs out of the forest to the nearest water course. Teak trees grow among large numbers of other and less valuable trees, and never in a forest by themselves. Before they are cut they are ring-barked, so that they dry where they stand. Teak is heavy, hard, close-grained wood that stands all weather, resists the ravages of insect pests, and defies the boring of marine worms. Hence its wide use in tropical lands and by the builders of ships.

Let us look at the Shwe Dagon, which sits on its hill like a great bell, on the other side of the Royal Lakes. Two thousand years ago there was only a simple village shrine on this hill; it was not until the sixteenth century that the great and glorious pagoda was erected. Its dome is heavily gilded with the gold leaf brought by pious Buddhists as an " act of merit." It is topped, like most other temples, with a metal umbrella-like *hti*. Around the base of the pagoda are many other shrines, outside which is a kind of paved courtyard shut in by halls and canopies, screens and arches, altars and shrines, and adorned with many images of Buddha.

The Burmese seem much shorter than the people of India—some, especially the women, almost doll-like in their coloured silks. Both men and women wear the *lungyi*—a sort of skirt skilfully folded about the waist without the use of buttons or pins; and the *eingyi*, a short jacket, generally white. Men wear bright silk scarves in turban fashion; women wear them thrown over the shoulders. Both men and women wear their black hair long —men gathering it into a top-knot, women coiling it on the crown of the head and ornamenting it with a flower placed jauntily over one ear.

A Burmese village is a collection of little brown houses; to avoid the damp, and crawling things, they are perched on stilts. The space below each house is used for numbers of purposes: as a store, as a fowl-house, or perhaps as a rubbish heap. Even to-day many villages are still protected by a stout fence or palisade, and are entered by a gateway which is carefully shut by the watchman every night. Around are the paddy fields in which ugly water-buffaloes work all day in the ploughing time—and dangerous animals they are to white folk, although they answer to the lightest word of the village boys.

Mandalay and Bhamo

A village home has little furniture: a mat and a bamboo pillow for each person, a few food vessels of earthenware or lacquer work, one or two tables 6 inches high, round which the people squat for their meals and their tea, some water-pots—and, of course, the family betel-box, for everyone chews betel just as he smokes cheroots. In the top partitions of the betel-box are the lime paste and the spices; in the second are tobacco leaves and areca (or betel) nuts, and in the bottom are the fresh green betel leaves. Betel-chewing stains the mouth crimson.

BURMA'S "LORD OF HEAVEN"

Will F. Taylor.

Burma has many bell-shaped pagodas, each containing its image of Buddha. Here is one such image, of giant proportions, before which offerings of hair, candles and flags have been placed. Compare the size of the figure with that of the Burmese standing at its base. Buddhism, the religion originating in Gautama Buddha—who was born about 560 B.C.—is widespread in the countries of the Far East where each of its different forms has its own sacred writings.

Far up the Irrawaddy is the old city of *Mandalay*, where we go to see the 450 white pagodas grouped in a square around the large gilded one in the centre; the palaces of the old kings and queens of Upper Burma; the Arakan Temple with its giant brass figure of the Buddha; and the moated Dufferin Fort—with its great square red walls, pierced on each side of the square by three gates—named after Lord Dufferin, who was the Viceroy of India when, in the middle of the nineteenth century, armed forces had to set Upper Burma in order and put down the tyrant King Theebaw.

Farther still up-stream is *Bhamo*, at the head of the Irrawaddy navigation, only twenty miles from China: in Bhamo's streets we can see Kachins from the hills, as well as Chinese from across the border.

Although the Burmese are mostly farmers, with rice as their main crop, the country has important mineral resources. Oil is produced at Chauk, Yenang-yaung and other centres. From the Tavoy region in the south, and from the highlands of the Salween comes tin. The silver ore from Bawdwin is smelted at Namtu. Mogok is noted for its ruby mines.

The only large towns in Burma are Rangoon, the capital, and Mandalay. Rangoon has a population of over half a million ; Mandalay, some 163,000. The port of Moulmein, at the mouth of the Salween river, comes third, with a population of over 71,000. Apart from these centres, only Bassein and Akyab contain more than 40,000 people.

Topical Press.

A SACRED BUILDING IN BURMA

This picture gives you an excellent idea of what a Burmese temple is like. It is the Shweh-mawdaw, a sacred building of Pegu, and is said to contain two hairs of the Buddha. Most Burmese temples, like this one, are topped with a metal, umbrella-like *hti*. From the *hti* hang the temple bells which, when swayed by the breeze, give forth a musical, tinkling sound.

The Story
of the
World and
its Peoples

In the
Ancient Empires
of the
Far East

Will F. Taylor.

THE GREAT WALL OF CHINA

Begun in 214 B.C. by the Emperor Shih Hwang-ti and designed to protect China from the Mongols, the Great Wall of China is 1500 miles long, averages 20 feet in breadth, and has over 20,000 towers and 10,000 watch-towers. It is said that one out of every three able-bodied men in China was pressed into service to complete this gigantic building feat.

CHINA

TO begin the story of the four hundred and seventy-four millions of people who to-day are members of the great Chinese Republic we must travel back to times before the dawn of written history, through legend to the twilight period of the Stone Age when the dwellers of the Hwang Ho, or Yellow River, valley were founding their own culture and civilisation.

Relics found in Honan province and elsewhere actually date from before this dim age; when Babylon was the centre of a mighty Empire and Stonehenge was yet new, the Chinese made pottery and bronzes and cultivated silk. Beginning as an inland people, they absorbed the more backward tribes by which they were surrounded,

reached the coastline of the Yellow Sea and expanded north and south.

Chinese legend-history goes back to Pan Ku, who is said to have been the first Chinese, and to Huang Ti, the Yellow Emperor, who is supposed to have ruled as long ago as 2698 B.C. But it is not until about twelve hundred years later, at a time when Greek literature and philosophy were at their greatest, that Chinese history really begins and we can speak with certainty of the feudal times of the Chou dynasty and of the great writers and philosophers of this great classical age such as Laotzu, Confucius, and Mencius.

The Chinese may well be proud of so ancient a heritage of learning and culture. For when Rome and Carthage were still young, the learning of China was gathered in State Libraries; from China has come one of the oldest books in the world, the *Sun Tzü Ping Fa*, a military textbook written in the sixth or fifth century B.C., which has survived, not only centuries of history, but the savage edict of the first Ch'in emperor who conquered the feudal princes and who, from sheer vanity, ordered all the books and records of past ages to be destroyed so that no man might challenge his claim to be the " First Sovereign Emperor." Tyrants have always feared learning and knowledge, and the harsh rule of Shih Hwang-ti and of his successors reminds us of the equally ruthless despotism of more modern dictators.

The Chinese Empire

The united empire took its name *China* from the dynasty which had brought about its union, the cost of which in learning and culture was redeemed by the later Han dynasty. The rule of the Han emperors was a Golden Age. Books that had been kept in hiding were now brought out and subjected to scholarly editing, poetry flourished, and art in all its forms was encouraged. These were times of historians and essayists, and of compilers of the early dictionaries. The lustre of the age has persisted to modern times, for even now Chinese like to think of themselves as " Sons of Han."

After the Hans, China was divided into three kingdoms for a time. Then came the short Sui dynasty from whose times survives the Yunho, or Grand Canal, which is over 1,200 miles long, reaches from Peking to Hangchow, and is the oldest and largest canal in existence.

Will F. Taylor.

THE TOWER ON TIGER HILL

China is known as a country of pagodas, and here is a picture of the famous Tiger Hill Pagoda at Soochow, about 50 miles from Shanghai. Pagodas are merely towers, and most of those built in China are eight-sided, possessing many storeys. There is a pagoda at Kew Gardens, near London.

CHINESE STREET VENDORS

They are hardly our idea of children's whistles, but that is what they are. This picture of the whistles and their rather serious-looking seller was taken in Peking.

What is the question these young Chinese seem to be asking as they watch the maker of paper cut-outs cleverly fashion some intricate design?

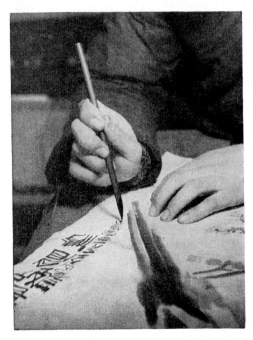

Photos: Hedda M. Morrison.

Many beautiful pictures have come from Chinese paint brushes, some in the old traditional style, others in the fashion of modern art.

Masks and ornate robes play an important part in the classical Chinese theatre as is shown by this picture of an actor representing a monkey.

Hedda M. Morrison.

ON THE BANKS OF THE GRAND CANAL

The Grand Canal is the largest and oldest in existence. Begun in 540 B.C., and built in sections, it is over 1200 miles long. The picture shows a cotton-seller on the banks of the Canal at Tsining in the province of Shantung.

No less renowned is the T'ang dynasty (618–907 A.D.) which was a period of brilliant cultural activity whence came some of the finest of Chinese poetry, painting, and sculpture. Under the rule of the T'angs, China saw the beginnings of its "Civil Service" which recruited by examination administrators for the Imperial domains. Under the T'angs, also, China had its

Hedda M. Morrison.

A SACRED MOUNTAIN LANDSCAPE

Hwashan, in Shensi Province, is one of the five sacred mountains in China. In early times, the Emperor would journey up these mountains to offer sacrifices to Heaven and Earth. The picture shows two priests gazing out over Hwashan's rugged grandeur.

first printed book (868 A.D.), the *Peking Gazette*, the first newspaper (712 A.D.), and began using bank notes.

The richness of Chinese culture and the beauties of Chinese civilisation were bound to be an irresistible lure to more warlike and barbarian peoples beyond the borders. Shih Hwang-ti, "First Sovereign Emperor," had been warned in a dream that disaster would fall upon

China from the north, and in 214 B.C. he began "The Long Rampart," a wall "one-twentieth of the circumference of the earth" which would protect China from the menace of the barbarians. It is said that nearly a third of China's male population was put to work upon the Great Wall which still stands as one of the wonders of the world. It runs from Shan-hai-kuan on the Gulf of Liau-tung to the Kiayu Pass on the threshold of the Tibetan mountains. It is 1,500 miles long and averages 20 feet in breadth. It has over 20,000 towers and 10,000 watch-towers.

The Mongol Invasion

But the Great Wall was not the impregnable barrier that Shih Hwang-ti intended. Long after his death, Genghis Khan led his Mongols into

Hedda M. Morrison.

A PILGRIM'S OFFERING

This painted wooden statue of Kuan Yin, the Goddess of Mercy, riding a horse can be seen in one of the temples of the sacred mountain of Hwashan, Shensi Province.

Hedda M. Morrison.

A TAOIST PRIEST

Tao means a road, way or method, and the Taoist beliefs which this thoughtful-looking priest holds date back to the sixth century B.C., when Lao Tzu is supposed to have laid the foundations of Taoism. Taoism, Confucianism, and Buddhism are the three most widespread religions in China.

China, making himself master of the empire and extending his conquest to Korea, Indo-China, and Burma. For nearly a century the Mongols ruled, at length to be driven out by a national uprising that was not to be equalled until the overthrow of the last Manchu Emperor in 1911. Under the new Ming dynasty, China recovered its old glories. Art and literature gained fresh life, porcelain became a national industry, and Peking, the Imperial capital which had so astounded Marco Polo, rose as cultural focus of the Empire.

But the grandeur of the dynasty declined. Under the last Ming Emperor, China was not only crippled by the cost of war, but ravaged by a terrible famine. Revolution spread across the land, and as anarchy loomed ahead the Manchus drove through the Great Wall to found a dynasty that was to last until 1911.

The modern Chinese Republic owes .

Hedda M. Morrison.

SPINNING COTTON YARN

Nearly all Chinese peasant farmers add to their small income by such pursuits as cotton spinning, rearing silkworms, and milling flour. But China does not rely upon such primitive methods as those shown above for her cotton. At such centres as Tientsin, she has thoroughly modern and well-equipped cotton mills.

its existence to the courage and fore-sight of one man whose concern for the welfare of his country turned him from medicine to the perilous life of a revolu-tionary national leader. He was Dr. Sun Yat-Sen—Dr. Sun, as we should call him: for in China the positions of surname and first name are reversed.

More clearly than anyone, Dr. Sun saw the ruin and chaos which crumbling Imperial rule had brought to China. His movement forced the abdication of the last Manchu emperor in 1911 and his party, the Kuomintang (People's Party) strove to unite the land and bring it the benefits of Western progress instead of the humiliation which hitherto had been the West's sole contribution to Chinese affairs.

The Chinese Nationalists were faced with a difficult task. After the fall of the Empire, China was torn apart by brutal military warlords, each of whom tried to carve out a dominion for himself. The Nationalists, too, were opposed by Chinese Communists, who wished to organise their country after the Russian pattern. Even more terrible was the shadow of Japan which later fell across the unhappy country. Japan had already profited by China's agonies to seize Manchuria and, in 1937, staged an "incident" which brought Chiang Kai-shek, Dr. Sun's successor in leadership of the Kuomintang, into a total war with the Japanese.

We remember only too well how that war became a part of the world conflagration of 1939 in which nearly all nations were involved, and how Chinese courage and heroism—which had already sustained her single-handed against a much more powerful foe—became a valuable weapon in the Allied arsenal. Freed from the menace of Japan, China was still ravaged by civil war. By January, 1949, the struggle had gone completely in favour of the Communists under their leader Mao Tse-tung. On January 21st, Chiang

Hedda M. Morrison.

CARPET WORKERS AT PEKING

This picture shows workers carpet trimming in a Peking factory. Carpets like the one shown in the picture are largely made from wool brought from the Gobi desert flocks and herds.

Hedda M. Morrison.

THE SPRINGTIME PATTERN OF CHINA'S FIELDS

Taken in the country west of Peking, this picture shows a typical northern landscape in spring when the green of growing things brings new colour to the fertile soil. Notice how the thrifty farmers have used every available patch of land.

Kai-shek gave up the Presidency of China. Later, he and the Nationalist government retired to Formosa (Taiwan), and in 1950 he assumed the title of President of the "National Republic of China."

The long struggle was virtually over and Mao Tse-tung established a Communist government in China, a change which raised many difficult problems for the United Nations Organisation.

Whatever the ultimate outcome may be, the world can but hope that China will at last find peace in which native culture and tradition may combine with the ways and machinery of the modern world to bring plenty and happiness to China's suffering millions.

The Build of China

China is by far the largest political division of the Asiatic continent. The main region of China, which has been called China Proper, is the historic land bounded by the high Tibetan plateau on the west and the Great Wall on the north-west and north. Around this core are the border provinces of Outer China.

China has lofty mountains like the Szechwanese cordillera whose peaks rise to over 25,000 feet, and some of her mountains are regarded as sacred and are focal points for pilgrims. Three major mountain systems divide the vast country into the sharply individual zones of North, Central and Southern China. Of these systems the greatest is the Tsinling Shan which runs into the very heart of China and forms, with lesser ranges, the Central Mountain Belt.

North and South are very different, not merely because of the mountain barrier but through fundamental differences in climate. The North has sharper, colder and longer winters, and has less rain than the more sheltered South. This has made the North a wheat and kaoliang (millet) region, and the South the rice region: and it has

Hedda M. Morrison.

ARTIST CRAFTSMEN AT WORK

The Chinese have a long tradition in the manufacture and creation of beautiful things and works of art. This picture shows cloisonné workers at their craft. Their designs are outlined by small strips of metal, and between these they put an enamel paste.

produced in the North a hardier, more conservative people to whom the icy winter spells bring unemployment unless they can turn themselves to village industries such as leatherwork and weaving.

The South is a much more diverse region consisting of the South-east with its sub-tropical coastal areas, its sparsely populated hill forests, and a life that centres on the seaport of Canton: and the tableland of the South-west, with its fertile plateaux at an average height of 6,000 feet above sea-level, its mountains that are the home grounds of primitive tribes, and its dangerous jungles.

On the map the great expanse of China suggests ample room for its enormous population. But much of the country is so high and so dry that many people cannot live there. There are also broad expanses of desert— the Gobi, which occupies the greater part of Mongolia: and farther to the south-west, the Takla-Makan in the Chinese province of Sinkiang. To the south are the towering peaks and high valleys of Tibet, whose priestly ruler, the Dalai Lama, rules over more than 3,500,000 people from his Potala, an incredible winter palace at Lhasa which is fifteen storeys high even though it was built over three hundred years ago. China has always regarded Tibet as Chinese territory, even when she was prepared to admit that the Dalai Lama did,

Pictorial Press.

A TIBETAN HOUSEWIFE IN HER KITCHEN

This Tibetan housewife smiles cheerfully as she prepares a meal. It will probably include tea mixed with rancid yak butter and salt, and *tsamba* (doughnuts made from ground barley and dipped in unsweetened tea). Although meat and vegetables are sometimes eaten, tea and *tsamba* are the chief food of many Tibetans.

in fact, enjoy independence. Tibet was called " a special territory." After Mao Tse-tung had established a Communist " People's Government " in China, his armies invaded Tibet and in 1951 an agreement was signed in Peking which, while it allowed Tibet to manage her own internal affairs, gave to China the control of her foreign affairs and defence. Later, the Dalai Lama and Panchen Lama were made members of the Consultative Conference of the Chinese People's Republic, an event which stressed that Tibet was now definitely a part of China.

Bordering Tibet is the Chinese province of Sikang, whose high mountains, on the edge of Szechwan province, are the home of the famous giant panda.

These fringes of China contain not one, but many races, as we might expect of frontier regions. In the north, in Mongolia, thin pasture-lands provide a hard life for nomad herdsmen with their flocks of sheep and horses. In Sinkiang, where the wooded slopes of the Ili river valley are welcome relief to the glaring barrenness of the great desert, Chinese interests embrace shepherd Kirghiz tribes; Tartar herdsmen roamers who pitch their tent-like *yurta* where fancy pleases them: and other tribes and people. In Tibet, " the roof of the world," yaks graze in the windswept valleys and the Tibetans astound the rare European visitor by their capacity for drinking tea or regale him with dances by fearsomely-masked performers whose gyrations are accompanied by a primitive " orchestra " and the raucous booming bass notes of the long prayer trumpets.

But China Proper—the home of most Chinese—is far away to the east where rich plains and valleys, busy ports and cities, provide a life that is hard and uncertain because eastern China is so overpopulated. The soil is fertile, the crops are plentiful and fast growing thanks to the summer rains, but only by incessant toil can the Chinese keep themselves alive. They are perhaps the hardest-working people in the world who, often in the midst of terrible poverty, exist for the soil and by the soil; and when the soil fails them, as it does sometimes, and the crops are poor, famine and disease stalk the land bringing slow death to countless millions at a time. Life for most Chinese is a grim and endless struggle against odds that to a weaker and less courageous people would seem insuperable.

E.N.A.

A TIBETAN FARMER AND HIS YAKS

The yak serves the Tibetan farmer in many ways. It provides butter, milk and meat. Its hide can be made into ropes and tents. In this picture we see two yaks pulling a crude wooden plough. The valley that they are helping to cultivate is some 13,000 feet above sea level.

IN "FORBIDDEN" TIBET

At Lhasa, the capital of Tibet, is the Potala, the palace-monastery of the Dalai Lama. The walls are white, except for those of the personal apartments of the Dalai Lama, which are a maroon colour (centre of building). On the roof are the tombs of previous Dalai Lamas.

Photos: Paul Popper.

Journeying along this road is the baggage train of an important Tibetan official, which by custom precedes its master when he travels. Stones line the roadway through the village. Near shrines and religious landmarks they will be elaborately decorated as offerings to the gods.

Eighty out of every hundred Chinese get their living from the land: and nearly all these peasant farmers supplement their tiny incomes by such pursuits as cotton spinning, rearing silkworms, and milling flour. In Chinese town and country, the *Chia* (family) is the most important unit whose elders are respected as the wisest and most experienced. The life of the Chinese peasant is the life of his *Chia* whose property he shares and for whose well-being he works.

Peasant Life

What sort of home does the Chinese peasant farmer have? Probably a house built of mud or clay and roofed with *kaoliang* (millet) stalks, or perhaps one made entirely from bamboo. In the colder north we should also find houses of stone and wood with tiled roofs, each with its long hollow brick bed, called a *kang*, which is centrally heated from a wood or charcoal fire and is a bed for the whole family during winter. The houses of the very poor will have no opening other than the doorway, for windows are very expensive.

In good times, our peasant farmer will eat three meals a day. His food and the way it is cooked will depend on the customs of the district where he lives, but his diet includes rice, vegetables, and fish. If he lives in the wheat-growing north, wheat flour noodles and pancakes will take the place of rice. If he is poorer than most, he will avoid such luxuries as meat and fish, and will live on vegetables and salted pickles.

Work in the fields is indescribably hard. The lucky few may have animals to pull and carry for them—sturdy ponies in the north, and water buffaloes in the south. But many will have to do all the work on the land themselves —and that means not only the men, but the women and children as well.

Will F. Taylor.

FORTRESS AND TRADING CENTRE

For centuries Tibet was a hidden land secluded from the world in the mountain fastnesses between India and China. This picture shows the ancient fortress town of Gyangtse which is also a trading centre. The town nestles at the foot of a rugged rock formation which is topped by the Gyangtse Jong, the old fortress.

WORK IN THE RICE FIELDS

This peasant farmer uses a water buffalo to pull his wooden plough. When the flooded land has been prepared in this way, the young rice shoots will be transplanted from the nursery plot, everyone in the family helping with this work.

Photos: L.E.A.

Rice planted in June is ready for harvesting in late October. Once again every member of the family helps. The rice is cut with a long sickle, then taken in bundles to the house, where it is threshed. The stalks are collected and sold for fuel.

Farm animals are few because they need fodder and there is hardly enough land to provide crops for the people themselves, let alone for any animals useful as they would be. Land is precious in China where every small patch must be made to yield something that will eventually fill hungry mouths. Even the fishponds are made to yield more than fish; from them come the water lily roots and watersnails that add tasty interest to Chinese meals.

In the Plain of Northern China, through which runs the great Yellow River (" the Sorrow of the Sons of Han," as it has been called through its disastrous floods), wheat is the main crop and food. The North has not so much rain as the South, and there is a dry season during which the crops must be safeguarded by irrigation. Irrigation is vital here because the soil is a dusty *loess* that would be useless to the farmer without plentiful water.

Rice-growing

But China is known as a land of rice, and this crop comes from Central and Southern China, from such provinces as " rice-bowl " Hunan, and from the river valleys of the Yangtze and the Si-kiang where cotton, tea, and silk are equally important products.

Go to the rice-fields in early July and you will see Chinese families planting the young rice-shoots which have been reared during the past month in nursery land patches. The shoots are planted in rows, six or seven shoots together. The peasants work in long lines at each row, singing as they plant because singing makes the work easier and the time pass more quickly. Rain, irrigation, manure and the hot July sun

Copyright.

RESTING FROM THEIR STUDIES

The Chinese have long been famous for their learning and though civil war has convulsed the country a great many universities and technical colleges have carried on training the China of the future. This picture shows a genial Professor of Law entertaining some of his students.

SCENES IN NANKING

This gaily-decorated gateway spans the road leading to the building that housed the National Assembly in the days when Nanking was the capital of Nationalist China. Nanking has some of the most modern buildings in China, but old habits and customs—including the ricksha—still persist.

Photos: Copyright.

These students seem happy and cheerful enough as they leave the domed Lecture Hall of the university at Nanking. Chinese universities were reorganised in 1952 and now teach in accordance with Communist principles. Much stress is laid on technical education, and new colleges devoted to technical subjects are being established.

make the young plants grow rapidly, and towards the end of September the fruit forms from the blossoms.

All this time, the peasant farmers have been carefully tending the crop—irrigating, weeding, and manuring; but now they can rest until the harvest in October. At harvest-time, the crop is reaped with long sickles, bundled and taken away to be threshed. Nothing is wasted; even the threshed stalks are gathered for fuel. Once the rice has been harvested and sent off to some marketing centre like Wuhu in Anhwei province, the fields are sown again—with rice for the family, or with beans, barley, or vegetables.

For many years, the Chinese wanted nothing from the western world and were content to live in their own traditional manner. But modern China is striving to develop her manufactures and heavy industry, especially in the north, where she has the necessary raw materials, such as coal and iron ore; where there are reasonable ports, such as *Tientsin*, the port for Peking and itself a growing industrial centre; and where the railways are better developed. An area where there has already been great development, and where development continues, is Manchuria, a Chinese province that was once coveted by both Russia and Japan. The important naval base of *Port Arthur* is under Soviet control.

Mukden, in southern Manchuria and on the north–south railway that links up with the Trans-Siberian Railway, is the main centre of engineering and heavy industry; since 1949, its population has doubled and now numbers about two millions. Within not far distant radius of the city are the coal and iron-ore towns of *Fushun* and *Penshi*, and the steel town of *Anshan*, which they supply. Hydro-electric power has been developed in the *Kirin* district and along the Yalu river, where it also powers the heavy industries of North Korea. Oil is now

Camera Press.

TAMING A CHINESE RIVER

These Chinese are preparing the site for the Junhochi Dam on the middle reaches of the Huai river. The Huai, or Hwai, used to flood regularly, but in 1951 work began on the Huai River Valley project, which will prevent flooding and provide power, irrigation and water communication for the provinces of Honan, Anhwei and Kiangsu. Similar projects are in hand for the Yangtze and Yungting rivers.

ALONG THE "BLUE RIVER"

These Chinese boatmen on the Yangtze river are driving their flock of ducks to market. Thin bamboo poles are used to keep the birds together, and although the journey may take a week or ten days it is a cheap and easy way of getting the flock to the market at Nanking.

Photos: Paul Popper.

These Chinese are working a treadmill to lift water from the River Yangtze to their farmlands. The Yangtze-kiang ("Blue River") is China's largest and most important river. The modern dam at Hasing Chaunshih now regulates its waters in the middle reaches. There are many farms in the fertile lower part of its valley.

being produced in southern Manchuria.

At the same time China has been improving her communications by road and rail with Sinkiang, where uranium ore is mined, and through Tihwa to the Soviet border to join up with the Trans-Siberian Railway system.

Manchuria, of course, is not the only part of China where there is important heavy industry. For example, nearly all the provinces in China Proper have coal-fields. The anthracite field of *Shansi* also has rich deposits of iron ore, and the iron industry in this province is said to be the oldest in the world. *Hopei*, *Shantung* and other provinces are rich in iron; the iron-ore deposits of *Tayeh*, near Hankow, which maintain the iron industry of *Hanyang*, are probably the richest in the world. China produces most of the world's tungsten; at *Mengtse*, in Yunnan, she has huge deposits of tin; she can produce all the manganese and mercury that she wants, and has considerable gold, zinc and copper resources.

It would be wrong, therefore, to think of China as a country of peasant farmers and primitive industry, and nothing else. Agriculture is primitive and so is some Chinese industry. But China is now undergoing rapid change. The process of development which was begun by the Europeans and Americans, and in which the Japanese later shared, is now being continued by the Chinese themselves, often with help from the Soviet Union. Among recent developments have been several concerned with flood control, irrigation and hydro-electric power. A typical example is the Huai river project, which was started in 1951. This river used to flood regularly, causing untold destruction to the homes and crops of some 50 million people. Now big reservoirs have been built along the upper river, and at Junhochi dams are being built for further control of the river waters. When the scheme is complete, water will be available for irrigation and navigation upon the river will be improved. The steel sluice gates used in part of this scheme were the first to be entirely made and fitted by Chinese workpeople.

Another river that has recently been subdued is the Yungting, which is now controlled by the dams and reservoirs at Juanging Gorge, more than sixty miles north-west of Peking. Since 1952 a modern dam has

Will F. Taylor.

TERRACED HILLSIDES IN YUNNAN

The curious ridges on the distant hillsides in this picture are terraces which have been carefully built by the local peasant farmers. They grow their crops upon the terraces, which prevent the rain from washing too much soil into the valleys and make the work of cultivating easier. This landscape is typical of the high parts of Yunnan province.

Mondiale.

THE HALL OF PRAYER, PEKING

This triple-roofed building, the Hall of Prayer, stands in the T'ien T'an (Altar of Heaven) at Peking. Built more than 500 years ago, it was the scene of spring prayers and sacrifices for rich harvests.

been built at Hasing Chaunshih, on the lakes in the middle Yangtze river. In this work the Chinese had the help of engineers from the Soviet Union.

China's Towns and Cities

British visitors to China in normal times choose *Shanghai* as their entry port if they wish to travel into the interior of the country. Shanghai, only a small fishing village many centuries ago and a nineteenth-century port for sea-going junks, is now the greatest port in China and a centre of the textile industry. Although it serves the Yangtze basin, it does not stand on the Yangtze river, but on a tidal creek fifty miles upstream. It is a fine maritime city, in every sense of the words, whose prosperity dates from the days when it was a British Treaty Port.

From Shanghai, we can travel by road, rail or river to *Nanking*, which has at times been the capital. It has some of the finest modern Chinese build-

ings and, on the south slope of the Purple Mountain, the imposing tomb of Sun Yat-Sen, the father of the Chinese Republic. From here a railway goes north to *Tientsin*, the great commercial and cotton city, and thence westwards to Peking and the terminal points for caravans from Siberia and Mongolia, or eastwards to *Mukden* and *Manchuria*.

But if we follow the Yangtze westwards from Nanking, we shall reach the steel city of *Hankow*, on the long north-south railway from Peking to *Canton*, the great city seaport of Southern China. Hankow is really three cities in one. North of the Yangtze are Hankow and Hanyang; south of the Yangtze is Wuchang. Together the three make the most important railway and commercial centre in China. The Yangtze river may one day be bridged in the Hankow district. In February 1954 plans were published of the new " double-decker " steel bridge which Soviet and Chinese engineers propose to put across the river. It was stated that the work of construction would begin in 1955.

Most famous for its architectural beauties is *Peking*. From 1928 to 1949 Peking ceased to be the capital and was later re-named Peiping. Its old name Peking, meaning Northern capital, has now been restored and the city is again the capital of China. Peking is not one, but five walled cities. There is the Tartar North City: the Chinese South City: the Legation Quarter: the Imperial City: and the moated Purple Forbidden City which contains some of the finest Chinese classical architecture.

Peking is a treasure-house of art and beauty whose parks and pleasure grounds, temples and palaces are lasting monuments to the great Ming and Manchu emperors whose capital it was. On all sides beauty abounds. Ornate and wonderfully carved pagodas of marble and other fine stone rear gracefully into the deep blue sky that is a roof to park and courtyard. We are amazed by the richly coloured Dragon Screen in the Tartar City and by the fearsome stone lion that mounts guard over the Gate of Heavenly Peace of the Forbidden City. Chinese sculptors were fond of taking animals as their subjects and as we approach the golden tiled Hall of Supreme Harmony we are confronted by a superbly fashioned bronze crane whose beak sticks proudly

Hedda M. Morrison.

WHERE EMPERORS RULED

These marble balustrades and bronze incense burners were photographed in the Forbidden City, Peking. Once the capital of the great Ming and Manchu emperors, Peking is still the cultural centre of Chinese life, even though the splendour of the Imperial Court no longer lives in its palaces and temples.

THE CHINESE WAY OF LIFE

Ewing Galloway.

If you lived in Peking, you might do your day-to-day shopping in such a street as this. The shop-keepers use signs, banners and awnings to advertise their wares. Outside one shop (*right*) a ricksha-man waits. Peking is divided into several cities; this street stands in the part of the capital known as the " Chinese City."

Aerofilms Library.

This Cantonese family have a houseboat on the Pearl river as their home. Sitting on the deck, they eat their bowls of rice and even the youngest member of the family seems able to manage his chopsticks. The Pearl river is part of the huge delta of the Si-kiang.

upwards as if he knows that he was made for imperial admiration.

Words cannot describe the grace, the richness, or the lustre of the ceremonial halls and temples in which Peking abounds. The very names chosen for these masterpieces suggest the ultimate in beauty. There is no ugliness in the sacred shrines of the Altar of Heaven whose many courts and temples are a tribute to the artistic genius of ancient craftsmen. Within the buildings are still greater wonders such as the Buddhas of the great Lama Temple in the Tartar City, and the intricately-carved Dragon Throne in the Forbidden City where once emperors sat in state.

Peking represents all that is finest in a race that has long been famous for the beauty of its works of art—for its carvings in jade and in ivory, and for its bronzes, its paintings, and its porcelains. Peking is a wonder city of the past, and it seems natural that a race which has great reverence for the past should regard Peking as a centre of modern Chinese intellect and culture. The city is the home of the National Academy which, with its seven institutes, ranked in Chinese higher education second only to the Academia Sinica. With other Chinese universities and places of learning, it has been reorganised by the Communist government.

Outer China and Formosa

" Outer China " is the term applied to the areas covered by the provinces of *Sinkiang* and *Manchuria*, the self-governing regions of *Inner Mongolia* and

Hedda M. Morrison.

A FLOATING " CITY " OF SAMPANS AT CANTON

In strange contrast to the modern buildings on the water-front at Canton are the massed sampans of the floating " city " that has hugged the banks of the Pearl river here for centuries. Canton is the great river port of southern China and stands about 80 miles from Hong Kong, the British colony at the mouth of the Canton river.

Hedda M. Morrison.

KITES FOR THE NEW YEAR

The Chinese are very skilful kite-flyers, but they display their skill only at the New Year. Notice the gaily coloured and fantastic designs on the kites, which make the English variety seem very dull and uninteresting.

Tibet, and the *Mongolian People's Republic*, which is entirely independent although it works closely with the Soviet Union and with China. Sinkiang, which was once called Chinese Turkestan, is divided into two parts by the lofty Tien Shan mountains, the larger part being the southern area, which is drained by the River Tarim. There are fertile valleys in Sinkiang where grains, cotton, fruits and other crops are grown, but much of the province is desert. Its chief town, *Tihwa* (formerly known as Urumchi) stands on the motor route from northern China to the Asiatic parts of the Soviet Union. The Mongolias are the home of herdsmen who move from place to place with their animals, according to the pastures and the seasons, and who live in felt tents called *yurta*. *Urga* (Ulan Batur) is the capital of the Mongolian People's Republic; it stands on the motor road linking China with Siberia.

The island of Formosa (Taiwan) was ceded to Japan by China in 1895, but was returned to China after the Second World War. It has a population of over 7½ millions. *Taipei* is the capital.

North and South Korea

It now seems strange that the name Korea should mean "Land of the the Morning Calm," for since 1950 this peninsula pointing south towards Japan has been the scene of bitter fighting and dispute. Korea was annexed by the Japanese, who call it Cho-sen, in 1910, but by the end of the Second World War all the peninsula north of the 38th parallel had been occupied by Russian troops, and the remainder by American troops. Later, the Allies withdrew and two separate republics were formed: in the north a "Korean People's Republic" emerged, with its capital at *Pyong-Yang*, while in the south a form of government more like those of the western nations was established. *Seoul* (*Keijo*) became the capital of South Korea.

In 1950 the North Koreans attacked without warning and swept into South Korea. The United Nations took swift action against this aggression and eventually drove the North Koreans back. But although, after a year of hard fighting, both sides agreed to a cease-fire, the move towards an armistice was painfully slow. Complete agreement between the North Koreans and Chinese Volunteer Army on the one hand and the South Koreans and United Nations forces on the other had not been reached by January, 1954.

South Korea has little industry; its people are small farmers growing rice, grain, cotton and tobacco. But there are valuable deposits of tungsten —said to be among the world's largest —at the Sandong Mine. North Korea is

Chinese Government Information Office.

OFF THE SHANTUNG COAST

Junks are still among the chief coastal craft of China. Their sails are made of fine matting stiffened with bamboo battens. Much farther south, in the South China Sea, junks such as this are armed with antiquated cannons as defence against the pirates which infest these waters.

Hedda M. Morrison.

A RESTING FISHERMAN OF HONG KONG ISLAND

This picture was taken at Shankiwan, one of the fishing communities of the British colony of Hong Kong. The colony includes the small mainland peninsula of Kowloon as well as Hong Kong Island. Fish forms an important part of the Chinese diet, and when the time comes to start work again this resting fisherman will find a ready market for his catch.

also rich in tungsten and has valuable coal-fields, and iron-ore deposits, and large hydro-electric stations along the Yalu river. The textile and chemical industries in this part of Korea were greatly developed by the Japanese.

Korea was once one of the most progressive countries in the world. Korean astronomers were studying the stars and recording comets and meteors a hundred years before the birth of Christ. Koreans were the first people of the Far East to devise a simple alphabet, and they used movable metal type for printing about fifty years before the famous Gutenberg. When war came, the Koreans had their secret weapons; in 1592, a " flying thunderbolt," which was in fact the world's first bomb, was used to strike terror in the hearts of the Japanese invaders. In this same war, the Koreans used a *ku-sun*, or " turtle boat," which was the invention of a Korean admiral. Protected by metal plating and equipped with rocket guns, it was probably the first armoured warship that the world had known.

The Korean Way of Life

To-day, most Koreans are farmers. Rice is their main crop, but they also grow wheat, barley, soya beans and vegetables. Silk and cotton materials woven by the womenfolk provide clothing.

The typical Korean farmhouse is of mud and thatch. The walls are whitewashed and the doors are paper-covered. Oiled paper is used instead of glass for the windows and may also be made into mats for the bare floors. The women's quarters are usually separated from the men's quarters by a courtyard. Hot smoke from the kitchen fire is carried by flues under the floors of the " winter section " of the house, providing the farmer with a cheap " central heating " system. There are no chairs. The farmer and his family sit on cushions on the floor and at night retire to beds of rugs and mattresses, with wooden blocks serving as pillows. About the farm, we shall be sure to see large jars in which the farmer stores his grain, pickled cabbage and other foodstuffs.

Koreans are very fond of pickled cabbage which, prepared with garlic, fish, red pepper and onions, forms a dish known as *Kimchi*. Pickled cabbage is also served with beans, mushrooms, pine kernels, seaweed, turnips and rice. *Saké*, a rice brandy, is the drink for special occasions; at other times, Koreans drink ginger tea.

Picture Post.

A STRANGE TENTED VILLAGE

These are *yurta*, or tents, made of felt, and they are inhabited by nomad Mongol herdsmen, who move from place to place with their flocks or herds according to the seasons and the pastures. Urga (Ulan Batur) is the chief town of Outer Mongolia.

The Story
of the
World and
its Peoples

In the Islands
of a
Once=Great
Empire

SUMMER IN JAPAN

E.N.A.

This picture gives us a charming idea of the scenery of Japan, with its leafy trees, trails of wistaria and typical style of architecture. The buildings at which we are looking form part of the Futawarasan Temple at Nikko, Japan. Nikko is a great centre of religious fervour, for it has many temples, as well as the tombs of Emperors.

JAPAN: THE LAND OF THE RISING SUN

THE name of Japan comes from two Chinese signs, or ideographs, pronounced Jih-pen, which mean the place where the sun rises. In Japan itself the country is called Nippon, which means the same as the Chinese word.

Before history began Japan was inhabited by people known as the Ainu. They were gradually driven out by the invaders from Siberia, though some descendants still survive in Japan. Eventually a great leader, Jimmu, became the first emperor of Japan and ever since those far-off days all emperors of Japan claim to trace their descent in an unbroken line from the great Jimmu. Jimmu himself was a direct descendant of the grandson of the Sun Goddess, the daughter of the creators of heaven and earth. Thus the Emperors of Japan have always claimed divine descent, though

this once firmly-held belief has been modified or weakened in very recent years.

In the present century Japan made great progress as a manufacturing and trading nation. She became, indeed, one of the great commercial powers of the world. Then from 1937 onwards Japan was at war with China in pursuance of her vast ambitions to build up a great Eastern empire. That war was still going on when in December, 1941, thinking that the right moment had come, her ruler made, without warning, a fierce attack upon American and British bases in the Pacific.

At first Japan met with very considerable success but by 1945 had lost much of the ground won earlier.

With the collapse of Germany, Japan's hopes of a vast Asiatic and Pacific empire faded away. Unconditional surrender on all fronts came in August, 1945. The armed forces of Japan surrendered and the Allies, under the American General MacArthur, occupied the mainland of Japan. The Emperor Hirohito still remained the ruler but under the stern eye of the Occupying Powers, whose resolve to make Japan a truly democratic country brought about the new constitution which came into force in 1947. An election, in which Japanese women had the vote as well as men, was held in that same year. On September 8th, 1951, the Peace Treaty with Japan was signed in San Francisco.

One of the most remarkable changes, indeed, which has taken place in Japan in recent years is the position women now occupy. They have the vote and they can become members of the Japanese Parliament, or Diet. Even so, most Japanese men still look upon women as inferior beings and it will be several generations before they regard their womenfolk as equals, as we do in the West. The change in women's dress is not so pronounced as in the case of the men. In the towns to-day it is unusual to see the national dress, though it can of course be seen in the country districts quite often. But the women, especially at holiday times, still prefer the national dress, and they look very lovely in their silk or cotton *kimonos*, each girdled by a highly-coloured silk sash called an *obi*.

It is the ambition of most Japanese to speak the English language as well as their own. For the younger people attending the high schools a two-years' course in English is compulsory. But many of the older Japanese are equally anxious to learn. There are, too, many technical and special schools, while elementary and secondary education is compulsory. There

By courtesy of Christmas Humphreys, Esq.

OLD AND NEW IN MODERN JAPAN

Japanese women cling more to the traditional dress than do their menfolk and probably even the girl in Western dress in the picture would wear the *kimono* and *obi* like her companions on national holidays and ceremonial occasions.

FESTIVAL TIME IN KYOTO

E.N.A.

The Gion Shrine Festival has been held regularly for more than a thousand years and includes grand processions of decorated cars and floats. In this picture we see a *Hoko*, or decorated tower-car. At the top of the tower, seated round the sacred page, is a drum and fife band. The fans held by the two men on the front of the car are used for signalling to the crowds and to the team of men pulling the car through the streets.

are six universities and five medical universities.

In the Real Japan

Although the Japanese Empire stretched from the cold and misty Kurile Islands to the forest-clad island of Formosa in the South, the real Japan was always in the main group of large islands between the Japan Sea and the deep Pacific. Honshu is the largest, and contains *Tokyo*, the capital with its port of *Yokohama; Osaka*, the biggest manufacturing city in Japan; *Kobe*, another great port, and several other of Japan's most important towns, many of which were shattered in the air raids of the war and are now being rebuilt. North of Honshu is Hokkaido, with Hakodate as its chief town and port.

South of the great main island, and shutting in the lovely inland sea with their northern coast-lines, are Shikoku and Kiushiu, with Nagasaki, the port which was almost completely destroyed in the last week of the Second World War.

Little remains of the Japanese Empire. Formosa, now the home of the Chinese Nationalist Government, has passed from Japanese control; so too have the Kuriles and Sakhalin, as well as many of Japan's mandated islands.

The Japanese islands are mostly very mountainous and all volcanic. They are, indeed, a long range of volcanic uplands partly sunken in the sea. You can trace this great line of volcanoes from the cold peninsula of Kamchatka in north-eastern Siberia, and through the Japanese islands to Formosa and on to the East Indies, where the island of Java has more volcanoes to the square mile than any other country in the world.

Japan is on what is called " a line of weakness " in the earth's crust, where the stupendous forces of volcanic eruptions and earthquakes are frequently active, proving that this part

Paul Popper.

PICKING TEA

Carrying their wicker baskets, the pickers work along the rows of tea bushes growing on the hillside, their clever fingers picking out the correct buds and leaves. In the valley, the flooded ricefields make a jigsaw pattern. Rice is Japan's most important crop.

FOR SHIPS AND TRAVELLERS

H. Armstrong Roberts.

One of the three principal ports of Japan is Kobe. Part of the large harbour is shown in this picture.
Kobe stands at the eastern end of the Seto Naikai (Inland Sea), on Osaka Bay, Honshu. In 1868, when
Kobe was founded, it was only a group of fishing villages. To-day, over 765,000 people live in this
busy industrial and shipping city.

E.N.A.

Japan was rapidly becoming "Westernised" before she plunged into war against the Western
Allies at the end of 1941. Since the occupation, mainly by American forces, the process has continued, but old customs and traditions still remain. Here is a wayside tavern in Japan with the
hostess standing at the entrance to welcome the traveller who desires rest and refreshment.

A TREE SHAPED LIKE A BOAT

Trained trees and magically dwarfed specimens are a feature of Japanese gardening, but the example shown is of outstanding interest. It is a spruce fir known to be centuries old; and, in the course of time, monks have cut and trained the branches till the whole tree has assumed the shape of a boat. The tree may be seen in the Kinkukuji Gardens at Kyoto.

Photos: E.N.A.

The many-storeyed structure here depicted is the castle at Nagoya in Japan, built by Katō Kiyomasa in 1611. The strangely curved eaves are a feature of Japanese architecture and we notice the same peculiarity in many of the pagodas.

ON THE ISLAND OF MIYAJIMA

E.N.A.

The curious structure in the water is known as a " torii." A Torii is a gateway built in front of a shrine and this one was originally made as a perch upon which the wild birds might rest to sing their morning greeting to the gods. The water is that of Japan's famous Inland Sea, in which a fifth of her national supply of fish is caught and which is used by ocean-going, coasting, and ferry steamers, though well-skilled pilots must be employed at the helm.

of the world is still " in the making."
Some of the most appalling volcanic out-
bursts the world has ever known have
occurred in Japan, and some of the
worst earthquake disasters. In 1923,
for example, the great city of Tokyo
was practically destroyed by an earthquake shock and by the fire that resulted.
In 1948, the rebuilt city of Fukui, 250
miles west of Tokyo, was destroyed in
one of the worst earthquakes that Japan
has suffered.

Japan's most famous volcano is
Fujiyama or Fujisan—" O Fuji," the
Japanese call it—" the Honourable
Mountain." You can see it on a clear
day as your steamer enters Tokyo Bay,
a perfect snowy cone of peerless beauty,
and at the sight, you understand once
and for all why Fuji appears in so many
Japanese pictures and decorations.

The greatest of all, however, is the
enormous old crater of Aso-san, which
is several miles across and which now
has many villages and fertile fields
within its broken rim of red and black
volcanic rock.

Skilful Farmers

So much of Japan is mountainous
that her crowded population must
make every possible use of the limited
amount of land fit for cultivation.
You will see not only the plains bearing
rice and other crops to the utmost
limit, but also the very hillsides
terraced far up to provide extra land
for growing things. Like the Chinese,
the Japanese farmers are hard and
patient workers, who have learned to
make use of everything and to waste
nothing.

By courtesy of Christmas Humphreys, Esq.

WHERE LIFE GOES ON UNCHANGED

While Western dress and customs are widespread in the towns and cities of Japan, life in the countryside shows us something of the Japan of old. This picture was taken in a village of Central Japan.
The clothes worn by the men are the same in style as those worn by their ancestors nearly a
thousand years ago.

SIGHTS AND SCENES IN JAPAN

E.N.A.

The national religion of Japan is Buddhism. This picture shows the famous Daibutsu, the great bronze Buddha, 50 feet high, at Kamakura, twelve miles from Yokohama.

Associated Press.

In this picture Japanese office workers are taking a lunch time rest on the lawn in front of the very modern National Diet Building in Tokyo, capital of Japan.

Pictorial Press.

Japan has long been famed for its geishas, girls who are trained from their early years in music, dancing, singing, and the art of witty and amusing conversation. The profession is tending to die out to-day and only the prosperous can afford the entertainment of their society. This photograph in modern Japan shows the well-bred, exquisitely-groomed geishas entertaining a party of merchants.

Because the land is so filled with mountains, the Japanese rivers are as a rule short and very swift—useful only for rafting down the timber from the highlands, or for providing cheap power for electricity. One of the thrills experienced by visitors to Japan is to shoot the rapids on one of the swift rivers in a boat that is by no means as clumsy as it looks.

The New Japan

The Japan about which we used to read in school books has changed a great deal within the last twenty years. Even before the war the Japanese of the large towns—especially the ports— had learned much from the Americans and Europeans. Electric trains and trams, motor cars, picture - houses, hotels, theatres and restaurants much like those you find in Europe and America are now common sights, for the Japanese are expert imitators.

Great up-to-date mills, factories, foundries and shipyards tell very plainly how well the Japanese have learned the business of modern manufacture. In Yokohama some of the business offices remind you distinctly of the skyscraper monsters of New York, Chicago and San Francisco ; the buildings are not so high, it is true, but the idea is unmistakably there. You will see Japanese business men dressed much as business men are in Europe and America hurrying off to their offices in the mornings ; and Japanese business girls, too, with clothes and hair styles similar to those of the West.

Associated Press.

HIROSHIMA RISES AGAIN FROM ITS ASHES

One of the most dramatic days in history was August 6th, 1945, when the first atomic bomb used in warfare fell on Hiroshima, city and port of Japan. It was largely responsible for bringing the final end of the Second World War. This photograph shows Hiroshima to-day as the city arises anew from the chaos and desolation left in the wake of that moment of devastation.

HEIR TO THE JAPANESE THRONE

On his nineteenth birthday the Crown Prince Akihito was formally invested as Heir to the Throne of his father, the Emperor Hirohito of Japan. In this photograph the Crown Prince is seen in the Imperial Palace at Tokyo reading his pledge to seek knowledge in order to discharge his duties to the Emperor and Empress. Standing behind the Crown Prince is the Grand Chamberlain.

Photos: Camera Press.

While the investment of the Crown Prince was performed in the traditional garb of old Japan, the procession through the capital was made in carriages and uniforms familiar in European countries. They were, in fact, eighteenth-century European in type and not unlike those used in Britain on similar occasions. In the Palace grounds 35,000 people assembled to acclaim the Crown Prince.

But in the country, away from the ports and the large cities, there is still the Old Japan with its fine old-world courtesy and love of beauty, that contrasts so sharply with the ferocious cruelty of the Japanese during the war, its wonderful old temples and fascinating houses, and its craftsmen and artists, who sometimes spend their whole lives on the creation of a single work of art.

Village and Farm

There, too, you can feel the real charm of Japan, enjoy the loveliness of the cherry blossom in spring, and see the gorgeous colours of the maples in autumn.

Life still flows fairly peacefully in the country villages of little brown houses, and in the thousands of tiny farms scattered in plain and valley. Unceasing work in the rice-fields or in the tea-gardens and mulberry groves on the hill-terraces, or wood-cutting and fuel-gathering on the upper slopes, fills the whole day for these patient toiling peasants. In the attics of the farm-houses live the silk-worms on their flat trays—greedy creatures that keep the girls and boys ever busy in gathering fresh mulberry leaves to satisfy the growing appetites of their crawling charges until the time comes when they spin their cocoons of wonderful lustrous silk and set their keepers the new task of gathering, unwinding and drying the silk and making it into pale yellow hanks to be sent to the silk factory in the town.

Yokohama

Those who come to Japan by sea usually enter the country at Yokohama, the chief port, which is virtually a joint

Associated Press.

JAPANESE YOUTHS TAKE AN ENGLISH LESSON

For many years past the Japanese have been keen students of foreign languages, and since the occupation by American forces the English language has been a compulsory subject at the secondary schools. Here we see the pupils at one of the High Schools in Tokyo learning how to translate English into Japanese.

city with Tokyo, where they are perhaps a little disappointed at first to find so many of the menfolk dressed in European garb and wearing hard bowler hats, but the bright clothes of the women and children make up for this. Over half Tokyo-Yokohama was destroyed in the war, but the concrete and steel buildings in the American style survived, and the Japanese were quick to begin rebuilding. New and the Old Japan flow through the streets in a mingling stream of motor cars while blue-clad coolies with mushroom hats may still be seen ; of rickshaws and bicycles ridden by schoolboys; of queer little lorries drawn by small shaggy ponies, and electric cars.

The Bronze Buddha

One of the places to visit from Yokohama is Kamakura. There people go to see the famous Bronze Buddha, which is nearly 50 feet high, and whose eyes are said to be of pure gold and its forehead of silver. Or if you wish to enjoy the beauty and peace of the countryside, you can go out to the Hakone Mountains, forty miles away. On this line is Gotemba, where you can leave the train to climb Fuji if you wish, leaving your hotel at three in the morning and reaching the summit in the late afternoon. You spend the night at one

Associated Press.

RECORDING THEIR VOTES IN TOKYO

One of the most remarkable changes in Japan during the past few years is the place women have come to occupy in national affairs. Here we have a scene outside one of the polling booths in Tokyo at a recent election. It will be noticed that the women are in some cases dressed in the old national costume, but the few men to be seen are all dressed in Western fashion, now the general attire for men in the towns and cities.

of the rest-houses and descend next morning.

Tokyo

Tokyo is only half an hour from Yokohama by electric train. It was practically a new city which arose out of the ruin caused by the terrible earthquake and fire of 1923, which left behind thousands of acres of smoking waste that only a week before had been a prosperous city. In six years the place was well rebuilt; "six new bridges spanning a river as wide as the Thames in London, 400 smaller bridges over the city's moats and inlets, 600 miles of new roads, three new parks, fifty-one open spaces, and houses, shops and factories." Three days of rejoicing were proclaimed in March, 1930. The Emperor himself drove through the city in his car at the head of a procession, and "paid reverence at the Hall of the Nameless Dead to the enshrined ashes of 33,000 people who perished in the flames."

Tokyo's principal shopping street is "the Ginza," which runs through the heart of the city; here you can buy anything that can be purchased in the great towns of Europe and America.

The Temples of Nikko

Nikko is a pleasant place at which to stay. It lies 100 miles north of Tokyo amid wonderful scenery, and is renowned for its beautiful temples some of which may be visited if you take off your boots or shoes before entering and wear the special slippers provided by the temple guardians. The famous Shrine to Iyeyasu bears the well-known carving which is copied in millions of Japanese trinkets, a carving in wood of three monkeys, one with his hand to his mouth, one with his hand to his eyes, and the other with his hands over his ears. "*Speak* no evil; *see* no evil; *hear* no evil." The Japanese think much of Nikko; they have a proverb that runs: "He who has not seen Nikko cannot say, 'beautiful!'"

E.N.A.

A FESTIVAL PROCESSION

The Japanese have many festivals, the most important being that of the New Year. Age is reckoned from the New Year, and only very young children celebrate on their actual birthday. Many of the religious festivals are occasions for great processions. The parade seen in this picture took place in Kyoto, until 1868 the capital of Japan.

AT THE SHRINE OF IYEYASU

By courtesy of Christmas Humphreys, Esq.

This picture shows the ornate gateway to the Shrine of Iyeyasu at Nikko. Iyeyasu was a shogun, or military leader, who brought peace and prosperity to feudal Japan in the early seventeenth century. Nikko, where Iyeyasu was buried in 1617, is one of the most famous religious centres of Japan, and has some of the finest work of Japanese craftsmen and artists as this picture shows.

Kyoto is another beautiful old city where you can see the Emperor's palace surrounded by its great wall with six gates, and in whose shops you find some of the most exquisite pottery and other works of art in the world. From Kyoto you can go up to lovely Lake Biwa, the biggest lake in Japan, which gets its name from the fact that it is shaped like a *biwa* or Japanese lute.

The wonderful old city of *Nara* was the centre of government a thousand years ago, and the ruins of palaces and temples there bear witness to its former greatness. *Osaka*, whose many water-ways make Europeans call it the "Venice of Japan," is a great manufacturing city with mills and factories on the most up-to-date lines. *Kobe* is its great port which, like Yokohama, is thoroughly modern.

Then there is the great seaport and dockyard of *Nagasaki*, standing on a bay on the island of Kiushiu.

Japan To-day

What would you find if you were able to visit Japan to-day? In the towns the ordinary Japanese have a hard struggle to keep life and home going. Food is a major problem because, since the war, the population has risen by more than 11,500,000 (of which 8,000,000 are Japanese who have returned home from abroad), to the amazing total of 85,500,000.

There is over-crowding in the cities and even a large family will probably have no more than a single room which it can call home. But outside the towns, the picture of life in present-day Japan is rather better: for the farmers and the fishermen have become comparatively prosperous since their harvests were needed to feed so many mouths.

Japan's industry has made great strides to recovery. Her great textile mills and factories are now producing almost as much as they did before the war. But while in 1940 Japan was exporting more than she imported, in 1952 her exports amounted to only about two-thirds of her imports.

E.N.A.

LARGEST IN THE WORLD

This is the largest suspended bell in the world, and it may be seen at the Chion-in Temple at Kyoto. Because of its historic treasures, Kyoto was never bombed during the Second World War. Although it is a busy city with modern streets and transport, as well as ancient shrines and temples, Kyoto is also a centre for age-old crafts, such as tapestry weaving.

The Story
of the
World and
its Peoples

A Great Nation
Whose History
Began With
the Pilgrim Fathers

H. Armstrong Roberts.

OUTWARD BOUND FROM NEW YORK

With a typical New York skyline as background, this cargo ship heads for open sea. New York harbour is a great sea gateway for the whole of the United States. It is a deep water harbour and unlike Montreal, in Canada, is never icebound.

THE UNITED STATES OF AMERICA

THE Federal Republic of the United States is not as large as Canada, but it has more than ten times as many people, for it lies in latitudes more favourable to the growth of a dense and busy population. More than 151 millions of people live in the United States and they are mainly of European descent; but whereas the inhabitants of Canada are chiefly British or French, those of the United States have come from almost every nation in Europe to form a united new people under the Stars and Stripes. Some 10 per cent. of the population of the United States are Negroes, the descendants of the slaves brought there to work in the plantations of the south-eastern States during the bad old days of slavery.

The peoples who came to America, as often as not, were fugitives from oppression and persecution, and were at first predominantly English. There were the Pilgrim Fathers, a little band of men, women, and children who fled from the bigotry of King James the First in 1620, in their tiny ship the *Mayflower*; there were Roman Catholics who began the first settlements in Maryland; Quakers in Pennsylvania: and debtors, rescued from prison by James Oglethorpe, in Georgia.

The Thirteen Colonies

By the time George III sat on the English throne, Britain had thirteen colonies in America—which she was soon to lose through the obstinate stupidity of George and his ministers.

How the colonists rose against British rule, united in Jefferson's Declaration

311

of Independence, and with George Washington as their leader fought successfully for their freedom, is told elsewhere. There were only some 4 million people in the United States when independence was won.

Immigrants still streamed in from Europe, and as the young Union became more closely knit together, self-confidence and a growing population brought about an extension of her frontiers. Louisiana was purchased from the French in 1803; frontier lands like Kentucky, Tennessee, Indiana, Missouri, and Illinois entered the Union; pioneers pushed westward —along the Santa Fé trail, along the river Missouri, and over the mountain ranges to the Pacific shore. Most of us know, from books and films, the colourful and romantic story of these pioneers—of the covered wagons, the encounters with hostile Indians, and the famous scouts of the plains.

The Civil War

But America was not yet one in spirit. The States of the North and those of the South had wide differences in outlook, particularly on the question of Negro plantation labour. Negro slaves worked the cotton and sugar plantations of the South; in the North slavery was detested as an affront to the morals of any civilised nation. The South, resolved to keep its slaves, wished to break away from the Union. The North, led by President Abraham Lincoln, one of the most famous of Americans, fought to preserve the Union.

Heroic deeds under very gallant leaders and terrible bloodshed characterised the Civil War which convulsed the United States for four long years. Abraham Lincoln, in accepting the challenge of the South,

Chesapeake and Ohio Rlys.

THE MOST VALUABLE STATUE IN AMERICA

This famous statue of George Washington, made from life by Jean Antoine Houdon, is said to be the most valuable piece of sculpture in the United States. It is to be seen in the graceful rotunda of the State Capitol of Virginia at Richmond. Friends and fellow-workers with Washington for American independence, such as Thomas Jefferson, testified to the likeness in appearance and spirit which the famous sculptor had recreated when the statue was finished.

UNITED STATES OF AMERICA

The United States of America is a federal republic of 48 States, governed by a Constitution which came into force in 1789. Washington is the capital and its most imposing and dominating building is the Capitol, seen in the photograph above. In the wings on the right and left of this building sit the Senate and the House of Representatives. The Capitol stands on an eminence 90 ft. high and its great dome is crowned by a statue of Freedom. George Washington chose the site and the foundation stone was laid in 1793, the Government moving into the building in 1800.

IN THE YOSEMITE VALLEY

In California, U.S.A., is the Yosemite National Park, covering over 1,500 square miles. Within this great area is the Yosemite Valley, a general view of which is seen above. The valley lies at the south-west base of the Sierra Nevada and is famed for its wildly picturesque scenery.

In the South-west of the U.S.A., is the State of Arizona and in this photograph we see some of the giant cacti and other remarkable plants which flourish in the wonderland of the Arizona desert.

Yellowstone Park in Wyoming was opened to the public as a national park in 1872. There are numerous hot springs and many magnificent geysers. Our photograph shows the Old Faithful Geyser.

FAMED IN AMERICA'S STORY

E.N.A.

Concord is a town of Massachusetts, U.S.A., 20 miles north-west of Boston. It is the most ancient of American inland towns and is famous, too, for its literary associations with writers such as Emerson, Thoreau and Hawthorne. Louisa M. Alcott, author of *Little Women*, lived at Orchard House, seen above.

E.N.A.

On the spot in Plymouth, Massachusetts, where the Pilgrim Fathers landed on December 21, 1620, to found the first settlement in New England, stands this statue of a Pilgrim maiden.

H. Armstrong Roberts

Carved by the sculptor, Gutzon Borglum, in the massive rocks standing in Mount Rushmere National Park, are these giant effigies of some of the great men who influenced American history.

FROM NEW YORK TO HOLLYWOOD

Lying almost entirely within the Great Basin, Nevada is one of the Western States of the U.S.A. Our photograph shows a view looking down on the lake and spillway of the famous Boulder Dam in Nevada.

Night-time in New York reveals a city of brilliance and of flashing lights. Our photograph shows Broadway and Times Square, looking north from Times Building. On the left is the Astor Hotel.

Hollywood, which has grown up in the golden atmosphere of sunny California, has for long been the capital of the film world. Here is a view of the residential part of the film stars' own town.

Los Angeles was among the pioneer centres of the film industry and from it Hollywood has developed. It has also a fruit-growing industry. Seen here is Los Angeles City Hall.

INDEPENDENCE HALL, PHILADELPHIA

Here the historic Second Congress met in 1775 ; here Washington was chosen as Commander-in-Chief of the Army; here the Constitution of the United States was approved and signed. Inside can be seen the ink-stand, quill-box and sand-shaker used for signing the Declaration of Independence. The statue is of Commodore Barry, one of the leading naval men of the War of Independence.

" saved the Union " by a war which he, more than anyone, had desperately hoped to avoid. It was only his earnest conviction that the very future of America depended on the preservation of the Union and his deep sense of human justice that led him to pay so terrible a price. And it *was* terrible—800,000 perished in the Civil War, and for many years there remained a bitter hatred between North and South, traces of which exist to this day.

The Mighty Mississippi

The wounds of war healed slowly, but not even they could stop the forward march of America. To highways and waterways were added railroads, and in 1869 the Union Pacific, spanning the vast continent, was completed.

New cities came to life, wildernesses were transformed by keen ploughshares, factories and great industries arose as the mineral wealth of the Union was revealed. The United States bustled on to greatness with the same pioneering spirit of enterprise and passionate love of freedom as the first settlers brought to her shores. These qualities still endure.

The central feature of the United States is a great and fertile plain with the mighty Mississippi—" Father of Waters "—draining it with its giant fan of tributaries; on the eastern side are the parallel ranges of the Appalachians and the Alleghany plateau with the great rich Appalachian valley between, and on the western side of the plains the Western Cordillera of high ranges,

THE WASHINGTON MEMORIAL

H. Armstrong Roberts.

This magnificent obelisk commemorates the most famous American of all—George Washington, the father of American Independence and the first President of the United States. For a long time there was no memorial to the great American in the national capital, but in 1848 the erection of a monument was approved by Congress. The Monument was dedicated in 1885 and stands on the very site that Washington himself selected as a suitable place for " A Monument to the American Revolution." It was designed by Robert Mills as " the noble offering of a nation to commemorate greatness, patriotism and virtue."

RELICS OF AMERICA'S PAST

In such a simple log cabin as this did Abraham Lincoln, one of America's greatest presidents, live his early years. Such pioneer homes of American history are carefully preserved at New Salem, Illinois, where Lincoln himself actually lived for a time.

Photos: F. G. Bailey.

This four-hundred-year-old house in St. Augustine, in the state of Florida, is the oldest in the United States. Over its door hang the flags of Spain, Britain, the Confederacy and the United States, indicating its varied history.

lofty plateaux and great valleys and basins, forming a tremendous complex system of mountainous country 1,500 miles wide, and containing some of the most majestic highland scenery on the globe. The eastern high range of the Western Cordillera is known as the Rocky Mountains, which extend into Canada.

Lakes and Great Plains

The northern part of the great plain of the United States is an extension of Southern Canada; there are the prairies golden with grain in summer and snow-swept in winter; there are the great cattle ranches of the drier prairies and the foothills; and around the southern and western sides of Lake Superior is part of the great "shield" of very hard old rocks containing the richest iron deposits in the world, where the ore is got out of huge open pits in the Mesabi ranges by monster grabs and electric shovels, taken in long lines of freight cars to the lake side, dumped into monster ore steamers and transported down the lakes to the big iron and steel works on the southern shores of Lake Michigan and Erie.

But the southern part of the great plains is very different. It is much warmer, for one thing, and in the moister eastern and south-eastern parts maize and tobacco, cotton, sugar, rice and subtropical fruits are grown in enormous quantities. The south-

Chesapeake and Ohio Rlys.

THE JEFFERSON MEMORIAL, WASHINGTON

Thomas Jefferson, the great American democrat who wrote the Declaration of Independence and later became the third President of the United States, is remembered as one of the fathers of his country in this beautiful memorial in Washington, the United States' capital. Jefferson himself was a skilled architect, and the limestone dome recalls Monticello, Jefferson's home, and the rotunda of the University of Virginia, both of which were built from his plans.

Planet News.

WASHINGTON GREETS A NEW AMERICAN PRESIDENT

Bands, banners, cars, and wedge-shaped formations of motor-cycle police are all part of the Washington scene on the day that a new President of the United States is inaugurated. This picture was taken as the procession moved down Pennsylvania Avenue to the White House reviewing stands where President Truman, elected for a further term of office, took the salute of detachments of the armed forces. The building in the background is the Capitol, where Congress meets.

western plains are very dry; parts, indeed, in Arizona and New Mexico are actual desert, although vast irrigation works have done a great deal in recent years to turn barren desert arid lands into fertile grain-lands and fruit orchards.

The Busiest Region

The busiest and most thickly-peopled part of the United States is in the north-east, where great cities manufacturing all kinds of goods and drawing to themselves the grain, cattle, ores and timber of the west give employment to many millions of people. South of them are the States where tobacco and cotton, rice and sugar have built up big business, and where other large cities flourish. West of all is the great basin of the Mississippi, with the great port of New Orleans near its mouth. West of the Mississippi Basin are the Mountain States, with their treasures of gold and silver, copper and lead and other minerals, and between these and the Pacific are the States of the Pacific seaboard, the best known of which is the lovely land of California, with its port of San Francisco on the Golden Gate.

The capital of all this rich country is *Washington* in the District of Columbia, on the high banks of the beautiful Potomac River, which comes down from the Blue Mountains. This magnificent city, "founded and planned by George Washington, the first President of the United States, long before it was born," has the stately Capitol as its centre, from which splendid avenues radiate like spokes from the hub of a wheel; fine Government buildings and monuments of marble appear amid their beautiful setting of trees and open spaces. Most of the people of Washington are employed in Government offices.

But the largest city in the United States is *New York*, which in 1950 had a population of nearly 8 millions, the population of " greater " New York being about 12½ millions. New York first grew up on the narrow rocky Manhattan Island and then overflowed to New Jersey, Brooklyn on Long Island and the Bronx, which to-day are linked together by many bridges. The first of these was the famous Brooklyn Bridge, built in 1883; since then more than fifty others of various sizes have been built.

City of Skyscrapers

Land became so dear, and room for building so restricted at the southern end of crowded Manhattan Island, that the only thing to do was to build *upwards*, since building outwards was

Chesapeake and Ohio Rlys.

THE WHITE HOUSE, HOME OF AMERICAN PRESIDENTS SINCE 1800

Washington, in the District of Columbia, is the capital of the United States, the nerve-centre of American government, and a beautiful city where famous Americans of the past are honoured by stately memorials. Its oldest public building is the White House, which has been the official home of every American President except the first, George Washington. Its historic name is " President's House."

impossible. That is why New York is the " City of Sky-scrapers," with streets like ribbons at the bottoms of great deep canyons of masonry, shut in by giant buildings of fifty storeys high and more, one of which may house ten or fifteen thousand people during the working hours. Fleets of street cars, three underground tunnels one above another, crowded ferries and thronged bridges can hardly take the millions of workers home each day and bring them all back next morning. All the chief railways of the North American continent focus on the city, and to its crowded wharves come the products of the whole vast land behind it away to the Pacific. It is one of the main centres for road haulage, about 10,000 long-distance trucks serving the port district each day.

H. Armstrong Roberts.

THE LINCOLN MEMORIAL, WASHINGTON

The memorial to Abraham Lincoln, the famous President who gave the slaves their freedom and, at the cost of war, preserved the Union, is a place of pilgrimage for Americans from near and far. Above his seated figure, which is 19 feet high, are engraved the words " In this temple as in the hearts of the people for whom he saved the Union, the memory of Abraham Lincoln is enshrined forever."

All nations have a home there. Fifth Avenue is the street of millionaire palaces, but in the lower quarters there are " great dingy box-like tenement houses where dwell the most motley mixture of human beings the world possesses."

The New York Waterfront

Those who come to the United States from Europe enter at New York, welcomed by the famous Statue of Liberty, which at night has great floodlights around its base and a gleaming torch on high. Behind it is Ellis Island, where immigrants are interviewed to see if they can be admitted to the country, and beyond is the waterfront—the most amazing in all the world, with its skyline broken by the soaring blocks and peaks of the skyscrapers.

America's Greatest Port

Americans will tell you that New York is the greatest port in the world.

It is actually made up of eight separate bays, and many of these alone are as large as most other ports. The shore frontage is more than 650 miles and can harbour more ships at any one time than any other port in the world. There is still space for this frontage to be extended. During a typical year, some 13,000 ships, carrying the flags of 125 steamship lines, will enter New York. Almost half of the foreign trade of the United States has New York as its sea gateway.

From New York, we can travel swiftly and comfortably by air to any part of the United States or, for that matter, of the world. For the United States has two great airlines that encompass the world—Trans-World Airways and Pan-American Airways—and what is more, has solved the problem of its own vast distances with numerous airlines which have " changed the unit of measurement from the mile to the minute." Such transcontinental companies as American Airlines, Eastern Airlines, United Airlines, and Transcontinental and Western Airlines can speed us wherever we may wish to go.

New York's largest airport, and one of the largest commercial airports in the world, is the New York International Airport at *Idlewild*, which was opened in 1948 as a terminal for nearly all overseas air services. The airport has ten miles of runways. Other New York airports are: *La Guardia*, the terminal for airlines serving towns and cities within a radius of about 500 miles; *Teterboro*, an important centre for air freight; and *Newark*, an airport used by regional air services.

The Black Country of the U.S.A.

North and west of New York is the busiest part of industrial America, where rich coal-fields and oil-wells, natural gas and water-power make manufacturing possible on a huge scale. The heart of this busy region is *Pittsburgh*, where " long lines of coal cars, huge ovens that turn coal into coke

for blast furnaces, smelting furnaces that look at night like volcanoes, clouds of smoke, streams of fiery metal shooting out into moulds, great presses and rollers at work shaping white-hot iron and steel, monster cranes, clanging metal, shrieking whistles and toiling men," make this city the most important metal-working centre in the world.

Along the Delaware

Pittsburgh is in the State of Pennsylvania, which was founded by the great Quaker, William Penn (1644–1718), who also planned the original city of Philadelphia, which is the state capital. In Penn's times, Philadelphia covered an area of only two square miles; to-day, the city covers over 150 square miles and is the third largest city in the United States, being surpassed only by Chicago and New York. Philadelphia stands on the banks of the Delaware river, and although more than a hundred miles from the sea, it is a busy port. Of growing importance are its refineries, which handle crude oil from the Gulf of Mexico, South America and the Near East. Among the many historic buildings in the city is the Independence Hall, where the Constitution of the United States was approved and signed.

Up river from Philadelphia, at Morrisville, a few miles from the New Jersey state capital of Trenton, is the new Fairless Steel Works, which has been built to handle iron ore from Venezuela and probably from the new fields of the Labrador-Quebec border in Canada. Canadian ore is said to be of higher quality than that from the Mesaba ridge in Minnesota, at the western end of Lake Superior, and it can be transported more cheaply. Another reason why American steel mills may look more to Canada for iron ore is that the rich surface deposits at Mesaba may be exhausted within the next ten or fifteen years. The transport of Canadian ore to Pittsburgh and other

AN ENGLISH "QUEEN" AT NEW YORK

Life Photo by Anareas Feininger

The " Queen " concerned is that pride of the Cunard fleet, the huge liner *Queen Elizabeth*, seen in this picture docking at her pier at New York. Notice how this noble ship dwarfs the buildings immediately facing on to the waterfront, and how she herself is dwarfed by the lofty skyscrapers in the background. The tallest of the buildings shown (left) is the Chrysler Building which has a height of 1,046 feet. New York's great harbour handles nearly half the entire foreign trade of the United States; the 1,800 docks of the harbour deal with about 13,000 ships each year.

steel centres in the north-eastern states will be made easier by the new St. Lawrence Seaway, when it is completed, but cargoes of ore may also be shipped to Boston and New London. *Boston* is second only to New York as an Atlantic seagate to America.

Another important centre of the American steel industry is *Gary*, Indiana, where there is one of the world's largest— if not the largest—steel plants. Add together the annual steel production of Britain, Russia, France, Japan, and pre-war Germany, and you will get some idea of the immense size of the American steel industry of which Pittsburgh remains the heart.

Pittsburgh, however, is only one of many important industrial and manufacturing centres in the busy northeast. Just as Pittsburgh is linked with steel, so Akron is linked with rubber, Holyoke with paper, Minneapolis with flour and Detroit with motor-cars.

Chicago

To the west of this great industrial region lies the rich Corn country, corn being the American name for maize. The centre of the Corn Belt is *Chicago*, on the shores of Lake Michigan—second largest city in the United States with over three and a half millions of people; its stockyards crammed with cattle and pigs from the western ranches or the surrounding maize country, awaiting their turn to be converted into canned meats, meat extracts, and all the animal products that modern science can devise. Other large towns in the surrounding country share in this tremendous meatpacking business. Chicago is a city of

Acme Photo.

NEW YORK BY NIGHT

Like some strangely modern fairyland, New York presents this amazing picture at night time. We are looking southwards from the Observation Roof of the Rockefeller Center. Upper left are strings of light marking the bridges over the East River to Brooklyn. In the far distance (right) an island pillar of light marks the Statue of Liberty. Immediately before us is the towering Empire State Building, surmounted by its unusual lighted shaft.

skyscrapers, too, a focal centre of road, rail, air and water communications, and the chief grain market for the Middle West. Other centres for meat-packing are Kansas City, Cincinnati, Omaha, St. Paul and St. Louis, but Chicago leads because of its key position in the great transport systems and because it has long been a centre for this work.

West of the Prairie States (Minnesota, Iowa, Missouri, North and South Dakota, Nebraska and Kansas) lies the most thinly populated part of the United States. Known as the Far West, this mountain region has the Rockies to the east, and the Sierra Nevada and Cascade Mountains to the west. The states of this region are Montana, Idaho, Wyoming, Colorado, Utah, Nevada, Arizona and New Mexico. The region is rich in minerals. There are copper mines (Montana, Utah, Colorado and Arizona), lead mines (Idaho, Colorado and Utah), gold mines (Colorado), and rich deposits of zinc and silver.

The northern Pacific States, Washington and Oregon, have fertile valleys providing apples and other fruits. Along their coasts are fruit and salmon canneries. *Portland*, on the Columbia River, and the Puget Sound ports of *Seattle* and *Tacoma* are the sea-gates of these north-western states.

In so vast a country as the United States, it is impossible for a traveller to see all the natural wonders—and there are, indeed, many. But there are two places in particular which visitors make a point of seeing on their journey across the continent—the beautiful Yellowstone Park and the Grand Canyon of the Colorado River in Arizona, both worthy of their places among the wonders of the world.

In Yellowstone Park

Yellowstone National Park is in the north-west corner of the State of Wyoming on the " Great Divide " of the Western Cordillera. Through it runs the Yellowstone tributary of the

H. Armstrong Roberts.

THE STATUE OF LIBERTY

One of the most famous landmarks in the world, this statue of " Liberty Enlightening the World " stands on Bedloe's Island at the entrance to New York Harbour. Designed by Bartholdi, the famous French sculptor, it took ten years to make and was presented by the French to the American nation in 1886. The height of the statue (not including the pedestal) is 151 feet.

Missouri in deep canyons. It is not only a region containing some of the most wonderful scenery in the United States, but also a sanctuary where trees and flowers, birds and animals, are strictly preserved from the risk of extinction. The geysers and hot springs however, are the most astonishing of all its wonders. Four thousand hot springs and over a hundred geysers provide spectacles which can be witnessed nowhere else, except in the North Island of New Zealand.

The Grand Canyon

The Grand Canyon of Arizona is easily reached by the " Sunshine Route " of the Southern Pacific; a branch line runs to the very edge of the Tonto Rim, where are large hotels for visitors.

The canyon itself is " a terrific trough 6,000 to 7,000 feet deep and from ten to twenty miles wide, and hundreds. of miles long, within which are hundreds of peaks higher than any mountain east of the Rockies, yet whose heads are below the floor level of the Colorado Plateau," in which this enormous gash has been cut by the power of running water. From its rim you can look down through a mile of clear air to the yellow ribbon of the Colorado River which has cut this mighty trench by age-long erosion. Its tributaries, too, have cut similar, but smaller canyons, which enter the main canyons, dissecting the dry plateau into a system of profound gorges.

Beyond the Great Basin, with Salt Lake City and its irrigated fields and gardens near Great Salt Lake, and over the Sierra Nevada, famous for its forest giants, the traveller descends into the rich valley of California—a land of flowers and luscious fruits, rich in grain and cattle—where careful irrigation during the dry summer makes it possible to grow things all the year round. California's great city is the port of *San Francisco* by the Golden Gate.

E.N.A

TIMES SQUARE, NEW YORK

Times Square is one of the best known centres of New York and is to that great city very much what Piccadilly Circus is to London. Linking Times Square and 52nd Street is Broadway, the city's theatreland, which at night is ablaze with light.

LOOKING UP AT THE ROCKEFELLER CENTER

H. Armstrong Roberts.

New York's Rockefeller Center consists of twelve towering limestone skyscrapers, of which the largest is the 70-storey RCA Building shown in this picture. The Center also has two theatres and forms the greatest broadcasting and business headquarters in the United States, as well as one of its most famous showplaces. Within the Center are restaurants, clubs, offices, roof gardens, and the Music Hall which is the largest theatre in the World. An army of workers is needed to keep the Center clean. There are 21,292 windows alone.

Golden California

Gold made San Francisco. But the land had greater riches than gold, and these—the wealth in timber and grain, cattle and fruit—were first developed by those who came seeking gold only to find much more lasting sources of income. Gold is still mined in the Sierras, and in the lowlands, where monster gold-dredges eat their slow way across country, extracting the gold and leaving behind them a desolate trail of waste gravel like strips of desert.

Between the Sierra Nevada and the Pacific lies the great Californian Valley, whose natural shelter and Mediterranean climate combine with scientific irrigation by farmers to make it ideal for fruit-growing. Here are acres of luxuriant orange groves, vineyards, apple orchards: luscious crops of grapes, figs, lemons, grapefruit, peaches and other fruit, which are shipped to all parts of the world from the Golden Gate port of San Francisco or sent by railroad in refrigeration cars to other parts of the United States.

H. Armstrong Roberts.

CROSSING THE GRAND CANYON

One of the most remarkable series of canyons in the world occurs on the Colorado River in the U.S.A. The finest of these is the Grand Canyon in Arizona, a gorge which extends for over 200 miles and which is between 3,000 and 6,000 feet in depth. Our picture shows a light suspension bridge across one of the narrowest parts of the Grand Canyon.

United States' Oil

In addition, California has oil, and is the second most important oil-producing State in the Union. Her 20,000 wells yield some 20 per cent. of the total U.S.A. oil production.

The United States actually produces nearly two-thirds of the world supply of petroleum. Her richest fields lie in Texas, Oklahoma, Louisiana, Arkansas, Kansas, but many other States are oil producers too. Most important of all is Texas which accounts for 45 per cent. of United States' oil production and whose " Big Inch " pipeline from Longville to Norris City, Illinois (530 miles), with its ten powerful pumping stations, pushes oil eastwards at a rate of 6 million barrels a month.

AMERICA'S MIGHTY INDUSTRIES

About sixty out of every hundred motor vehicles made in the United States come from the State of Michigan. This picture shows one of the large factories where mass production methods are used. It is at Dearborn, not far from Detroit, and is operated by the great Ford company.

In the foreground of this picture are the pleasant, tree-lined streets of Birmingham, Alabama; in the background, the grey smoke of the iron and steel works which make Birmingham the " Pittsburgh of the South." The Birmingham district is the only area in the United States where the iron, coal and limestone for steel-making are found together in worthwhile quantities.

WHERE STEEL IS MADE

H. Armstrong Roberts.

The United States produces amazing quantities of steel each year from mills such as the one seen in this picture. Pittsburgh, in the state of Pennsylvania, is the greatest steel centre, but Gary, Indiana, also has one of the world's largest steel plants.

E.N.A

This picture shows the interior of an American steel plant. Stainless steel ingots are being poured into a huge electric furnace. More than ninety million tons of steel ingots are produced each year by this great American industry.

PENNSYLVANIAN FARM AND CITY

On a previous page there is a picture of the historic Independence Hall in Philadelphia, Pennsylvania, but this city is as modern as any in the United States. This is how it appears from the Art Museum which stands on Parkway.

Photos: H. Armstrong Roberts.

Here is a view of another part of the same state, which is one of the thirteen original states in the Union. Steel and coal are important industries, but so is farming, and the farmstead seen in this picture is typical.

Texas is also America's leading state in the raising of beef cattle. Her farms and ranches carry about 8 million head of cattle. Within the state is the largest cattle ranch in America. This is King Ranch, which occupies 900,000 acres of south-eastern Texas. The ranch employs no fewer than 750 hands, many of them Spanish-American vaqueros now in the third generation, for King Ranch likes " to raise its own help."

But let us return to California, to *Los Angeles*, the largest city in the state and a traditional centre of the fruit-growing industry. Not far away is Hollywood, whose clear air and brilliant sunshine make it an ideal " home of the movies." To the east and south lies real desert country, with weird flowering cacti and primitive Indian tribes who still live in their *pueblos* or communal houses of sun-baked adobe or clay, much as their forefathers lived a thousand years ago.

Cotton

United States lands bordering the Gulf of Mexico are districts of cotton-fields, rice-fields, and sugar plantations. Texas, the biggest of the States, is also the largest cotton producer. Next in importance are New Mexico, Arizona and California. Together, these four states grew nearly half the total American crop in 1951. The great cotton ports are New Orleans, Galveston and Mobile on the Gulf, and Charleston and Savannah on the Atlantic.

In recent years the cotton-producing states, while still providing a lot of raw cotton for export, have ceased to rely on the mills of the northern states for turning the home share of the crop into textiles. The South now has its own textile industry and makes about three-quarters of the total textile production of the United States. The new mills and factories that have been built in the southern states produce not only cotton goods, but materials in orlon, nylon and rayon. Other industries, too, have sprung up in the south: *Birmingham*,

Alabama, one of the few places in America where the basic raw materials for steel (iron ore, coal and limestone) are found together, is a town of furnaces and rolling mills; at *Lufkin*, Texas, and along the Coosa River in Alabama, paper is produced from the wood of the forests of the South; agricultural machinery, glass and furniture are some of the other products of the newly industrialised southern states.

Cotton-growing itself is changing. Where hand labour once planted, cultivated and harvested the crop, machines are now often used.

" Father of Waters "

One of the busiest ports in the South is New Orleans. The old French and Spanish houses of this city remind us of the people who founded it and first made it a place of importance. But New Orleans has now a growing horizon of skyscrapers that recall those of the other great American cities of the north-east. It stands nearly 100 miles up the winding Mississippi.

The Mississippi, " Father of Waters," is—with its tributary, the Missouri—the longest river in the world. It comes from Lake Itasca and from the Western Cordillera, flowing slowly across a vast plain, confined in its lower course by great embankments called levees which sometimes give way causing terrible floods. Its streams and tributaries extend into the wheatlands of the north, the cattlelands flanking the Western Cordillera, and the maize and cotton belts around St. Louis and New Orleans respectively.

South-east of St. Louis are the largest tobacco plantations in the world, many of them in the states of Virginia, Tennessee, and Kentucky. These states, with Georgia, North Carolina and South Carolina, produce about 90 per cent. of the American tobacco crop. North Carolina is the leading state. The chief tobacco centre is *Richmond*, and exports go via such ports as Wilmington, Norfolk, and Baltimore.

CARVED IN THE ROCK

Keystone.

The Black Hills of South Dakota, named after their dark carpet of firs and pines, contain an unusual monument to four of America's great men. On Mount Rushmore, carved from the mountainside, are gigantic memorials to Washington, Lincoln, Jefferson and Theodore Roosevelt. You can form some idea of the size of these effigies by comparing the face of George Washington (above) with the hut on the skyline.

STRANGE CITIES, OLD AND NEW

H. Armstrong Roberts.

In Mesa Verde National Park, Colorado, you can see this centuries-old cliff village that was once the home of primitive Indians. Droughts in the thirteenth century caused the Indians to forsake this and other similar homes at Mesa Verde.

Keystone.

Oak Ridge, Tennessee, is one of the chief centres of atomic research in the United States. Materials produced here are used for making plutonium at Hanford, Washington. This picture shows the hospital and dormitories used by workpeople at Oak Ridge.

SOME AMERICAN UNIVERSITIES

Harvard University, at Cambridge, Massachusetts, is the oldest in the United States, and dates from 1636. It is named after John Harvard, who left half his estate to the college. One of its buildings (called Halls) is seen here.

Photos: E.N.A.

This is the Harkness Tower of Yale University at New Haven, Connecticut, which university has produced notable scientific scholars.

This is Blair Hall, part of the University of Princeton, New Jersey, which until 1896 was called " The College of New Jersey."

WHERE THE TUOLUMNE FLOWS

H. Armstrong Roberts.

The United States has many beautiful National Parks where thousands of Americans go each year
for holidays amidst superb scenery. Among the best known is the Yosemite National Park in the
Sierra Nevada, about a hundred and forty miles from San Francisco. The Park has an area of
1,176 square miles, through which flows the Tuolumne River; and its falls, giant trees, rocky peaks
and domes provide such scenes of natural grandeur as are seldom surpassed.

YELLOWSTONE NATIONAL PARK

H. Armstrong Roberts.

On the borders of Mon'ana and Idaho, but mostly in Wyoming, are the 3,472 square miles of Yellowstone National Park, one of the most beautiful and incredible places in the United States, which is visited by nearly half a million tourists every year. Within the Park are hot springs and geysers, mountains made of sulphur and of black volcanic glass, and the wonderful canyon whose steep yellow walls hem in the turbulent Yellowstone river. It is here that the river leaps over a cliff 308 feet high, forming the Lower Falls seen in this picture

SCENES AT A RODEO

Maybe the American West is not so wild these days, but you will still find cowboys there—and cow-girls too. Their skill is often displayed in rodeos in which such events as roping the calf (above) always find a place in the programme

Photos: E.N.A.

Riding a lively mount such as this is a severe test of horsemanship and endurance for this Californian cowboy.

This picture shows us the ornate dress and harness that a cowboy might favour for some very special occasion.

Photo : Wolffsohn.

FISHING NEAR JAPAN'S SACRED MOUNTAIN

Of the countless picturesque scenes in Japan this is perhaps the most renowned, and it is known all over the world. The peak of Fujiyama is invariably capped with snow, but pilgrims come in their thousands to ascend the slopes. The earliest Europeans to visit Japan were Portuguese, so long ago as 1542. The first Englishman to reach these islands of " Cipangu " was William Adams, of Gillingham, Kent, who arrived there in a Dutch vessel towards the end of the sixteenth century.

THE OCEAN VOYAGER'S FIRST GLIMPSE OF THE NEW WORLD TO-DAY

It is these skyscrapers at the end of Manhattan Island that give the traveller by sea his first impression of the New World to-day. These skyscrapers of downtown New York should not be confused with those in the midtown section some miles away where the Empire State Building and other famous skyscrapers stand. Behind the tall structures seen in this picture are Wall Street and Broadway. The Hudson River flows in the foreground and it is along this busy waterway that the Trans-Atlantic liners arrive and depart. The district in front of the skyscrapers is known as the Battery, recalling the British fort built in 1693. New York Harbour is not the most beautiful in the world but its skyline is probably the most impressive.

COTTON "DOWN SOUTH"

Texas, the largest of the states of the U.S.A., leads in cotton production, but large crops are also produced in New Mexico, Arizona and California. This picture shows Negroes picking cotton by hand, but nowadays more and more machinery is being used for this work.

Photos: H. Armstrong Roberts.

This bonny Negro child, standing amid picked cotton, evidently means to lose no time in starting his career as a picker.

This mechanical cotton picker can pick a bale of cotton in one and a half hours. It would take a man seventy-five hours to pick a bale by hand.

WHERE THE TOBACCO GROWS

These are the Portland Canal locks on the Ohio river at Louisville, Kentucky. Kentucky, famous for its horses, is an important agricultural state with tobacco as the chief crop, of which nearly 500 million pounds are produced annually.

Photos: H. Armstrong Roberts.

Tennessee and Virginia also have some of the largest tobacco plantations in the world, the town of Richmond, Virginia, being the chief tobacco centre. This picture shows a typical plantation scene, with experts examining the tobacco as it grows.

FROM CALIFORNIA TO HAWAII

A wide variety of climate, scenery, trees and flowers is found in California, the Golden State of the U.S.A., which extends for nearly 800 miles from north to south. This picture shows the famous Joshua Trees (*Yucca Brevifolia*) growing in the so-called desert lands of California.

The twenty Hawaiian Islands lying in the North Pacific together form the Territory of Hawaii of the United States. The capital is Honolulu, on the island of Oahu. Next to sugar, pineapples (seen above) are the most important produce. Each plant gives fruit for about four years in succession.

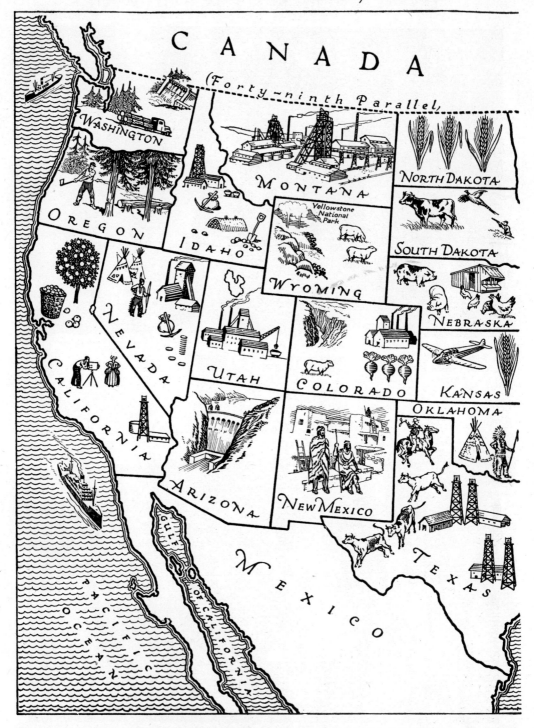

The Stars and Stripes, which is the National Flag of the United States of America, has six rows of stars in its top left-hand corner, with eight stars in every row. Each of these stars represents one State in the Union. This pictorial map shows the different States and some of the major activities or sights which belong to each. The largest state of all is Texas which is double the size of the United Kingdom; the smallest is Rhode Island, which is bounded by Massachusetts and Connecticut. Washington, the Federal capital, stands in the District of Columbia between Maryland and Virginia.

Specially drawn for this work.

That portion of the United States formed by Maine, New Hampshire, Vermont, Connecticut and Massachusetts has a climate not unlike our own, and these states are sometimes collectively known as the New England states. South of them are the Atlantic states, and still further south the states where cotton and other tropical crops flourish and labour is largely in the hands of the descendants of Negro slaves. States such as Iowa and Missouri form the Middle West and are followed by Kansas, Texas, Colorado and others known as the Western states. In the far west are the Pacific states of California, Washington and Oregon.

341

The south-east is the home of one of the greatest and most beneficial schemes ever undertaken by a United States' government—the Tennessee Valley Authority, which was set up in 1933 to control and harness the flow of that " worst river," the Tennessee. The area controlled by T.V.A. is as large as the island of Cuba and extends beyond Tennessee into the states of Kentucky, Virginia, North Carolina, Georgia, Alabama and Mississippi.

The Work of T.V.A.

Muscle Shoals Dam was given to T.V.A. and many other dams and power stations have since been built. The eighteenth T.V.A. dam was completed in 1951. Besides controlling the river and so preventing erosion, the dams have provided electric power for farms and industries. The navigation of the river also has improved. Reafforestation has been carried out, special fertilizers provided, and industry encouraged. Among the new industries are the huge aluminium mills at Alcoa, south of Knoxville: the big copper plant, near Ducktown: and the paper mills and plastics industry of Kingsport. Farmers have been helped by the scientists and soil experts of T.V.A., by cheap loans, and in many other ways. In fact, the Authority, which began with the task of harnessing the river, has now become " a regional welfare authority, co-ordinating the work of other Federal and local agencies throughout the valley."

Mondiale.

IN A CALIFORNIAN ORANGE GROVE

Between the Sierra Nevada and the Pacific lies the great Californian Valley with its endless acres of orange groves, vineyards and apple orchards. Here we see part of the rich orange harvest being gathered. The fruit is carefully cut, not picked, from the trees, and is cleansed with mild soap and borax before it is packed for sending away.

F. G. Bailey.

A MIAMI BEACH

The Atlantic shores of Florida, the southernmost state of the United States, are studded with sea-side resorts and winter beaches where it seems as if the sun shines all the year round. Miami is among the best-known of its world-famous pleasure grounds, and looking at this picture of sun-kissed Matheson Beach, Miami, we can understand why these shores are so popular with people from the colder north.

Many Americans believe an Authority similar to the T.V.A. should be set up for the Missouri river, " Big Muddy " as it is called, but as yet the M.V.A. has not come into being.

Water power is highly developed in many parts of the United States. One of the most famous dams is the Boulder Dam across the Colorado River. Another gigantic hydro-electric scheme is on the Columbia river, where the Bonneville and Grand Coulee Dams create vast supplies of power from the snow and ice waters from the Rockies. Power from these dams feeds light industry in the West and supplies the plutonium plant at Hanford, Washington, which was actually sited there because of the availability of limitless power. You can read more about Hanford and other American atomic energy plants in another volume.

Florida—Southernmost State

Lovely Florida, whose peninsula, like a projecting thumb, points southwards into the warm waters of the Gulf Stream, rivals California in the production of fruits. Its Atlantic shores are studded with seaside resorts and winter beaches popular with Americans from the colder north—Palm Beach, Miami, and Daytona Beach, the last famous as the scene of record-breaking motor trials. In Florida, too, you could buy a baby alligator if you wanted one, or seek out the aloof Seminoles, a people who live apart and are still a law unto themselves.

The United States has also responsibilities beyond her immediate borders, for she has several outlying territories—Alaska, Hawaii, Puerto Rico, the Virgin Islands, Guam, and American Samoa. Before long some of these territories may be granted statehood. Early in 1954, the Senate approved a proposal to grant statehood to Hawaii and Alaska.

"The Roof of North America"

Americans sometimes refer to *Alaska*, their territory in the far north-west, as " the roof of North America," and if you travel up the great Alaskan Highway (about which you can read in Volume Three) to the high mountains near Cape Spencer it is easy to understand this description. For here are some of the highest peaks of the North American continent, Mount Fairweather (15,300 ft.), Mount St. Elias (18,008 ft.), and Mount Logan (19,850 ft.). But the highest of all lies much farther north; that is Mount McKinley whose snowy cap rises to 20,300 ft. *Anchorage*, with a population of over 11,000, is the largest town of Alaska, but *Juneau* is the seat of government. At Juneau you can see a gold mine whose shafts run *upwards*. It is the Alaska Juneau mine which penetrates Roberts Mountain. *Fairbanks*, the Alaskan terminus of the great Highway, is only 120 miles south of the Arctic Circle, but is quite a modern town. Linked with Seward and Whittier, on the Pacific coast, by railway, it is of great strategic importance.

One of the most unusual places in Alaska and a natural wonder of the world is Lake George, which has been called " the lake that drains itself." For most of the year, the outlet of Lake George is barred by the Knik Glacier. Melted snow, rain and water from the glacier collect in the lake until, by about July,

THE RAINBOW NATURAL BRIDGE
H. Armstrong Roberts.
In south-eastern Utah, from the Arches National Monument to the Navajo Indian Reservation on the Arizona border, is a desert wonderland where Nature has carved the long reefs of sandstone rock into a thousand and one curious shapes and formations. Pictured here is the Rainbow Bridge which is 300 feet high and was held to be sacred by the Navajo Indians.

STATES AND TERRITORIES

Besides the states in the Union, American territory includes Alaska, Hawaii, Puerto Rico, and certain islands. The picture above shows us the Childs Glacier on Copper River in the Territory of Alaska where salmon-fishing and mining are the chief industries.

Photos: H. Armstrong Roberts.

This youngster is standing quite happily amid a Puerto Rico sugar cane crop. Molasses, tobacco, coffee and pineapples are also major products.

This picture takes us back to the United States proper, to the state of Maine, and shows how maple syrup is collected from the trees.

there is enough water to flood across the ice barrier. Once this happens, the flow is enough to drive a channel through the deep glacier down to the Knik Valley and Cook Inlet. Before long, the lake is completely drained. But with the return of cold weather, the ice barrier is once more formed and the whole process starts anew. Another interesting place is Point Hope, some 200 miles north of the Bering Strait, where archæologists have discovered a buried city which was inhabited in the years before Christ by a highly cultured people.

Alaska is by no means solely a region of snow and ice. The Alaskan summer brings long hours of sunshine, beautiful flowers, and pleasant times on the bathing beaches. But it cannot hope to rival *Hawaii* in such things. Here the traveller is greeted with those garlands of flowers known the world over as *leis*. There are more than twenty islands in the group which we call Hawaii, but only eight of them are inhabited. They are old volcanic islands, and the oldest is Kauai, where Captain Cook landed in 1778. The largest of the islands is Hawaii; but the capital, *Honolulu*, is on the island of Oahu, and is the chief port.

Hawaii's chief industry is farming, the staple crops being pineapples and sugarcane.

Puerto Rico

Puerto Rico is an island of the West Indies, and *San Juan* is its chief town and one of the oldest cities in the New World. In its sixteenth-century cathedral rest the ashes of Ponce de León, the first governor and the discoverer of Florida. Sugar is the island's main crop.

H. Armstrong Roberts.

PAINTING THE DESIGNS ON POTTERY

Under the admiring gaze of the little girl, this Pueblo Indian artist of New Mexico paints gay designs on her pottery. Her brush is probably made from a few hairs pulled from a dog's tail and twisted round a stick. The pots are soft-baked and are so porous that they must be water-proofed inside before they can be used.

The Story
of the
World and
its Peoples

Countries
along the
Pan=American
Highway

FLOATING GARDENS IN MEXICO

H. Armstrong Roberts.

His striped, blanket-like *serape* slung across one shoulder, this Mexican *peon* (peasant farmer) poles
his primitive craft across the still waters of Xochimilco's floating gardens.   The Mexican Republic, of
which he is a citizen, takes its name from the old capital of the Aztec empire.

MEXICO AND CENTRAL AMERICA

THE PAN-AMERICAN HIGH-
WAY, the great motor road that
is to link the United States with
Colombia, and so with South America,
will run across the narrow and mountainous isthmus that contains the countries of Mexico, Guatemala, El Salvador,
Honduras, Nicaragua, Costa Rica and
Panama.   These lands of the old Spanish
Main are the historic home of ancient
Indian cultures many of which survive
to-day in the manners and customs of
the peoples of Mexico and Central
America.   In some parts, Indians are
still the most numerous inhabitants, and
here and elsewhere traces of the ancient

Mayas, Toltecs, and Aztecs can be
found: slight maybe, but discernible
nevertheless.

One of the reasons why these ancient
peoples have not survived to a greater
extent is that the Spaniards brought
to Central America, not only an insati-
able lust for gold and Christianity at its
most fanatical, but also European
diseases which wrought havoc among
the native peoples of the isthmus lands.

The great centres of Spanish coloni-
sation were Guadalajara in the Mexican
Highlands, and Mexico City which was
the capital of the Vice-royalty of New
Spain.   Other centres from which

347

Spanish power spread were Guatemala City, and Panama which commanded the gold route across the isthmus and became almost legendary in its fame as a rich commercial city that was a constant lure to such buccaneers as Morgan. But the Spanish adventurers were comparatively few, and despite the dreadful epidemics the surviving Indians more than outnumbered them. Population is still thickest where it was before the Spaniards came, and Europeans are more than outnumbered by pure Indians, and by *mestizos*—people with both Spanish and Indian blood in their veins.

For three centuries Mexico and Central America were ruled by Spain, except for the British colony of Honduras on the northern coast of the Gulf of Honduras. The breakaway from Spain between 1819 and 1823 began a long period of civil war, of bad government, of groupings and regroupings of the Central American republics as we now know them, and in the case of Mexico, a desperate struggle against Napoleon the Third of France, who attempted to place Archduke Maximilian of Austria upon the throne of a Mexican empire. From such turmoil arose the modern Mexico and its neighbouring republics of Central America (except for Panama, which was part of Colombia until 1903).

In Mexico and its Capital

Estados Unidos Mexicanos, the United States of Mexico, is the full name of the land called after the old capital of the Aztec empire. For Mexico consists of twenty-nine states, two Territories, and a Federal District around *Mexico City*, the capital. Mexico is a land of mountain backbone from whose Mount Zempoaltepec both the Pacific Ocean and the Gulf of Mexico can be seen. Across the country runs a volcanic belt, some of whose peaks rise so high that they are always clad in snow. Most of Mexico is high table-land, but there are narrow coastal plains and also the low

peninsula of Yucatán. There is no cold as we know it; the Mexican climate is kind and creates ideal conditions for life and agriculture, although the country cannot grow enough food for its people.

The population of nearly 27 millions, it is said, includes over two million Indians. At least sixty-five out of every hundred Mexicans live from the land. On the coastal plains, there are verdant forests of mahogany and other woods, and plantations where sugar-cane, bananas, rice, rubber, cocoa, and other tropical crops are grown. On the higher ground, coffee, cotton, tobacco, maize, and vines flourish. On the high plateau land, root crops and fruit are grown, and here the farmers' asses, sheep, and goats are pastured. From the Yucatán comes about half the world's supply of sisal.

But only about half of Mexico's land is of real use to her farming people, and arable land is actually only 8 per cent. of her total area. Formerly, Mexican farmland was chiefly divided among the *haciendas* (estates) of the wealthy landowners and worked by poor *peons* (peasants). *Haciendas*, and their small brothers, the *ranchos*, still exist, but most of the big estates have been broken up and the land shared among the *peons*, under the *ejido* system of the rural village community. President Cárdenas, especially, took a lead in this redistribution of land, and it was he who gave the Laguna cotton region a £2,500,000 irrigation scheme and introduced collective farming there.

The market centre and focus of social life in Mexico is the village, where the people gather on market-days, feast-days, and holidays. Most probably they are farmers, or miners from the silver, gold, copper, zinc, or other mines, or workers from the oilfields and factories. For Mexico has important mineral resources, and the first centres to be established by the Spanish colonists, after Mexico City and Guadalajara, were mining towns. These old

SCENES IN MEXICO

In 1943, a simple Indian farmer of the Mexican village of Paricutin was ploughing his fields when he heard a rumble and just behind him appeared a spiral of white smoke. So began this volcano which is the only active crater in the volcanic chain that runs across Mexico.

Photos: E.N.A.

This is part of Mexico City's Paseo de la Reforma, one of the most splendid boulevards in the world, which leads to Chapultepec Park, the home of Mexico's rulers since the days of the Aztec Empire. Mexico City, with its population of nearly 2¼ millions, has been called the oldest city in North America.

Dorien Leigh.

MEXICO'S INDEPENDENCE MONUMENT

This fine monument stands in Mexico City's Paseo de la Reforma and commemorates the emergence of Mexico from three centuries of bondage. At the top stands winged Victory with a laurel wreath, and holding in her left hand the broken chains of enslavement.

centres are still being worked and one of them, Pachuca, is still the richest silver town in the world. Mexico produces nearly half the world's silver and is the fourth largest producer of gold. Lead from Chihuahua and Nuevo Leon makes her the second of the world's lead producing countries. Mexican oil comes from *Tampico*, on the Panuco river, on the Gulf of Mexico, whence have come more than 2,000 million barrels of oil since the fields were first discovered in 1901, and from the Tuxpan and Tehuantepec areas. The isthmus of Tehuantepec is now crossed by a pipeline which links the Atlantic port of Minatitlan with the Pacific port of Salina Cruz. New oil-fields have recently been discovered in the isthmus and in the state of Tabasco.

Nearly three-fifths of Mexico's people are *mestizos*, of mixed Spanish and Indian blood. Most Mexicans live in the plateau country, especially round the capital, Mexico City, which has a population of over two millions.

The historical centre of Mexico City is a square, or *plaza*, called the *Zocalo*, with the government buildings and the old cathedral, built on the site of an Aztec war temple. From this nucleus the present fine capital, with modern buildings, busy office blocks, spacious avenues like the Paseo de la Reforma, and busy industrial suburbs, has developed. Mexico City is not only the geographical capital of Mexico; it is the country's spiritual capital, a centre of cultural and social life as well as of industry and commerce.

Guatemala and its Gum

Guatemala is the northernmost of the Central American republics, bordering Mexico with a region of dense jungle where *chicle*, the gum that is used in chewing gum, is tapped from massive trees. The mountains of Mexico continue their southwards thrust in Guatemala, forming the *Altos* (Highlands) where most Guatemalans live " in the shadow of sleeping volcanoes."

GUATEMALA'S ANCIENT CAPITAL

Until 1776, La Antigua was the capital of Guatemala. To-day it is a sleepy old town rich in such architectural gems as the cathedral church of La Merced shown in this picture. The modern capital is Guatemala City, clean, spacious, and thoroughly up to date.

Photos: E.N.A.

Guatemala's Lake Atitlan is one of the most beautiful lakes in the world. Its waters are the deepest blue and are fringed by such volcanoes as Atitlan Volcano seen in the background of this picture. The lake is thirteen miles long and, in places, is fifteen hundred feet deep.

Actually, some of the volcanoes are far from sleepy; Fuego Volcano, near Antigua the former capital, is always steaming and now and again spews red-hot lava from the sulphur-streaked sides of its active crater. The land surface of Guatemala is mostly covered with ash from these volcanic giants, except in the east towards the Caribbean. Mount Tajamulco is the highest Guatemalan volcano, rising nearly 14,000 feet above sea-level.

Since 1776, *Guatemala City* has been the capital. Before then, the capital was at La Antigua, " the Very Noble and Very Loyal City of St. James of the Gentlemen of Guatemala," which three times in its cultured history was destroyed by earthquake and flood. To-day, La Antigua is a sleepy old town rich in architectural gems of the days when Guatemala was Spanish. Her Palace of the Captains-General is considered to be one of the finest examples of Spanish colonial architecture in the Americas.

Guatemala City was once itself a town of quaint cobbled streets, but these—and the old houses and buildings—have now yielded to modern thoroughfares and fine buildings like the National Palace. Guatemala City is spacious, modern, and clean, but along its streets you can see gaily dressed Indians carrying loads upon their backs as they do in all parts of the country, for Guatemala's population is predominantly pure-blooded Indian.

Coffee is the prime export crop of Guatemala which is an agricultural country with many corn-producing Indian small-holders. The villages are famous for their weaves of cloth and for the brilliance of their native costumes. In Guatemala, too, is one of the most beautiful lakes in the world—Lake Atitlan, which legend says is bordered by twelve villages each bearing the name of an Apostle. The waters of the lake are even more blue than those of the Mediterranean or Adriatic. Looking at the placid blue surface beneath the mighty peaks of extinct volcanoes, you are almost tempted to believe in the accuracy of the gorgeous technicolour you see in your cinemas at home: and it seems impossible that when the *chocomil*

E.N.A.

ON AN EL SALVADOR COFFEE PLANTATION

El Salvador's prosperity depends upon coffee, the most famous of its national products. The coffee is harvested at Christmas and is brought to the mills by every possible means, by train, by lorries, and by wagons such as those seen in this picture (right). Sometimes as many as 14,000 berries are gathered from one tree!

Royal Mail Lines Ltd.

IN THE CAPITAL OF BRAZIL, RIO DE JANEIRO

Brazil, the largest of the South American countries and the fourth largest in the world, belonged at first to Portugal, but has been an independent republic since 1889. Its capital, Rio de Janeiro (River of January), takes its name from the date of its discovery on January 1st, 1502, though there is no river of that name. The modern city, largely rebuilt in this century, is remarkably spacious, with many splendid buildings, especially along the Avenida Rio Branco which runs for over a mile from the waterfront until it incorporates the palm-lined canal, seen in the picture above, now known as the Canal do Mangue.

World Wide Magazine.

FISHING WITH BOW AND ARROW

In South America the native Indians in the neighbourhood of the Rio Negro, which joins the Amazon in Brazil, and of the Upper Orinoco in Venezuela, use bows and arrows instead of rods and lines for their fishing. The arrows are made of long straight stalks of wild cane, fitted with iron arrow-heads in such a way that the barbed head comes off when it pierces the fish but remains attached to the arrow by the cord. Silver-scaled fish called " cartabac " and the more golden-coloured " pacu " are caught as they feed near the surface of the water.

wind comes, the lake stillness is lashed into waves 12 feet high.

Coffee in El Salvador

If you received a letter from El Salvador, the postage stamp would probably have " El Salvador's coffee is the best in the world " upon it, but in Spanish. For the industrious little farming state of El Salvador owes its prosperity to coffee, which is the famed national product. El Salvador is densely populated, and it has been calculated that there are sixty-five coffee trees to each one of its 1,855,000 inhabitants. There are coffee plantations everywhere, on level ground and over the slopes of extinct or sleeping volcanoes whose volcanic soil produces the best of El Salvador's fine coffees.

The finest coffee is called *Malacara*, which comes from one of the largest and most modern coffee mills in the world, that of Santa Ana on the Pan-American Highway, forty-eight miles from San Salvador, capital of this little coffee state. At Christmas when the crop is harvested, coffee is brought to this mill, *El Molino*, as it is called, by railway, by lorries, and by ox-carts: and shift workers at the mill toil night and day to cope with the streams of ripe red berries that come by the load from the plantations. Sometimes as many as 14,000 berries are gathered from one tree!

El Salvador is mountainous, and its slopes and valleys are climbed and crossed by first-class metalled roads which are maintained publicly by the *Vialidad* system. San Salvador, the capital, is also the centre of population and is overlooked by San Salvador Volcano, which suddenly burst into terrible life in June, 1927, after 258 years of inactivity. This dreadful eruption, which went on until November, was accompanied by earthquakes and much of the capital was laid in ruins.

Even such little countries sometimes follow the examples of richer and more powerful states which have all the means to develop their territories. In 1950,

Fox Photos.

IN EL SALVADOR'S CAPITAL

San Salvador, the capital of El Salvador, has a population of over 160,000. It is a modern city with lovely parks and handsome buildings like the new church which is shown here. No less renowned are its beautiful tropical flowers and colourful religious festivals.

El Salvador began work on what is probably her most ambitious national project—the building of a dam across the Lempa river, about thirty-five miles north-east of the capital. The completion of this dam will double the output of electric power in the country.

Honduras the Mountainous

Although its area makes Honduras the second largest of the Central American republics, its population

THE CHURCH AT CORINTO

Corinto is the chief Pacific Port and Pacific railway terminus of Nicaragua and the gateway to Managua, the capital. It is a small place with a population of over 5,000, but it is from here that Nicaragua's coffee, sugar, hides and wood are exported.

numbers less than 1½ millions. One reason for this is that Honduras is among the most mountainous of the Central American states; for a long time her people were scattered in isolated communities with slow-moving ox-carts and rough mountain tracks as their only ways of reaching one another. To-day, however, Honduras makes up for its lack of road and rail communications by airlines which, in hours, do the journeys that ox-cart and pack mule would do in days.

What coffee is to El Salvador, bananas are to Honduras. The big banana farms are along the north coast. Honduras also has one of the largest gold and silver mines in the world, the Rosario Mine, near *Tegucigalpa*, the capital. Copper, iron, lead, zinc, and coal are also mined.

The people of Honduras are mostly *mestizos*, but along the north coast there are communities of Jamaican Negroes who were brought in to supplement local labour on the miles of banana plantations that have been carved from the jungle.

Nicaragua

A chain of twenty-three volcanoes, six of them active, runs down the western side of Nicaragua, the largest of the Central American states. Most famous of these is Momotombo, on the shores of Lake Managua, which was immortalised in Victor Hugo's poem *Les Raisons du Momotombo*. At the southern end of the same lake is *Managua*, capital of Nicaragua, a city which was devastated in the earthquake of 1931 but which has now been entirely rebuilt. The largest lake is Lake Nicaragua, which is a hundred miles long; a canal has long been planned to join the lake with the Pacific coast, thus providing a water highway from the Pacific down the San Juan river to San Juan del Norte (Greytown) on the Caribbean shore.

Nicaragua exports coffee and bananas and, in her eastern areas, produces more rubber than any of her neighbours, for here rubber trees were planted to give shade to the coffee crop. In contrast to the Spanish Nicaraguans of the west, the people of the eastern coast are predominantly Indian and Negro. Most famous of the Indians are the Miskito tribe, whose name was corrupted and given to the eastern coast. The Mosquito Coast, it was called, and for two hundred years it was a British protectorate. Nicaragua itself takes its name from Nicarao, an Indian chief who lived on the shores of Cocibolca, the Great Lake, which is to-day Lake Nicaragua.

Costa Rica, a Land of Flowers

Costa Rica, " the Rich Coast," is one of the smallest American republics. It is largely a country of coastal plains, with highlands and mountains rising to more than 6,000 feet above sea level as the central core of the country where are the four lofty volcanic mountains, Poás and Barba (both over 9,000 feet high), and Irazú and Turrialba (both over 11,000 feet high). Costa Rica's area of 23,000 square miles is inhabited by some 800,000 people, 75 per cent. of whom live on the Central Plateau. Unlike the other peoples of Central and Latin America, the Costa Ricans are of pure Spanish stock, people whose ancestors came from Galicia, Aragon, and Biscay. Costa Rica has less than 4,000 Indians.

Costa Rica is a farming country whose main crop is coffee. But she produces also bananas, cacao, copra, and rubber, and rears beef cattle on the plains of the north-west. Hers is a green fertile land whose rich soils led to the establishment of the Inter-American Institute of Agricultural Sciences at Turrialba. Hers is, too, a land of flowers and in the famous Orchid Garden at *San José* you can see one of the finest botanical collections. San José, a modern city whose electricity comes from hydro-electric plant on the mountain rivers, is the new capital of Costa Rica, and is about a hundred miles from her Atlantic seaport of Puerto Limón. The original capital was Cartago, a little over ten miles to the east of San José.

Panama

When we speak of Panama, we think more of the great canal joining Atlantic and Pacific than of the little state whose name comes from an Indian word meaning " plenty of fish." In its natural interest for the Canal, the world tends to overlook Panama and

Fox Photos.

WHERE SPAIN ONCE RULED

The old buildings of the Central American republics remind us that these isthmus lands were once part of a mighty Spanish empire in the New World. This fine old church can be seen at León, once the capital of Nicaragua and now its second city.

its 805,000 inhabitants tucked away on the edge of the great international sea route. Columbus came this way and reported to his Queen that he had seen natives " adorned with ropes of pearls." Pearl-diving is still romantic enough and has sufficient hopes of reward to induce the Indians of Panama Bay to brave the terrors of the deep—the devil fish, the mud crabs, and the electric eels—and dive down to the oyster beds where a fortune may be awaiting them.

23-2

To Panama came Vasco Nuñez de Balboa, discoverer of the Pacific who may well have given Panama its name. To-day, the Panama dollar is called the *balboa*, and Balboa's statue looks out from one of the *plazas* of Panama City across the ocean that he discovered.

Panama's chief product is bananas, but standing as she does at one of the great international crossroads, she handles manufactures and products from many other countries and is a clearing house for trade from all points of the compass. As her trade is international in the widest sense, so is the population of Panama's towns and cities. For *Panama City*, the capital, and Colón, and other western towns live by the Canal and through the Canal. In the interior are small villages where women still wear the *pollera* or the *tumbahombre*, where native Indians still paint their faces, where plantains and palm nuts are crushed for food with primitive implements, and where there are still expanses of unmapped jungle and legends of buried treasure.

The Panama Canal

The great Canal that bears the shipping of all nations stretches for nearly fifty-one miles from Balboa on the Pacific to Cristóbal on the Atlantic through the United States Canal Zone. First conceived as long ago as 1534 and rejected by the Spanish Inquisition as "impious," it was championed in later years by French astronomers, and later still by von Humboldt the great German naturalist and his famous countryman, the poet Goethe. In 1904 the United States occupied the Canal Zone and work began under the direction of Colonel George Goethals and Colonel William Gorgas. It was a superhuman task involving the damming of the Chagres river and the forming of the 160 square miles of the Gatun Lake as a reservoir for the water fed to the electrically-operated locks: the building of the locks themselves: and the construction of generating stations, observation stations, and all sorts of ancillary establishments. 35,000 workers and the largest array of constructing machinery the world had seen were used, and the herculean task took ten years to complete. In 1914, the Panama Canal was opened, and the sea routes between New York and San Francisco and Liverpool and

E.N.A.

THE BARREN SUMMIT OF MOMOTOMBO

The most famous peak in Nicaragua's volcano chain is Momotombo, over four thousand feet high. As we see it in this picture we can understand why Victor Hugo, the great French writer, called it a "bald and nude colossus." It was long known as the "rebel volcano" because it resisted the attempts of climbers, those who tried to ascend the peak never returning.

E.N.A.

THE AIRPORT OF COSTA RICA'S CAPITAL

San José, the capital of Costa Rica, is served by the airport of La Sabena, which is about a mile from the city. Most of the traffic is in the hands of the big international airlines, such as Pan-American Airways, TACA (Central American Air Transport) and KLM (Royal Dutch Airlines), who also control companies operating within the country.

San Francisco were shortened by 8,000 miles and 6,000 miles respectively.

Republics of The Spanish Main

Now let us swiftly cross the Caribbean Sea to the island republics of Cuba and Haiti and to the Dominican Republic.

Cuba is famous for its cane-sugar industry, and for its cigars which take their name from *Havana*, the capital. But while cane-sugar and tobacco are the best-known of Cuban products, the republic also has large market-garden and cattle-raising industries and large deposits of iron, copper, and other ores. Cuba is a favourite holiday country for tourists from the Americas and is an important air crossroads, the airports of Camagüey and Havana being used by aircraft of ten nations. Spanish is the language of its population of nearly five millions.

To the east and separated by the Windward Passage from Cuba is the forested and mountainous island of Hispaniola, two-thirds of which is occupied by the Dominican Republic. The capital is *Ciudad Trujillo* which, except for a few historic buildings, was destroyed by hurricane in 1930, and which is now a rebuilt and thoroughly modern city. In the old cathedral, they will still show you the glass-fronted box which Dominicans declare to contain the remains of Christopher Columbus, and at one end of the city they will point out an old ceiba tree as being one of those to which Columbus moored his ships. The Republic has a population of more than two millions and exports sugar, cocoa beans, coffee, molasses, cattle, and salt.

The western third of Hispaniola is the Negro Republic of Haiti, the only state in the Americas where French is the official language. Space does not permit an account of the violence and bloodshed which characterised the birth

IN THE STEPS OF BALBOA

H. Armstrong Roberts.

The city of Colón stands at the Atlantic entrance to the Panama Canal, being the twin city of Cristóbal, which is the entry port for the Canal in the Canal Zone. Looking at this pleasant road with its palms and houses it is hard to believe that this district was once a hotbed of yellow fever.

E.N.A.

In 1513, after a 25-day march across the Isthmus of Panama, Vasco Nuñez de Balboa, the famous Spanish explorer, beheld the Pacific. His discovery is commemorated by this fine bronze statue standing in the Santo Tomás Hospital plaza at Panama City.

IN THE "SUGAR=BOWL" REPUBLIC

H. Armstrong Roberts.

This swimming pool is in Havana, the beautiful Cuban capital, and borders the Malecon, a spacious avenue joining the city to its suburbs. The monument in the background is to the victims of the American battleship *Maine*, mysteriously destroyed in Havana harbour.

E.N.A.

Wielding sharp-edged machetes (cutlasses) these Cuban harvesters move up the steep slope lopping the luxuriant sugar cane as they go. Cuba is often called the "sugar bowl" of the Americas because its sugar production is immense; 85 per cent. of the crop goes to the United States.

of the republic or of the romantic, brave, and often tyrannical, leaders such as Toussaint L'Ouverture, the slave who became a general in the French army, and Henri Christophe, the Negro King whose grim and desolate citadel frowns down from the steep mountainside.

Christophe's Grim Citadel

Henri Christophe was the first President of the Haitian republic that was proclaimed in 1806 and subsequently exchanged his title of president for that more splendid one—" king."

He was efficient, but ruthless, forcing his subjects to develop the country by such cruel means that his rule seemed like a return to the slavery they had just thrown off. In the building of his great citadel thousands of slaves were employed in dragging the vast quantities of building materials to the mountain site chosen by the Negro king. These luckless men and women toiled ceaselessly under the stern eyes of Christophe's overseers, knowing full well that they would be killed if they did not work hard enough or fast enough.

Tier by tier the stones rose on the mountainside, but before the fortress was finished, Christophe's slaves were in revolt and, fearing what might happen if he fell into their hands, the crazied monarch shot himself. His tomb can still be seen in the vast courtyard of his unfinished citadel.

Port au Prince is the capital of the Republic which has an estimated population of three millions. Sisal, coffee, sugar-cane, and bananas are produced.

E.N.A.

THE GRIM CITADEL OF A NEGRO KING

During the French Revolution, Negro slaves on the French island of Hispaniola won their independence, and their leader—Toussaint L'Ouverture—founded a kingdom. Last of the Haitian kings was Henri Christophe whose mountain citadel, seen in this picture, was built at a terrible cost in human life and misery. Its walls, twenty feet thick, have within them the grave of their despotic architect, whose violent death in 1820 heralded the foundation of the modern Haitian Republic.

The Story
of the
World and
its Peoples

Through
the Republics
of
South America

H. Armstrong Roberts.

THE PRESIDENTIAL PALACE, RIO DE JANEIRO

Stately palms flank the approach to the Guanabara Palace, which is the private residence of the President of the Republic of Brazil. The palace is only one of the many fine buildings in the Brazilian capital which is a tribute to architects and landscape gardeners who made this lovely city out of an old town of slums and swamps.

THE LAND OF THE MIGHTY AMAZON

THE first glimpse of South America that most of us get on coming out from Britain is of that high shoulder of tropical Brazil which heaves itself out of the Atlantic at Cape San Roque. It was this same shoulder which de Cabral, the old Portuguese navigator, saw when he discovered Brazil in the first half of the sixteenth century.

Rio de Janeiro

Eighteen days out of Southampton our steamer calls at the beautiful harbour of *Rio de Janeiro*, the Brazilian capital, which has a population of over 2,400,000 people. Its lovely islands are dotted with the white villas of wealthy Brazilians, and the tall Sugar Loaf that rears its strange cone over the bay forms a fitting approach to the city's wide curving promenades planted with palms, its straight trees and fine open squares, and its pretty houses on the rising ground behind the business quarters of the city. A wonderful view of Rio can be got from the Corcovado, a mountain behind the city, or from the giddy peak of the Sugar Loaf itself, which has a cableway to its summit, and which at night is brilliantly lighted.

Rio is one of the great coffee ports of Brazil, as well as its splendid capital. But even more coffee comes out of *Santos*, the next port at which we call on our voyage south. A few miles inland from Santos is the coffee capital of *São Paulo*, a city whose fortunes depend as much on coffee as those of Kuala Lumpur on rubber, or Kimberley on diamonds.

São Paulo is considered one of the finest cities in South America. At the back of it and in most of the hill country of the Sierra do Mar right away to Rio there is the rich *terra roxa*, the red soil on the well-drained slopes ideal for coffee-growing.

The workers on the coffee *fazendas* (estates) are Brazilians, or Negroes, or Indians, or immigrants into Brazil from Spain, Portugal and Italy. A *fazenda* may support as many as five or six thousand people, for not only does it grow coffee, but it has its own cattle pastures, its own grain-lands, and its own gardens and fruit plantations, as well as its own mills, bakeries, repair shops, blacksmiths' shops, and its store where the thousands who live on the *fazenda* can buy anything they require. A really up-to-date *fazenda* in Brazil is a world in itself.

It is a wonderful sight when the green of the myriads of neat rows of coffee bushes changes to a delicate white in blossom-time, filling the air with deep perfume. It is the beginning of a story that ends (so far as South America is concerned) at Santos, where we see dock labourers— black, brown, yellow or olive-skinned — carrying the heavy sacks of coffee " beans " to transporters for the waiting steamers.

Interior Brazil

This is only the rich " doorstep " of Brazil. If you go inland and north from the coffee-lands, you come first to high tropical grasslands with many cattle and with great flat tablelands of bare rock here and there. Down in the deep valleys of their southern edges are gold-mines and gravel-beds that yield diamonds and other precious stones. Go on beyond the high grass-lands and you come at

H. Armstrong Roberts.

ASCENDING THE SUGAR LOAF

The world-famous Sugar Loaf Mountain at Rio de Janeiro, shown on the opposite page, can be ascended by this cable railway. In this view we can see part of the shores of Botafogo Bay and, beyond, the Christ Statue on top of towering Corcovado.

TWO CITIES OF BRAZIL

Rio de Janeiro is a city of peaks, palms, sea, and sunshine. In this picture we are looking across the Praça Paris, a fine promenade and gardens built on land reclaimed from the sea, to the Sugar Loaf, the most famous of Rio's peaks.

Photos: H. Armstrong Roberts.

The second largest city in Brazil is São Paulo, which has a population of over 2 millions. A city of skyscrapers and wide arterial roadways, São Paulo's prosperity is founded upon the coffee plantations and the cotton and citrus fruit plantations. Santos is the port for São Paulo.

Will F. Taylor.

BY THE "RIVER OF JANUARY"

Rio de Janeiro," River of January," was the name selected by an early discoverer for the vast bay upon which the Brazilian capital stands, because he wrongly believed this beautiful stretch of water to be the mouth of a river. Here is a general view of this city of perpetual sunshine.

last to the greatest forest in the world, the Selvas of the Amazon Basin, where trees and creepers grow so luxuriantly that they almost crowd out men and animals, and where the only easy way of getting about is by canoe or river-steamer along the giant waterways.

The best way to see what the forests of the Amazon are like is to take the steamer (from Liverpool) that will bear you across the equatorial Atlantic to the city-gate of the forests at *Pará*, and then up the mighty yellow flood of the Amazon as far as *Manaus*, the modern city in the very heart of the Selvas on the Rio Negro, tributary of the " mother of waters."

The Mighty Amazon

Your ship may be steaming up the Amazon without your realising it, for in places nearer its mouth this vast river is so wide that you cannot see its banks if you are in mid-stream. It is only when your ship follows the deep

channels as they swing near to the shore that you realise what this forest is, and begin to wonder what awful secrets it holds behind that steep precipice of living vegetation which faces you with its myriad shades of green in a wall 200 feet high.

Great flowering creepers fling carpets of scarlet or yellow over the forest wall; flights of brilliant birds wheel out and back again into the depths of the forest, giant butterflies with five or six inches of delicate blue wing-span flit across the deck, and in the yellow swirling flood, swarms of alligators float like almost submerged logs, or great tangled floating islands drift by. You know that beneath that smooth surface full of blinding sun reflections there lurk shoals of savage *piranhas*—saw-toothed fish that would strip the flesh from your bones in a few minutes—and that along the edges of the river where water and vegetation mingle in a gloomy tangle there are probably anacondas 30 feet long awaiting easy prey.

SNAPSHOTS FROM RIO DE JANEIRO

Capital of Brazil and one of the principal seaports of South America, Rio de Janeiro stands on one of the finest natural harbours in the world and is justly famed for the beauty of its position. The city is well served by rail, steamship and air services. Above is a view of the waterfront seen from the roof of the Noite Building.

Photos : H. Armstrong Roberts.

Besides being a prosperous seaport Rio de Janeiro is one of the healthiest cities in the tropics, and it has its pleasure beaches where the city workers and their families can enjoy all the pleasures of a seaside resort. Our photograph is of Flamingo Beach, with the Sugar Loaf Mountain, 1,230 feet high, in the background.

Yet in the heart of all this there is the city-port of Manaus; its busy wharves accommodate large steamers from European and American seaports and are the loading point for cargoes of rubber, Brazil nuts, timber and cacao. For that is the function of Manaus. The city is not the centre of an agricultural region or a place with much industry; it is a collecting centre for produce from an area extending into Bolivia, Colombia and Peru. The city is of such importance that it has a population of more than 110,000 and modern streets, buildings and public services.

The Rubber Gatherers

Down the dark Amazon streams comes the rubber collected in the forest depths by sweating *seringueiros* who brave the fevers and the forest dangers to earn a scanty living by tapping the rubber-trees and smoking the white juice on paddle blades to turn it into thick balls of brown and black rubber. Some goes by river steamer or dug-out canoe, some in great rafts of floating balls of solid rubber, to the port of Manaus for shipment. But wild rubber is not as important as the much finer plantation rubber for which countries such as Malaya are famous. At one time more than 80 per cent. of the world's rubber came from the Amazon country, and it was the development of the Malayan plantations that struck so hard at the rubber growers of the Amazon, whose previous prosperity had built the city-port of Manaus. Then, in the nineteen-thirties, the great Ford Company bought huge stretches of land in Amazonia, two great estates which were called Fordlandia and Belterra, and there began anew the cultivation of rubber. Unfortunately, the trees were attacked by blight and at length the Ford Company, which had spent five million pounds in developing the plantations, sold them to the Brazilian Government. Since then, trees that will resist the blight have been developed and the amount of rubber produced in Amazonia is increasing. Scientists are studying the Amazon lands and are helping colonists to establish farms on the rich soil that is being reclaimed from the jungle.

The "Great Diagonal"

The greatest development project of all is known to the Brazilians as "the Great Diagonal." This scheme promises nothing less than a 3,000-miles-long chain of new towns and airports across the jungle lands from Rio de Janeiro in Brazil to Caracas in Venezuela. Aircraft are taking an important part in blazing this path of civilisation through the wilderness, conveying men and equipment, even giant tractors and bulldozers, to the interior to work on town sites and airfields, the sites for which have been partly cleared by men and machines dropped by parachute. Then, as the towns rise, roads are driven through the jungle to link the new

H. Armstrong Roberts.

BUILDING A PAVEMENT

Rio's pavements are made of innumerable black and white stones carefully worked in intricate patterns by such workers as this Brazilian road-maker.

Brazilian Government Trade Bureau.

PART OF A TYPICAL COFFEE FAZENDA

Nearly 60 per cent. of the world's coffee is grown in Brazil. Coffee is her most important export, most of the crop going to the countries of North America and Europe. This picture shows part of a typical *fazenda* (estate) in Brazil. Some of these estates are as large as 30,000 acres and employ 5,000 workers.

communities with one another and with the rest of the country. Typical of these new cities is *Goiânia*, capital of the state of Goias.

The Great Diagonal, Brazilians believe, is where the future prosperity of their great country lies. In time, it is said, Rio de Janeiro will cease to be the Brazilian capital and its place will be taken by Brazilia, an entirely new city far in the interior of the country. Already the land has been earmarked and the plan prepared.

The Amazon lands, which are already attracting large numbers of colonists, contain fabulous riches—vast deposits of manganese, iron ore, copper, tin, silver and other metals, as well as valuable trees such as the babaçu palm, which yields a glycerine oil, and the

carnáuba, which provides wax, and mahogany and rosewood and other precious timber. Quartz crystal, gold and diamonds also are among the treasures of Amazonia. And recently, at Blue Goose Dome in the Peruvian part of the Amazon basin, an important oilfield was discovered.

The Selvas

Despite the changes which are now taking place so rapidly, the Amazon is still the home of primitive peoples.

Some of the natives of the Selvas live in thatched villages by the riverside, growing cassava roots from which the *farinha*, used everywhere for making bread and cakes, is made, and also maize plantains, cacao, sugar-cane and cotton from which the native cloth is woven. Others are primitive savages and head-hunters living in the remote parts of the forest, building great houses called *malokas* in which a whole tribe lives, each family in its own little compartment, with a great open floor of split logs for general meetings of the tribe in the middle.

This forest of the Selvas fills the whole of the great heart of South America ; it is mainly in Brazil, but stretches into the Guianas, Peru, Colombia, Venezuela, and Bolivia as well. Its heavy rains and hot sunshine give it a steamy, unhealthy climate, and its hordes of stinging and biting insects make life a misery to all except those who come prepared with mosquito nets to sleep beneath, mosquito veils to their sun helmets, and mosquito boots to protect their ankles from the winged pests. Yet now it is being tamed by " the Great Diagonal "—a scheme which may, in time, give the Amazon basin a population of a thousand millions of people.

The Treasure-House State

It is not possible here to describe all the riches of so vast a country as Brazil, but before we travel southwards let us look briefly at the Brazilian state of Minas Geraes (" General Mines "), which covers a high plateau behind Rio and the coastal range and which, as its name suggests, is a treasure-house of mineral wealth. Within this state there are literally whole mountains of iron ore; huge deposits of manganese, bauxite, mica and other minerals ; and great quantities of quartz crystal, gold and diamonds. *Belo Horizonte* is the state capital, and it stands within what Brazilians call " the iron quadrangle."

It is not hard to discover the reason for this name. At *Itabira*, not far from the capital, is one of the richest iron-ore deposits in the world. Caué Peak, near Itabira, is a mountain knob that is composed entirely of the ore, and mining consists mainly in taking slice after slice off the top of the mountain. From Itabira ore goes to the large new steel works at *Volta Redonda*, which was established in 1948 to provide more than half the steel needed in Brazil.

Volta Redonda lies in the Paraiba Valley, in the state of Rio de Janeiro, and is linked by electric railway with the iron ore mines of Itabira, 235 miles distant. Coal from Tuberao is shipped to Rio and thence sent by rail to Volta Redonda, where it is mixed with imported coal before coking. In 1951, Volta Redonda supplied more than two-thirds of Brazil's total production of steel ingots and nearly half her rolled steel and pig iron. But not all the Itabira iron goes to Volta Redonda; large quantities are sent by rail to the port of Vitória for export. More than $1\frac{1}{4}$ million tons were exported in 1951.

Minas Geraes has been known for its mineral wealth for many centuries. If you want to see what the state was like in the days when Brazil belonged to Portugal and a Portuguese nobleman was " Captain-General of the Mines," you must travel to the old state capital of *Ouro Prêto* (Black Gold), which has so many wonderful old buildings that the Brazilian Government has declared the city to be a national monument. Here, too, you can see the statue of " the Tooth Puller " (Tiradentes), a young Brazilian dentist who, in 1789, was a leader of an unsuccessful revolt against Portuguese rule.

Continuing this voyage southwards from Santos, the South American liners proceed to *Montevideo*, the capital and port of Uruguay, the smallest republic in South America, and *Buenos Aires*, the capital of Argentina and the largest city in the southern hemisphere. Both are the great ports of the Plate River, which is Nature's gateway to the grasslands of the Pampas and their cattle-lands, sheep farms and granaries.

The pleasant modern city of Montevideo has a population of 850,000. Besides being the capital of Uruguay, it is a very fashionable holiday resort with a chain of fine bathing beaches of gleaming white sand.

By courtesy of M. Bertrand Flornoy.

For many years the true source of the Amazon, the mightiest river in the world, has been the subject of discussion. M. Bertrand Flornoy, President of the Society of French Explorers and Travellers, has led three expeditions to the Andes and eventually traced the great river to its source. This photograph shows the stripling Amazon some 62 miles from its beginning. To follow its course the explorers were forced to take the tracks which run several hundreds of yards above the river. In its earlier stages, and before it is joined by the river Ucayali, the river is known as the Marañon.

Uruguay has been described as " the only ' welfare state ' in Latin America." Railways and public services are owned by the state, which also controls insurance, petrol, broadcasting and other enterprises. Uruguay has its state health service, which is free, provides free schooling for the young and pensions for the aged, and protects its workpeople. In all these respects Uruguay is much in advance of many other South American countries.

The wealth of Uruguay lies in her pastures. Nearly all the land is devoted to grazing, and in 1951 the republic had more than 8 million head of cattle and 23 million sheep as well as large numbers of horses, mules, goats and pigs. The Uruguayan ranch owner, or *estanciero*, usually lives in a rambling, single-storey house built of brick covered with plaster and standing within a garden where oranges, peaches, flowers and vegetables are grown. Around this " home farm " extend the pastures of the estancia, with the thatched adobe houses of the *puesteros* (herdsmen) here and there. Near the house of the ranch-owner are the barns and sheds where the sheep will be sheared and the wool stored, stables and cattle pens, the homes of the *peons* (labourers) and similar buildings. The main food of the workpeople on an estancia is mutton, and it is said that one *peon* and his family will eat a hundred sheep during a year.

Buenos Aires, like many other great cities of the New World, is laid out on the chessboard plan into fine streets intersecting at right angles. Here and there are beautiful *plazas* or squares adorned with statues and fountains, and shady parks. Museums, theatres and galleries and magnificent shops make Buenos Aires the most splendid city in South America. Six great terminal stations receive the many lines that converge upon it, and its docks are crowded with ships from all parts of the world. Its chief business is in meat, grain, linseed and wool from the Pampas.

H. Armstrong Roberts.

IN THE LOWER TOWN AT SALVADOR

Salvador, which is sometimes called Bahia, is the fourth city of Brazil and capital of the state of Bahia. It has a population of more than 424,000. Its upper and lower districts are linked by steep motor roads and by public lifts. One of the latter is seen in this picture. Until 1763 Salvador was the capital of Brazil. It is noted for its cigars and cigarettes.

THE SOURCE OF THE AMAZON

In this photograph we are nearing the source of the Amazon and are looking down on Lake Tincicocha, one of the string of seven lakes which leads up to the source. To reach it the explorers had to pass between rivers of lava at a height of some 15,420 feet, then descended to camp near the lake at night, close to one of the glaciers which feed the lake.

Photos by courtesy of M. Bertrand Flornoy.

This is the true beginning of the Amazon, in Lake Nincocha, the " infant's lake," as the Indian guide called it. From this tiny lake at the foot of a glacier 15,912 feet above sea-level, the first waters of the Amazon flow, to drain an immense area, which comprises nearly one-half of South America, as it flows eastward for some 4,000 miles to discharge its immense volume of water into the Atlantic.

24—2

"The great ocean of waving grasses rearing their silvery plumes to a height of eight or nine feet," seen by the Spaniards when they first visited the country, is now partly turned into grain-lands or into pastures for huge herds of cattle and flocks of fine sheep, which have displaced the native herds of deer and guanaco.

Estancias and Frigorificos

The large *estancias*, some covering half a million acres, centre upon the homes of their owners or managers, around which trees have been planted, and ranges of sheds and corrals built. For the families of the *peons* and the *gauchos* (cowboys) there are adobe huts further away from the home paddocks. The *gauchos* themselves, like the Canadian cowboys and the Australian stockmen, may be absent for many days, or even weeks, tending cattle and horses on these great estates, branding the animals or rounding them up for other purposes, and seeing that the long wire fences are kept in good repair.

In the neighbourhood of the Plate River ports are large freezing establishments called *frigorificos*, where the flesh of the animals reared on the Pampas is prepared for export as chilled or frozen beef or frozen mutton. There are great factories, too, which can the meat, make meat extract, and pack tongues into glass containers. Cattle flourish on the warmer and moister parts of the Pampas, sheep on the cooler and drier lands towards the south. You will find busy *frigorificos* even on the Straits of Magellan and on the lonely isle of Tierra del Fuego.

It is warm enough in parts of north-western Argentina for tropical crops to be grown. On the plantations there,

H. Armstrong Roberts.

WHITE SANDS OF THE URUGUAYAN CAPITAL

Uruguay is the smallest of the South American republics, but its capital of Montevideo is one of the finest South American cities and a favourite holiday resort. Here, lapped by azure blue seas, are the clean, white sands of Pocitos Beach, one of the most popular of the many beaches for which the capital is famous.

H. Armstrong Roberts.

IN THE COFFEE EXCHANGE, SANTOS

Coffee is Brazil's most famous product and while Rio de Janeiro, the Brazilian capital, is an important coffee port, even more coffee is shipped from Santos, 200 miles to the south. The most important building in Santos is the Bolsa, or coffee exchange, the interior of which is seen in this picture.

especially in the region of Tucuman, cotton and sugar-cane are grown, as well as maize and fruits, but in the unsettled region of the Gran Chaco, in the far north, native South American Indians live by hunting and fishing or growing grains and fruits.

Over the High Andes

From Buenos Aires we can take a train across the Pampas and over the high Andes to Chile and the port of *Valparaiso* on the Pacific. Leaving the San Martin Station at Buenos Aires at 10.20 either on Sunday or Thursday, we arrive at Valparaiso either on the following Monday or Friday at about 23.42 Chilean time, which is forty-four minutes slow of Argentine time. The first part of this journey is over the Pampas, whose level expanse is broken here and there by the trees round the buildings of the great *estancias*. Enormous herds of cattle and wide areas golden with grain or blue with the flower of the flax tell of the wealth being made there.

Next morning we are in Mendoza, "The Garden of the Andes," a city in a fertile valley of vines and fruit trees, within twelve miles of the foot-hills of the Andes. Changing here into the narrow-gauge train, we begin to climb in steep curves up to the great tunnels at the top of the Uspallata Pass, 12,000 feet above sea-level, catching glimpses of Aconcagua (23,000 feet) and of other snowy giants of the Andes up side valleys, and doing our best to accustom ourselves to the thin air at this height. We stop at Puente del Inca on the way to see the famous statue of Christ upon the Cumbre Pass where Argentina meets Chile; on its pedestal is an inscription which, translated, reads:

"Sooner shall these mountains crumble into dust than the peoples of Argentina and Chile break the peace which at the feet of Christ the Redeemer they have sworn to maintain."

At Los Andes we change into the Chilean train, and after a quick run of four hours from Andean snows to the flowers and orange groves of the lowlands we reach the port of Valparaiso on the sunny Pacific.

A new link in the Chilean railway system was completed in February, 1948, joining the Chilean nitrate port of *Antofagasta* with *Salta* in Argentina. This new Trans-Andean railway was built over some of the most difficult territory in the world : over the barren highlands that Spanish explorers called "the land of death and despair," over the desolate *salinas*, or salt deserts, fourteen thousand feet above sea-level, through steely barriers of mountain rock, during the dusty heat of summer and the icy snow winds of winter. The railway provides an all-rail route to Buenos Aires by which the products of the Chilean nitrate fields and the meat, grain, and manufactures from the Plate River can travel. Before the railway was built, transport of goods between Buenos Aires and Antofagasta involved a long sea voyage of over 500 miles to Valparaiso.

An even faster crossing of the Andes can be made by plane from Buenos Aires to Santiago. The many important cities and commercial centres of Latin America and the vast distances which often separate them have made the South American States very air conscious, and all the great places of the continent are in speedy touch with one another and with the outside world by the swift airborne transport of this modern age.

H. Armstrong Roberts.

THE COLUMBUS MONUMENT, BUENOS AIRES

Many South American cities are generously equipped with memorials to the great men of the past. Among those in Buenos Aires is this monument to Columbus. As we might guess from its name the capital of Argentina is a very healthy city.

Dorien Leigh.

THE PLAZO DE MAYO, HEART OF THE ARGENTINE CAPITAL

Buenos Aires, capital of the Argentine Republic, has a population of more than three millions and is the largest city in the Southern Hemisphere. It is a city of tall, modern buildings and pleasant squares and open places, one of the most famous of which is the Plaza de Mayo. The gardens (left) adjoin the Presidential Palace, which is known as " La Casa Rosada " because its walls have been colour-washed in rose-pink.

Chile

Chile is a country remarkable for its narrowness and its great length, for it is squeezed in the small space between the Pacific and the high Andes. It has many different climates, for it extends from within the Tropics to cool, temperate latitudes like those of the north of Scotland.

Northern Chile is a thirsty land. Much of it belongs to the Desert of Atacamà, where rain hardly ever falls. Yet if we look at the map we see along its shores a string of ports of which Iquique and Antofagasta are the chief, and cannot help wondering what it is that makes men live in a land that is by nature rainless and barren. But if we visit some of these towns we learn their secret. There we see large vessels being loaded with nitrates from the desert to fertilise the fields and plantations of Europe and many other parts of the world. We are astonished, too, to see fruits and pleasant gardens here and there, and soon discover that, like the people who live there, they get the life-giving water from the Andes, many miles away, through long pipes.

Nitrate Factories

The factories or *oficinas* where the nitrates are prepared lie out in the open desert, and have thousands of men and their families living in their many buildings. Some are splendidly equipped with libraries, gymnasiums, and even swimming baths. They are little centres of busy life, like islands in a barren desert. The nitrate is prepared from the hard rocky material which lies several feet below ground and must be broken by blasting before it can be removed to the factory. From this stuff, not only the fertilising nitrate, but iodine also is prepared. Formerly, about 90 per cent. of the world's nitrate fertiliser was supplied by Chile, but nowadays an increasing quantity is produced artificially by chemical and electrical processes. But the *oficinas* still produce about 69 per cent. of the world's iodine.

The nitrate ports, especially Tocopilla and Antofagasta, ship copper from the rich mines of the north, which are worked by American companies. Iron ore is mined also at such centres as El Tofo, which provides ore for the new Chilean steel plant of Huachipato, near Concepción.

Middle Chile is a different land altogether. Here rain comes in the winter, but the summers are long and dry and the grain-growers and fruit-farmers must carefully irrigate their land in order to ensure rich crops. The most fertile lands are in the Central Valley, where vineyards and orange groves, wheat-fields and maize-fields, vegetable gardens and olive groves flourish.

Southern Chile is yet another different land, where heavy rains fall, and dense forests clothe the slopes ; where the coast is broken into myriads of inlets and fringed with thousands of islands, and where Indian fishermen have their villages.

Along the southern coast are many *frigorificos*, which handle the millions of

Ewing Galloway, N.Y.

WORK IN A NITRATE FACTORY

Chile's wealth lies mainly in her mineral deposits, especially gold, silver, copper and nitrate. The latter comes mainly from the desert regions of Tarapaca and Antofagasta. In this picture we see the crushing plant in one of the refineries. Nitrate's main use is as a fertiliser, but it has important by-products such as iodine.

THE SIGN OF THE CROSS

H. J. Shepstone.

The great mountain chain of the Andes, stretching almost from end to end of the continent, forms the backbone of South America. It is among these mountains, at La Cumbre Pass on the Argentine and Chilean frontier, that this noble statue of Christ may be seen.

sheep that are raised on the southern pastures. *Punta Arenas* (Magallanes), the southernmost town in Chile, is a port of call for most ships passing from one ocean to the other and the chief centre of this important sheep-rearing region. In the Chilean part of Tierra del Fuego oil-fields are now in production.

The southern part of South America is often called " Patagonia." This name comes from the nickname *Patagones* (Big Feet), which early Spanish explorers gave to the primitive tribesmen whom they found in the south.

Robinson Crusoe's Island

In the Pacific, 370 miles off the Chilean coast, are the islands of Juan Fernandez, where Alexander Selkirk (the original of " Robinson Crusoe ") lived for nearly five years. Visitors can still see on Más a Tierra Island the cave in which he made his home.

North of Chile is the country of Peru, famous in history as the home of the Inca people whom the Spaniards of the sixteenth century found living in cities adorned with splendid temples and palaces. It was a wealthy and prosperous land among the plateaux of the Andes, where great roads linked the towns and a happy people lived upon the produce of their well-tilled farms and their pastures. But Pizarro, the Spanish adventurer, was greedy for gold and treacherously ordered Inca Atahualpa to be slain, although the Inca had caused his prison to be filled with gold from stripped palaces and temples as the price of freedom. All that remain to tell of the past glories of the land of the Incas are the ruins of mighty temples and giant walls made

Mondiale.

THE WORLD'S LARGEST COPPER MINE

This picture was taken at Chuquicamata, Chile, about 100 miles north-east of Antofagasta. Though it is called a mine, there are no underground workings. The copper-ore is obtained by blasting the face of the mountain, as the picture shows. Every day, trains take over 40,000 tons of ore to the nearby crushers.

SOUTH AMERICAN MARKETS

All the local people seem to meet at the market in South America, and the Sunday market at Huncayo, Peru (above), brings in the Indians from surrounding districts. Huncayo is the centre of a grain growing and mining district.

Photos: E.N.A.

This is the market at Popayán in Colombia. This town stands on a tributary of the river Cauca and contains many beautiful monasteries and churches, for it is an important religious and academic centre. Its Holy Week processions are justly famous.

ECUADOR AND TIERRA DEL FUEGO

E.N.A.

Few of the rivers of Ecuador are navigable. The principal river is the Guayas, seen above with typical houseboats moored to its banks. Ecuador is the chief world source of balsa wood and also produces the " Jipijapa " hats, better known to us as Panamas.

Dorien Leigh.

Half of the island of Tierra del Fuego belongs to the Argentine and half to Chile. The island has good, peaty soil and rich pastures, and supports large flocks of sheep. Oil is produced in the Chilean part of the island. Ushuaia, which is seen in this picture, is capital of the Argentine part.

SCENES IN COLOMBIA

Medellin, the second city of Colombia, is often referred to as the Manchester of that republic on account of its important textile factories. North-east of the city are these mountains with the thatched houses of small villages on their lower slopes. Colombia is best known for her mineral riches, which include gold, silver, and emerald mines. In Colombia, too, are the remarkable salt mines of Zipaquirá.

Photos: E.N.A.

This bridge is the Puente de Occidente in Colombia, and the river it crosses is the Cauca. The road is the Western Trunk Highway which runs from the Ecuadorean border through Medellin, an important manufacturing centre, to Yarumal and Puerto Valdivia. The bridge has a span of 940 feet. Main roads are good but comparatively few, because the country is so mountainous.

La Paz, in Bolivia, is often called " the highest capital in the world." It stands 12,000 feet above the sea and is built in a series of " ups and downs " as this picture shows.

This is another view of La Paz which, however, is not the legal capital of the republic. Sucre, over three hundred miles to the southeast, is the legal capital.

Photos: Will F. Taylor.

Ecuador, as its name suggests, stands on the Equator and has a long seaboard to the Pacific. Here is a home typical of the remoter parts of the republic.

Some seventy per cent. of the population of Ecuador is Indian and mestizo, and you will find both at such Sunday morning markets as the one seen in this picture.

A STRANGE RACE IN VENEZUELA

The extraordinary figure here depicted is a member of the Pishauko tribe. The tribe lives in almost impassable jungle and the men are most warlike among themselves and towards all their neighbours. If these people are overtaken by illness they resort to self-torture as a cure, and this strange custom is known to prevail among other savage races in different parts of the world. The queer fellow seen above is a dancer in full regalia on the occasion of a festival.

of worked stones and so wonderfully fixed together without mortar or cement that they have defied the winds and the weather of the centuries. Peru is still an important silver producer. To-day most of her silver comes by extraction from the lead ores of Morococha and Casapalca, and from the copper ores of Cerro de Pasco. Her reserves of the precious metal are " beyond calculation." Nevertheless, her copper, oil and iron are more important, although the large iron ore deposits have still to be fully developed. Two of the chief Peruvian oilfields are Negritos and Lobitos, both served by the port of Talara. *Cuzco*, the old capital of the Incas, stands at a height of 11,400 feet above sea-level. There you may see the cathedral built by the conquerors, and around the city the mighty ruins of the empire they destroyed.

Pizarro's bones you can see for yourself in their glass-fronted coffin in the great cathedral at *Lima*, founded by him in 1535. Lima is the capital of Peru ; its port is *Callao* on the Pacific, only eight miles away.

Sugar-cane and cotton are important Peruvian crops, especially in the irrigated coastal regions where fertile areas close to the barren uplands each have their own ports from which their produce may be shipped.

From the Peruvian and Chilean ports wonderful mountain railways make their way up to the high plateaux among the Andes to the shores of Lake Titicaca, 12,000 feet above the sea, and to the rich tin and cattle country of Bolivia and its capital of *La Paz*. These high Andean lands are the home of the llama, which is the chief beast of burden, and the alpaca and the vicuna kept for their soft wool. Railways run along the length of the Peruvian plateau—perhaps the highest railways in the world and far above the clouds.

E.N.A.

A LLAMA PACK TRAIN IN PERU

In the high Andes, the llama is the traditional beast of burden and carries loads weighing a hundredweight up to fourteen miles each day. This scene of a llama pack-train in Peru is typical. Notice the wayside cross and the rough state of this lower Andes road.

E.N.A.

ON ONE OF THE WORLD'S HIGHEST RAILWAYS

This is a scene on one of the highest standard gauge railways in the world—the Central Railway from Callao to Huancayo in Peru. This picture shows the climb to the highest point, La Cima, which is 15,705 feet above sea level.

Bordering Bolivia on the south-east is the republic of Paraguay, whose capital is *Asunción*. Cattle products, especially hides, are important and much valuable timber is exported. From Paraguay, also, comes *yerba maté*, a strongly flavoured type of tea.

The Northern Republics

The giant volcanoes of the Andes are chiefly in Ecuador, where Chimborazo and Cotopaxi rear their mighty cones ; but Sorata, who lifts his snowy head over 21,000 feet above the sea, is in Bolivia. Ecuador, whose capital is *Quito*—a city of eternal spring nearly 10,000 feet up—is the real home of the so-called " panama " hats, made by the Indians from the fan-leaves of a kind of palm tree.

The northern countries of South America—Colombia, Venezuela and the Guianas—are lands of cacao and sugar, of cotton and tobacco, of bananas and rubber. Dense forests clothe the mountain slopes and deep valleys, although parts of Colombia and Venezuela fall within the Llanos of the Orinoco—great tropical grass-lands. Colombia, too, is famous for the fine emeralds which have been mined intermittently since the days of the Spanish Conquistadors, and is second only to Brazil in the amount of coffee produced.

Colombia is rich in minerals, especially gold, silver, coal and iron. A national iron and steel industry is now being developed in the Paz de Rio region. There are also important oilfields, and most of the crude oil is refined at Barranca. Platinum has been worked in Colombia for more than 200 years, and

THE LAGUNILLAS OILFIELD

Lagunillas, one of the most extensive oilfields in Venezuela, lies on the eastern shore of the lake of Maracaibo. As the picture shows, drilling is carried out in the lake itself, often in considerable depth of water. The lake is about 120 miles long and, in places, 60 miles wide. Four channels, one of which is navigable, link it to the sea.

Photos: Shell Photographic Unit.

At Lagunillas the oil company maintains a school for the children of the oilfields staff and work-people. Six hundred children attend the school. This large outline model of the Americas is one of their geography projects.

CHIEF CITIES OF VENEZUELA

In the past thirty years Venezuela has become one of the world's largest producers of petroleum. The chief city and capital of this South American republic is Caracas, which was founded in 1567 and has suffered severely from earthquakes in times gone by. To-day it has become a modern city and this photograph shows how building development is spreading towards the hills that surround it.

Photos: Topical Press.

Maracaibo, a fortified town, was once the scene of one of the most daring exploits of the famous buccaneer, Sir Henry Morgan. In 1918 it still remained a primitive town, little changed since Morgan's time. To-day it is the second city and chief centre of the oil industry in Venezuela, with all the amenities of modern life. Above is a view of the Plaza Baralt in the heart of the city.

her deposits of this valuable mineral are the largest in the world.

In these hot countries most people live on the highland plateaux, where the climate is cooler. *Bogotá*, the capital of Colombia, is over 8,000 feet above the sea, and *Caracas*, the capital of Venezuela, is in an upland valley at an altitude of over 3,000 feet. An air service connects Bogotá with its ports of Barranquilla and Cartagena on the Caribbean Sea.

Venezuelan Oil

In 1951, Venezuela produced nearly 100 million tons of oil chiefly from the Lake Maracaibo basin. She is the second largest oil-producer in the world and the leading oil-exporting country. One of the newest refineries is at *Cardon*, on the Paraguana Peninsula, where a new town and port have sprung up almost overnight. Much of the material

for this new oil centre was sent from Britain, and the company promoting the development represents British interests.

Venezuela has important gold mines south-east of Ciudad Bolivar and rich deposits of iron-ore at Cerro Bolivar. Iron-ore from El Pao, in the state of Bolivar, is exported by way of the new railway and port of Palua to the Bethlehem steel plant in the United States.

The Wonders of South America

While the mighty Amazon itself must remain the greatest and most impressive of the natural wonders of South America, it is not the only remarkable spectacle for visitors to that distant continent. In the wild territory where the frontiers of Argentina, Brazil and Paraguay run close together are the Iguassu Falls, amazing in size and unsurpassed in beauty. They stand in the midst of untamed

Shell Photographic Unit.

CARDON, AN IMPORTANT OIL REFINERY

One of the newest oil refineries in Venezuela is Cardon, on the Paraguana Peninsula. The refinery covers about 810 acres; and the town, built to house the staff and workpeople, nearly 1,500 acres. Our picture shows one of the two schools built by the oil company for the children of the refinery workers. In the background are the oil storage tanks.

MORE MAJESTIC THAN NIAGARA

In the Misiones Territory of Argentina bordering Paraguay and Brazil are these cataracts of the Iguassu River. They are three times as wide as, and some 60 feet higher than, Niagara. The principal San Martin Fall is on the left. The Misiones Territory was so called because it contained several old Jesuit missions. The ruins of these can still be seen, the most noteworthy being those of San Ignacio.

Photos: E.N.A.

Clouds of spray rise from the cataract of the Iguassu known as the " Devil's Throat," sometimes reaching a height of 600 feet. The roar of the tumbling torrent is so great that you cannot hear yourself speak. Beyond the falls are exotic orchids, flowering lianas, begonias, palms and bamboos.

forest where orchids, flowering lianas, begonias and other exotic jungle growths blaze in an incredible mass of vivid colour.

The Iguassu River is a tributary of the River Parana and its famous falls extend for some two miles above a drop 200 feet high. There are actually several falls and each is named.

Another beauty spot worth visiting is the Nahuel Huapi National Park in the southern lakes of Argentina.

Peru offers a railway journey that can scarcely be paralleled—a journey on the central line from Callao to Huancayo. The distance involved is only some 300 miles, but the central line is one of the highest standard gauge railways in the world. Through tunnels and across bridges it climbs to La Cima, a point 15,705 feet above the sea. At times the mountainside is so steep that the train zig-zags, travelling slowly upwards in one direction and then reversing to travel upwards once more along the second arm of the zig-zag. This is a journey through some of the most magnificent mountain scenery in the world, to be compared in its majesty with that of the Swiss Alps.

Wild Life in South America

Anyone who has read the books of W. H. Hudson, the great naturalist who lived part of his life near Buenos Aires, knows of the interesting birds and animals to be found in South America. One of the animals, the guanaco, provides one of the exciting sports in South America, for it can be hunted in certain parts of the Southern Andes.

The guanaco is a member of the llama family, larger and wilder than the tame pack llama. Guanaco graze in herds, and can be hunted with the rifle or with the traditional *boladeros* and lasso. The *boladeros* consist of weighted thongs, knotted together, which are whirled above the head and then thrown so that they bind themselves round the prey, bringing it to the ground.

H. Armstrong Roberts.

WORKING IN BUTTERFLIES

There are over 30,000 different kinds of Brazilian butterflies, and many are so beautiful, especially those of the "morpho" and "blue silk" kinds, that they are preserved and used in the making of jewellery and ornaments. This picture shows a Brazilian at work on an intricately-patterned butterfly tray.

Telling of the
Products
We Send to
Other Countries

And About
the Goods
They Send
Us in Return

Specially drawn for this work.

FROM THE FOUR CORNERS OF THE EARTH

There was a time when the people of Britain lived on the produce of their own land. With the growth of population and as new worlds across the seas were opened up, this country gradually became a great trading nation—a nation of shopkeepers as Napoleon once termed us. Food and raw material were brought from other lands and in exchange we sold them the products of our own works and factories.

OUR TRADE WITH THE WORLD

HOW many of you envy Robinson Crusoe? What an exciting time he had on that desert island! But have you thought of all the things he had to do without and what a hard life he led? Would you really like to be marooned on an island all by yourself, and have to grow your own food, make your own clothes, and build your own house, in fact, do and make everything for yourself? When you sit down to your next meal, pause and think of all the things on the table that you would not be able to grow or make for yourself, simply because you would have neither the means, the opportunity, nor the time. Then think whence all these things come.

The bread may be made from wheat which once grew on the prairies of Canada, the butter may have been made in New Zealand, the marmalade, no doubt, contains oranges from South Africa, while the bacon and egg have come from Denmark, the tea grew in

After the painting by Lord Leighton, P.R.A.

PHŒNICIANS TRADING WITH THE EARLY BRITONS

The earliest of all maritime trading nations were the Phœnicians. They were the first navigators to sail out of the Mediterranean, along the coasts of Spain and France, and so to Britain where they traded with the " Tin Islands "—the Scilly Isles and Cornwall. This picture, which is on the walls of the Royal Exchange, London, shows Phœnician merchants exchanging purple cloth with the Britons for skins. They brought beads and jewellery as well, and received lead and tin, besides skins, in exchange.

India, and the sugar is from the West Indies. Of all the things you had for breakfast, perhaps only the milk originated in this country.

Every Corner of the Earth

Think also of the clothes you are wearing: your jacket was probably manufactured in Yorkshire, with wool

Specially drawn for this work.

ENGLISH TRADERS IN WOOL AND CLOTH

In the Middle Ages England produced the best wool in Europe and the trade in this, then later in cloth, was developed between this country and the Continent, particularly the market towns of Flanders where the English merchants established their headquarters in Antwerp.

that came all the way from Australia; or your cotton dress, made in Lancashire from cotton grown in the United States of America or India; your shoes may have the name of a Northampton firm, but the leather from which they were made came from West Africa, or the Argentine, as raw hides, and the heels first started their life on a rubber plantation in Malaya. So, you see, we eat and use things each day that come from every corner of the globe. Yet there was a time when the people of Britain had to depend on their own efforts for everything, just as Robinson Crusoe did.

In Britain, from the time of the Romans until the end of the eighteenth century, trade with other countries was conducted on a comparatively small scale: that is to say, by comparison with the vast flow of our trade to-day. Even within Britain, there was

no swift movement of commerce. The main reason for this was that the roads were extremely bad, and it was very difficult to transport goods from one place to another.

England's Woollen Goods

However, as Britain has a long coastline and many good harbours, her people have always earned a living from the sea. From the time of Alfred the Great we had a navy, and as transport by sea was much easier than by land, it was only to be expected that a certain amount of trade grew up between our ports and foreign lands. In fact, in the Middle Ages we had begun to be an important trading nation, and we were especially noted for our export of wool.

We produced the best wool in Europe, and for several hundreds of years wool from England was sent to weavers in

Flanders and Italy. Gradually it was found that more money could be obtained for woollen cloth than for raw wool, and so the English people turned to making cloth. This was carried on in the homes of the villagers, and not in large factories as it is now.

The raw wool and woollen cloth were taken at certain times of the year to local market towns, where they were bought by merchants, who gave good prices for them. Those parts of England which were good sheep-rearing areas became very rich. The Cotswold region has numerous relics of this old trade. The merchants who bought the wool had to take it along the bad roads by strings of pack horses to the ports and thence by ship to the main wool market in Europe at Calais.

There, other merchants bought the produce and the English traders returned with silk goods and other luxuries from France.

Fresh Lands and New Markets

Eventually the English merchants formed themselves into trading companies, and were known as the Merchant Adventurers. They had a charter granted to them in 1404, and established their headquarters in Antwerp.

As time went on, the people of Europe made woollen goods themselves, and so we had to look around for other countries who would buy the things we made. About this time America was discovered, and small groups of people were leaving Europe to settle in these new lands. These settlers provided the new markets we were looking for, and

Specially drawn for this work.

THE EAST INDIA COMPANY AT SURAT

Various groups of English merchants formed themselves into trading companies known as Merchant Adventurers and in due course they went much farther afield than the countries of Europe. Perhaps the best known of all was the East India Company to whom Queen Elizabeth I granted a charter on the last day of 1600. Their first factory or trading station was established at Surat on the west coast of India in 1612.

Specially drawn for this work.

ADVENTURERS OF ENGLAND TRADING WITH INDIANS

In 1670 Charles II granted a charter to the " Company of Adventurers trading into Hudson Bay " in North America. Trading posts were built at the mouths of the rivers running into Hudson Bay, and the picture above depicts the scene at one of the Company's early posts, Fort Charles, when the Indians arrived in their canoes bringing furs in exchange for the goods the English traders had to offer.

before long a thriving trade grew up with our colonies.

New trading companies were formed such as the Hudson Bay Company and the East India Company. The latter was formed in 1600, and had trading posts in India; the sailing ships, laden with silks and spices, took three months to do the journey from India to England. The discovery of new lands brought the discovery of new commodities; rice, tobacco, cotton, potatoes, and a host of other things, which now we take very much for granted.

Until the eighteenth century, our main exports were woollen goods, followed by leather and iron, while our imports included sugar, rice, ginger and tobacco from America, tea and silks from the Far East, wine and fruit from the Mediterranean lands, and wines and brandy from France.

The Industrial Revolution

Towards the end of the eighteenth century and early in the nineteenth, a vast change in the way people lived and worked, took place in England— so big a change that it has been called a revolution—the Industrial Revolution. Many clever inventions were devised, so that instead of goods being made slowly by hand, they were made much more quickly by machines.

About this time, too, a rapid improvement in the means of communication took place in Britain. Canals were constructed, railways were built, so that now the coal, raw materials and finished goods could be moved about the country with comparative ease. All these changes in the way things were made had several effects on the way the people lived.

Till this time, England was an

agricultural country, and grew all the food she required. Now, however, a large number of the farm workers found that more money could be made by working in the large factories that were springing up, and so the population gathered round these centres of industry and Britain soon became a nation of town dwellers. To-day, four out of every five of the total number of people living in England and Wales are to be found in towns, and over half the total number live in fourteen large urban areas. Now let us see how these changes affected the trade of Britain.

As the people became town dwellers, and as the population grew rapidly from only nine millions in 1780 to twenty-one millions in 1851 (to-day over fifty millions), it became quite impossible to grow sufficient food in these islands to feed such a vast number. So from this time onwards a very large proportion of the essential food for the nation had to be imported from other countries. Also, because we had begun to manufacture a much larger number of goods, it became necessary to import raw materials, for the only one we have in sufficient quantities is coal, and even with coal we are not always able to mine the quantities we need. Very soon cargoes of wool, cotton and iron were being unloaded at our ports. Goods made cheaply in the factories were sold cheaply in other lands, and our export trade increased rapidly.

Growth of Shipping

We imported more and more raw materials and food, and paid for them (and made a good profit) by selling manufactured textile, iron and steel

Specially drawn for this work.

DOWN IN THE COTTON FIELDS

Early in the history of British settlers in America the growing of cotton became an important industry. To meet the demand for the large amount of cheap labour required, a big trade in slaves from Africa developed. It was not until after the American Civil War of 1861–65 that this system of slavery on the big cotton plantations came to an end, though the slave trade itself had been abolished long before then.

goods to countries which needed them. The workers in the factories received higher wages, and were able to buy more and better food, and so the standard of living in Britain rose. We became a prosperous trading nation. Naturally many ships were required to carry all these goods and raw materials, and our shipbuilding industry increased accordingly. The time came when we had more ships than any other country. We carried goods and raw materials for those nations having few ships, and for this service we were paid in their currency. So we accumulated wealth in other lands.

British engineering firms also built railways, bridges and various large projects of this nature for other countries. All the railways in the Argentine are of British construction. Money to pay for them was raised in Britain, and loaned to the Argentine, who paid us interest on it each year. As we were selling more to foreign lands than we were buying from them, our wealth or resources in those lands gradually increased. A country which exports more than it imports is said to have a favourable balance of trade, and this means that more can be spent on necessities and luxuries; consequently the standard of living rises.

This state of affairs existed until gradually other countries began to learn how to manufacture goods for

Specially drawn for this work.

BRITISH ENGINEERS BUILD RAILWAYS ABROAD

Following the development of a railway system in our own country, British manufacturers, and in many cases, British capital, undertook the building of railways and bridges in many other countries. Here we see the work of laying the railway tracks in Argentina in progress. These remained British-owned until recent years.

themselves. We exported machinery to them and showed them how to use it, but of course our export trade to these lands declined, as they made more and more things for themselves. Then as soon as they had a surplus they competed with us in other markets, and we lost even more of our trade. Countries such as Japan were able to make their goods more cheaply than we could, because their workpeople had a much lower standard of living than our own people and received very much less in wages.

So, by 1939, we had become a great industrial nation with a population approaching fifty millions. But we could not produce enough food, clothing or raw materials in the British Isles to satisfy our wants. We had to import and, of course, we had to pay for what we imported.

Paying for Imports

Now it is no use my travelling to America with a suit-case full of pound-notes, hoping to buy wheat from a farmer there to send to England, because the Americans do not have pound-notes: they use dollars. Instead, I must take some goods manufactured in England, something the Americans want, sell the goods over there, and so get a supply of dollars. Then I can go to the farmer and buy the wheat, since I can now pay him with American money. In other words, our imports must be paid for by our exports. Trade between countries is not usually as simple as this. A third, or even a fourth, country may be brought into the picture. If, for example, America did not want my British goods, I should have to look round for another buyer. The sort of buyer I should need would be one who, trading with America, had more American money than he needed—and one who wanted my goods and so was prepared to pay me for them in American money.

Port of London Authority.

GENERAL QUAY SCENE AT KING GEORGE V DOCK

For centuries London has been one of the greatest ports of the world. In this photograph we have a general view of the scene at King George V Dock, which was first opened in 1921. To this modern dock come the vessels of famous shipping lines bringing their cargoes of meat, grain, fruit, tobacco and other commodities we need from abroad and then re-loading with the manufactured goods made by Britain's workmen and bought by customers in lands across the seas.

Central Press.

FOR A SOUTH AMERICAN OIL REFINERY

Varied are the cargoes loaded in London's many miles of docks. This picture shows a giant pipe, 83 feet long, 10 feet in diameter, and weighing 108 tons, being loaded at the Royal Albert Dock for transport to a South American oil refinery. This pipe was the largest of its kind ever to be exported.

Other ways have been mentioned by which we obtain credit, or purchasing power, abroad—for example, we receive dollars for carrying goods or passengers from one country to another in our ships, if we do it for the U.S.A. Money earned in this way, before 1939, paid for about one tenth of our imports. The interest on our foreign investments, such as the Argentine Railway, paid for about a quarter of our imports.

Unfortunately, the War came along, and we had for a time to give up making things to sell abroad, and turn to the manufacture of armaments and equipment for our Navy, Army and Air Force. However, we still had to import food and raw materials, and had to pay for them with our foreign capital and by borrowing money from other countries. Thus, the railways were sold to the Argentine and the money used for paying for imports of meat. We lost many ships during the War, and in any case could not earn money with them as they were needed to carry our own goods, war material and armed forces.

We were no longer able to pay for a quarter of our imports with the interest received from money invested abroad. Nor were we able to make up for this at once by manufacturing more goods for export. For during the War, little could be done to provide our factories with new machines to replace those that were wearing out. Our output of goods was therefore less. Even coal production had fallen seriously, although the demand had risen, and we were forced to bring in coal from other countries.

That is why Britain has had to work

hard in recent years to make more goods for export and to find countries abroad that will buy them. Only by doing this can we get the foreign currency to buy all the things we need. We have succeeded in sending more goods abroad; in 1949, we exported goods to the value of nearly £1,845,000,000, but in 1952 we exported more than £2,693,000,000 worth. We must continue to work hard to produce goods at the lowest possible prices, because once again we are faced with competition from countries such as Germany and Japan, who are recovering rapidly from their defeat in the Second World War.

One difficulty in trade to-day is that a country may want to buy goods from us, but not have the British money—or the equivalent value in goods that Britain wants—to pay for them. For example, the farmers of Brazil would like to buy farm machinery made in Britain, but they cannot do so because Brazil has at present no way of paying for this machinery. Our manufacturers, of course, would like to sell to Brazil, but we have no suitable foreign currency with which to buy Brazilian products. Currency restrictions, therefore, often make trade between countries uncertain to-day; indeed, at times trade between two countries may be brought to a standstill, and the markets may be closed until enough of the right currency has been earned by one or other of the countries concerned.

How We Trade with the World

In other sections of "Pictorial Knowledge" you may read about other countries and learn from the pictures what interesting places there are to be seen. In this section we shall again visit many of these countries of the World to discover what they produce for us, and what we send to them in normal times.

Let us first turn to our nearest neighbour, France, and find out with what

David Brown Corporation (Sales) Ltd.

FOR WORK IN FLOODED RICE FIELDS

British machines are made for work in many parts of the world where conditions are quite unlike those at home. Here, for example, are a British tractor and rotary cultivator being operated in a partly-drained lake. This demonstration was carried out for the benefit of a Burmese trade delegation and showed that the equipment would be quite suitable for work in flooded rice fields.

Fox.

LORRIES FOR FINLAND

Loaded at London's Surrey Docks, these lorry chassis pack the after deck of a Finnish merchant-
man bound for Helsinki.   Finland, who provides us with valuable timber from her vast forests,
has received large numbers of these lorries from Britain in the past few years.

things she could provide us.   Probably one of the most familiar commodities (at least in name) is the sparkling wine, Champagne.   But we obtain many other popular and well-known French wines, which, like Champagne, Burgundy and Bordeaux wines, receive their names from that part of the country in which they are made.   They differ for many reasons.   One is because of the different varieties of grapes which are grown, and another is the varied soils in which the vines are cultivated.   Yet another reason is the climate, which affects the flavour of the grapes.   Wherever the vine is grown, it requires strong continuous sunshine before the autumn harvest, and so in Britain we cannot grow grapes

successfully, except in hothouses.   In 1953, we imported in bulk over $1\frac{1}{4}$ million gallons of French wines.

What France Supplies

Nearly one-fifth of France is covered with forests; compare this with England, where only about one-twentieth is forestland.   Wood from these forests is burned in pits, or kilns.   The wood charcoal thus obtained is very useful for hardening steel, refining sugar and producing penicillin.   For these and similar purposes, we require much charcoal in the United Kingdom.

Nearly all of you, at one time or another, will have heard of " French Chalk "—perhaps when you have been to the tailor's to buy a suit or have an overcoat made, for tailors use " French Chalk " for marking cloth. The real name for this substance is Steatite, or Soapstone, because it has a soapy feel. It is also used in the manufacture of electrical switchboards and acid-proof table tops. When it is in a very pure form it is called talc, and it is the main constituent of talcum powder. When sprinkled on inner tubes and rubber gloves it prevents them from sticking, and it is also employed as a " filler " in high quality paper, oilcloth and textiles. These are only a few of the uses to which it is put in the various industries of Britain. The largest deposit of talc in Europe is found on the northern slopes of the Pyrenees, those high mountain ranges between France and Spain.

France also helps to provide us with silk. The centre of her silk industry is the ancient city of Lyons. Some of the raw silk is obtained from Far Eastern countries, and some from silkworms reared locally on the leaves of the mulberry trees, which abound in this part of France. We buy some of the silk in the form of cloth and some as dresses made by famous French fashion houses. Paris fashions are now finding London fashions a serious rival, for during the occupation of France by the Germans, only women on the continent of Europe could obtain the French model clothes, while we were free to develop our export trade of dresses, shoes and hats with the Commonwealth and the countries in North and South America.

For the Glass Makers

British fabrics have an excellent reputation abroad, as we specialise in high quality woollen and cotton cloth, having lost most of our markets for cheap goods as a result of competition by Japan and India. What is more,

Central Press.

ENGINES FOR EUROPE'S RAILWAYS

London Docks are by no means the only outlet for Britain's vital exports. Here we see a " Liberation " locomotive being loaded at Gladstone Dock, Liverpool. Built at Newton-le-Willows, Lancashire, it formed part of a consignment shipped shortly after the end of the war to help in the re-equipment of Europe's shattered railways.

Central Press.

BRITISH ENGINEERING SKILL SERVES THE WORLD

Behind the ports where British goods are loaded for markets abroad are the factories where the goods are made. This picture shows car parts being made ready for shipment to Australia. British cars and other products of our great engineering craftsmanship are justly world-famous and play an important part in our trade with the world.

we have had to import from France to provide sufficient material for the dresses and suits we need. These fabrics are manufactured in North-East France around Lille, where there is an important coalfield. Some of the raw wool used here is bought from London, the world's chief wool market.

When one considers the vast amount of glass that must be needed for the windows of all the buildings in Britain, for all the tumblers, mirrors, pictures, laboratory equipment, and the hundred and one other glass objects used by the British people, it is not surprising that a large quantity of sand suitable for making glass has to be imported. France is one of our sources of supply.

Other small, but essential, things which we buy from France because we have not enough here include pigments for giving yellow, brown and red tints to paint, and rosin, which also is used in the paint industry and in the paper, soap and linoleum industries.

Before 1939 we bought diamond dies from France. These are diamonds mounted in a frame, and through each diamond is bored a tiny hole. Very fine wires are made by drawing metal through these holes. Thousands of miles of wire were required during the War, and so our production of dies increased to meet all our own requirements, with even a small surplus for export. However, since the War we have once again begun

26-2

to buy abroad a small number of diamond dies, particularly of the smaller sizes.

Other manufactured articles we buy from France include artificial abrasives used for grinding and polishing wood and metal; and chemicals, which are used as alloys in our important iron and steel industries of the Midlands and Sheffield.

As you have read in another section of "Pictorial Knowledge," France has many ancient towns and buildings, and she is rich in scenic beauty, especially in the Alpine region and the south coast. The latter, known as the Riviera, enjoys a very pleasant sunny climate even in our winter. All these things attract British tourists. The money they spend enables British exports to be bought in France. For similar reasons we in Britain are advertising abroad the interesting and beautiful sights to be seen in these islands, so that visitors, particularly from America, may be attracted here.

In the Netherlands

Belgium is only a small country, but the most densely populated in Europe. Many of the people, however, have a low standard of living, which enables cheap manufactured goods to be produced. Glass and glassware, cotton goods, iron and steel bars are made on the coalfield, which is an extension of that in N.E. France mentioned previously. The coal seams are very contorted, which makes them difficult and expensive to work. Indeed, the average British miner normally has an output twice that of his Belgian counterpart. Belgium has insufficient coal for her requirements, and, like her neighbour France, imports coal from Britain as well as from the German Ruhr. The more coal we can export, the more goods we can buy from her.

Paul Popper.

LUMBER AT A SWEDISH MILL

About half Sweden is forestland, whence comes the timber for furniture, pit props, matches and wood-pulp. Nearly half her exports consist of timber products, and in this commodity Britain is Sweden's best customer. The picture shows lumber at the Vifstavarf sawmills.

Associated Press.

PLOESTI, RUMANIA'S GREATEST OILFIELDS

Oil is one of the most important of world commodities. The Ploesti fields in Rumania have a comparatively small output compared with the United States, Venezuela, and the Middle East, but are the largest in Europe. The oil that comes from the refineries shown here is at present going mainly to Russia and the countries within her sphere of influence.

Belgium is also our chief supplier of flax, which goes to Northern Ireland to make linen. Beside the streams which cross the Belgian plain, grow willow trees, and from them we get rods and sticks for making baskets and furniture.

In return for these raw materials and manufactured articles Belgium buys machinery and woollen goods from us. Once again we see how vital the textile industry is to our trade.

Belgium's next door neighbour, Holland, is, as you may read elsewhere, very low-lying, especially those parts called polders, which have been reclaimed from the sea. Often the land is sandy, but this does not prevent cattle and pigs being reared, for nowadays the cattle are fed on root crops and imported cattle-cake. The Netherlands are famous for their dairy produce which, once bought widely by us, still comes to this country in such quantities as our earnings of foreign currency will permit.

Where Bulbs are Grown

Were you to visit the little town of Alkmaar in northern Holland on a Friday morning, a colourful scene would present itself. This is market day, and from the farms and dairies of the district are brought the round, shining red cheeses for which Holland is famous. The workers in the market wear white coats and red, green or some other coloured ribbon in their hats, to represent the firm employing them. Have a look next time you go into the grocer's shop and you may see one of these cheeses, for they are popular in England. Ask your greengrocer if he ever sells things from Holland. He will reply, " Yes, plenty. We get thousands of good, sound tomatoes from there, and cucumbers, and even peaches and grapes, early in the year, too." This is because most of the plants are grown under glass in hothouses.

Onions, too, we buy from the Dutch to increase our food supply. The onion is an edible bulb with a rather curious looking flower, but the people of Holland are specialists in growing bulbs which produce very beautiful flowers. The most common are tulips, hyacinths and daffodils. It may be that some of the flowers in your garden came from a field near the Dutch town of Haarlem.

We must not forget that Holland has industries very similar to those of Belgium. Her tiny coalfield in the province of Limburg, in southern Holland, is really a continuation of the Sambre-Meuse coalfield of Belgium. The coal is costly to mine and Rotterdam in normal times imports quantities from Tyneside in northern Britain, finding the sea-borne coal much cheaper.

In return for the dairy produce, vegetables, bulbs and flax, we send to Holland, besides coal, cotton yarn for weaving into cloth, and jute sacks from Dundee. Holland, like England, is a country with a large mercantile fleet, and she needs large quantities of jute cloth to bring home sugar, coffee and so on from the East Indies.

On Dutch Roads

Nearly everyone in Holland rides a bicycle, for it is ideal cycling country, with no hills, where special "roads" have been built for cyclists. Many of our British cycle manufacturers sell their goods to the Dutch people, who appreciate the reliable quality of our machines. British-made motor cars are also to be seen on the roads of Holland. If we can export more and more cycles, cars, lorries and tractors, it will enable us to buy more and more of the things we need.

Denmark, another low-lying country, is famous for its dairy produce. The rich farmlands and pastures, especially those of middle and eastern Denmark, enable the farmers to breed fine dairy cattle, pigs and poultry. Co-operative creameries and bacon factories turn the farm products into rich butter and cheese or first-rate bacon.

We buy butter, cheese, eggs and bacon from Denmark, who ships these goods to us through the port of Esbjerg. In 1953, more than £54,800,000 worth of dairy produce came to us from Denmark, who was second only to New Zealand in the amount of dairy stuffs sent to Great Britain.

Diatomite from Denmark

One interesting mineral we buy from Denmark is called Diatomite. This consists of the fossil remains of microscopic water plants. A cubic inch of Diatomite has been estimated to contain between forty and seventy millions of these diatoms. Diatomite resembles chalk in appearance and is capable of absorbing about three times its own weight of water. This property makes it important as a filter, in the process of sugar refining and in the making of malt extracts and fruit juices. It is used also for filtering petrol, sewage and perfumes, and is put into metal polishes as a mild abrasive.

Denmark has neither coal nor iron, so these materials, and goods made from iron, such as agricultural machinery and motor cars, she normally buys from us.

Like Great Britain, Germany is a manufacturing country, for she has large, rich coalfields, and highlands in the south where cheap electricity is produced. Before 1939 the policy of the Nazi government was to make her as self-sufficient as possible, relying on imports from other countries to the minimum extent. Some things, however, Germany has always had to import. From Great Britain she

E.N.A.

GREEK CURRANTS DRYING

Currants form over half our imports from Greece. The picture shows trays of currants drying in the sun. The little huts in the shade of the trees in the background are used for drying " shade " currants which are the most expensive variety. The chief centre of the industry is Patras, on the southern shores of the gulf of that name.

obtained cotton and woollen yarn and re-exported raw wool. In return, she supplied us with textiles, paper goods, iron and steel goods, machinery, glass and chemicals.

From the earliest times when the ancient Vikings voyaged abroad the people of Norway have turned to the sea for their livelihood, because the interior of their country is bleak and inhospitable; there is very little flat or fertile land. Fishing fleets visit the shallow waters of the Dogger Bank, the cold waters of the Arctic Ocean, as well as the sheltered waters of the fjords behind the skerrygard. They catch far more fish than the three and a quarter million Norwegians require, and the surplus is exported. Next time you have brisling (like small sardines) for tea, look on the label, and you will probably see that they were canned in the small port of Stavanger.

Norway has innumerable water falls,

which are used to generate cheap electricity. We have already seen that this is essential in the production of aluminium, but it is needed also for the manufacture of artificial abrasives, and certain mineral compounds known as ferro-alloys. Ferro-alloys are absolutely vital to the manufacture of steel, different alloys being used according to the special purpose for which the steel is required. These alloys, as well as aluminium, we obtain from Norway.

In addition she can provide us with many other minerals, which are the raw materials of many of our industries. Graphite is used amongst other things for making stove polish. Titanium, a black mineral, oddly enough gives the best white pigment used in the paint industry. Quartz is employed in the manufacture of cheap jewellery, radio sets and telephone instruments. Pyrites, an iron ore containing a high percentage of sulphur, is used in the production of sulphuric acid.

Some parts of Norway, where the slopes are not too steep, are clothed with coniferous forest. The soft wood from these spruce and pine trees is much in demand in Britain, where it appears as pit props, boxwood and pulp for the making of paper.

In return for these raw materials we supply Norway with the manufactured goods she is unable to make herself. These include woollen and cotton cloth, motor cars, radios, domestic and factory machinery.

A Land of Forests

Approximately one-half of Sweden is covered with evergreen forest. It is therefore not surprising that nearly one-half of her exports consists of timber products. Look on the label of a box of matches and see if it has come from Sweden. We buy thousands of boxes from her, in fact the safety match was a Swedish invention. The timber from her vast forests is used for furniture and pit props, much of it is ground into pulp for the manufacture of paper, while Swedish spruce is used in the manufacture of the " man-made silk " that is called rayon. As you can imagine, we need these timber products in Britain and are Sweden's chief customer for timber.

Southern Sweden is largely beautiful rolling farmland with lakes, streams and spotlessly clean farms. Here, where the climate is more sunny than in the rest of Scandinavia, oats, wheat, potatoes and sugar beet are grown, and

E.N.A.

SORTING TOBACCO LEAF AT A TURKISH FACTORY

Turkey has given its name to a special kind of cigarette, made from tobacco grown on the Mediterranean coastlands. This picture shows girl workers in one of the great Government factories examining and sorting tobacco leaf. Some of this tobacco will eventually find its way into cigarettes to be sold in our own country.

Tea Bureau.

TEA FOR BRITAIN AND THE WORLD

Until about 1830, all the world's tea came from China. But the greatest exporter of tea in the modern world is India. Much of India's best tea is grown on the lower slopes of the Himalayas, around Darjeeling. This general view of a tea estate shows the tea factory and the buildings in which the workers live.

dairy cattle are bred. As in Denmark there is a co-operative marketing scheme, efficiently run, and from the central creameries we buy quantities of butter. Your breakfast eggs and bacon may also have come from Sweden.

In the lonely north, where the long dark winters are illuminated by the Aurora Borealis, are whole mountains made of rich iron ore. This raw material is much in demand by the great iron and steel manufacturing countries of Europe. We use large quantities in the blast furnaces at Middlesbrough and the steel works at Sheffield.

About twenty-five years ago, a great mass of arsenic ore, the largest in the world, was discovered near Boliden, in northern Sweden. This mine alone could provide all the world with every bit of arsenic it requires. We import some for making weedkiller, insecticides and sheep and cattle dips.

Sweden is noted for the manufacture of high quality steel goods, requiring highly skilled labour. We import ball-bearings, electrical appliances, and Primus stoves, the latter being a Swedish invention.

In return for these vital products of Sweden's forests, fields and mines, we supply her with coal. This comes very largely from our Scottish mines in Lanarkshire, Fifeshire and Midlothian. She also imports pig-iron, having no coking coal with which to smelt her own ore. Machinery for her textile mills and other factories is also imported from Britain and other countries.

Some of you may have been down a coalmine. It is a rather frightening experience until one gets used to it. Think of those long dark tunnels, with hundreds of feet of solid rock above them—small wonder that stout pit-props are needed to support the roof. In many mines steel supports are used, but a large number of miners hate working in these mines, preferring those which still use wooden props. This is surprising until one knows the reason. If the steel props can no longer support the roof, one will snap suddenly, and the miners may be caught and crushed to death, but a wooden prop gives a warning cra-a-a-ack, giving the miners a fraction of a minute in which to dodge to safety.

Before 1939 we bought hundreds of thousands of pit-props each year from Finland, and although this trade was halted during the war years, we are again buying large quantities of timber from her vast forests.

The Union of Soviet Socialist Republics

The U.S.S.R. extends for thousands of miles, from the Baltic Sea in the west to the Pacific Ocean in the east. Within this great area many types of climate are experienced, and so the people can grow nearly every kind of crop which they require. This vast territory also contains tremendous reserves of coal, iron, platinum, gold and practically every mineral used by man.

It is therefore only to be expected that Russia, as she is familiarly known, is to a very great degree self-supporting, and even has a surplus of some things which she desires to export. Such things include wheat, timber, flax and furs; these we buy from her in exchange for machinery of various kinds, iron, steel and wool. How frequently we find these same British exports occurring. Our iron and steel goods of all kinds, from ships and railway trains to nuts and screws, are always in demand.

Tea Bureau.

TEA PLUCKING

Picking the tiny leaves is a very delicate operation done by Indian women as this picture shows. They can fill their large baskets many times each day. After the leaves have been dried and rolled they will be sent—probably to London—in lead-lined chests.

Mondiale.

JUTE FOR CALCUTTA AND DUNDEE

Calcutta and Dundee are the two great sack-making towns of the Commonwealth. Sacks and sailcloth are made from jute and the picture shows jute-cutting in India, whose Ganges delta is one of the places where the plant grows best.

Rumania and Bulgaria

The people of Rumania are mainly peasant farmers growing sufficient food for their own needs, with a small surplus of wheat and maize for export, some of which we buy from them, when the harvest is good. Since 1939, however, our trade with this country has largely disappeared, and Rumania now trades more with Eastern Europe than she does with the West.

A visit to the rose gardens of the upper Tundja valley, in the Balkan mountains, when the roses are ready for picking in May is an unforgettable experience. The roses are picked very early in the morning, when their perfume is at its best, and about three million blossoms go to make 2 pounds of essence, known as attar of roses. This therefore makes very expensive perfume. Since all kinds of scent can now be distilled cheaply from coal, our import of attar of roses from Bulgaria is only very small.

The most valuable crop grown here is tobacco of the Turkish variety. The dry climate aids the cultivation of the plants and the drying of the leaves, giving a high quality tobacco. In normal times, some of this tobacco was exported to us direct, while some went to Greece and was re-exported to us as Greek tobacco. Table grapes and tomato purée are other commodities of Bulgaria's trade, for it is with the luxuries of life, rather than with the necessities, that she can provide the countries with which she trades.

Greece and the Balkans

Christmas would not be complete without plum pudding and mince pies. We have to thank the Greeks for one ingredient, namely, currants, although, when speaking of currants, we must not forget the great Commonwealth of Australia. These small, dried, seedless grapes were once called Corinths, after the city near which most of them were cultivated. They constitute over half our imports from Greece, while raisins and tobacco make up the bulk of the remainder.

From Naxos, in the Grecian Archipelago, comes emery, an abrasive used for making grinding wheels; and from Euboea comes magnesite, the raw material used for fire-proof, non-slip surfaced floors, found in hospitals, kitchens and the like. Sponges, similar to the one in your bathroom, are widely used in pottery making, in certain kinds of printing and photography, in glass and leather working, and in the cleaning of vehicles. Quite a number of these come from Greece and the small islands of the Dodecanese.

Products of Cyprus

The island of Cyprus, which is only 148 miles long, is a British colony, and we have helped the Cypriots to produce many of the commodities which they sell to us. One of these is pyrites; 6 per cent. of the world's production of this iron and sulphur ore is mined in Cyprus. Good quality sponges and a gum from the locust bean (an ingredient in paint and varnish) are also supplied to us.

Trade of the tiny republic of Albania is largely confined to the export of tobacco, which is of good quality and grown throughout the country. Again, it is manufactured goods that are required by the Albanians, but the mode of life of most of them is very primitive, and they cannot afford to buy the wireless sets and motor cars which we might sell them.

Sometimes you may see a " plumpudding " dog, or, to call it by its correct name, a Dalmatian, being taken out for exercise by its owner. Originally, these dogs came from Yugoslavia—Dalmatia being the name of that part of the country near the Adriatic coast. This region is a barren, mountainous area, but the interior of the country is low-lying and fertile.

It contains numerous farms, and mile upon mile of orchards, where fruits such as we can grow in England, apples, pears and plums, are cultivated. Much of the fruit, after being picked, is dried in the hot sunshine. Perhaps the prunes you had for dinner were once plums in these orchards.

We also buy timber from Yugoslavia, while she buys iron, steel, machinery and textiles from us, having few mills or factories of her own.

From Hungary and Austria

Hungary is another country which may have contributed to your Christmas dinner. Each December we get thousands of turkeys from the Hungarian plain. On the excellent farmland of this region, wheat of a high quality is grown, and some of this in normal years is exported to Britain.

The people of Austria are working hard to reorganise their agriculture and industries, so that they may once again share in world prosperity. We are able to supply some of the things she needs, such as machinery for her factories, clothes and household goods for her people, and vehicles of all kinds. In exchange for these things, she can send to us iron and steel, minerals such as magnesium, timber products, including furniture, and other goods requiring much skill but little raw material in their manufacture, notably jewellery.

Switzerland

What wonderful pictures the name of this little country among the Alps conjures up in our minds! We think of beautiful valleys set amid snow-capped peaks, with brilliant flowers adorning the slopes. We think of ice-skating, ski-ing and rock-climbing, of magnificent hotels and a happy people. All these things bring wealth to the Swiss people, for each year many thousands of tourists from all parts of the world spend their holidays in Switzerland.

COCONUT PALMS IN CEYLON

Paul Popper.

Large numbers of these sturdy palms grow in Ceylon. From the white kernel of their nuts, copra is obtained: while the tight, brown coir fibres round the nut are used to make coconut matting, door mats, and in upholstery work. Copra yields coconut oil which is essential in the manufacture of margarine and hair shampoos, although similar oil can be obtained from such other vegetable sources as groundnuts.

Paul Popper.

GIANT BAMBOOS IN CEYLON

Tea is the most important and best-known of our imports from Ceylon, but bamboos which have an endless variety of uses grow to great stature there, as this picture of giant bamboos at Peradeniya shows. The figure of the man is a scale by which their size can be measured.

people of other lands to spend their holidays in Britain.

Lemons from Sicily

There are literally dozens of varieties of cheese peculiar to individual countries. We have already met some in dealing with Holland. The dairy farmers of the North Italian plain are experts at making Gorgonzola and Parmesan cheeses, which are widely known. They are also good at making their hard variety of wheat into macaroni and spaghetti, which we eat quite often in one way or another. Nearly all the world's lemons come from the groves on the plains of Sicily. Many of these groves were severely damaged during the War, but as they are restored, an increasing number of lemons can be sent to us for use in our homes, and in the making of marmalade and soft drinks.

Does your watch keep good time? If it does it probably bears the words " Swiss Made," which are the hall-mark of excellent craftsmanship. With the money she obtains from British tourists, and from the sale of watches and clocks to this country, the Swiss buy goods they cannot make for themselves through lack of coal and iron. These things include motor cars, aeroplanes and woollen cloth. You will note that even holidays abroad must be balanced by exports, or by encouraging the

An old-fashioned remedy for various ailments was brimstone and treacle. Brimstone is the old name for sulphur, and it is widely used in the manufacture of sulphuric acid. Masses of this substance are to be found on the slopes of Mount Etna, an active volcano in Sicily.

Borax is mined in Tuscany, in the form of boric acid. Laundries use large amounts of it for softening water, but its chief use is for the enamel coating of baths and stoves, and in the making of Pyrex and similar ware. For these purposes, and for making ointment, toothpaste and cosmetics, we have to import tons of this mineral from Italy. Mercury also is mined in Tuscany, and other Italian minerals we buy include talc, graphite and barytes. Italy, like Southern France, is famous for silk, some of which is sent to Macclesfield in Cheshire, to be woven into cloth.

Racing cars of Italian make are famous the world over. Having little iron and no coal, the raw materials for the automobile industry are imported in the form of scrap iron. Numbers of our obsolete ships and tanks, as well as old iron bedsteads, have in the past found their way to Italy.

Rich Iron Mines of Spain

Spain has given its name to a variety of onion, and a kind of liquorice, but these are by no means the most important products of the country. Small sour Seville oranges make excellent marmalade. Lemons, almonds and table grapes also come to us from Spain. The latter are carefully packed in cork dust. Cork is simply the bark of the cork-oak tree, which grows in these lands of southern Europe. It is put to a large number of uses.

What molten metal can you plunge your hand into without burning yourself? The answer is, of course, Mercury, which is a liquid at ordinary temperatures. It is rarely found as a liquid in the ground, but nearly always occurs as a compound with sulphur, known as cinnabar. One of the deepest quicksilver (the ancient name for mercury) mines in the world is at Almaden, in southern Spain, where the workings go down nearly a quarter of a mile.

The vermilion paint in your paint-

Paul Popper.

BURMESE TEAK RAFTS

Burma's dense monsoon forests are rich in such valuable hardwood as teak. Much of the timber felled in the forests is floated down the mighty Irrawaddy river to Rangoon in rafts of the kind shown in this picture. Notice the banding of the logs and the " dwelling hut " for the raftsmen whose tiny figures can be seen aft steering their ungainly vessel.

box comes from a mercury compound, as does the red paint used on the hulls of ships. Yet another compound is used for ammunition detonators, and there are many more uses for this fascinating mineral, so familiar to us in the thermometer and barometer.

In the mountains of northern Spain, rich iron-ore is mined. Thousands of tons are shipped annually to ports in the British Isles, such as Belfast and Barrow-in-Furness, for use in ship-building, and to Swansea for the tin-plate industry. The ore from around the little port of Bilbao is reddish in colour, and is known as hematite, after a Greek word meaning " blood."

In southern Spain another type of iron-ore is found which, because of its colour, is known as fool's gold. This is Pyrites, and Spain has the largest deposit of it in the world, in the famous Rio Tinto mines. As pyrites is nearly half sulphur, most of what we buy from Spain is used to make sulphuric acid

and fertilisers. Other minerals from Spain include copper and lead, and for the manufacture of good quality paper we import esparto grass, which grows on the Meseta—the dry plateau of the interior.

We have found that most of the countries in Europe buy motor cars, machinery, electrical apparatus, coal and coke from us, and Spain is no exception.

Portugal's Sardines for Motor Cars

Port wine is the product most people associate with Portugal. This wine takes its name from Oporto, near which the grapes are cultivated. Leixões is the outport for Oporto. The metal tungsten is of the greatest value in modern industry. Tungsten ore, known as wolfram, is mined at Panasqueira, where there is one of the largest deposits of this ore in Europe.

Nearly all the tungsten brought to Britain is used in the steel industry for

Malayan Information Agency.

MALAYAN RUBBER FOR WORLD MARKETS

Malaya's rubber plantations include many owned by famous tyre-manufacturing firms. This picture shows crepe rubber drying on a Johore plantation. It is dried for ten days, then packed in wooden cases for shipment.

Associated Press.

A MALAYAN RUBBER-PLANTER'S HOME

If you were a Malayan rubber-planter you would probably live in a house of this sort. The workers on your plantation would probably be Tamils from South India. The rubber you grew would command world-wide markets and swell the flow of trade between the nations.

making high-speed cutting tools, which even when red-hot will cut through ordinary steel as a knife cuts through butter. Razor blades, hacksaw blades and motor-car springs contain tungsten, and the filaments for a hundred million electric light bulbs can be supplied by less than two tons of this metal.

You may have noticed that most of the tinned sardines we eat come from Portugal. On one occasion in recent years when it seemed we would be unable to afford this delicacy, the Portuguese government said that if this happened they would have to stop buying our motor cars.

Other imports from Portugal are similar to those from Spain, particularly cork and pyrites. Our exports to her consist, in the main, of metal goods, machinery and coal. Time and again we have seen how vital is our production of coal, not only for export, but also for making the goods for export.

Turkey is rapidly becoming Western-ised. The homes of the people and their schools are steadily becoming more like our own and are furnished with a great variety of things, from wireless sets to inkwells, made in England.

From Turkey

Turkey has given its name to a special variety of cigarette, made from tobacco grown on the coastlands of the Mediterranean and Black Seas. In the same regions also are cultivated certain kinds of grapes, which when dried are called sultanas.

You may not have heard of gall nuts, but you have certainly heard of ink! Turkey is one of our principal suppliers of the oak apples, or gall nuts, which are the source of ink. If you live in the country, you know how useful binder twine is to the farmer. This, and other kinds of string and cord, are made from soft hemp. These Turkish exports, as well as borax and emery, enable her to buy all that she needs from us.

As the small country of Syria was once a French colony, most of its trade is still with France. Nevertheless, there is some trade with England, in gall nuts, hemp, citrous fruits—especially oranges—and silk. The silk cloth of Damascus is very beautiful, but very expensive!

How lovely is a juicy Jaffa orange! A giant among oranges! We buy as many of them as we can, particularly at Christmas time, when they are shipped to us through the ports of Jaffa and Haifa, in the Holy Land. Grapefruit, too, are grown in Israel, and exported to this country by the shipload, while the people of this troubled land buy in return such things as cotton and woollen cloth, machinery for their farms, and rubber tyres for their vehicles.

In the well-watered areas of Iraq, near the rivers Tigris and Euphrates, date palms are grown on plantations, and we obtain tons of their fruit each year through Basra, the chief port. The country contains rich oilfields, and much of the petroleum is pumped along iron pipes to Tripoli in Syria and Banias in the Lebanon, whence it comes to England to be refined.

Although the nomad peoples of the Arabian peninsula produce dates, hides and livestock for export, the most valuable Arabian product is oil. There are rich oilfields in the kingdom of Saudi-

Hedda M. Morrison.

A GREAT CLEARING HOUSE FOR FAR-EAST TRADE

Among the great trading centres of the world is the British colony of Hong Kong, which lies east of the Pearl river estuary and south of Canton. Its harbour, which is seen in this picture from Victoria Peak, and waterways cover seventeen square miles and form one of the finest anchorages in the world. In normal times, most of the export and import trade of south China is handled by Hong Kong.

E.N.A.

CLEANING EGYPTIAN COTTON

These Egyptian workers are cleaning cotton which will probably be exported, by way of Alexandria, to the United Kingdom. In our great mills in Lancashire it will be made into the beautiful cotton fabrics for which Britain is world-famous. Egypt is one of the chief cotton-producing countries and Britain is her most important customer.

Arabia, whence oil is piped to Sidon, on the Mediterranean, or to the refineries at Ras Tanura or Bahrein Island. A joint British-American company operates the important oilfield of Kuwait. The development of these oilfields has created a demand for machines and equipment for the public buildings, hospitals and schools which are being built in the new oilfield towns. Britain has a share in providing for these new centres.

The Oil Wells of Persia

Iran, which resumed its former name of Persia in 1949, supplies Persian carpets. They are woven from wool obtained from sheep kept by the nomadic tribesmen, and are famous for their colours and intricate designs. Lambskins, too, are much sought after by the wealthy ladies of Great Britain, who wear them as fur coats.

Iran possesses vast resources of oil, which were developed by the Anglo-Iranian Oil Company. In normal times, the crude oil is sent by pipeline to the head of the Persian Gulf, where there is the great oil refinery of Abadan.

Between Persia and Pakistan lies the small mountainous country of Afghanistan. Nearly all its trade is with Pakistan and India, but it sends us a few things in normal times, notably carpets and lambskins.

India and Pakistan

Every home in England uses at least one commodity from India, namely, tea. Most of the world's tea comes from shrubs grown on plantations on the lower slopes of the Himalayas, around Darjeeling. Picking the tiny leaves, at just the right stage, is a very delicate operation, but the Indian women are expert at this. They can fill the large baskets, carried on their heads or backs, many times each day. After the leaves have been dried and rolled, they are packed in lead-lined chests and shipped to London. Here they are sold by auction to large firms, who blend different varieties of tea, which eventually appear in the familiar packets we see in the grocer's store.

Hundreds of thousands of years ago, the great plateau of southern India was cracked in the north by earthquakes. The molten lava which welled up through the cracks solidified at the surface, and has since weathered to give a very fertile, black soil, excellent for the cultivation of cotton. Most of this is used to-day in Indian factories, but a surplus is available for the mills of Lancashire.

Jute from East Pakistan

Every farmer uses a large number of sacks, and not only the farmer, but the greengrocer, the corn chandler and countless other people. Nearly all the sacks and similar material, such as the backing of linoleum, are made in two towns. One is Calcutta in India, and the other is Dundee in Scotland. The substance used for making these sacks and sailcloth is called jute. Although other fibres could be used, this is the cheapest.

The plant grows best in the delta region of the Ganges, especially in East Pakistan, and despite the hot, steamy atmosphere the farmers work very hard to harvest the crop. Jute grows to a height of about twelve feet, with most of its leaves and branches near the top of the plant. After about three months' growth, the blossoms appear and the plant is then ready for cutting. It is

Copyright.

GROWING TOBACCO IN THE RHODESIAS

These African workers are watering tobacco seed-beds. The crop that will be grown may well come to Britain as Empire tobacco, for nearly all Empire leaf comes from Northern and Southern Rhodesia. Tobacco growing is the most important agricultural activity in Southern Rhodesia, and tobacco is the most valuable export. In 1951 more than 67 million pounds were exported.

E.N.A.

LOADING IVORY AT MOMBASA

Ivory is obtained chiefly from the "dentine" which covers the tusks of certain elephants. Less than a fifth of the ivory now exported from Kenya comes from animals killed recently. Most comes from stores gathered over the years, or from tusks found in the jungle.

lopped off close to the ground, stripped, and bundled. The pith and outer bark are allowed to rot so that the fibres are loosened, and the dried stems are then beaten until only the fibre is left. This is baled, marketed, and then sent to the mills in lengths 10 to 15 feet long which are cut into shorter lengths to be made ready for spinning and weaving.

The number of uses to which jute can be put is amazing. Not only does it provide sacks and bags, but aprons, canvas, cords, meat wrappers, tarpaulins and tapestries. Before the war, jute manufacturers at Dundee could list more than ninety products which came from their factories.

A Fibre of Many Uses

Kapok is a fluffy fibre similar to cotton. It grows in pods on tall trees in India, Ceylon and the East Indies, and harvesting it is a very perilous occupation. The chief use of this remarkable fibre is in saving life at sea, for it is five times as buoyant as cork, and does not become saturated in sea water. Many steamship companies use mattresses and pillows, as well as lifebelts, stuffed with kapok, as they will support thirty times their own weight in water.

It is used also in padding airmen's flying suits, eiderdowns, tea-cosies, dressing-gowns and so on, having the added advantage of being mothproof. Film and broadcasting studios are padded with this fibre to make them soundproof, and it has many other uses. No wonder we in Britain buy large quantities of it.

Fishing nets and submarine cables are treated with rot-proof material known as cutch, an extract obtained from several different plants grown in India.

Hides and Cane

Have you ever had to take a dose of castor oil? This is an extract from another Indian plant. Most castor oil imported into this country is used as a drying oil in paint and varnish.

Hides are sent to Britain to be made into innumerable leather goods such as satchels, handbags and saddlery. The bones, horns and hooves are not wasted. Just imagine, your coat button may have been part of a cow somewhere in India or Pakistan! Knife handles, combs, fertilisers, glue and gelatine are all by-products of the cow.

The cane from which your shopping basket is made quite probably came from India, as do the rattans which are used for seats of chairs. The brushes in your home, shoe brushes, hair brushes, paint brushes, and so on, may also be made of bristles and fibres brought all the way from the Far East.

India, being rich in minerals, sends us a variety of unusual ores. Artificial

E.N.A.

HUSKING COCONUTS IN THE SEYCHELLES

The coconut is one of the most wonderful nuts in the world, for it can provide food, clothing, shelter, and fuel. Cord, rope, and mats can be made from the coir fibre; the shell can be used for spoons and buttons, or burned as fuel. The dried nut-meat becomes copra which yields oil for margarine and soap.

frost, which glistens on the Christmas tree, is really tiny flakes of mica, but of course there are far more important uses for this mineral. In fact, about 90 per cent. of mica is used in the electrical industry, as it is a good insulator; telephones, dynamos, electric irons and most electrical appliances contain it. The best kind of mica is found at Bihar and Madras.

Everyone has seen and probably used a pocket lighter. The metal which gives the spark is an alloy of iron and a little-known metal, called cerium. Cerium is used also for searchlights and electric arc-lamps. Monazite (cerium ore) is obtained from the sands on the beaches of Travancore. Nine-tenths of the world's supply comes from this area, as also does another unfamiliar mineral, called titanium. This is an ingredient in white paint, and is employed in making linoleum, toilet preparations and stainless steel. Titanium can now be produced as a metal. It is much lighter than but just as strong as steel.

Talc and magnesium, previously mentioned elsewhere, also come from India. Sparking plugs, bricks, cement and glass which have to withstand high temperatures contain kyanite, from the Khasi hills of Assam.

The Useful Coconut

The people in the towns of India and Pakistan are learning to work in factories and thus to produce many of their own manufactured goods. Some of the machinery which they need is bought from Britain.

Large numbers of coconut palms grow in Ceylon, where the white kernel is removed from the nuts and laid out in the sun to dry. It is then known as copra. This is sent to Britain, where it is crushed and the coconut oil used in shampoos and margarine. The bulky residue is made into cattle-cake. When the coconut was growing at the top of a tall, straight, palm tree, it looked very different from those we sometimes see in fairgrounds. For one thing, it was very much larger. Around the nut were tight layers of a coarse, brown fibre known as coir—there is usually a tuft remaining at the top of the nuts we see at the greengrocer's.

This coir is most useful for coconut matting, door mats and upholstery, while some of the coarser fibres are used in brushes.

The Importance of Graphite

It may surprise you to learn that the lead pencil you use each day has no lead in it at all. The black substance through the centre of the pencil is obtained by baking a fine clay with a mineral called graphite at a temperature of 2,000 degrees Fahrenheit. When a hammer, an anchor, or any other metal casting is made, the molten metal is poured into a mould and allowed to set. To prevent sticking, the mould is sometimes dusted with graphite, mixed with talc. We require much graphite, for, as we have seen, iron and steel goods form a very important part of our exports. In Ceylon is a great vein of this mineral,

E.N.A.

CUTTING SISAL ON A KENYA PLANTATION
String and rope are made from the fibre of the agave plant which is known to us as sisal hemp. Sisal plantations are found, not only in East Africa, but in Mexico, Central America, and the West and East Indies.

Mondiale.

AFRICAN SISAL FOR STRING AND ROPE
This picture shows washed sisal being dried on a Tanganyika drying ground. The highlands and coastlands of East Africa have many plantation crops cultivated by African workers under white managers.

and for a long time we have obtained the bulk of our supplies from her.

Most important as well as the best known of the exports from Ceylon is tea. In 1953 Ceylon supplied over 116 million pounds of tea to Britain.

From Burma and Malaya

The dense monsoon forests of Burma contain vast resources of valuable timber, much of which is hardwood, such as teak. Where the forests come down to the coast and rivers, felling is fairly easy, and it is a common sight to see Indian elephants wielding huge logs as a boy might wield a cricket bat. Most of the timber is floated down the mighty Irrawaddy and its tributaries to Rangoon, whence it is transhipped to Britain.

Burma is famous for its beautiful rubies and emeralds, which are mined in the wild mountainous country near the Chinese frontier.

Tin, which is one of our most useful metals, is one of the chief products of Malaya. Bronze, gun-metal, Britannia metal and pewter are all alloys of tin. The dyeing of silk stockings, and the rustling finish given to silk cloth, are aided by the addition of tin. However, the most important use of tin is in plating thin sheets of steel to make tin cans.

Famous tyre-manufacturing firms have their own rubber plantations in Malaya. Tamils from South India work on these plantations, usually under a European manager. The raw rubber, or latex, rather like dirty milk in appearance, is found just under the bark of the rubber tree. A V-shaped cut is made in the trunk, from which the latex runs into a small vessel. One Tamil worker will look after as many as three hundred trees in one day. The liquid is collected and taken on bullock carts to the factory, where acid is added to make it solidify. Then it is rolled, dried and smoked to form

E.N.A.

PICKING GROUNDNUTS IN NIGERIA

The groundnut is an important source of the oil from which margarine is made. As the picture shows, groundnuts, or peanuts, are cultivated in Nigeria. Another source of supply is East Africa though developments in this area are not on so large a scale as first planned.

E.N.A.

THRESHING GROUNDNUTS IN GAMBIA

Groundnuts are also grown in Sierra Leone and Gambia. In Gambia, they are the chief export. The groundnut plant is small and forms its fruit above the ground. But the green pods gradually bend down until they are buried just below the surface. Here the pod ripens to a yellow colour. Within each pod are two or three brown-skinned kernels.

sheets of crepe rubber, which are packed in bales and sent to Britain. There are hundreds of uses to which rubber is put. See how long a list you can compile.

Gum Manila and Gum Damar are two natural resins which come from Malaya and are important in the manufacture of paint, varnish and lacquers. Derris and other roots growing in this tropical land are valuable to us as pesticides, used in sheep dips, weed killers and insecticidal dusts.

Other commodities arriving from Malaya include canes, rattans, shellac, cutch, tungsten and tinned pineapples.

Indonesia

The innumerable islands of the archipelago between Asia and Australia include uninhabited coral atolls, active volcanoes, as well as the most densely populated island in the world—Java. A great variety of crops is grown, but not all of them enter into our trade, for Indonesia has close associations with the Netherlands. Can you remember what things we make with canes, rattans, cutch, resin, kapok, derris, rubber and tin ? These commodities, together with tea, pepper and spices, we import from Indonesia.

The Philippine Islands

The capital of the Philippine Islands, Manila, has given its name to a very strong hemp, which we import. Most of the trade of the Philippine Republic is, however, conducted with the United States of America.

Thailand, the land of free people,

A TURKISH COTTON FACTORY

Kaiseriyeh is one of the industrial centres of modern Turkey. In addition to its aircraft assembly factory, the town has the largest cotton mill in the Middle East. The mill, which is seen in this picture, was planned by Russian experts.

Photos: E.N.A.

As this picture shows, the cotton *kombinat* at Kaiseriyeh employs thoroughly modern machinery for treating the raw cotton. By 1951, cotton had overtaken tobacco, figs and raisins, and wheat, and had become Turkey's most important export crop. Kaiseriyeh, which stands in the heart of Anatolia, is sometimes called Kayseri.

PRODUCTS OF INDONESIA

Java is the chief source of cinchona bark, from which quinine is produced. Cinchona culture was introduced into Java during the nineteenth century, in the western district of Preanger, of which Bandoeng is the chief centre. In this picture we see samples being taken from bales of cinchona bark at the factory there.

Photos : Paul Popper.

This Balinese boy and his young brother are standing amid bundles of harvested rice which have been put out to dry. In the background is the open-side store for the threshed grain. Rice is an important crop to the many peasant farmers of Indonesia.

for that is what "thai" means, is also known by its older name of Siam. From her we buy rubber and shellac, and from us she gets machinery and much of the equipment needed for building and developing her schools, hospitals and mines.

Formerly grouped with Laos and Cambodia as French Indo-China, the republic of Viet Nam is another Asiatic country from which we buy rubber, and in times of plenty, rice.

Goods from China

China is almost the same size and has approximately the same population as Europe. It is not surprising, therefore, that her products and requirements are large and varied. Most Chinese are extremely poor, living under conditions that would not be allowed in England. They receive very low wages for the work they do, and hence the goods they produce are very cheap, even when the transport charges to Britain have been paid.

We would not enjoy eating the millions of eggs we buy each year from China, because they are not always as fresh as we like them. They are canned raw, and are used in many industries, particularly those connected with paper, book-binding and textiles. Curiously enough, only a very small amount of the famous China tea actually comes from China. To-day most of it is grown in India.

Roast pork is a great delicacy in China, and all peasants keep at least one pig to be eaten on feast-days. Pigs' bristles make good-quality brushes, and the hair, when spun and curled, provides a material for stuffing upholstery.

Canes, rattans, gall-nuts, tung oil (a vegetable oil used as a drier in paint) all come from China. Ramie, another fibre, is needed for gas mantles, and as a substitute for flax in the manufacture of such things as parachute cords.

The mountains of South-west China are rich in a great variety of metallic ores. One of these is antimony, long used by Eastern damsels for blacking their eyelids. To-day, antimony, when alloyed with lead, is employed in accumulators, pipes and shrapnel shells. The type used for printing this book also contained antimony, and the sulphide of the metal is used in the heads of safety matches, and the striking surface on the box. Tin and tungsten also are found in this region.

In the peninsula of Shantung, a special kind of silk is made. Shantung silk differs from ordinary silk cloth, because the silk-worms—which incidentally are not worms but caterpillars—are fed on leaves from the oak and not from the mulberry tree.

China has been struggling hard for several decades to come nearer to a Western standard of life. Factories are developing, roads and railways are being built, schools and hospitals are being established in many parts. At first much of the equipment for these projects was obtained from the United States and—to a lesser degree—Britain, but now China looks more to the Soviet Union, who is helping her to develop her heavy industries, especially in Manchuria. The millions of her population, whose standard of living has yet to be raised, may yet provide a big market for the machinery and goods that Britain is able to sell.

Made in Japan

Between the two World Wars, the people of Japan built a great number of modern well-equipped factories. British firms not only supplied the machinery for many of these, but also taught the Japanese how to use it. The fact that the workers are paid low wages means that the cotton and silk cloth, paper sunshades, wooden toys, china and a host of other goods turned out by the factories, can be sold very cheaply. Since 1945 Japanese manufacturers have made a rapid recovery and we may expect to see an increasing number of articles bearing the stamp "Made in Japan."

FRUIT FROM SOUTH AFRICA

South Africa Information Office.

The Union of South Africa sends us such delicious fruits as oranges, peaches, pineapples, pears and sultanas. This picture shows workers on a fruit farm inspecting and packing choice pears. One of the attractions, to us, of South African fruits is that they can be sent to us when, like other northern hemisphere countries, we have no fruit of our own.

South Africa Information Office.

This picture shows trolley-loads of packed fruit in the storage chambers of a South African pre-cooling station where the fruit will be kept until shipped in vessels equipped with cool chambers. These precautions ensure that the fruit does not over-ripen, but arrives at its destination in prime condition.

Morocco, Algeria and Tunisia, which collectively stand for France in North Africa, naturally conduct most of their trade across the Mediterranean Sea with that country. There are, however, a number of vital products with which they supply us. We cannot live without the mineral phosphorus, nor can other living creatures, including plants. Grain removes large amounts of phosphorus from the soil, and in order to get good crops it must be put back in the form of a fertiliser. That is why we import thousands of tons of phosphate rock from North Africa, for it is essential that we make every British acre produce as much food as possible.

Our factories, too, must produce to the maximum, but over-worked machines become worn out and must be renewed. We have insufficient iron-ore in Britain to meet these requirements and to make iron and steel goods for export, so we buy large quantities from North Africa.

Esparto Grass and Cotton

Many things, from old rags to stinging nettles, can be used for making paper. Esparto grass which grows in the Barbary States is used for making good-quality paper, and we import it for this purpose.

Less important exports from this region include Red Squill (a poisonous root used for killing rats), cork, diatomite and cobalt.

The finest and softest handkerchiefs are made from cotton grown in the land of the Pyramids. The raw cotton we buy from India consists of short fibres, which can only be made into cheaper quality cloth, whereas the long fibres of the Egyptian variety can be spun into a silky thread, resulting in the beautiful fine cotton goods which other countries like to buy from us. We buy quantities of onions from Egypt each year and at one time we also obtained rice from her and may do so again.

Stamp collectors show considerable interest in the face of a stamp, but ignore the back. Unless this is properly

Paul Popper

A GOLD COAST COCOA FARM

Cocoa was an expensive drink until peasant farmers on West Africa's Gold Coast were encouraged to grow large crops. The picture shows how the farmer has cleared a little land from the high surrounding bush. Tall trees have been left standing to provide shade. In the centre of the clearing, cocoa beans have been put out on the mats to dry.

coated with gum the stamp will not do its job. The gum for this, and many other purposes, comes from the Sudan, in the form of Gum Arabic. This is exuded from thorny acacia trees, growing in the dry parts of this territory.

In 1925, the great Makwar dam was built near Sennar, on the Blue Nile. This enabled a plentiful supply of water to be provided for the cotton plantations of the Gezira Plain, between the White and Blue Niles. The cotton grown is the good quality Egyptian variety, and in normal times most of it is exported to England through Port Sudan on the Red Sea coast.

On some of the hill slopes of the wild mountainous country of Abyssinia coffee is grown for export to European countries, such as Britain. This coffee, and hides, skins and beeswax, form the most valuable exports of this country. In common with French North Africa, Egypt and the Sudan, Abyssinia buys from us cheap cotton cloth, building materials, soap, motor cars and machinery.

British East Africa

The only parts of Uganda, Kenya, Tanganyika and Nyasaland, in British East Africa, where the white man can live comfortably, are in the highlands or by the sea. Thus, it is in these parts that most of the plantation crops are to be found growing, for nearly all plantations have white managers and African workers.

From the small islands of Zanzibar and Pemba, we buy the dried flower buds of the clove trees, so useful for flavouring our stewed apples. On the plateau are cultivated kapok, cotton and sisal hemp, the latter being used for rope binder twine.

On the slopes of Mount Kenya, and in Uganda, are many tea and coffee plantations, some of which are owned by well-known British firms. Derris root and Pyrethrum flowers, used as insecticides, and beeswax contained in floor polish and cosmetics, are also

Paul Popper.

A COCOA FARMER AT WORK

Armed with his sharp cutlass, this Gold Coast farmer cuts the golden-yellow pods which grow directly from the stem of the cocoa tree.

supplied to the United Kingdom. From us, the people of East Africa require cotton cloth, corrugated iron, enamel bowls, railway rolling stock, lorries and many other manufactured goods.

Mozambique, or Portuguese East Africa, has large areas of lowland covered by dense forests and mangrove swamps. Some tropical crops, including sugar-cane, hemp and pineapples, are grown on estates owned and developed by Portuguese and British trading companies. In addition to these products, beeswax is imported by us.

Through Northern Rhodesia

Empire tobacco comes almost exclusively from the two colonies, Northern and Southern Rhodesia, where there are great possibilities for future development.

In the heart of the tropical forest of Northern Rhodesia, near the Belgian Congo frontier, is one of the richest mining areas in the world. Special railways have been built for hundreds of miles through dense jungle to get the copper and cobalt to the coast. About a quarter of all the copper produced in the world is used by the electrical industry, mainly as wire.

When another metal is alloyed with copper, it is hardened. Bronze used in ancient times for knives, axes and ornaments, is copper alloyed with tin. Brass, a copper-zinc alloy, is much needed in war-time for shell and cartridge cases, but it also has numerous peace-time uses. Look around you and see what a variety of articles are made of brass. Most brass and copper ware is made in the " Black Country," around Birmingham, and it eventually finds its way all over the world.

Southern Rhodesia, too, is very rich in minerals ; those we buy in Britain include asbestos, chrome and zinc ores. Asbestos has two remarkable properties. Firstly, it splits up extremely easily into fibres, which can be spun and woven into cloth. Secondly, it will not burn, melt, or allow electricity to pass through it, and is not affected by chemicals. Naturally, this useful mineral is employed here in safety curtains, firemen's clothes, brake linings, cable covering, gas fires, acid filters, roofing tiles and flat and corrugated sheets for building.

Modern steel goods, from bicycles to furniture, have a chromium-plated finish. Most chromium is, however, alloyed with steel for special purposes such as stainless cutlery, and parts of cars, railway carriages, aircraft and bridges. You can see, then, that these Rhodesian ores are of vital importance to a large number of our industries, for without them we would have few manufactured goods for export.

Union of South Africa

Sparkling wines, golden oranges, luscious peaches, sun-dried sultanas, juicy pineapples, are some of the delicious things which come to us from this sunny Dominion. This, too, is a land rich in gold, platinum, diamonds and many other minerals.

Nearly all the gold, mined a mile beneath the streets of Johannesburg, in the Rand, is used as the real wealth behind the paper and baser metal currencies of most countries, but a number of other uses include jewellery, pen-nibs and dental fillings. From the Transvaal also comes platinum, another precious metal used in jewellery, and employed in electrical and laboratory apparatus.

Asbestos, chrome-ore, manganese, uranium and mica are additional minerals we receive from South Africa.

Are you one of the people who enjoy gazing into a jeweller's shop window at the glittering gems ? Many of the diamonds you see there must have come from South Africa. Near Kimberley, and also in Pretoria, a blue clay is quarried. From the clay are washed rough diamonds, which look like pieces of glass until they are skilfully cut and polished. Those

WEST AFRICAN TRADING SCENES

E.N.A.

Another Nigerian crop is cotton, which is grown mainly in the north. The picture shows us bales of cotton being offered for sale in the famous walled city of Kano, a Hausa town with a long history as a trading centre. Most of the $13\frac{1}{2}$ millions of people living in the Northern Region are Mohammedans. Kano, their chief town, is linked by railway with the port of Lagos.

E.N.A.

This picture shows a busy wharf scene at Iddo, a sister-port of Lagos and Apapa where the main Nigerian railway comes down from Kano. Once swampland, the shore between Iddo and Apapa is now a busy dock area of wharves and warehouses where goods for export are handled and stored.

unsuitable for jewellery are of great value in many British industries as parts of cutting tools. The ostrich feather, as a feminine adornment, enjoys spells of popularity. Farms on the South African Karroos supply the world with this commodity. Quantity, not quality, is the aim of the African cattle farmer on the Veldt. Hence there is always a large number of hides and skins available for export. Millions of sheep, too, are reared on the plateau. Wool is therefore another valuable export to the United Kingdom.

Cape Town is the outlet for most of the products of the Union, and has elevators especially built for loading the locally grown wheat. Here, in the shadow of Table Mountain, ships are constantly arriving from Britain with cargoes of mining machinery, cars, locomotives and cotton and woollen goods.

Fireworks and signal lights owe their crimson flame to lithium chloride. Lithium is one of the very few products of the dry, barren mandated territory of South-West Africa.

Uranium, used in the production of atomic energy, comes from the Katanga region of the Belgian Congo. Here, also, are mined copper and cobalt which we sometimes buy, although most of the trade of this land is with the mother country, Belgium, and with the United States.

On the Gold Coast

Chocolates are a fairly recent invention. Until the African peasant farmers of the Gold Coast were encouraged to grow large crops, cocoa remained an expensive beverage. This self-governing Commonwealth territory now produces more than any other country in the world, the bulk of it being sent to cocoa and chocolate factories at Bournville (Birmingham), York and Bristol.

Africans use palmoil instead of butter. The fruit of

Paul Popper.

SPLITTING COCOA PODS ON THE GOLD COAST

When all the trees are stripped of their pods, the whole family set to work. The men and boys pick up the pods and with a swift stroke split them open with their long knives. The women and children scoop out the white pulpy beans and throw them into the baskets.

National Film Board.

TIMBER STARTS ITS JOURNEY TO THE MILLS

Logs from Canada's forests are hauled to the river and then floated downstream to the mills. Armed with peavies—long, hooked poles—these lumberjacks are seen moving the logs into the river to join millions of others all moving downstream towards the mills.

the oil-palm resembles small plums. The outside is fleshy and yields palm-oil; inside is a hard nut, the kernel of which, when crushed, gives palm-kernel oil. Margarine and soap are made in England from these oils.

Coconut palms, from which come copra and coir, also thrive in these tropical coastlands, while from Kano, an ancient walled city in northern Nigeria, come groundnuts grown locally by African farmers. Hides and skins from their animals, and tin from the nearby mines, are also sent by rail to Lagos, the chief port. Ships bound for Britain pick up cargoes of manganese from the Gold Coast and iron-ore from Sierra Leone.

In West Africa we have a ready market for bicycles, sewing machines, gramophones and cheap cotton cloth.

Although France receives most of the products of her colonies in French West Africa, we trade with the French Cameroons for titanium ore (rutile), used in dentistry to give a natural colour to false teeth.

Canada and Newfoundland

Wide open spaces—unlimited resources—comparatively few inhabitants! All this adds up to the fact that Canada has a large surplus of food and raw materials. Without the wheat from the Canadian Prairies, bread, cake, biscuits and breakfast cereals would almost disappear from our tables. Bacon, butter and eggs, too, come from the dairy farms of the St. Lawrence lowlands, while thousands of boxes of apples are shipped to us from Nova Scotia in the east and British Columbia in the west. The latter State also provides us with nearly all the tinned salmon to be seen in our shops.

You can read in the section on Canada, of the vast forests stretching from the Atlantic to the Pacific, and of all that happens to the timber before it reaches this country. The demand for the raw material for newsprint has become tremendous. Cellulose made from timber is being used in the manufacture of substitutes for silk, cotton, wool, metals, motor car bodies and wheels. Goods and food that were sold unwrapped a few years ago are now calling for forests of timber.

Red fox, silver fox, musk-rat, beaver, ermine and mink, are some of the animals living in these forests. The furs of these animals are made into costly coats and capes.

The rocks underlying the forest belt of the Dominion are some of the oldest in the world, and contain rich mineral deposits. You can read of the important recent discoveries of uranium, iron-ore and other minerals elsewhere in this work. The asbestos mine at Thetford, Quebec, the lead-zinc mine at Sullivan, British Columbia, and the nickel mine at Sudbury, Ontario, are the largest of their kinds in the world, and each sends a large proportion of its output to Britain. The uses to which asbestos and zinc can be put have been mentioned elsewhere; lead is needed in this country for accumu-

National Film Board.

BRITISH COLUMBIAN SALMON HARVEST

Nearly 25,000 workers are employed every year to deal with the great mid-summer salmon run. Nets, traps, and troll-lines supply a rich harvest to the score or more West Coast canneries. The picture shows seine net fishermen loading their catch into scows which take it to the canneries

National Film Board.

NEWSPRINT FROM CANADA

Canada's vast forests help to satisfy the tremendous world demand for paper for our daily newspapers. This picture shows rolls of paper awaiting shipment from the docks on Powell River, British Columbia. Canadian timber also supplies cellulose for silk substitutes, and for motor car bodies and wheels.

lator plates, cable covering, paint and plumbing, while nickel is important for strengthening steel, the heating coils of electric radiators and toasters, machine tools, nickel plating and other purposes.

Mica quarried 100 miles from Ottawa is capable of withstanding temperatures of 1,000 degrees Centigrade, and is therefore invaluable for furnace and oven windows. Copper, cobalt, cerium, platinum and talc likewise occur in this region. Cadmium and selenium are valuable by-products when zinc and copper ores are smelted. Silver is hardened by the addition of cadmium, and is then known as Sterling Silver.

Only about 300 tons of selenium are used throughout the world every year, but it has a very large number of fascinating applications. When a racehorse, or a burglar, intercepts a beam of light shining on a selenium cell, the effect is immediately registered electrically. It is used in television, cinematography, and the devices whereby street lamps, buoys, electric signs, etc., are automatically switched on at dusk and off at dawn. We get one metal from Canada which is not mined there! Bauxite from British Guiana is refined at Arvida, on the Saguenay river in Quebec, and comes to us in the form of aluminium. In order that our pottery and glass industries may continue to supply the world with their much-demanded products, we must import quantities of feldspar from Canada for glazing.

The industrial cities of the Dominion supply her with some manufactured goods, but more come across the border from the U.S.A. We only provide about 15 per cent. of Canada's imports, and of this, woollen, cotton and artificial silk goods, spirits and tea, are the chief items.

A four-page newspaper with a circulation of a million uses, in one week, pulp from four thousand trees! Every day, huge rolls of newsprint from Newfoundland can be seen entering newspaper offices in Fleet Street. This is by far our largest import from this part of Canada, but next in importance comes fish. Fish to a Newfoundlander means cod, caught in their thousands in the shallow waters of the Grand Bank. The Catholic countries of Europe buy most of this, while we prefer salmon from Newfoundland's streams and from British Columbia. Ships bringing these commodities and small amounts of iron-ore and zinc concentrates across the Atlantic Ocean, return from our shores laden with the products of our factories.

United States of America

The United States is one of the most productive countries in the world. She grows three-quarters of the maize, half the cotton and a fifth of the wheat of the world, and she produces over half the world's petroleum, and more than a third of the world's coal and iron-ore. American commodities stand high on our list of imports.

Foodstuffs form an important part of these imports. Wheat comes from

Mondiale.

SORTING SALMON AT A CANADIAN CANNERY
The salmon fisheries of Alaska and British Columbia are far more valuable to Canadian trade than even the great cod fisheries of the Grand Bank. Fine fish such as these are caught, cleaned, cut, tinned, and cooked and sent to Britain and all parts of the world.

the Prairies adjoining Canada, and must be carried hundreds of miles by rail to the Atlantic coast ports. Cargoes of grapefruit are brought from Texas and Florida, while canned and dried fruits, especially peaches, prunes and raisins, are brought from California, via the Panama Canal. The towns of the Middle West specialise in the canning of pork and beef, and in the production of by-products such as lard.

On the rich, black soils of some of the southern States, where the climate is warm and moist, cotton is grown. Negroes, descended from slaves, work on the plantations, planting, weeding and picking the cotton which is sent to a ginnery where the seed is separated from the fibres. The white fluffy fibres are packed in 500-pound bales, many of which are sent to Liverpool, Manchester and Glasgow, for distribution to the British cotton mills. Oil, extracted from the seeds, is used for frying fish and chips, while the residue is made into cattle cake, both of which are needed in Britain.

Tobacco smoking is said to have been introduced into Britain by Sir Walter Raleigh. To-day, millions of pounds are spent annually on this " fragrant weed." Most British cigarette smokers prefer the Virginian variety, grown on plantations

Mondiale.

POWDERED MILK IN THE MAKING

Everyone is familiar with the cans of powdered milk which the grocer can provide to supplement what the milkman brings. More often than not these cans will bear the name of an American firm, and the picture shows a superheated tank in an Idaho, U.S.A., factory where the milk is dried by the circulation of heated air.

in Kentucky and neighbouring States.

Rare Minerals from America

Although America is extremely rich in nearly all varieties of minerals, only small quantities are available for export, as the major part of her output is required for her own factories. However, some rare minerals are only obtainable from the U.S.A., and these include a natural asphalt which is resistant to chemical action and hence invaluable for acid-resisting flooring, battery boxes and cable covering; carbon black used in the rubber

the interior, and brush fibre and sisal from Yucatan. In exchange for them we ship industrial machinery, cotton goods, varnishes and paints.

Our trade with each of the seven tiny countries between Mexico and South America, which together are only twice the size of the British Isles, is mainly confined to timber and tree products. Most homes contain at least one article of furniture made of mahogany. This is one of the hardwoods we import from British Honduras. From the forested lowlands, around the Caribbean Sea, come bananas and chicle. The latter is a yellowish-white sticky juice, collected in the same way as raw rubber, and is the main ingredient of chewing-gum.

Costa Rica sends us small amounts of coffee, grown on the volcanic soils of the plateau.

Once again it is our manufactured goods, such as textiles, which enable us to pay for these products.

The climate and soils of Cuba are specially favourable to the large-scale cultivation of sugar cane. Molasses obtained from the cane is a source of industrial alcohol, needed for the production of methylated spirits, plastics, dyes, drugs, perfumes and cosmetics. In Jamaica, rum is distilled from the cane juice.

Havana, the capital of Cuba, has given its name to high quality cigar tobacco, grown in this and neighbouring islands. These tropical islands also produce much fruit. Ships equipped with special refrigerators bring bananas by the million from the plantations of Jamaica to the docks at Avonmouth. We also enjoy Jamaican grapefruit and oranges. The latter can be recognised in the shops by their rather yellowish skins. Considerable quantities of honey are sent to us from this British possession, while her Blue Mountain coffee commands a high price in the British market.

Sea Island, the finest variety of cotton in the world, is grown in the small

E.N.A.

SCARRING PINE TREES FOR TURPENTINE

The United States supplies us with much turpentine for our paint and varnish factories. Here we see pine trees being scarred so that the turpentine can collect in the iron gutters shown in the picture.

islands which form the eastern boundary of the Caribbean Sea. Barbados sugar is so called from the island in which the cane is grown. We receive the bulk of these products, together with nutmegs from Grenada. Dominica has many British-owned lime plantations, in fact, she is the world's chief producer of limes and lime-juice.

The best-known product of Trinidad is natural asphalt from the famous Pitch Lake. This unique natural wonder covers only one hundred acres, but as the pitch is dug out, the holes fill up again from below. At the present rate of consumption, it is estimated that it will last for four hundred years. Oilfields near the Pitch Lake produce petroleum. One further item of export from these islands is cocoa, which is increasing in importance, as it replaces bananas on plantations ravaged by disease.

Sponges, turtles and tortoises (important for their shells) abound in the warm waters of the coral islands known as the Bahamas, and are exported to us.

Through South America

Of the three Guianas, British Guiana is the richest, mainly on account of the deposits of bauxite found there. This is the sole British Commonwealth territory in the South American Continent, and most of her trade is with Britain. Much of the brown sugar to be bought at our grocer's is called Demerara, after the river valley of that name in which it is cultivated. Molasses from the sugar cane is also taken by Britain.

One of the more important products of the dense equatorial forests of the Guianas is balata, a rubber-like gum used to make belts for machinery and as a substitute for gutta percha. From the forests come hardwoods, one of the more valuable being greenheart, which, because it contains an oil disliked by marine worms, is extensively used in ship-building. We supply Guiana with machinery for mining bauxite and refining sugar, and other manufactured goods which her people require.

Brazil has normally a considerable trade with this country, sending us a wide range of products. Some of these have assumed an increasing importance in recent years, especially cotton, sugar and beef. Large numbers of cattle are reared on the grasslands of the plateau, and Brazil rivals Argentina in supplying us with chilled and canned beef. Hides, hair, especially that from the tails of the cattle, which is curled and used in mattresses, and other valuable by-products are shipped to England. Brazil is the chief producer of quartz, over half her output coming to Great Britain. She also provides some of our coffee.

Quartz, or rock crystal, is used in cheap jewellery, for making optical glass and parts of radio and telephone instruments. This country, the largest in South America, is our main source of cotton linters, employed in making paper, plastics, bedding, surgical dressings and rayon, and cotton waste, mainly used for furnishing fabrics and towels. Shoe polish and floor polish, found in every home here, contain vegetable waxes, probably originating in Brazil. These waxes are derived from the protective coating on the leaves of certain palm trees. In order to make paints and varnishes dry quickly, a special oil is used, which comes from the Oiticica tree of Brazil.

Brush fibres, ramie, derris root and pyrethrum flowers are additional Brazilian exports.

You have read that we import thousands of hides from other countries which are made into leather in our tanneries. At one time all the tannic acid used in this process came from British oak trees, but now we import a large proportion of tannin from Paraguay. It is derived from the very hard and heavy wood of the quebracho tree, growing in the forests of the Gran Chaco, and enables leather to be tanned quickly and cheaply.

On the Pampas

Fray Bentos and Paysandu are two towns in Uruguay which have given their names to two products popular here, namely, corned beef and ox-tongue. Besides cattle, the grasslands of Uruguay are ideally suited to the rearing of sheep, some of the wool from which is shipped to London.

The grasslands, or Pampas, of Uruguay extend into the Argentine, where they are used for similar purposes. Large droves of sheep and cattle are slaughtered and prepared for export in the *frigorificos* of the Plate River estuary. As in Uruguay, wool and other numerous by-products of the animal industry are important as articles of trade.

We also buy wheat and some cotton, which grow in the more fertile regions.

These vital imports of food and raw materials from Argentina are again paid

WEST INDIAN OIL AND SUGAR

Near La Brea, and not far from the famous Pitch Lake, Trinidad, are these oilfields. There are other fields near Guayaguayare. The production of oil is one of the colony's chief industries and provides nearly 80 per cent. of the exports of the island. The refineries of Trinidad also process crude oil imported from Venezuela.

Sugar, molasses, and cotton are the chief exports of Barbados. This picture shows an ox-wagon taking cane to the factory for crushing. This squeezes out the rich juice which will be boiled in another part of the factory to obtain the sugar. Though Barbados sugar is important, one of the largest sugar plantations in the Commonwealth is on the island of Trinidad.

for by the machinery and other manufactured goods we send to her.

The Copper Mines of Chile

In the Atacama desert of Northern Chile are found the world's chief deposits of nitrates. High in the Andes of this part of Chile is the world's largest copper mine, ore from which is sometimes imported by Britain. The " head " on a glass of beer, and the foam from a fire extinguisher, are produced by saponin. This substance is obtained from quillaia bark, of which Chile is the sole supplier.

The small country of Bolivia, set high in the Andes, is very rich in a variety of minerals. Of these we receive tin, antimony and tungsten.

The Alpaca is a cousin of our old-world camel, but is much smaller and lives in Peru on the mountain pastures of the Andes. Its hair is soft and silky, and is in great demand here for making the light, hard-wearing cloth known as alpaca.

Ecuador was the first country in which Panama hats were made. This form of headgear, woven from the fibres of the toquilla palm, remains one of the chief exports of this country. The bark of the cinchona tree, growing in the remote forests of eastern Ecuador, is supplied to us for the manufacture of quinine, a drug used to combat malaria and for other medical purposes.

Venezuela is the second largest oil producing country in the world and the world's largest petroleum exporting country. The oil may be refined at Port Cardon, Venezuela, or on the Dutch

E.N.A.

HUSKING TRINIDAD COCOA PODS

Eastern Trinidad has much the same climate as the Gold Coast of West Africa, and is a rich cocoa-growing region. Here we see workers husking cocoa pods. The beans thus obtained are allowed to ferment and are dried before being bagged for sale.

E.N.A.

JAMAICAN TOBACCO

Jamaican cigars rival those of Havana for their excellence and we have seen many more of them in Britain since our shortage of dollars made it difficult for us to obtain the Havana variety. Here we see a field of tobacco growing under cheesecloth which has a mellowing effect.

islands of Curaçao and Aruba. Large quantities are sent to Britain.

Australia and New Zealand

All men, even those in the hottest countries, need to wear clothes, except the most primitive peoples. One of the most common things of which clothes are made is wool. The chief wool-producing country in the world is Australia, which has more than 117,000,000 sheep. Most of these are merino sheep. The merino's wrinkled skin enables it to carry an astonishing amount of wool, which is finer and more silky than that of sheep of any other kind. The fleeces, which may weigh as much as 40 pounds, are packed in bales and taken to ports such as Geelong and Sydney, where they are graded and shipped overseas, especially to London,

which is the world's chief wool market. From there they are sent to the woollen mills of Yorkshire, or re-exported to countries on the continent of Europe.

In many parts of Australia, especially the north, there are vast cattle " stations " (ranches) where fine-quality beef cattle are raised. In 1953, Australia was Britain's leading supplier of beef. Thousands of dairy cattle too are reared, especially on the east coast lowlands, where the climate is moist. More butter, cheese and eggs, too, are produced than the Australians require, and they sell their quite considerable surplus to the mother country.

From Australia's rich farmlands come wheat and barley; from her orchards, fruit. Apples will keep sufficiently long to be sold fresh when they arrive in

Britain, but soft fruits such as peaches and plums are best canned, or made into jam, or even dried. Australian grapes are not only dried to make sultanas, raisins and currants, but are also made into wines. All these things are consumed daily by the people of our islands.

Australia has very little forest-land. In the south-west tip are found forests of hardwoods such as jarrah and karri. These woods are tough, heavy and resistant to weather and boring creatures, and so are extremely useful. From the wattle, another Australian tree, valuable tannin is obtained, while other trees yield resin. Both these items are imported into Britain.

Many of the early settlers in Australia went there seeking gold. Gold is still mined in considerable quantities, but much more valuable are the vast deposits of uranium ore which are now being developed. Australia also produces a variety of other metals, including lead, tin, zinc, cadmium, titanium and tungsten; the uses to which each is put have been described elsewhere.

Australia is largely a producer of pastoral and agricultural products. Although the number of her industrial enterprises is increasing, she must still buy a considerable quantity of factory-made goods from abroad. Most of these she gets from us.

Two important inventions, namely, the steamship and the refrigerator, enabled New Zealand to climb rapidly to its present rank as one of the world's outstanding pastoral countries. No

Australian News and Information Bureau.

PREPARING AUSTRALIAN CHEESE

Australia is known throughout the world for her dairy and agricultural products. The fine dairy herds of New South Wales, Queensland and Victoria provide the raw materials for the well-equipped cheese factories. The picture shows us cheeses being prepared for blending in the maturing room of a typical factory.

one thought of sending mutton to Britain in slow sailing ships that took three months to do the journey! In 1952, New Zealand had over 35 million sheep and more than five million cattle. It is therefore not surprising to find that animal products of all kinds account for more than nine-tenths of the islands' exports. We, in Britain, are her best customer, particularly for wool, meat and dairy produce.

The character of the country is so varied that in some parts one breed of sheep, such as the merino (for wool), does well; in others, another breed, such as the Southdown (for mutton), does best. The Corriedale, originally evolved in New Zealand, is a dual purpose sheep, producing wool and mutton.

Inspectors, employed by the government of New Zealand, mark "Canterbury Lamb" and dairy produce with the national emblem, a fern frond, as a guarantee of their purity. Look out for this sign on the things you buy in the shops. You may even see it on a jar of honey or a box of apples.

Ready-made clothes, cotton and woollen cloth, cigarettes, boots and shoes, iron and steel plates and wire for fencing are our chief contributions

Australian News and Information Bureau.

LOGGING IN NEW SOUTH WALES

When it comes to timber, Australia is best known for her hardwoods—jarrah and karri from West Australia; ironbark, grey gum and red gum from Victoria and New South Wales; blue gum from Tasmania. Here we see a 10-ton blackbutt log being towed away in Wauchope Forest on the north coast of New South Wales.

to the imports of New Zealand, of which we supply about half.

Britain's trade reaches out to almost every country of the world. We are utterly dependent on other lands for all kinds of foods and for a host of minerals and other raw materials, needed to make the things we use each day and the manufactures we sell abroad. All these imports, it must be remembered, have to be paid for almost entirely by money earned by our exports. We have advanced far from the way of life of Robinson Crusoe, but unless we maintain and increase our flow of exports, we shall find ourselves without not only the luxuries but the very necessities of life.

Our Changing Trade

Like many things in our day-to-day life, trade undergoes change, sometimes quite suddenly. For example, the development of new resources or the building of a new industry in a country may enable it to make for itself goods which were previously imported from another country. War, currency difficulties, the protection of home industries from foreign competition—these and many other factors may determine the volume and nature of trade.

We are exporting much more now than we did in 1938. Our exports of aircraft, machinery, motor vehicles, electrical goods and chemicals are more important nowadays than our exports of cotton and woollen goods, although the latter are still very important. We are also exporting much less coal. Before the war, about 35 million tons of coal were shipped from our islands every year; but in the period 1950–52, the yearly average was only 11 million tons. Our imports of raw materials for industry have increased considerably, while our imports of food, drink and tobacco have fallen.

Catering for visitors is a growing British industry and, as we have seen, is an important form of trade. In 1952 nearly three-quarters of a million foreign tourists came to our country and spent about £80 million during their stay.

High Commissioner for New Zealand.

NEW ZEALAND APPLES FOR BRITAIN

Next time you visit the greengrocer look at the apple boxes and see if they bear a fern frond mark. If they do, the apples will have come from New Zealand, whose national emblem—widely used on the Dominion's produce—is the fern frond. Here we see crated apples being loaded for shipment to Britain.